BOOK ONE

NO SHADOW OF TURNING

BOOK ONE

NO SHADOW OF TURNING

REFINER'S FIRE

JOAN CULLINS FOUNTAIN

Xulon Press

Xulon Press
2301 Lucien Way #415
Maitland, FL 32751
407.339.4217
www.xulonpress.com

Unless otherwise indicated, Scripture quotations taken from the King James
Version (KJV) – *public domain.*

Printed in the United States of America.

ISBN-13: 978-1-54562-085-4

For my parents Rebecca and Alvin Cullins
My brother George
And friends Laura Miller Thomas and Barbara Reinmuth Hollman

Their inspiration helped to create this story

ACKNOWLEDGEMENTS

Many thanks to the people who helped to make this story possible:

- The knowledgeable staff of the State Museum and the Nelson Museum of the West, Cheyenne, WY.
- The Laramie Plains Museum, Invinson Mansion, Laramie, WY.
- Christy Smith, M.A., and the fine docents at the Grand Encampment Museum, Encampment, WY.
- John Waggener, M.A., The American Heritage Center, University of Wyoming, Laramie, and the excellent staff in the research center.
- Nita Engen at the Museum in Centennial, WY, and Melanie Marie O'Hara of Centennial, for information on the history and people of the Snowy Range; Sue Ann Shaffer at Bailey Ranch for sharing anecdotal family history; and Ed Winslow for the invaluable reference to Mel Duncan's Mining Book of the Medicine Bow Range.
- The talented staff and docents at the Frontier Culture Museum of the Shenandoah Valley, Staunton, VA.
- The New Market Battle Field Visitors Center and Museum, New Market, VA.
- The staff and excellent museum at the Virginia Military Institute, Lexington, VA.
- The park rangers and historians at the Harper's Ferry Dry Goods Store and Ammunition Depot, Harper's Ferry National Park, Harper's Ferry, WV, for information on 19th Century textiles, guns, and ammunition.
- Dr. Deborah Fusco for invaluable time in directing the storyline and editing.
- Britta Hart for the outstanding character illustrations.
- Walter Fountain, my amazing and patient husband, for encouragement, expedition planning skills, and proofreading.
- Insight into the soldiers and people of the Civil War period was derived in part from the outstanding information and exhibits at the historic Wilderness Battlefield in Virginia and the Antietam Battlefield in Maryland. Many state and national parks provided the wilderness experiences necessary for the telling of the story.
- The characters in this novel are compilations of my son, Bryan, a gifted and talented singer-songwriter; his talented daughter, Mia; and my daughter Patricia and her husband Mike, excellent parents who early on gave me

the privilege of helping to homeschool my granddaughters, Kaitlyn and Lauren. The girls are now college-aged women who love the Lord. Their friends and the youth at our church have provided insight into the generations of young people who experience joys and struggles as they strive to live by the timeless, unchanging commands and doctrines of the Word of God in a world that is constantly changing, as well as insight into the lives of those who make a different choice.

All glory and honor are given to the magnificent God of the Bible and to His Only Son, Jesus Christ.

CAST OF CHARACTERS

THIS NOVEL FEATURES fictional characters who interact with historical figures and participate in both real and fictional events of the period. The timeline of 1849-1871 is meant to be accurate, with the exception of the socio-economic representation of the fictional town of Sideling, which in this context has been advanced from a small timber-tie camp to a newly-settled town for the purposes of keeping the fictional character, Johnny McLane, at the age of 15 during the 1864 American Civil War Battle of New Market, Virginia.

The town of Sideling is set in the foothills of the Rocky Mountains, southeast of the Snowy Range and beside the Big Laramie River, in today's Jelm-Laramie region of Wyoming.

While the political figures of Governor John Campbell, President Ulysses S. Grant, Louisa Gardner Swain, and members of the first territorial government are historical figures, the lawmen (with the exception of Nathaniel Boswell) are fictitious, and are a compilation of many territorial lawmen of the times. The outlaw Judd Barrow is fictitious.

The cities of Laramie and Cheyenne, the capital city, are historical, as well as the references to the military forts in Wyoming.

By 1866, the Wells Fargo Enterprises combined with all the major stagecoach, steamship, and railroad ventures transporting and guarding mail and merchandise throughout the west. The Plains Relay Station is meant to be a fictional representation of a small business.

The political conversations concerning the American Civil War, the reconstruction efforts in the southern states, and state of the territorial government of Wyoming are gleaned from historical writings. While accurate to a point, they are meant to reflect the views of the fictional characters and are not meant as political commentary.

Many of my family names were used randomly and given to the fictional characters in this novel, but do not represent the actual lives of the historical figures. In the novel, the fictional John Robert McLane is a compilation of my great-great grandfathers, Joseph Edward McLane (a businessman and founding father of the Mt. Carmel Church in Walters, Virginia) and Elijah Everett Whitley (who historically lived at the Mill Pond and was a miller-farmer during the Civil War, serving for the Confederacy). The historical figures of John Robert McLane and his wife, Rebecca Keaton Scott, are my great grandparents, who resided in the towns of Courtland and Franklin,

Virginia, and were the parents of five daughters. When John Robert's fifth child was a daughter, he gave up trying for a son and named her Rebecca John. She was a favorite great aunt, and was nicked named "Johnnie".

The fictional McLane Mill farm and store are a combination of historic Winborne's Mill, near Sunbeam, Virginia, and the prosperous store of the Holland family (related to the Whitley's by marriage), which sat at the top of the hill above the mill pond until succumbing to ruin during the Civil War era.

ABOUT THE AUTHOR

JOAN FOUNTAIN IS a Registered Nurse and lives with her husband, Walter, on their small "homestead" in Howard County, Maryland. Joan volunteers as a Challenger leader for the Pioneer Girl program, an arm of the Christian Service Brigade, mentoring and teaching outdoor and life skills to 7th through 12th grade teens. She also serves as a teen mission leader at her church. The Fountain "farm" is home to horses, chickens, ducks, cats, and a pig named "Addie." Joan and Walter have an open-door policy, holding Bible studies and mentoring sessions, and using their home as a meeting place for college students and young adults. Joan's hobbies include the study of history, back-packing, canoeing, and everything "out-of-doors," with a focus on the Mid-Atlantic region. Since the age of four she has been drawn to the West and her adopted states of Wyoming and Colorado.

The *No Shadow of Turning* triology will continue with book two, *Freedom's Song,* which is currently available, and book three, *Above the Mist*, which will follow.

INTRODUCTION

JOHNNY MCLANE WAS born the son of a prosperous farmer and miller in the tidewater county of Southampton, Virginia, on the eve of the turbulent decade before the American Civil War. Thrown by fate as a youth into the conflict, having to endure the horrors of a divided nation as a military cadet in the battle-torn Shenandoah Valley of Virginia, then orphaned on a journey across the country during the westward expansion, he encounters many personal struggles. Forced to come to grips with shattered dreams and devastating losses, he journeys onward, facing the realms of intimate relationships, social, spiritual, and political responsibilities. He must choose between the mores of his upbringing or make the difficult decision to face the fledgling, territorial society of Wyoming with a biblical-based worldview, controversial even during the restless years of the mid-19th century.

In the 21st century, we face a similar task. To make no spiritual decision is actually a decision, and failure to acknowledge this has very real and lasting consequences. At the top of today's best seller list rests the Holy Bible, as it has since it was first printed more than 500 years ago. More than a volume of stories and rules, it is an instructional manual, containing wisdom sufficient to navigate successfully through the most difficult circumstances of our lives. One person cannot fully translate the meaning of a scripture passage for another, because this revelation is personal, inspired, and appointed by God for individual benefit, and given by God at the appropriate moment.

Intermingled throughout this story, the scriptures references are meant to pertain to the storyline and should give insight into the decisions made by the characters involved. It is hoped that they will stir in the reader a desire to delve deeper into the rich, always unfolding "Living Word" of the Bible. If the story is read only for pleasure, it is my prayer that it will point to God's truths. God sees, guides, and directs—with great mercy and grace—those who are willing to follow Him, and His expectations of our personal accountability and responsibility remain the same, for all societies, in all centuries, throughout time.

> "Every good gift and every perfect gift is from above, and cometh down from the Father of lights, with whom there is no variableness, neither shadow of turning." James 1:17 KJV

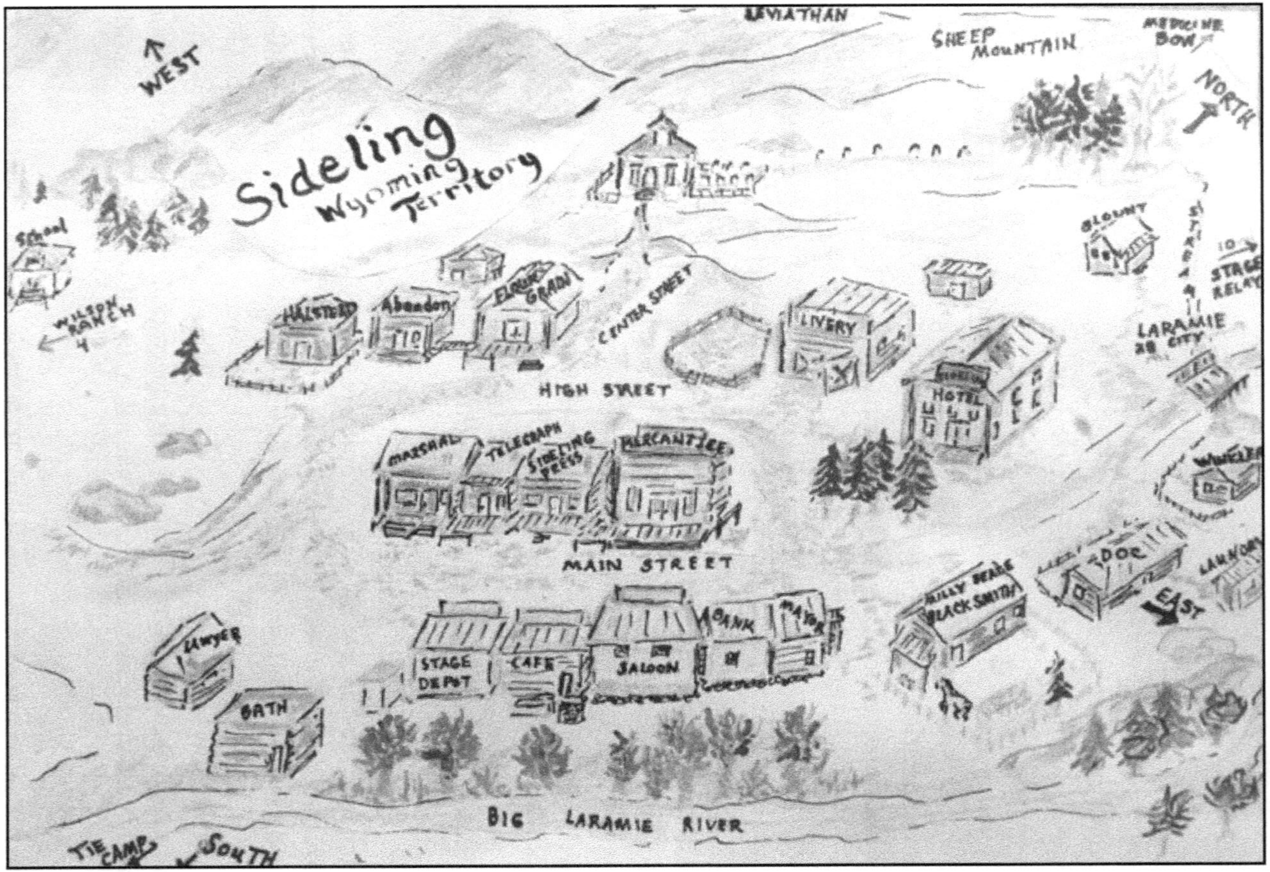
Sideling
Wyoming Territory
WEST
NORTH
EAST
SOUTH
SHEEP MOUNTAIN
MEDICINE BOW
LARAMIE CITY
STAGE RELAY
School
WILSON RANCH
HALSTEAD
Abandon
HIGH STREET
CENTER STREET
MAIN STREET
LIVERY
HOTEL
BLOUNT
MARSHAL
TELEGRAPH
SIDELING PRESS
MERCANTILE
STAGE DEPOT
CAFE
SALOON
BANK
MAYOR
BLACKSMITH
DOC
LAUNDRY
LAWYER
BATH
BIG LARAMIE RIVER
TIE CAMP

BOOK ONE

REFINER'S FIRE

1

THE WARP

LIFTED BY THE currents, the hawk sailed silently along the banks of the Big Laramie River, his watchful eye ever fixed on the underbrush, spying for signs of prey and finding none. Suddenly, he soared higher, riding the currents and circling over the prairie lands below, veering westward, while searching the foothills of the Medicine Bow Range. Reaching a small town nestled between the mountains and the winding riverbank, the hawk sank low, his keen eye focused on the highest roof of a rough-hewn building.

A mouse scurried along the slanted eave, unaware of the rapidly descending predator. As the hawk dropped swiftly, a shotgun blast shattered the still morning air, along with the window on the newly constructed second floor of the Sideling Hotel, sending the hawk to a rapid ascent.

"And just what in blazes do you think you're doin', Beau Brenner? Hold it right there!"

Johnny McLane caught the surprised youth by an arm, yanking the shotgun from his hands. "Let me be Deputy, I didn't hurt nobody!"

Attempting to pull his arm free, Beau's eyes cut to narrow slits, lost in his scowl, as his large bulky frame struggled against Johnny's tight grip.

"You just can't walk into the middle of town and blast off a shotgun for no reason!" Johnny growled. "What's the matter, have you lost your mind?"

Attempting to keep his grip on the boy, Johnny struggled with the surly youth. At five feet nine inches, Beau was just slightly shorter than the deputy, but outweighed him by a good twenty pounds. Nearly losing his balance, Johnny yanked Beau hard, twisting Beau's arm up behind his muscular back. The boy moaned.

"Aw, I was shootin' at an ole hawk! He was bound to kill somebody's chickens... ow! Quit! I'm just doin' somebody a favor!" Beau cursed and spit in the dusty street.

"Yeah? We'll just see what the marshal thinks about this 'favor'!"

They struggled forward as Johnny manipulated the angry youth down the wide, dusty street. "You're supposed to be workin' or in school... so what are you doing out here?"

Before Beau could answer, Johnny shoved him onto the plankboard porch before the city marshal's office. Kicking the door wide with a booted foot, he pushed Beau roughly through the doorway and wrangled him into a nearby chair, slamming the heavy door shut behind them.

Sam Brett stood passively, watching the ruckus.

"Looks like you bought yourself some trouble, Mr. Brenner," Sam reflected mildly, watching Johnny place the shotgun across the large office desk then turn to face the perpetrator. "The middle of town isn't generally where people go to hunt, is it?"

Beau scowled at Sam's question and tilted his head, cutting his eyes to glare up at the marshal. "That stinkin' deputy just has it out for me! I ain't done nothin' and I ain't hurt nobody...now let me loose!" Beau railed, attempting to rise from his chair.

Johnny shoved him down again. "Marshal Brett's not finished talkin'! Sit still," he growled.

Emptying the shotgun, Sam Brett leaned it against the far corner wall.

"School opens in thirty minutes, and if that's where you're supposed to be today, you better get to it," Sam said, glancing at the clock on the wall. "Your pa can pick up the gun later."

Sam returned his attention to the correspondence he held and addressed his deputy dismissively. "Be sure he gets inside the schoolhouse, Johnny."

Johnny McLane

Johnny stood, indecisive for a moment, and his eyes tracked between the marshal and the sullen youth. He shook his head and held his tongue.

"Yes sir," he grunted, hauling Beau to his feet. Opening the door, he pushed the boy back through the doorway and onto the porch.

With a jerk, Beau freed his arm and muttered sullenly, "Alright, alright! I'm goin'. You don't gotta drag me!"

Managing to maintain control of the boy and still engaging in banter, Johnny escorted Beau erratically down Main Street, toward the white clapboard schoolhouse, which lay on the southwestern fringe of town. Myra Davis' rig was tied to the hitching post at the side of the structure.

Johnny held the boy, eyeing him intently. "Looks like your teacher's here, Beau, git inside. The marshal cut you a break this time, but don't be expectin' it again!"

With a curse and a wicked sneer, Beau pulled away.

Although desiring to be rid of the morning's annoyance, Johnny became cognizant of his own tactlessness and remembered his position. "Hold up a minute!" He grabbed Beau by his shirt sleeve, turning the youth to face him.

"Just look around you, Beau," he reasoned, indicating the two small boys playing marbles in the dirt by the schoolhouse steps. "They don't need older fellows runnin' crazy through the town, settin' bad examples for them. Think about that, can't ya?"

For a moment, Johnny tried to search beyond the arrogance and obstinacy of Beau's expression. Concentrating on Beau's gray eyes, he hoped to find at least a flicker of remorse within. Instead, through Beau's defiant, dull glare, a sickening sense of being absorbed into the hollow vacuum engulfed him.

Johnny's gut tightened and his defenses rose against the repulsive harbinger. In his haste to be rid of the boy, he shucked off the omen and spun Beau around roughly. Releasing him, Johnny tipped his head smartly toward the schoolhouse.

"Go on git...now! You get the shotgun back when your pa comes for it."

Beau turned and kicked at a rock with the toe of his boot, sending it to ricochet off the side of the building. He sauntered defiantly toward the stairs, stomping noisily upward and stopping in the doorway to look back over his shoulder.

Johnny shook his head disgustedly. He turned to walk back up Main Street, glad to be rid of the annoyance and wondering how Myra Davis could manage the kid or even tolerate him in her classroom.

"Hey Deputy!" called Tad Smith, running up to Johnny after having shot his Aggie and taking the prize of his opponent's marbles.

"Hey yourself, Tad Smith. How are you this mornin'?"

The seven-year-old towhead squinted his eyes against the rising sun as he looked up at the deputy.

"Look what I just won. Looky here!" he exclaimed excitedly. Johnny crouched down beside the small boy.

"That's fine, Tad, you made quite a haul for yourself!"

"You after a robber or somethin' or just makin' your rounds?" Tad's eyes narrowed with intrigue.

"Maybe a little of both," Johnny chuckled. "Say, how's that pup of yours? Did Doc fix his leg?"

"Yes, sir. He cleaned it up, stuck a bandage on it, but Liberty gnawed it clean off. Ma says if he licks it, it'll heal. It sure scared me though." Tad's wide eyes were so earnest, Johnny had to laugh.

"I'm glad things are lookin' up for Liberty; he'll make a fine huntin' dog one day."

"We can go huntin' can't we? Real soon, can we?" Tad asked, eyes bright with the notion. The bell clanged from the wooden finial above the doorway.

"Gotta go, Deputy. Don't forget our huntin' trip! See ya later." Stuffing the marbles into his pocket, he took off in a mad scamper, joining his classmates who laughed and joked as they filed through the doorway.

Myra Davis, the young schoolmarm, greeted each child as they entered. She paused to wave at Johnny. Her bright blue dress stood out crisply against the whitewashed boards of the recently constructed building, and her blonde hair was caught up on the crown of her head.

He returned her greeting with a quick tip of his hat. 'So prettily packaged,' Johnny thought, remembering their first meeting well over a year ago.

He had come down from Montana, looking for work and was just about to enter the marshal's office on the corner of Main Street. As Myra exited the office, Johnny tipped his hat to her upturned face and asked if the marshal was in.

He saw interest spark in her eyes. He had seen that expression many times before as he had marched with the corps of cadets through the streets of Virginia: the tilt of the head, tempting bow of the lips, and the subtle lowering of the eyelids flickering innocently as they peered up through long lashes. At the time, a lad of fifteen, with an outward swagger bolstered by numbers and lack of opportunity, he had been exhilarated in the fray of young women and simultaneously unsettled by the many unknowns he was sure to encounter both on and off the battlefield.

With a coy smile Myra had breathed, "Yes, the marshal is available."

'Later, maybe,' Johnny thought, looking after her as she had brushed past him, but her touch had been the strike of flint to match, and the spark caught him off guard, surprising him. She seemed aware and had turned again to smile.

Myra and Johnny found themselves reconnected during a fall frolic in town the next week. Myra admitted her disenchantment with the small town in which she was raised, close to an Amish farming community in Ohio. In 1867, she had come west for the adventure of a new society. Once in Denver, she had read of the need for teachers in the Dakota Territory and had traveled north to Sideling where she found a position. In 1868, as Sideling had become part of the newly organized Wyoming Territory, Myra found herself restless once again, for she was still bound by the constraints of a society couched in mores similar to those which had repressed her in Ohio. However, she purposely left this fact out of her intimate discussion with Johnny.

Among the war-torn soldiers, misfits, and fortune seekers who had come westward were many God-fearing, industrious Americans and foreigners seeking new opportunities. They had fled the depressed post-war economy of the "states", oppression, and famine on foreign shores. Such were the early founders of Sideling.

Settled years before as a French trapper outpost, the tiny community of Sideling formed around a single old log structure known at the time as "Sideling House". It nestled in a valley among the southeastern foothills of the vast mountain wilderness called the Medicine Bow Range. During the 1830s until about 1860, the establishment was an isolated supply station for trappers and a center for the trading of beaver, wolf, and other pelts. In 1867, when railroad construction brought the need for tie camps into the timbered mountain areas, McGreavey's tie camp sprang up directly across the narrow river, along the eastern bank of the Big Laramie, which flowed to the north past Sideling House.

The mighty Union Pacific railroad inched westward from Cheyenne, almost forty miles to the north, through the rugged terrain and often brutal weather of the high plains. In a race to join its counterpart being constructed eastward from California, railroad ties were hewn at McGreavey's camp in winter and floated down river with the spring thaw to Laramie City, bringing settlement westward and growth to the community of Sideling.

On that distant night, admid the fall frolic, Myra had danced exclusively with Johnny, then allowed him to kiss her at the end of the evening. When he tried to see her later in the week, she was unavailable during the little spare time he found. At that time, he had been penniless and in desperate need of a job. Reflecting on the odd circumstances of his life, Johnny had counted pursuit as hopeless and held off the notion.

Before his sixteenth birthday, Johnny had been taken in by the Casey family, traveling with them from Nebraska to the Montana Territory. He worked alongside Ord Casey and his two sons clearing land, constructing a log cabin, a barn, and helping to secure cattle for the pioneering family. After more than three years, the long hours, longer frigid winters, and the increasing desire to strike out on his own had driven Johnny to ride southward in pursuit of his life's ambition.

But over the months, as the remnant of his dream seemed to evaporate like a vapor, Johnny found that his hopes of learning to read law would likely not be realized, and he was forced to change his plans.

The "War of Northern Aggression", as it had often been referred to by Johnny and his compatriots, had seen to that, and because of it and in spite of it, he had decided to find work as a lawman. Also, owing to the war, he was a fast draw, a good shot, steady under pressure, and sorrowfully inept at expressing his attributes.

The interview with Marshal Brett in Sideling on that early spring day of 1869 had not gone well. After a brief introduction, a flicker of what might have been perceived as interest lit the steely gray eyes of the tall, older man, but was gone just as rapidly as the marshal dropped his pencil on his desk and proclaimed flatly that the budget and size of the town "at this time" could not support another lawman. It seemed to Johnny that the marshal considered him to be a risk, for he told him in no uncertain terms that in a shootout he didn't want to worry about having to defend both of them.

"From what little you've told me about youself, I reckon you're a few weeks shy of twenty years. Why don't you save some money, homestead and raise a family, son?" The question was delivered more as a command than a suggestion.

"I'm not a cattleman, sir," was Johnny's simple response as he stood before the stoic marshal that day, feeling foolish.

Following the discouraging interview with the marshal and in sore need of a hot meal, Johnny found work as a substitute kitchen boy in Frances Kelly's café across the street from the marshal's office. But in three weeks' time, he was replaced by the rightful employee and took work as a "tie hack", spending the summer and fall lean, bearded, and gaining muscle by hewing timber into ties at McGreavey's tie camp.

Johnny dwelt with the men in the tie hack log cabin, and took meals in the cook house, rarely leaving the rowdy camp. Occasionally, he would take the camp canoe, cross the river and make a "run" into Sideling for some missed supplies, catching site of Myra Davis. He never called out to her, and she would not have recognized him, for his unruly hair hid his eyes, and unkempt, he remained a nondescript figure among a confrere of men.

With the early summer thaws, he spent countless hours at the river, sometimes helping to dam up its flow only to release the flood needed to float the ties which jammed the shallow, cold, river waters. He struggled along with the men as they fought tie jams in mid-stream, balancing perilously on the ties and prodding them for miles along the swollen river.

Amidst the turmoil of his days, Johnny remained amicable but withdrew increasingly from attachments of any meaningful sort. Vaguely conscious of a void within, he suffered from a lack of desire to define it. In want of how to fill it, he was consequently haunted by recurring dreams from his past, for although he had survived the turbulence of those earlier years, the warrior and the sojourner had been little more than a child.

He worked until worn out, saved his pay, withstood most forms of temptation and managed to hold onto his one valued and highly sought after possession, his exceptional horse, Traveller.

Losing little of monetary value in the constant nightly card games, he lost himself and dulled his inner conflictions in the intense art of gambling. But often, in the black hours before dawning, he would awaken in a sweat, unable to forget Myra's kiss, and struggling with thoughts of what could have followed, prayed to the heavens that he could survive until the passions receded into the exhaustions of his days.

(Psalm 106:35-36)

Johnny grew increasingly restless, and unable to hold out on his dream of becoming a law officer, found himself shaven and shorn and on the street in Sideling one fall evening in 1869, ready to leave town with the coming of the dawn.

There were few jobs to be had as clerk or shopkeeper along the one block that composed Sideling's Main Street, and less opportunity in the two stores and the livery in the block with its sprinkling of cabins and an abandoned building that made up High Street to the rear of Main.

As more cattle were driven northward from Texas to fatten on the high plains of the Wyoming Territory, before being shipped eastward by rail for market, cattle ranching had slowly begun to increase. Cowhands were needed out on the plains as cattle were being crossbred, enabling the resulting heartier "beheeves" to withstand the harsh territorial winters. Still, none of this interested Johnny.

In the waning of that fall evening, in the middle of Main Street, just outside the door of the Watering Hole Saloon, two gunmen drew down on the marshal. Marshal Brett shot one of them and by mere coincidence, Johnny, who had been tolerating the boredom of the slow evening on a bench outside of the Sideling Café, fired his Colt .44 straight into the heart of the second gunman, dropping him in the dust.

After an agreeable conversation, the marshal hired Johnny immediately. By early spring, and almost twenty-one, Johnny had proven himself an asset to the office and to the community in general.

Sam Brett took Johnny under his wing, advising him in the profession of law officer. Orphaned since his mid-teen years, Johnny accepted willingly the guidance of the honest, moral, and just man who was more than twenty years his senior. With this, the void in Johnny's soul seemed to be narrowing.

(Psalms 106:44-45)

———————◆———————

Myra had proven to have other suitors, and Johnny had tried but lacked the time it took to court the sought-after young woman who had seemingly mastered the art of seduction, while successfully deflecting occasional inquiries from the elderly three-member school board.

During the occasional dance, and when he could afford dinner, she had flattered him, thrown all her attentions his way, then hinted he was "wasting himself" on his occupation. He took her comment like the gentleman he was, quietly deciding to prove her wrong, and went about his business, pouring his energy into his work and keeping his goals to the forefront.

But he found himself unable to stay away, and she toyed and tempted artfully, making him believe that he was the pursuer, and sending so many mixed signals that he became uncomfortable and frustrated.

One evening, after she had him just where she wanted him, he had kissed her again and she responded passionately, then pushed him away, advising him she was "unavailable" in the next week due to "previous engagements". He left her at her doorstep then, promising himself never to see her again.

(Hosea 2:6-7a)

In the days and months that followed, they were never quite able to stay apart, inexplicably drawn to one another like flame to substance, singeing and irritating but never consuming one another. When she drew him to her once again, handing him the same excuses, although inflamed by her external sensuality, Johnny managed to regain his senses long enough to figure that Myra seemed to lack internal substance. Resolute for a season, he placed romance to simmer on the back burner again, and attended to the business of studying the law, and to the rigors of taming a frontier town while Myra, unable to draw him in again, and fascinated by him, watched him jealously.

(Proverbs 4:1-9)

Being a young man of good moral character and descending from a long line of Virginian patriots, Johnny was quick to catch Sam's vision of eventual statehood. Only a year had passed since Wyoming had become a territory, carved out of the larger Dakota Territory. Gamblers and crooked politicians roamed, circuiting the few towns sprinkled on the plains as far as railroads and horses would carry them.

Tucked between mountain ranges in the foothills of the Rockies, although almost forty miles from the railroad lines, Sideling's proximity to timber, readily available water, and the discovery of precious metals from nearby mountain ranges made it attractive in a land where much of the environment was harsh; winter could last through the spring season. The security of a community did not rest in its environment alone, for there was inherent unrest in the hearts of men. Some struggled with the paradox between an insistence on living in complete self-reliance as they had back in the "states", no matter the cost to others, and the current essential need to depend on neighbors for survival.

While Sideling's resources were attractive, its proximal location inadvertently provided an out-of-the-way shelter for wandering gunslingers, horse and cattle rustlers, or an occasional road agent, all eager to make a fortune or fame for themselves. From a trail through a valley of narrow mountains, which split off from the newer 1850 Cherokee trail crossing the Colorado border and winding to the north, the main road through Sideling continued northeastward toward Laramie City.

Regardless of where they were situated, the strong hands of good lawmen and honest officials were needed to build the kind of towns where citizens could settle, bringing in families, and increasing the numbers that would allow the territory to become eligible for statehood.

(Isaiah 62:10)

Upon re-entering the office, Johnny whipped off his hat, tossing it at the wall nearest the empty cell, where it caught by the rim on the peg. Marshal Brett watched him sink into the chair across from the desk where the marshal sat filling out the monthly report.

"I just can't figure that boy out, Mr. Brett. He always seems to be looking for trouble. If I hadn't been making rounds and run across Beau, there is no telling what he may have done with that shotgun. Do you believe his story about shootin' at a hawk?"

Still writing, the monotone voice of the marshal interrupted the pause, breaking the silence. "Did you see a hawk?"

"No, I never gave his story any credence. Guess I was just too angry with him for being so stupid. Besides, if there had been a hawk it would've been long gone after that blast," Johnny said, tipping his chair back on two legs.

"Or dead." Sam Brett stood and stretched. "You might want to go and see if there's a hawk lying somewhere near that hotel. At least then you could tell his pa he wasn't trying to shoot up the town."

"Maybe he needs a little shakin' up. Maybe then his pa would keep him in line," Johnny countered.

"I doubt he meant to hurt anyone, although he sure could have. Boys his age tend not to think before they act. Beau will have to explain the shotgun episode to his father, and although I doubt the man cares enough about what his son does, ole man Brenner will have to pay for that shattered window. That will come down hard on Beau, and most likely he'll think before he acts next time. The only law he broke was destroying private property and maybe disturbing the peace."

"He might have benefited by spendin' the day in jail instead of in school, Mr. Brett. It's only September and even at seventeen, he's required by territorial law to put his 2-3 months in class. If he's not there, isn't he supposed to be workin' for Mr. Jones at the mercantile?" Johnny asked, raising his brow.

"Bradford Jones has been doing Beau's pa a favor. Letting that boy work for him was Bradford's sister's idea...maybe I never told you that. You know Beau is Brad's nephew, but I doubt you know that Beau only has the job at the mercantile because his ma is so fragile...mentally, and she can't deal with him. Beau's pa is a strange one also; the townsfolk leave them be for the most part. Beau will be eighteen soon and whichever way he plays it, whether going to school or working, the situation is best left between him and his father. We won't hold him on a technicality, and without a shotgun he's not a danger to himself or to anyone else. We don't judge, boy, and the way I see it the law is

14

being enforced. Working probably teaches him as much as staring out the window of Myra Davis' classroom. I'm gonna get some breakfast. You comin'?"

"Sure, after if I check if there is any hawk." Johnny stood and moved to pick up his hat, which had fallen to the floor. 'This day could have started out better,' he mused.

Rounding the hotel, Johnny picked up the shards of broken glass which had exploded from the window and tossed them into a box of scrap lumber and rusty tin cans at the rear of the mercantile. As he crossed High Street and walked around the hotel, Euphony Brown poked her head through the sash of the blown-out window and hollered down at him.

"You're gonna fix that window, aren't you Johnny McLane? Hyrum will be home this evening and he'll be plenty mad when he finds out that you let hoodlum boys run through the streets of Sideling with shotguns, blowing out brand new windows!"

Johnny knew the woman all too well. He took a breath and collected himself. "Yes ma'am, I'm on my way back to the mercantile to see if I can get some glass. Tell Mr. Brown he is welcome to come by the office and file charges if he wants, when he gets back to town."

Leaning further out of the window she pointed a skinny finger at Johnny.

"I saw you take that Beau Brenner to jail. That's just where he and his kind belong," she barked.

"He's currently in school and his..." But before Johnny could finish, Mrs. Brown fired back, hard brown eyes snapping in her weathered face.

"What? You let that heathen out of the jailhouse?"

"I'll take care of the window ma'am, good morning to you," he replied diplomatically, dodging her barrage of insults by tipping his hat and turning on his heel.

Her anger had worked to fuel his own. "Yankee!" he murmured spuriously, before he even had time to correct the thought, and lacking the proper contrition when he did. Johnny simmered, pacifying himself with the notion that salt air in the coastal New England town from which Euphony and her husband hailed, had likely dried up their souls as well as their withering frames to viciousness, for Hyrum Brown was as contentious as his wife.

He sighed and looked at the sky. White clouds billowed across the blue canvas: a beautiful day and he'd be stuck fixing a window for a sour, old soul. He wanted to go to the school and haul the kid out to fix the window. That was just the problem. The boy never atoned for any of his misdeeds, not as far as Johnny knew. He just got off, continuing to terrorize dogs, hawks, and any other living thing that got in his fractious way.

Johnny stepped onto the porch of the mercantile and noticed the smear of blood on his pant-leg and with anger abating, began to feel the throbbing in his right thumb. As he entered the store he examined the wound, wrapping his bandana around it, relieved there was no glass embedded within.

"Howdy, Johnny, what can I do for you?" Bradford Jones stood behind the counter, sorting nails.

"I need four standard panes for the hotel window," Johnny replied without returning the jovial proprietor's greeting.

"It must have to do with the shotgun blast earlier. What happened?"

Johnny shook his head and frowned. "Just a kid messing around," he said not wishing to explain again.

"Let me check the backroom, I'll see if I have them. Be right back."

Johnny applied pressure to his aching thumb. The store was quiet and dark, and it took his eyes some time to adjust from the brilliant mid-morning sun. The log-beamed ceiling of the original cabin called "Sideling House" held the cool of the early morning hours and the warm, pungent scent of years of wood smoke from the large potbellied stove in the center of the room. He relaxed and took in the rows of shelves along the walls. They were stacked with almost every supply a homesteader could use. He liked the smell of the herbs and tobacco as well as the order and efficiency of the place. Seemingly anything a body would need to keep life running smoothly was here in this one place.

The thought took him back to a faraway time, to another general store, much like this one, now gone forever. 'People,' he thought, 'people are what take the order out of life.'

He reflected on a gristmill and the grinding of the kernels of corn between huge mill-stones. As a child, he had snitched handfuls of the cornmeal, warm and sweet from the grinding, then secreted himself away behind the mill with Moses as they ate and watched the dark water tumble from the pond, over the huge wooden wheel into the milltail. Gone also.

The door of the mercantile swung open, spilling sunlight across the wide-planked floor, dissolving his reverie.

"Hey Jess! What brings you to town today?" Johnny enquired of the tall, blond, young man, entering. "I haven't seen you in weeks."

"I was lookin' for you. I heard ole Euphony Brown hollerin' at ya, and I thought you were probably headed this way. What's up? Not managin' to stay out of trouble, I'll wager."

"Trouble seems to follow me like one of ole Eb Smith's hounds lately. Comes with the job, I reckon," Johnny laughed, giving Jess a crooked grin.

"I gotta get supplies for the relay station, and I was thinking maybe we'd go fishin' if the marshal could cut ya lose for the afternoon. I heard the cutthroat trout are bitin' good."

Jess Bryant had an easy way about him, and Johnny found himself hoping he could find some time to spend fishing with his friend.

"I'll check with the marshal as soon as I fix the window, Jess."

"Good, I'm gonna load up the wagon and get something to drink, and I'll check with ya at the office, say, afternoon?"

"See you then," Johnny replied.

Only two panes were found and replaced, and the lower sections had to be fitted with a board. Mrs. Brown had glared only briefly at Johnny, having otherwise left him in peace to finish the task. His stomach rumbled, and he realized he had forgotten to eat breakfast.

It was past noon when the marshal returned to the office, finding Johnny munching on a sourdough biscuit and drinking coffee.

"I made rounds, seems like it's gonna be a quiet day." Hanging his holster on the peg behind the desk, Sam asked, "You find the hawk, boy?"

"No, sir, but I did fix the window and appease Miz Brown. She's unhappy and says her husband will come over this evening. As usual, she was angry." He raised an eyebrow and added pointedly, "Says we should have kept Beau in jail."

"I expect she was madder that the window was broken and more anxious to get it fixed than anything else. She and Hyrum don't like to spend a penny they don't have to. I expect she'll forget the window when Hyrum returns and set her venoms on something else." Sam pulled out the rolling, swivel chair and settled himself behind the desk.

"So Beau gets off scot-free again," Johnny said in disgust.

The marshal regarded him thoughtfully. "Just what is it you have against that kid, Johnny? How do you let him get to you so easily?"

Pauses in conversation between the two men were not rare. Often Sam would ask a question then seem oblivious to anything except what lingered on the desk before him, but Johnny knew this not to be the case. Johnny sometimes took a while to formulate thoughts, consciously or unconsciously expressing or suppressing the deepest of them, and Sam respected this in his deputy.

But now, as Johnny recalled his earlier gut feeling regarding Beau, he was tempted to explore its cause and admit his speculations. The truth was that over the last six months, on occasion, that same unsettled feeling had disturbed him during his day-to-day interactions with a handful of Sideling's citizens. He hadn't attempted to analyze or speak of those brief premonitions, had let them pass, and had moved on. Lately his encounters with Beau were neither subtle nor fleeting as was usually the case with the others. When Beau challenged Johnny's authority to intervene, Johnny found it easy to lash out at Beau's blatant disrespect and never cared to understand him.

"He's always in trouble and I don't like him... don't trust him either." The explanation sounded too simple, even to himself. He tried again.

"There's somethin' in his eyes, I think. Or rather, something's missin', kind of... well, maybe akin to lackin' a soul. I just can't explain it."

Having tired of soul searching, and suddenly inspired by being able to dodge the issue, Johnny declared, "I almost forgot! Jess stopped by and wants to go fishin' this afternoon. Can you spare me for a few hours?"

"Reckon that'll be fine," Sam said, considering the request. "You'll not be far from the bridge if I need you?"

"No, sir, and I'll be back for evenin' rounds."

He made a dash for the backroom, retrieving his fishing pole, and was out the door before Jess reached the porch. Johnny swung easily into the saddle. His big, gray gelding, Traveller, nickered as Johnny touched him gently with his spurs, sending him forward, just behind Jess' bay gelding. The horse tossed his head, its silver-white mane blowing with the wind, glad to be released from the hitching post. The two men held to a jog, riding abreast down the road toward the bridge crossing the Big Laramie River. The afternoon sun was bright, the day breezy and cool, just perfect for fishing.

The road wound to the southwest as they passed the schoolhouse. Johnny glanced toward the boys who were tossing a ball in the schoolyard, thinking he might get a glimpse of the Brenner boy and hoping that the kid had stayed in school instead of running off. Jess' gaze followed Johnny's as the deputy slowed Traveller, turning slightly in the saddle.

"Who is that?" Johnny asked emphatically.

Three girls stood in the middle of the schoolyard near a huge oak. Two of the girls were shaded by the autumn leaves, while the third girl stood in the sunshine, her head tilting back in laughter; long wavy, auburn hair shining like copper in the sunlight, while the breeze blew wisps across her brow. Gracefully, she raised her arm to push the curls away from her eyes. She was slender, but her figure was perfect under her fitted, lavender, calico dress. The girls smiled at the fisherman, two of them waving, but the girl in the lavender did not. She held a book in her hand, and watched the men ride past. Johnny tipped his hat, then tipped it forward over his brow embarrassed for having stared at the girl so openly.

"Who is who?" Jess asked, glancing sidelong at Johnny.

"Didn't you see her? The girl in the lavender dress... the one with the beautiful hair?" His voice trailed off as he unwittingly turned back to see if he could catch a last glimpse of her. The girls had begun their entrance into the schoolhouse, and the lavender, copper-haired girl was gone.

Johnny turned to stare at Jess. "Don't tell me you didn't notice her," Johnny declared incredulously.

"Are you talking about little Cassie? Dodge Wilkerson's oldest daughter? Why she ain't nothing but a kid! Fifteen or sixteen years at the most!"

"Go on!" Johnny scoffed, "I know Dodge Wilkerson's daughters. I've seen 'em all at church and I'm sayin' that girl can't be Cassie Wilkerson. That kid wears pigtails and has freckles."

"You really need to get out more, son. She is Cassie Wilkerson; she just looks a little different today. Maybe she let her hair down or bought a new dress or somethin'. Anyway, she is a schoolgirl, and too young for the likes of us. Boy, you better start pickin' from the ladies in town, or see if you can squeeze back in line for Myra Davis again. She kinda fancies you anyway, don't she? All of 'em are easy for lawmen, married are not. Why in blazes do you think I wear the badge when you need extra help? D'ya think I enjoy being shot at?"

Lost in thought, Johnny didn't reply. Heedlessly, he spurred Traveller on, racing to the river with Jess trailing by a length. The rocks and the boulders near the bridge provided eddies away from the main current, which the trout favored. The men fished the afternoon away, occasionally getting a nibble, then a strike, and wrestling in the gamefish which would provide dinner for the men at the stage relay station, ten miles northeast of Sideling. Johnny's meals were taken in the café or the Watering Hole Saloon, and opportunities for frying fish presented themselves only when he camped on the trail or went hunting. He reluctantly relinquished his right to half of the fish.

"Too bad you can't come to the relay for dinner, we'll be making some good sinkers to eat with these ole boys," Jess grinned, toting the fish in a rucksack, and tying it to his saddle horn. He mounted his bay.

Johnny stood by the horse, handing Jess his fishing pole. "Well," he quipped, "one of us has to have a real job, Bryant. Just remember you owe me big. Save me a biscuit, and say hey to Sodie for me." He returned Jess' lazy grin.

"I sure will, when I see her. She's kinda put out with me now, well, you know women!"

Johnny laughed," I don't wonder, the way you string her along!"

"Hey, I keep her guessin'. Women like a little mystery! I'll see you later. We'll go huntin' soon." Jess wheeled the bay around, cantering off with a salute in Johnny's direction.

The sun set over the mountains, casting a golden glow which rippled across the water. Johnny sat on a rock, watching its slow descent. He and Jess had not talked much. Jess was easy that way when they hunted or fished, and Johnny had appreciated the time spent quietly with only the splash of fish breaking water, the rush of the river, or the plaintive call of a distant hawk. He stretched out, fitting his five foot, eleven-inch frame on an accommodating boulder, and looked at the sky. It was so blue he felt as though he could fall into its depths... if he could only let go of the earth.

He thought about Sodie, the girl Jess had courted for over a year now. He knew the comely brunette was anxious to take the next step in their lengthy relationship, and commit to Jess, but Jess dragged his heels. Johnny supposed Jess loved her well enough, but he also knew that Jess would have a hard time settling down. Riding the countryside, breaking horses, playing cards, and almost anything in a skirt made a man like Jess come alive. As proprietor and owner of the Plains Relay Station, contracted to the prosperous freighting magnets, Wells and Fargo, he lived facilely with a couple of bachelors. Jess could come and go as he pleased which suited him fine. A wheelwright by trade, he enjoyed his work.

But Johnny knew Jess needed Sodie. She was the glue that held him together, the one constant in his life. Both Sodie and Jess were his friends, and he didn't want to see either of them hurt.

He closed his eyes, tired of thinking. The image of Cassie Wilkerson laughing in the sunshine, her dazzling smile and graceful figure cut through his thoughts. Could she really be as young as fifteen? Twenty-one as of mid-May, he had never formed any deep attachment with a young lady. His recent encounters with Myra had done nothing to help settle his sorrow-shot heart. The only real experience he could confess was hidden, buried deep in the recesses of his mind, and he could not allow himself to dwell on it. It had been in a time of great difficulty, sorrow, guilt and fear-a time of great loss.

Now, lying quietly, he began to experience the loneliness that sometimes crept over him in the rare times he could relax. Feelings of being disconnected and alone increasingly haunted him. He liked the town and his job, but maybe it wasn't enough for a lifetime. No set schedule, little sleep and constantly having to stay alert took most of his energy and all of his time.

How had Sam Brett been alone and done this job for all these years? He had alluded to having been married once and had simply commented that his wife had died. The marshal never mentioned it again, and Johnny had asked no more questions.

Johnny felt the old wave of loss descend as he thought of his own mama. She had been so pretty, always with a warm smile for everyone, so full of life until the war, then gone with the accident on the wagon train. Was it only four years ago? No, it had been more than five.

He was fifteen at the time, a handsome, tall youth with a quick smile and lively blue-green eyes, brown hair streaked with blond from exposure to the summer sun. He and Julia McLane had been a good team, having left the war-ravaged countryside of southern Virginia. They had come west as the number of wagon trains dwindled, before western expansion became easier by rail as the Union Pacific railroad stretched farther and farther across the country.

Convincing Johnny of the need to go west in the summer of 1864 had not been easy, and if not for her decimated condition and desperate insistence amid much pleading, he would have resisted completely. Ultimately realizing that he had no choice in the matter, he joined her as she sought to fulfill the life-long dream of his father, John Robert, for what was now only a remnant of the McLane famiy: a dream of life far from war, soldiering and slavery, and from the cotton and peanut fields, all of which drained a man's body and claimed his soul.

It had been a hard journey and very different from the harsh realities of the agonizing struggle in Virginia. With one son missing, one daughter taken in illness, and another married to a Confederate officer with the war still raging, the death of Johnny's father had been the real beginning of Julia McLane's decline. John Robert McLane had been correct. Life in Virginia as they knew it would be no more, so with the last of her remaining strength, she set her mind on a new course.

She grew stronger with the experience as new purpose took hold, and she watched the change in her son as he slowly began to heal from the rigors, devastating losses, and idealistic emptiness of the past few years. She valued the experience as an instructional time for Johnny and treasured the examples of courageous men and all the challenges and lessons which came to her son as the wagon train moved westward.

Julia shared her love for God and instructed the boy with the Bible, using examples of the Israelite patriarchs and their struggle to reach the promised land of Canaan. They moved as they were directed by a loving God, her God. Her faith was great and Johnny seemed to catch it. Julia had a new strength about her then, and she flourished in the great adventure.

Life for Julia had ended in a flash as a wagon broke loose from its traces, rolling backward, crushing her under its huge wheels. Her slight frame had been covered by a blue, calico quilt by the time Johnny had returned from hunting game with the men. He remembered that quilt, and was relentlessly haunted by the vision of her pale face and vacant eyes. They buried her in the wide expanse of the grassy prairie, while the wind blew from nowhere, rushing on to who knew where. Even now, when the wind howled down from the mountains at night, Johnny remembered that terrible day and he missed her sorely.

Cassie Wilkerson

Blocking the warmth of the sun, a shadow crossed his chest. He sensed it and opened his eyes just in time for Traveller to deliver a wet snort, his huge head just inches from Johnny's face. Bolting upright, he wiped his face with his sleeve and nearly fell off the rock.

"Alright, alright, I reckon you must be hungry." He stroked Traveller's neck, placing his forehead briefly against the horse, breathing in the warm, comforting scent he loved so much. "Good boy, I'll get you home. I guess the marshal will wonder what's become of us."

Picking up the gun belt, which he had tucked between the rocks, buckling it on and tying the holster end at his thigh, the young man became the lawman once again. Mounting, he spurred Traveller toward Sideling just as twilight fell, and the shadow of the mountains stretched wide across the prairie.

2

THE WEFT

THE TWO DRUNKS who had been secured in the jail overnight, sobered up enough to be release by 8:00 a.m. It had been a long night, and Johnny slept little on the cot in the backroom, kept awake by the snoring of the inebriated men. The marshal, having arrived at the office early, sent his deputy to the café for breakfast. The coffee was strong and just what he needed to jolt him awake for the new day.

Returning to the office, he swept the front cell, and cleaned the back cell which reeked of vomit. He washed up in the backroom, shaving by the reflection of the small mirror over the washbasin. After changing his shirt, Johnny reentered the office to find Sam Brett, shirt sleeves rolled up, reading the latest wanted posters.

"You should take a look at these, boy, there are a few new faces here. We'll need to take some of the old ones down. Glad to see that at least some of these men have been apprehended," he said, thrusting the posters into Johnny's hands as he walked toward the door and stepped outside. "Gonna make rounds."

Sam Brett was a man of few words. Only occasionally did he feel the need to expound upon some point of law or some injustice done, but when he did, Johnny knew it was time to listen and to listen well.

He walked to the desk sinking into the swivel chair. Just then, the bark and growl of a dog followed by loud cursing and the squeal of a frightened horse broke the tranquility of the morning. He jumped to his feet and vaulted over the railing in front of the desk. Out of the doorway at a run, he collided with a stack of hat boxes.

As he slammed into the bearer of the boxes, box tops and boxes flew in all directions. Worst of all, a tumble of jumbled skirts surrounded a form on the ground. Surprised and confused, Johnny helped the dazed lady to her feet, trying to straighten and brush the dust off her skirts. Realizing he was making an awkward situation worse, he quit.

"I'm sorry ma'am, I didn't see you. Are you alright?"

Her bonnet sat lopsided, covering her forehead and eyes. Clumsily, Johnny pushed it back off her face and to his astonishment, found himself staring directly into the deep blue eyes of Miss Cassie Wilkerson. His hands dropped to his sides.

Looking a little dazed, she took a wobbly step back, and he caught her elbows as she almost toppled over the hatbox which lay on its side behind her.

"Let me help you; why don't you sit down for a minute." Flustered, he attempted to guide her up onto the porch, offering her the chair beside the office door.

She resisted and seeing the destruction at her feet, whirled around and exclaimed, "Oh the bonnets! What will Miss Olivia think?"

She began to pick up the wayward bonnets, and Johnny moved to help her replace them in the three boxes, recapping the boxes with the dented, dusty lids.

Expressing genuine concern, Johnny asked, "Where were you goin' with these, Miss Wilkerson? I'll carry them for you...sure you are alright?"

"No, no, thank you, I can manage. I...I was just heading over to Miss Olivia's," she stammered, still trying to brush the dust off her sleeves and shoulders, and attempting to straighten her skirts. Embarrassed, she would not look directly at him as he held her arm, and she seemed to be measuring the distance between them and Olivia's cabin which sat along High Street to the rear and diagonally from the corner of his office.

Her long, auburn hair had escaped the confines of her bonnet, and she took it in both hands, gathered it together, then twisted it into a spiral and placed it over her right shoulder. He watched her, fascinated. Her eyes met his, and she blushed under his gaze.

"If you'll just help me balance these boxes...," he realized with a jolt that she was speaking and he was staring.

"I'll be glad to help you. I could carry these," he said apologetically, "It's no real trouble. Are you sure you are not hurt?"

He perused her disheveled gown, looking for signs of injury. She was such a comical sight he couldn't help but grin, his right eyebrow arching involuntarily as it did when he was amused.

He caught her indignant glare and repented quickly, losing his mirth. "I'm really sorry, but you look so..."

She straightened her bonnet, shook her head and snapped, "I don't think this is humorous!" She held out her hands. "If you really want to help, stack these boxes on my arms!" She flushed then faltered under his gaze, adding, "Please." Johnny stacked them.

Shoulders erect, she turned and walked off, favoring her right foot. A hatbox jutted out from each elbow, and another visibly bobbed over one shoulder. Johnny stared after her and wondered how it could be that she was even more attractive cloaked in anger. Maybe it was the heightened color in her cheeks or the flash of lightning in her eyes, and because he had laughed at her, maybe he would never have another chance to figure this out.

Marshal Brett finished rounds and rode out to the Smith homestead to assess a disturbed area on the southwest range. Smith believed that there were some "slicks" stolen from his small herd. Always a problem for lawmen, Marshal Brett reminded the homesteader that Wyoming law stated that calves must wear a brand before they became yearlings.

Smith had lowered his eyes, cursed, and tried to argue the point. Upon hearing the story, Johnny knew that the marshal would have no arguments from the man as "the law was the law". It could never be proven that those slicks belong to Smith even if they were found, for he had never branded them. The marshal, a true peace officer at heart, might take the time to placate the angry man, but would never bend the law.

Johnny finished sorting through the wanted posters, throwing out pictures of the poor unfortunates who had been captured or met up with the wrong end of a bounty hunter's gun. He was glad for the menial chore as he was having a hard time concentrating, his mind wandering off to drown in Miss Wilkerson's deep blue eyes. He wanted to know if she was recovering and needed to explain his laughter and search those marvelous eyes again.

Suppose the bonnets were ruined? He should find out if Olivia Halstead knew what had happened and understood that Cassie was not to blame for the accident. What was Cassie doing with all those hatboxes? Wasn't she supposed to be in school? He convinced himself that he should investigate. He should take a chance and rectify his behavior toward the young woman, make amends for his insensitivities, and most of all get another glimpse of her. Deciding he wasn't doing himself any good by just obsessing over the incident, he took his hat, placed it on his head, strapped on his gun belt and headed across High Street to Olivia Halstead's cabin.

A bell jingled as he tentatively entered the front gate, passing through the small yard to the front porch. Out of place and uncomfortable, he realized he had never set foot in this part of Sideling's real estate. He knocked on the door.

"Just a moment please," Olivia called, then appeared in the doorway.

Olivia Halstead was a spinster but not in the severest sense of the word. She had spent the last of her third decade and the beginning of her fourth, caring for her aged mother. Upon the old lady's demise, Olivia found that she could not bear to send her saintly mother off to glory in a simple pine box.

So beautiful were the posies she had carefully selected, arranged and placed on the old woman's bosom as she lay in silent repose. So elegant was the positioning of the swag of pine and flora bedecking the stark coffin, and so sincere were the mourners' words of consolation and admiration for the presentation of the departed, that Olivia promptly buried her mother, cleared out the sick room, and transformed the eight foot by eight-foot space into a floral shop of sorts.

Her talents soon found their way onto the bodices and bonnets of Sideling matrons. Her little endeavor was so remarkable that Olivia found a source for artificial flowers in Cheyenne, used the pittance of her proceeds and had small quantities shipped by train to Laramie City, then freighted to Sideling.

After Kate Wilkerson expressed concern that perhaps her eldest daughter was lacking in the feminine arts of sewing and design, Olivia 'selected' Cassie from her handful of Sunday school girls. With much prompting and no small measure of reserve, Cassie agreed to give her a hand in the tiny, blossoming enterprise.

"May I help you, sir?" Olivia inquired, with a slight twinkle in her eye. "Come in, come in! We don't get many gentlemen visitors," she cooed affably, taking his arm at his reluctance. "Are you looking for anything in particular?"

Stepping through the doorway, Johnny found he didn't know what to say.

"Would you like to see some hats? Are you looking for one for a young lady, perhaps?"

Olivia tilted her head and smiled broadly at the young man she knew to be deputy but had never had occasion to address besides a casual, passing "good day".

He stood speechless for a moment and the tin star on his jacket was the only sign of life as it reflected the dancing light from a candle. "You must be the reason for my injured young apprentice and my damaged goods."

Johnny colored, recovering his tongue. "Well, yes ma'am, I am and I'm sorry for any trouble I've caused you. How is Miss Wilkerson? Is she about?" he asked, wishing he was anywhere else in the world other than being held captive by the woman's firm grasp and her astute observations.

Olivia also held her smile. "Cassie is fine and not much damage was done. She limped off to school just before you arrived. Perhaps you could find her there."

Johnny knew he would not hunt for Cassie at school and confounded, realized he would have to find her another time.

"Thank you, ma'am. Could you tell her I stopped by to see if she was alright?"

It occurred to him that he handled damage complaints all the time, it was his job. Johnny took a breath, focused and continued.

"I'd be glad to pay for those damages. It was my fault if the bonnets were ruined, not Miss Wilkerson's. I ran into her and knocked them out of her hands."

"I am sure everything is fine. Only minor things, a little spot cleaning here and there," Olivia replied. "But thank you for stopping by."

She released his arm and clasped her hands before her, smiling genuinely as though she found the incident somehow amusing.

"You're welcome, ma'am, and if there is anything I can do, please let me know... thank you, ma'am."

Johnny turned and walked out, closing the door, grateful to leave the unfamiliar world of budding millinery behind him.

3

THE MIRE

"WHERE HAVE YA been, boy?" Marshal Brett was cleaning one of the six Spencer rifles kept locked in the wall cabinet behind the desk. When Johnny didn't answer, he continued. "You remember Pete Worrell's trial is the day after tomorrow?"

"Uh, yes sir. I suppose I'll leave for Laramie City early tomorrow afternoon," Johnny replied, removing his hat and gunbelt. He sank into the chair opposite Sam Brett. Thoughts of the trial had loomed over him all summer long, and he didn't relish thinking about it now.

"I sure hate to testify against him. I know what I saw that night, but Pete still denies killing an unarmed man. He's been a good friend to me... now he calls me a liar."

"Are you?" Brett asked without emotion.

Surprised at the direct examination, Johnny continued. "Well, no...you know we never found a gun on Conner's body, not near it, not anywhere. Pete says he saw him reaching for what he thought was a gun, said he saw a flash of metal. It seems wrong to lock up a man for something like that. A mistake was what it was. He just misjudged the situation," Johnny said, leaning forward, elbows on his knees.

"What does your badge tell you?" Sam asked.

Johnny sat back in the chair, rubbing his hands over his eyes and dropping them on his lap.

"To believe in the facts, just what I witnessed, I know. But what about his little brother? Matt is hardly old enough to take care of himself and Betsy is even younger. What about them? He's their only living relative."

"Guess you know that their lives lie in the hands of the judge and jury," the marshal said, laying down the rifle. He placed the cleaning rag and the rod next to it and looked squarely at Johnny. "You gonna have a problem with that?"

Johnny stood up and walked across the room, placing another stick of wood through the doorway of the potbelly stove. Orange light from the crackling fire dispelled the gloom of twilight. He slammed the door shut and lit the gas wall lamp. The coffee was strong and hot. He poured it into a tin cup, blew on it and took a sip, then turned to face the marshal. "I hope not," was all he could manage.

The sun was high and warm on his shoulders as Johnny and Traveller loped to the outskirts of Sideling. The almost three-hour ride would be pleasant as the fall day was beautiful, and a light breeze played with the leaves on the cottonwood trees. Johnny could feel Traveller's excitement and knew the gelding loved the trail as much as his master did. Now and then Traveller would toss his head and sidestep. "Well son, we got a ways to go. I know you are anxious, good ole boy!" He stroked Traveller's soft, grey neck and the horse calmed, snorting contentedly.

Just passing the Sideling schoolhouse, Johnny noticed Dodge Wilkerson and Eric Flynn nailing boards to a half-formed table under the trees to the left of the school building. He called out "hey" and waved. Dodge Wilkerson waved and walked toward the horse and rider, raising both arms in greeting.

"Well Deputy! Would you have time to give us a hand?" Eric walked up behind Dodge. One of the older boys, Eric was a pleasant, sturdy youth, and the son of Sideling's other prominent cattleman. Johnny had seen him around town with Beau Brenner on occasion and at church with his family.

Dodge Wilkerson was well known to Johnny as a deacon of the church, respected town council member, and cattle rancher. He had the largest spread, 10,000 acres, four miles southwest of town, and he was the father of five daughters, the oldest being Cassie Wilkerson.

"We could use an extra hand! Got an hour to spare for the Fall Festival? Best way we know to raise money for books and supplies!" Dodge prompted amiably, looking up at Johnny.

Johnny dismounted, leaving Traveller to graze. "Guess I have a little time, sir. I am on my way to Laramie City on business," he answered, shaking Mr. Wilkerson's hand.

"Hey Eric," he added, nodding to the young man.

"Fine then, fine! Grab a hammer," Dodge exclaimed, turning to lead the way. "We can make short work of this project."

Johnny rolled up his sleeves, discarded his hat and other accoutrements, and then hauled boards off the stack of timbers. Taking up a hammer, he took a turn at nailing as Eric held the table erect, and Dodge stabilized the far end of the long bench.

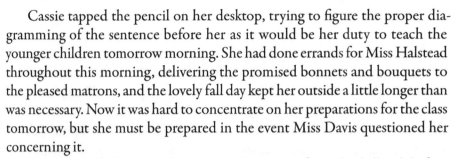

Cassie tapped the pencil on her desktop, trying to figure the proper diagramming of the sentence before her as it would be her duty to teach the younger children tomorrow morning. She had done errands for Miss Halstead throughout this morning, delivering the promised bonnets and bouquets to the pleased matrons, and the lovely fall day kept her outside a little longer than was necessary. Now it was hard to concentrate on her preparations for the class tomorrow, but she must be prepared in the event Miss Davis questioned her concerning it.

The sound of a hammer drew her musings away from the dull task before her to the open window beside her desk. In the sunlight, a large silver-gray, riderless horse stood grazing. A coat was rolled up and attached behind the cantle. A metal object on the coat caught the sunlight, flashing with the lazy movement of the horse. Recognizing the horse, Cassie's gaze swept the schoolyard.

Johnny, right leg against a log and leaning forward, sawed at a board. She took in the mesmerizing scene and watched him as he worked. The muscles in his upper arms and the pull of his shirt against his shoulders pleased her. His brown hair tumbled slightly over his forehead, and he stood to wipe his brow with an arm and leaned back against the side of the tree.

She was struck by how handsome he was, how free and boyish he appeared as he laughed with her pa and Eric, free from gunbelt, hat, and badge.

She placed a hand absently to finger the cross hanging from the chain around her neck and stared. She had thought of him frequently, ever since her embarrassing tumble into the street in front of the marshal's office. She felt small and clumsy then, but remembered the strength of his hands as he had kept her from falling backward over the hatboxes. She flushed as she remembered how he had looked at her, first concerned, then seemingly amused. What had he thought of her?

"Cassie Wilkerson, I've dismissed the class, are you feeling unwell?" Myra Davis asked, startling Cassie back to reality.

"Oh, no. I'm fine," Cassie exclaimed, collecting her paper and pencil, and retrieving her poetry book which had fallen to the floor. Feeling foolish, she attempted to collect her thoughts as Miss Davis continued.

"Your pa is outside with Eric, I believe, and they have finished the booth for our festival.

Remember, you are teaching the younger grades in the morning, and are also to be here early Friday evening. You and Millie didn't forget our last fall frolic meeting tomorrow night, did you?"

"No ma'am. We're planning on being there," Cassie replied, smiling and thankful for the reminder as she had truly forgotten the meeting.

Before Myra could finish, Millie Beale poked her head into the room, her body hidden by the wall dividing the coatroom closet from the classroom. "What's taking so long, Cassie? I've got to get to Miss Emma's for my piano lesson. Can't wait. I'll talk to you later! 'Bye!" She disappeared rapidly, shutting the front door with a slam.

"Gracious!" exclaimed Myra. "What a whirlwind that girl is!" Turning to Cassie she added, "Please take a pail of freshwater outside to your pa and Eric. I believe they're almost finished and are probably parched. Thank you."

With her book and bonnet in one hand, Cassie kept her eyes glued to each step as she carried the pail, trying not to spill the water as she descended the front steps, but it sloshed over the rim and down the front of her dress onto her shoes. At the base of the steps, she lifted her skirts, wiping the toe of one black-laced boot against the stocking of her opposite leg and with a critical eye, noticed that the other boot was now heavily speckled with water and dirt. She took a step just as a gloved hand lifted the pail from hers.

His eyes were an intense blue-green, leaving her breathless as she glanced up, finding them just inches from hers. As he smiled at her, she recalled the mischievous twinkle, and she blushed, instantly angry with herself for doing so.

"Let me help you, seems your hands are full again," Johnny said, laughing softly. He wore the same disconcerting expression he had worn the day of their collision and it set her at sea.

"Thank you," Cassie said simply. She attempted a smile, but the corners of her mouth had gone numb.

"Good afternoon, daughter," Dodge Wilkerson greeted. "How do you like our handiwork?" He swung an arm wide and smiled.

"Do you think the table is long enough to accommodate all those boxed dinners you girls will be cooking up?" Cassie had not noticed her father walking up behind Johnny and was relieved by his familiar presence.

"It's fine Pa, should be just the right size." She smiled, focusing on her father's accomplishment.

"Thanks to the deputy and Eric we got it done in one afternoon. I am obliged to you, McLane."

Lost in Cassie's aura, Johnny remembered himself and drew to attention, turning to her father.

"My pleasure, sir. Glad I could help, and I really need to be getting down the road. I hope to make Laramie City before dark." But standing just inches from her, he was unwilling to move. Framed by lovely auburn hair, amidst a sweet expression, her blue eyes sparkled, and Johnny allowed himself another few seconds, beholding the girl before him. Neither of them spoke and as a faint blush rose to her cheeks, he searched her eyes, enchanted, until Dodge Wilkerson's deep voice interrupted.

"Hopefully your journey is a good one. Maybe you will get back in town before Friday night. We'll look for you; don't want you to miss the bazaar!"

He held his hand out and shook Johnny's firmly. "Thanks again, son, God speed."

"You're welcome, sir," and addressing Cassie, "Nice to see you again, Miss Wilkerson." Placing his hat on his head, he stepped back and whistled for Traveller.

Cassie watched curiously and from around the side of the schoolhouse, with a nicker and a shake of his thick mane, Traveller came trotting up to them. Cassie stroked Traveller's velvet muzzle and watched as Johnny mounted.

Mr. Wilkerson put his arm protectively around Cassie's shoulders, and they stepped back as Johnny touched the brim of his hat in salute, his spurs to Traveller's flanks, wheeling the horse about and cantering off. Dodge and Cassie walked behind the schoolhouse to the buggy.

"Sam Brett's got himself a good man, maybe young, but he is a fine fellow. What do you think about that horse, daughter? Pretty smart animal I'd say."

"I wonder how he trained him to come at a whistle." Cassie climbed into the buggy, assisted by her pa.

"Time and patience, time and patience," repeated Mr. Wilkerson, as he circled to the other side of the rig, taking up the reins and clucking the horse forward.

'Strength and gentleness' was Cassie's silent assessment as they drove from the schoolyard for home. 'If a man has those things, his horse will have them also.' Cassie knew about horses. They were animals of prey and had to learn to trust. A tame horse was still a strong horse, and his strength could be used to serve a man well, especially in this rugged country.

As they drove through the afternoon, the shadows lengthened. Cassie pondered these things, wondering not only at the emerging feelings which had overswept and taken her by surprise, but at the spirit of the beautiful, gray horse, and most especially, about the deputy who unsettled her so.

Four miles southwest of town they reached the yard of the Wilkerson ranch with plenty of daylight to spare.

"I'll put the rig away and meet you in the barn," Pa told her, slowing by the porch.

Hopping down from the buggy, Cassie dashed up the four front steps, taking them two at a time, her skirt bunched in one hand and a schoolbook in the other, unaware of her sister at the window above.

The house was a simple two-story, rectanglular log cabin with a wide, covered front porch. Four small windows were aligned across the second floor, and little Juney had been waving wildly at them from an opened window as the white lace curtains blew in the breeze. She clutched her baby doll in one hand, and leaned precariously out of the window frame. Cassie was through the large front door before she even noticed Juney, but Dodge pulled the horses up quickly, reprimanding his youngest daughter. "You get back inside that window, gal. I've told you not to lean out, screaming like a banshee! You'll break your neck!" Before he could finish the last of his words, Juney had disappeared.

Dodge unhitched the horses, threw them hay, and was beginning to check the water buckets when he realized that Cassie had not joined him.

Being the eldest now, Cassie had taken on the bulk of the barn chores since her only brother had died three years earlier. With a great love for the outdoors, she had learned to ride when she was barely old enough to sit a horse, and Dodge was proud of her. Willowy but strong, she was as high-spirited as any of their riding horses. She had an innate way with animals. Ever since his son had died of pneumonia that cold winter, Dodge had allowed Cassie to become his "right-hand man", and she helped to ease his broken heart. Sometimes as he watched her, he wondered if he had done the right thing. Should he continue to allow her to be so self-reliant, so free to ride the countryside, or should he insist that she become more like the other young ladies in her circle of friends? His own dear Kate told him that Cassie would settle herself on her own, over the course of time. He wasn't as sure.

Where was she now? He finished the task of watering the horses just as Juney came running through the open barn doors.

"Ma wants you for supper," she piped, running to him. He swung her light six-year-old frame high into the air and held her in his arms for a moment.

"Tell her I'll be right in, and give me a tight hug," he cajoled. She complied and he stood her on the ground, turning her with a light swat to her behind. She ran back to the house, strawberry-blonde braids bouncing behind her.

Kate Wilkerson had the chicken fricassee warming on the stove. Martha and Annie, aged eleven and eight respectively, finished setting out the dinnerware, happily chatting about their day in school.

Fourteen-year-old Mary came through the back door with a pail of fresh milk. "Pa's looking for Cassie, Ma says she has not been to the barn."

"Good gracious," Kate sighed, replacing the coffee pot on the back burner. Drying her hands on her apron, she left the kitchen, crossing the hall to the wide staircase. The door to the room shared by Cassie and Mary was partially opened. Tapping lightly, "Cassie, may I come in?"

Kate entered the room. Cassie sat on her bed with her hairbrush in one hand and multiple colored ribbons lying across her bed. She looked up at her mother without speaking.

"What are you doing, Cassie? Your father has been looking for you. Dinner is ready now, and I believe you've forgotten your barn chores and the animals."

Cassie stood reluctantly and faced the mirror. She pivoted slowly from side to side, firming her lips.

"Ma, do you think I am pretty?" She pulled the brush through her hair and turned back to face her mother. "Am I?"

Kate stepped forward taking her hand. "What brought all this on, Cassie? It is not like you to fret about such things."

Studying her daughter's knit brow, she stood quietly for a long moment, puzzled by Cassie's frank self-examination. Cassie was an unusually sunny child, seldom overly concerned with matters of appearance and in whom Kate found natural beauty. Kate touched her cheek and smoothed her hair.

"Of course you're pretty. Folks say you look a lot like me," she teased. The corners of Cassie's mouth turned up and Kate watched a lone tear slip down Cassie's cheek as her daughter forced a slight smile.

"We'll talk about this later. For now, everyone is waiting on us." Kate put her arm about Cassie's waist and they went down to supper.

(Proverbs 31:25-31)

It was almost dark when Johnny reached Laramie City. Keeping Traveller at a steady pace, he made good time. The exhilaration he had experienced during his earlier encounter with Cassie had faded in the last few miles as he began to contemplate the upcoming trial, the reason for this sojourn.

Pete had been a cowhand and had become a good friend. They met almost immediately after Pete came to Sideling, just after Johnny had become deputy.

In the times Johnny found to attend church functions and a few dances, Pete and Johnny vied for the same young lady, until she dumped them both for another transient cowhand. Seeing the humor in this, they decided most girls were fickle and became fishing and hunting comrades. In the month that followed, Pete was left to parent his thirteen-year-old brother, Matt, and eight-year-old sister, Betsy. He relocated them from Denver to Sideling after their mother died suddenly with the fever. Pete's father had been killed in the Indian wars a few years before. After the death of his mother, Pete had become an angry man, drinking heavily at times. Johnny tried to encourage him, and remained a friend, but Pete's temper and the alcohol made it difficult.

At the time of the shooting, Johnny had been in Laramie assigned to pick up funds destined for the Sideling bank. Pete had come to Laramie City to purchase a fancy cowpony which had caught his eye, and Johnny met Pete for dinner that spring evening. The promised pony had been sold for a higher bid, and angry, Pete drank steadily for about an hour as he and Johnny discussed his recent losses. Pete began to argue with another patron at the bar over some remark that was made which Pete had misunderstood. Johnny and two others kept a fight from breaking out between the two men, and while Pete and Johnny stayed in the bar, the other man left.

Shortly afterward, as Pete walked out of the bar through the swinging doors, he spotted the man he had argued with walking toward him. Johnny walked behind Pete, slightly to his left as Pete stopped at the edge of the porch, drew his gun, and shot and killed Brad Conner on the spot. Johnny was the only witness, and it had happened in the blink of an eye. Now he was summoned to appear as a witness for the prosecution. The whole mess made him sick.

He spent most of the past summer trying to decide what his responsibility to Pete was and how he would testify. He had visited with Pete's siblings on occasion and both children were convinced that Johnny would help prove their brother innocent, and even though he had tried to tell them the truth, they would not accept it. Matt had argued and Betsy had broken into tears, so upset that Mrs. Chanette, the widow woman who had come temporarily to care for them, sent Johnny away. He had tried to see Matt again, but the boy refused to talk with him.

After stabling Traveller in the livery, Johnny walked through the dark to the Union Pacific Hotel to register. His stomach rumbled as he lit the gas lamp in the hotel room. Flinging his saddle bag onto the bed he left the room for the bar.

Upon entering the bar, he was struck with an eerie sensation; this fall night was about the same temperature and void of stars and moon just as that distant spring evening. He shook off the feeling and as he waited at the bar, a pretty blonde in a provocative black lace dress approached him.

"Buy me a drink, honey?" She placed a hand on his, smiling at him.

"Sorry," he replied, turning toward her, revealing the star on the breast of his coat. "I'm here on business."

"Lawman? Well, everyone needs a little relaxation," she said moving her hand to his arm and looking into his eyes.

"I just need some food," Johnny stated flatly, attempting to discourage her attentions. "That's all."

"I'll see what is left in the kitchen for you. My name is Suzanne. I'll be right back. Have a seat over there."

She indicated a small table at the side of the crowded bar. Overrun by weariness he sat down, but immediately got up, went back to the bar, and ordered a beer. Coffee might keep him awake. He wanted only to sleep and have tomorrow over as quickly as possible. This nightmare needed to end.

Suzanne came back with a plate of beef stew and two sourdough biscuits. "May I join you?" she asked, indicating the empty chair at the table.

"It's a waste of your time. I won't be good company," he answered, realizing she wasn't going to give up easily. Not bothering to try to dissuade her, he nodded toward the empty chair and took a forkful of stew.

She talked of inconsequential things, asking about Sideling and whether or not Johnny liked his job. She told him about the family she had left behind, hoping he would understand that this was only a temporary job for her as she would move on as soon as she could. The food and the beer and the dull conversation made him drowsy. He finished his dinner, bought Suzanne a drink for her trouble and excusing himself, walked out of the bar. He had told the truth; he had not been good company. Suzanne watched him leave.

The night air was crisp, and he stood for a long moment in the dark on the hotel porch. Taking a deep breath, he tried to clear his head. He found himself walking in the direction of the livery, thinking he might check on Traveller once more. The horse nickered as he entered the barn. Johnny stroked his neck, his hands passing over the hair which had dried stiffly from the sweat of the saddle during the afternoon's ride to town. Noticing a curry comb and a brush in the box nailed to the wall, he began to clean Traveller's coat.

"Sorry, son," he said softly. "Looks like I neglected you this afternoon. Don't worry, by tomorrow night this time, we'll be home."

Traveller turned his head, nudging Johnny's shoulder. The smell of the barn and the warmth of the horse was comforting, and Johnny felt the tensions of the day begin to drain away.

"Home," he whispered, and loneliness fell heavily, pressing to the depth of his being and he trembled under the weight of it. He had a gun, a badge, and some friends in a town named Sideling, but no real home. Traveller was his only true possession, the only living thing that belonged solely to him. He felt empty.

'Oh, God,' he thought, 'Now, I am responsible for a friend possibly losing his life.'

He prayed for strength but felt only despair. He thought of the God of his father and mother. When he allowed himself to think back on those years, on the atrocities that had changed their lives so drastically, he wondered if God remembered him, or even saw him at all.

He walked through the moonless night, back to the hotel. The lobby was dimly lit and seemingly empty. As he headed for the stairs, Suzanne stepped from the shadows, blocking his pathway. She looked up at him provocatively.

"I thought you seemed like you could use some company tonight, Deputy. I am available if you like," she breathed, artfully resting her hand upon his arm.

Johnny felt her step to his side. He inhaled her perfume, and stood quietly, looking down into her upturned face. She moved her arm to his shoulder, her fingers lightly stroking the back of his neck as she drew nearer. His body began to respond and he closed his eyes, unable to concentrate. Images rose from a time long gone, bringing a flood of emotion. The haunting of that desperate time, uncomfortable and cruel, came stealing in and he caught his breath sharply. Gently, he lifted her arm from his shoulder and stepped back.

"I can't...I won't," he whispered thickly, more to himself than to her.

She clutched his forearm, searching his eyes intently. "I'll be around-if you change your mind." She watched as he turned and climbed the stairs.

On the landing, turning to look back over his shoulder, he saw that she had gone. The lobby was empty. He shook his head to clear his mind and focused on the hallway before him.

(Proverbs 27:12)

Johnny tossed and turned much of the night. Distorted images of guns and war, of wagon wheels and lost innocence filled the long, dark restless hours, and just before dawn, he slept. The jingle of traces and rumble of wagons dragged him up through the heavy gray of deep sleep. Bright sunlight spilled through the windows, and he opened his eyes.

He groaned as he became aware of where he was: the trial and Pete, followed by the remembrance of the woman in the shadows. He stretched and threw a pillow over his face to block out the daylight. Five more minutes. He dreaded rising but experience had taught him that lying in bed worrying was usually far worse than being up, awake, and chasing whatever difficulty lay ahead. He took his time dressing, shaved and went for breakfast.

Entering the small restaurant, adjoining the bar, he found only a few men lingering over coffee and one reading a newspaper. The woman was nowhere to be seen, and he was relieved.

With little appetite, he finished only half of the eggs and sausage. He tried to form a logical testimony. Be brief, concise, just answer the questions. Would the judge see through the evidence? Could Johnny convince the jury that under his tough exterior Pete was a responsible man who had fallen on hard times and was burdened with caring for his young siblings? He was not a menace to society, he had just made an error in judgment. Should he walk over to the jail and try to see Pete? No, he supposed, was the answers to the questions, and most especially to the last one.

He finished breakfast, went to the livery to saddle up Traveller, and went for a ride in the chilly morning. By 11 o'clock he was back in town. The trial, to be held in the saloon nearest the sheriff's office, was set for noon. With saddlebags packed, he left the hotel. There would be no staying around town after he testified; he was sure of that.

The circuit judge for the fall trial session was a tired looking old man in a rumpled black suit. Johnny had never seen him before. The defense attorney and the prosecutor spoke as though they did not care one way or the other about the outcome of this trial. Six men and three women made up the jury: nondescript middle-aged citizens, all fed up with random killings on the streets, all wanting to have this trial over as quickly as possible. Pete's heavy responsibilities might sway the hearts of the jurors... some of them. However, Johnny had seen this play out before. The people of this upstart hamlet were not much different than those of Sideling. They were decent people who desired to raise their families and birth their businesses in peace. Pete had been that kind of man.

Johnny took in the faces of the jurors. With sinking heart, he realized they would never know who Pete was. How long would they be willing to listen? Or would they set upon him with their harsh judgments, and shatter his life like a leaning wall or tottering fence?

Pete sat, hands clasped before him, as he gave his account of the events of that dark spring evening. "Yes," he had seen a shiny object as Conner came toward him in the street and lifted his hand toward his coat pocket. "Yes," he believed that Conner was going for his gun. Desperation in his voice and despair in his eyes created a pathetic picture.

Then it was Johnny's turn to testify. Keenly aware of the growing expression of disbelief on Pete's face and the flash of wrath in his eyes, Johnny told what he had observed on that night. He answered each question directly. "Yes," Pete had been drinking. "Yes," Pete had become angry when he thought he had been challenged by Conner. "Yes," he had walked out of the saloon, onto the porch, had drawn his gun and shot Conner dead. There had been no gun on the dead man, no gun on the ground around him, and no other eyewitnesses. Laramie City's marshal, Eli Tucker, had been the next one at the scene and found no further evidence.

The judge dismissed Johnny. There had been little cross examination and no new evidence presented, so the jury was sent out to deliberate. The city marshal stood and pulled Pete to his feet, guiding him to the back of the small courtroom.

In a fit of anger, Pete turned, shouting, "You lie, McLane! You are the one lying, not me. You know I can't go to jail! You're sending me away! Who'll take care of Matt and Betsy when I'm in prison? I thought you were my friend! Liar!" When the marshal tried to hold him, he jerked his arm away, but the marshal held him securely.

Johnny came toward him, hoping to say something, anything, to settle Pete down, but Pete became more agitated. His eyes were wild. Tearing away from the marshal's grip, Pete lurched forward as Johnny stepped up to help the marshal restrain him. In a split second, Pete swung his cuffed hands in a wild arc, striking a hard blow to the left side of Johnny's face, sending him crashing into the bar. The back of his head struck the corner hard and he crumpled to the floor. The attorneys and the marshal's deputy tackled Pete and dragged him screaming and cursing from the room.

A few of the citizens who had remained in the courthouse came to Johnny's assistance, calling for the doctor. Blood flowed from a gaping wound along the cheekbone under Johnny's left eye, where the force of the handcuffs had caught him. Someone applied pressure with a handkerchief to stop the bleeding, but the skin was split to the bone. Johnny wasn't conscious when the doctor arrived, but as they lifted him, he groaned, muttering unintelligibly.

At the marshal's command, Johnny was carried by three men across the street to the doctor's office. Goldie Asher readied the only examination table in the small room as the men lay Johnny upon it. Blood seeped through the handkerchief, and although it was held firmly to the wound, it dripped onto the clean sheet below.

Sedating him with morphine, Doc Asher cleaned the wound and when the bleeding stopped, spent the next half hour placing sixteen sutures at the gash above Johnny's cheek bone.

"You don't think he will lose his vision do you, Doc?" Mrs. Asher asked her husband, as she held the deputy's face upright. The left side of Johnny's face was bruising rapidly, and his eye began to swell shut.

"Don't think so, Mother. I didn't see any damage to the eye itself. He'll have one devil of a headache, though. Hold his head steady, now. You'll have to get a telegram off to the marshal in Sideling. This boy won't be going back anytime soon."

"The morphine injection knocked him for a loop. You didn't give him much." Mrs. Asher cleaned the blood from around the sutured area and observed, "He is still out."

"I'll have the deputy help me move him to the back bedroom. He'll have to stay here for a couple of days." Doc stood to rinse the blood from his hands.

In the early morning hours, Johnny awoke in the dimly lit room, unaware of where he was. His face ached and his head pounded, and raising himself slightly on his elbows, he was plagued by dizziness and nausea. He sank weakly back into the pillow. He placed a hand on his swollen face then groaned as the touch sent waves of pain through his cheek.

In less than a minute Goldie Asher's thin frame entered through the doorway. She turned the kerosene lamp wick higher. The light stung as it pierced Johnny's partially opened eye and tears ran down his left cheek. His tongue was parched, his lips stiff, and he mumbled in confusion.

Goldie Asher leaned over him as she struggled to hear. "Easy does it, son, you had an accident. Doc is taking good care of you. You will be alright. Don't worry, we've telegraphed your marshal and he knows where you are."

"My horse," Johnny rasped. Mrs. Asher answered soothingly as she lay her hand on his forehead.

"The horse is being seen to. Doc went to the livery and explained everything. They'll take good care of him. Try to rest now."

She held a cup, spooning water into Johnny's mouth. It was cool but mingled with the metallic, bitter taste of blood. Any slight movement brought back the dizziness and nausea so he lay still. Throughout the night he slept fitfully, waking to the pounding pain, then being medicated into a strange, floating state of semi-consciousness.

The next day passed in much the same way, but by evening Johnny could sit up without the nausea, although he found himself unable to move without becoming dizzy. Doc discontinued the morphine, and Johnny was able to take some soup.

Doc sat by the bedside. "Don't know how wise it is to allow women to serve on juries. Since the organizers and legislators of this great territory deemed it fittin', and stranger yet, gave them the vote, well, I guess in this instance at least, it served your friend quite well. The young man was convicted of second-degree murder, but only sentenced to ten years imprisonment. I am sorry, but it's better than a hangin', son. I heard you two had been good friends."

The remark struck Johnny like a kick in the gut, and he did not comment.

"It is not draining now so I'll leave your wound uncovered... try not to touch it." He swabbed a liquid on the sutures and Johnny flinched.

"My friend has a young brother and sister. They're staying with a widow woman, but I don't know if she can raise them up or even how long they can remain in her care."

"Sometimes we don't get to know all the ins and outs of a situation. You did what you had to do, leave the rest to Providence. It is all you can do," Doc replied. "Can't be easy, doing what you do for a living. How old are you?"

He and Johnny talked for a while and Johnny liked him. He had kind eyes and able, gentle hands. Johnny was impressed by how well Doc and Goldie worked together. They laughed easily and seemed to anticipate each other's needs without words being spoken. Their love for one another recalled his childhood and the small farm where he was raised before the war had torn Virginia apart, along with everything he had known. He remembered his mama, full of laughter, and the gentle way his papa loved to tease her. The pounding pain having lessened and exhaustion overtaking him, he turned his face away and slept.

(Proverbs 27:6)

When Doc returned to check on him early the next morning, he found Johnny hunting through his saddlebags for a clean shirt. Dizzy and unstable when he turned too quickly, his movements were slow and deliberate.

"What do you think you are doing, son? You don't need to dress; you aren't going anywhere."

"Back to Sideling, sir, the marshal needs me. I've been away too long." Johnny perched carefully on the edge of the bed. Swollen to a slit, his left eye watered, and he dabbed it with his shirt sleeve frequently and tried not to touch his swollen, painful cheek.

"You will never make it to Sideling, you're too weak, and the ride will start your head pounding. Give it another day; you will be better by tomorrow," Doc admonished.

"I need to go, sir. I'll take it easy. I am not much good at lyin' around."

The physician placed a hand on Johnny's shoulder. "Listen son, you'll still be lying around, only it won't be in the bed. It'll be along the side of the trail, and that won't get you back to Sideling."

"I appreciate all you've done. You and Miz Asher have surely been kind, but I'm heading back," Johnny refuted, determination set in his tone and upon his face.

"Well, you're as stubborn as they come," the practitioner conceded tiredly, cautioning, "You know we had a snowfall last night. It turned colder."

The fall weather had given way to an early winter day, and light snow blanketed the ground. Johnny left the livery, and although the bright daylight forced him to keep his left eye shut, the lacy snowflakes felt cool against his hot cheek.

He pulled his hat low to shade his eyes. He was glad for Traveller's strength as he mounted, barely able to lift himself onto the saddle after tacking the horse. He did not go to the jail, knowing he couldn't tolerate the agonizing ordeal of seeing Pete. He knew what the man thought of him and didn't have the strength to face him. That he had told the truth had to be enough for now.

The Doc was correct. The young horse was not used to a constant slow pace and strained against his master's reluctant hand, causing Johnny's head to pound, and the dizziness and nausea returned. After an hour of the jolting ride, Johnny stopped by a stream along the trail and sliding down from the saddle, staggered to the edge of the stream, fell to his knees, vomited, then rolled onto his back in the snow. He closed his eyes, catching his breath and waiting for the dizziness and nausea to pass. Snow fell softly on his face, cooling his sweating brow.

He awakened with Traveller's cold muzzle pressed to his ear, and sitting up slowly, managed to get on his feet. He mounted and rode on, head down against the wind.

Sam Brett turned the key in the cell door, securing the two inebriated cowhands who watched numbly as Johnny came through the front door. Pale and trembling, Johnny pulled his hat off and slid into the nearest chair, resting his head against the wall. Sam threw the keys on the desk, reaching Johnny in two great strides, grabbing him by the shoulders to keep him from sliding from the chair.

"What are you doing here, boy? How did you manage the ride?"

Johnny mumbled unintelligibly, and Sam raised his deputy's arm, placed it around his shoulders and pulling Johnny to his feet, helped him to the cot in the backroom. Johnny sank onto the mattress as Sam lifted his legs to the cot, covering him with an army blanket.

"I'll get Doc, stay put." Sam ordered.

"No," Johnny whispered, "I'm alright; just take care of Traveller. I couldn't make it to the barn." He peered at Sam through swollen eyes, and Sam swore softly.

"Stay put. I'll take care of the horse, and I am getting Doc."

"Not goin' anywhere," Johnny breathed, just able to raise both hands to his throbbing temples.

Doc came, bringing laudanum. "Let's have a look." He examined the wound. "You've got quite a headache, don't you?"

Johnny lay quietly. From under the heavy lid of his uninjured eye, Johnny watched Doc Cullins mix the medicine. With the clink of the spoon against the glass, he closed his eyes, too sick to protest. Doc lifted Johnny's head while he administered the liquid, and Johnny prayed silently that somehow this time it would be different. Perhaps this time the visions and the voices he could consciously repress in his waking hours wouldn't overcome him, and the laudanum would just ease the pain and let him sleep.

As he cleaned the wound, Doc conceded, "Ole Doc Asher did a good job with the sutures, but you're darn lucky you didn't fall off that horse and bust your cheek wide open again. You'll sleep now." Using an ophthalmoscope, he examined Johnny's swollen eye. "You see the light, don't you, boy?"

Johnny flinched at Doc's touch. "Yes sir," he murmured weakly, and turned his face toward the wall. Sam leaned against the wall at the foot of the cot, arms folded across his chest as he watched them. Doc stood up, catching the question in Sam's eyes and the deep concern etched in his face.

"He'll be fine, but he's got to stay down, at least until his dizziness passes. See to it, Sam."

Doc fixed his eyes on Johnny. "Hear me son? Stay put!"

But Johnny did not comprehend, and as he slipped away, Doc and Sam's voices grew faint. He tried to catch himself, but there was only darkness and pain about him. Tumbling into the effects of the laudanum, he was unable to stop the terrifying freefall. Deeper and deeper into the blackness, passing grotesque, distorted figures with hollow eyes and outstretched grasping fingers, while blood red fragments exploded around him amidst reverberating cannon fire, and into the horrendous din of battle.

———————◦•◦———————

"Tell me, tell me, weary soldier... from the rude and stirring wars
Was my brother in the battle where you gained those noble scars?
He was ever brave and valiant and I know he never fled.
Was his name among the wounded, or
numbered with the dead?"
(*Was My Brother in the Battle*, Stephen Foster)

4

THE RAT

The Shenandoah Valley, 1864

CAPTAIN SCOTT SHIP'S bay gelding, dappled with the pale early morning light, cut through the ranks of the marching cadets. "Keep up lads, just one more day! General Breckenridge is depending on us!"

Johnny was weary. His soggy leather boots were beginning to rub through the heels of his woolen socks. Rain ran off his forage cap and down the back of his neck adding moisture to sweat under the weight of his gray wool jacket. The water, scraps of bacon and cornmeal he had consumed, only an hour before, hardly kept his belly from rumbling. The young cadet commander kept the boys in step; excitement, even anticipation of facing battle drove them forward.

"We'll take them Yanks and drive 'em back, make 'em sorry they ever came to the Valley!" cried an excited youth, receiving cheers in response.

Bantering and bravado filled the morning air. Some of the lads remained strangely silent, nervously gripping their muskets. With trembling lips, they forced weak smiles at the jesting of their boisterous comrades. Johnny hoisted his musket to his shoulder and grimaced at his friend, Saxby, who gave him a tight-lipped smile in return.

"We can do this, we'll make them sorry they came to the Valley!" someone yelled.

Deemed fit, and chosen by his commanders on the day of his fifteenth birthday, Johnny marched with the 247 cadets from the Virginia Military Institute. Having left Lexington three days earlier, the cadets marched onward, anxious to complete the eighty-mile march up the Shenandoah Valley to join with the Confederate troops under General Breckenridge near the town of New Market, Virginia.

The intent was to assist the troops by halting the advancement of the Union army under the command of General Franz Sigel. The soil of the Shenandoah Valley, rich and fertile, provided not only a road north through the valley, but produced a fine crop of wheat that would help sustain the starving Confederate troops if the Yankees could be held off and kept from destroying the crops.

"Hold the Valley!" had been the command of Robert E. Lee. "Guard the industries and railroads in the towns of Lynchburg, Staunton, and Lexington!" Among the General's goals was the preservation of the ultimate prize: the capture of the Confederate capital of Richmond. Another was to run the Yanks back up north just as far and as fast as possible.

Along the Valley Pike, rain soaked wheat fields lay, some still bearing the crop of early spring planting. Occasional farmhouses, some burned and others standing bleakly against the mire, contrasted sharply with the peaceful blue-gray rolling mountains of the Shenandoah range, stretching off into the distance on the eastern side of the Valley.

Johnny did not feel brave. He had almost stopped feeling anything at all except for a nagging uncertainty of what lay ahead. Virginia was his home and for generations had always been the home-place of his family. Just as his forefathers defended her against the British during the American Revolution, he would stand with his father and brother and defend his home and his family from the northern aggressors, who so brutally violated everything she was.

"We are a band of brothers and native to the soil,
Fighting for our liberty with treasure, blood and toil"

Some of the boys had taken up the tune of the Bonnie Blue Flag, breaking into Johnny's thoughts. His clear tenor voice, and his courage rose. He joined the chorus as they tramped along the soggy macadam-surfaced road.

"Hurrah, for the Bonnie Blue flag that bears the single star!"

The long anticipated meeting with the foe and the repelling of the Yankee troops would soon be realized.

'The soil and preservation of our way of life; that is what the fight is for,' he reflected. Slavery had not been the issue for his family. Papa had talked openly with him about that many an evening as they sat on the wide front porch of their home which lay on 100 acres across the Blue Ridge and far to the east of this vast, fertile valley of the Shenandoah. The flatlands, sandy soil, and swamps of extreme southeastern Virginia, known as the Tidewater, had never supported the huge plantations found in the fertile soils of the deeper south where cotton was "King" and the slave trade flourished.

The McLane's family grist mill, mill pond, and general store, which housed a post office that bore the stamp of McLane's Mill, Virginia, lay in Southampton County near the North Carolina border. Johnny's ancestors had come to Virginia from Ireland, Scotland, and Wales in the 1600s. The economic waxing and waning of those early years in the new country were borne by generations of the McLane clan. Through hard work and perseverance, they had managed to make a stable living and attain some degree of prominence in the community and the countryside.

Sparsely populated, farms in the county were relatively small, calculated in the hundreds of acres, and those who owned slaves, owned few. However, Johnny's father had told him that the area had not been free of violence, for one hot summer night in 1832, under a huge blood moon, a rebellious band of slaves rose up and slew many white men, women, and children as they rampaged through Southampton County. A young, literate, black preacher by the name of Nat Turner was convicted of leading the band, and many guilty and innocent coloreds had been hunted down in the swamp and forests. Turner was eventually caught, quickly tried at the county courthouse in Jerusalem, and hanged with the others to the relief of the horrified population, fearful of the same reprisal from other oppressed slaves. Terror seized the entire South.

Every boy in Johnny's school told that old story over and over again, around campfires in the pine forests, and at the edge of the swamps where they often camped. Each telling became more and more gruesome as the boy's imaginations ran wild, and they spit, crossed their hearts, and swore that the dense swamp still concealed the ghostly bodies of old, murderous, wild-eyed men.

Sometimes, even on sweaty humid nights when the inevitable cool, dank mist rose from the swamp and spread like a hand across the bottomland, Johnny could feel the icy cold, dead fingers crawl up his neck. He would shiver them off and then lead the boys in a rousing chorus of "John Brown's body lies a molderin' in the grave", another campfire favorite.

Julia McLane thought little of John Brown's moldering body, and refused to have the telling of it sung in her presence. Having received a sharp whack with a broom across his backside, Johnny learned to confine the songs to the campfire and trapping treks with his buddies. Papa however, laughed at their folly, and enjoyed the telling of the stories almost as much as the boys.

Now, through the din of singing cadets, Johnny thought about Papa and missed him.

As far back as he could remember, he would sit on his papa's lap, listening as John Robert read the newspaper accounts of the goings on in the Tidewater and beyond. Johnny loved the smell of the cherry tobacco, pushed deep into Papa's wooden pipe bowl, with the match striking brightly in the evening twilight. A few deep puffs and the air would fill with the wonderful aroma. Papa always had time for Johnny's questions, explaining the words he did not understand: impressment, agrarian, legislative. He talked of all the political unrest between the states to the north and the states lying south of Washington City, and of territorial lands that were to be admitted to the Union: new states to the west where a man might travel to be free and equal before the law.

John Robert believed in the equality of man as held forth in God's Word. He studied the Bible and made it a part of his family's daily morning and evening devotions without fail. Johnny loved the stories of David and the villainous Goliath, and of Joseph and Samson, which came alive with the telling. Papa had spoken like he knew Jesus and loved Him passionately, and Johnny had believed that there were no better men than his papa and the man, Jesus, in whom Papa trusted.

As he grew, Johnny worked in the store alongside his papa stocking shelves, taking inventory, and putting into practice ciphering skills learned in the room Aunt India Carr used for schooling the children at her home, just down the road and across the fields. Often times, he worked at mending tools used to farm the peanut, cotton, and tobacco fields, singing melancholy songs about freedom, faith, and hope alongside Big Jim and his boy, Moses, who were freed blacks that worked for Johnny's papa.

Moses and Johnny had grown up together, fishing and trapping beaver in the swamps and creeks near the Nottoway River. They had been good friends, almost like brothers, except that Moses lived with his family in a small cabin near the edge of the mill pond. Gensey and Catty, mother and sister, helped Julia McLane in the "big house".

Papa and Johnny's evening talks turned to more serious issues in 1860, as a new president had been elected, and war seemed likely. Papa believed that without the slave population to harvest fields and care for the plantations, the South would struggle to stand.

"I declare, our state spends so much time defending slavery, the politicians can't get anything done! We ought to be building railroads instead of depending on our waterways for hauling goods. I tell you, son, no man can ever really 'own' another, and Virginia's pride will be her downfall. The Good Book says, 'Pride goeth before the fall and a haughty spirit before destruction.'"

Johnny lay on his bed that night, the upstairs window to his room opened to the swath of a million stars forming a thin white cloud, spreading across the sky, uniform and majestic, and mocking the whole human race with its mortal frailties. He played his harmonica, a slow, haunting tune he had learned from Moses and Big Jim, and thought about the newly elected president, Mr. Lincoln. Moses had argued that Lincoln was a black man who would free all Negro people as soon as the war started. Papa said that wasn't true; Lincoln was a white man, an Illinois lawyer who would make certain that any new state admitted to the Union would be a free state.

But Papa was not so sure Mr. Lincoln would actually free the slaves, for although the northern states worked together closely, bound by industrial factories and concerns, their factories depended on the goods that the South provided. Papa liked the new president, but kept his thoughts at home, for his opinions were not popular, and he was unsure that the new administration would guarantee the rights of the states to govern themselves, which was something he believed in strongly. On the times Johnny had accompanied Papa to the county courthouse in Jerusalem, he had witnessed the loud exchanges between the farmers and businessmen. Most thought a war could be won quickly by the South, although some did not. One thing was certain though--all believed war would come.

That same night, as he lay on his bed, Johnny had pondered all these things, wondering what the future might hold for them...for him. Picking up his harmonica, he began the tune he loved the most, and the clear, sweet strains floated through his opened window.

"Steal away, steal away, steal away to Jesus..."

Tired from the day, Johnny lay his harmonica on the bed, crossed his arms behind his head, and finished the song with his clear, melodic tenor.

"Green leaves are bendin', poor sinners stand a tremblin'
The trumpet sounds within my soul, I ain't got long to stay here."

Johnny had not known Papa still rocked on the porch beneath his window, listening to the distant, sweet refrain of his song. John Robert puffed on his pipe, and deep sadness filled his breast as he reflected on the chorus of the song he knew all too well.

"The trumpet sounds within my soul, I ain't got long to stay here," he whispered. The great, deep bellows of the bullfrogs from the pond, and the whispering of the wind through the pines were the only response to the overwhelming questions welling up in his soul.

In 1861 the war had come, and within a year John Robert got up a regiment of local volunteers, became their colonel, and went off to defend the homeland. Joseph, Johnny's older brother, had gone off a month earlier. Being only eleven, Johnny, and his thirteen-year-old sister, Mary Annie, were left with Julia to keep the home-place, assisted by Moses, Gensey, and Big Jim.

In January of 1863 the war raged on, and Johnny was sent west to the Virginia Military Institute in Lexington. The Institute had just recently reopened its doors, and if conscription was disallowed for the cadets as Governor Letcher had declared, Johnny would be able to complete his education in relative safety. Julia had protested these events, but Papa had believed in the goal of the institute: "to strengthen the nation by producing strong men with leadership qualities and good moral character," he had declared. "'Citizen soldiers' as they are known, my dear. It is an educational institute, Julia, and not a military target." The issue was settled.

Mama and Mary Annie were left at home to run what remained of their store. Supplies and food were hard to come. The Union army blockaded what little travel there had been along the roads and the river systems which wound inland from the seaport of Norfolk to the east, and the Albemarle Sound to the south. The Nottaway, Blackwater, and Meherrin Rivers meandering not far from the town of Jerusalem, and the city of Petersburg, which lay 40 miles to the west, were cut off by Union troops. By 1863 the area was in desperate need of provisions, and the mill sat dormant. Cotton could not feed the families of the south, nor could tobacco.

At first, Julia tried to keep her letters to Johnny lighthearted. News that Johnny's oldest sister, Rebecca Keaton, had married to her long-time beau and distant cousin, Jet Scott, was welcomed. While Johnny was elated that Jet had been elected Lieutenant and was engaged with the Army of the Potomac under the command of Robert E. Lee, Julia was not, for she struggled under the burden of the farm and the mill.

Julia and Mary Annie attempted to farm with the help of Big Jim, for Moses had gone off to join the Union forces. Most of what they produced was taken by impressment agents for the good of the "Cause".

It had always been John Robert's practice to follow the Lord's instruction from the book of Leviticus. "Do not strip your fields bare, or pick up fallen grapes." Faithfully he had insisted on this, believing such should be left for the poor and the sojourners. What little was left in the fields was trampled by the Union cavalry regiments or gleaned by hungry Rebel infantry passing through. Julia had tried to live by her Christian convictions, helping the wounded men and giving what she had, but she had almost nothing left and little strength with which to give it. Lack of basic supplies could only mean Mary Annie and Julia had nothing to sell and little for themselves.

Johnny missed them terribly, but what seemed even worse was that Mama had only asked him to pray for Papa and Joe. She never said where they were... or if she had seen them.

(Leviticus 19:10)

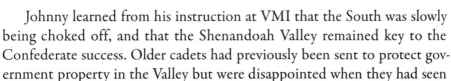

Johnny learned from his instruction at VMI that the South was slowly being choked off, and that the Shenandoah Valley remained key to the Confederate success. Older cadets had previously been sent to protect government property in the Valley but were disappointed when they had seen only traces of action. This march would be different. Now, the singing and bantering of the boys was barely audible through the rain as the tramping of soggy, worn boots met the tough, rutted, macadam turnpike before them.

Eighty long miles, hour after hour, Johnny tramped numbly along, thinking about his father, imagining him in the distance on a big black stallion riding high above the heads of the marching youth. Maybe he would see him tomorrow--maybe Papa would be with the troops who were engaged along the road leading to the north of the Valley.

"The Road of Warriors" it had been called, for great Indian chiefs and explorers had traveled it for centuries. Johnny had heard it led all the way to Philadelphia. Maybe Papa would be riding with General Lee and the general's big gray horse, Traveller. Maybe they, with the help of the cadets, could chase the Yankees north again and end the war. Mist mingled with his stinging tears, and he quickly wiped his sleeve across his face.

Rain hung over the valley as the exhausted cadets stopped for the night, and rain continued as they reached the hills surrounding New Market the following day, joining with the Confederate regulars encamped there. The streets of the town of New Market lay deserted as citizens huddled in fear in their homes throughout the day. By midnight, as Johnny and a few of the cadets sat by the campfire guarding federal prisoners, just south of New Market, a courier from General Breckenridge arrived with orders, and the VMI corps began to form up. Some of the cadets had crawled through the windows of a nearby Presbyterian Church to escape the rain, sleeping on the wooden pews until the roll of drums awakened them and drew them out into the dark. Though clouds hung in the night sky, the cadets followed the Confederate veteran brigade, marching before their own artillery. As they marched in relative silence through the storm, Johnny swore he had never seen a more eerie sight. Distant campfires, burning on a far ridge, appeared to be suspended in the dark sky, and embers burst and flamed like hellish demons.

Through the rain, Johnny listened to the sounds of the cavalry as they met in skirmishes on the hillsides, and in his diary after the battle, gave an account of the events as best he could recall them.

May 15, 1864, Dawn: *General Breckenridge has been unsuccessful in drawing the Federal cavalry out, having used his troops only defensively from a fortified position in the hills. Now he greeted our corp of cadets, and with the combined forces of guns drawn by cannon limbers up to the rise of the hill, Breckenridge ordered the Federal troops fired upon. The Federals answered with gunfire of their own, and the cannons exchanged fire between the rises of the hills for two hours. Suddenly an enemy shell tore open the center of the Confederate ranks, and we cadets were ordered into battle, marching in perfect alignment down Shirley's Hill.*

When Captain Shipp ordered, "Battalion close ranks!" we unified, closing the gap created by the wounded and dead regulars. We marched across the field by a farmhouse, as mini balls and shells rained down and flew around us like angry hornets from a hive. Finally, reaching a fence line just to the north of the orchard, we sheltered behind it, dropping and firing from the knee.

Julia knew little of what had transpired that day. Communication was slow in coming and sometimes non-existent, for skirmishes and battles raged throughout the South. It was, however, Johnny's letter written from the Institute on June 28, 1864, over a month after the battle, which drove Julia in desperation to take the next drastic step.

> *Dear Mama,*
> *28 June, 1864*
>
> *I pray that all is well as can be for you. Have you heard from Papa and Joe? How are Mary Annie and Rebecca? Has Rebecca heard from Jet? I don't know if the letters I write to you now get through for I have not received any from home for the last two months. Have you heard the news from Lexington?*
>
> *Our involvement in the battle at New Market with General Breckenridge's troops was a fearsome one. But we met the challenge*

with honor. We were called up to support the Confederate troops if needed, and we were indeed called to fight.

During the battle, an enemy shell tore open the center of the Confederate ranks. We were ordered to move in as a huge thunderstorm with blinding rain convened upon us and we charged the enemy line just as our Confederate brigade lost ground.

Crossing a muddy depression, my right shoe was sucked from my foot, and as we advanced steadily and not faltering, I was wounded in my right leg, below the knee. Confusion, smoke, shot and shell rained down, but I was able to keep advancing with what was left of our company. We fired a volley at the Union battery's horses, dropping some of them. Union General Von Klieser's fire diminished then and he limbered out all but one Yankee gun. Then the whole Federal line retreated! We pursued them, capturing many and were commended by General Breckenridge.

The able-bodied boys helped lay the bodies of our own wounded and dead across the artillery limber. Soon rendered helpless, I was laid upon a limber as well.

We were taken to Staunton, some of us in wagons. My wound was dressed and has healed. From Staunton, we were placed on a train to Richmond. Stopping in Charlottesville, the atmosphere was joyful and we cleaned out the ice cream parlors of their fare and were celebrated by the citizens, with many pretty girls in company!

Upon reaching Richmond we were commended by the Congress and received new Enfield rifles from President Jeff Davis. But we were soon needed again as Union Lt. General David Hunt marched down the Valley and captured and ransacked Staunton, destroying the railroad and much of the town.

Though sent by rail to assist our troops and protect Lynchburg, we returned immediately to Lexington, warned that Hunter might turn for Lexington in retaliation for our victory at New Market. Then on the 9th of June, General Carsland failed to hold

*off Hunter at Midway and word came to prepare the newly con-
structed river bridge coming into Lexington for destruction. Papa
will remember the stone bridge as he and I crossed it, coming over
the canal and the Maury River, when we first entered VMI by
the north post, just down from the hospital.*

*I was one of the Cadets chosen to go to the bridge with Captain
Wise. ("Old Chinook" we call him, respectfully) with a howitzer and guns. Superintendent General Smith and other cadets
loaded the wagons and canal boats with school records and property to take them to safety.*

*Before dawn on June 11, our troops crossed the bridge to cover
the retreat of our rearguard. As our men were chased back across
the bridge by the Federal advance, we fired on the advance and
turned them back. We had hay bales soaked with turpentine and
piled around the bridge and under it, then fired them up and
used the howitzer on the bridge pilings to weaken them, effectively destroying the bridge.*

*Afterward, we "doubled quick" back to the barracks thinking to
be quite safe, however General Hunter proceeded to shell the
barracks and school, with artillery from the high hills north of
the river. Brick and mortar rained down, and we were moved
quickly to Washington College. The fire was fearsome. We vet-
erans of the New Market Battle tore our Colors, and each took a
fragment with which to remember our victory and our honorable
school, now gone up in flames.*

*We marched west toward the mountains to a place called Balcony
Falls and there, threw up breastworks to protect the citizens who
had fled from Lexington in the event that Hunter would follow.*

*On freight boats, we traveled the James River toward Lynchburg
again and made ready to support General Jubal Early in defense
of that city. We arrived on June 15, marching in darkness and
silence at night to relieve exhausted Confederate troops. We lay
all night in trenches in red, doughy mud, each with a gun across
his lap, wrapped in blankets, waiting. In the early a.m. we saw*

that the enemy had retreated and were told that Hunter had taken his Yanks west. We were not needed and on June 24 we arrived back at Lexington.

We now live on the school grounds, in tents for the fourth class cadets, or "rats" as we are called because of our gray uniform coats, and in cabins for the first class whose graduation day we are anxiously awaiting. It is hard to have lost our comrades to battle, but we stay strong with drill and busy with cleanup of the destroyed Institute. The interior is gone but the walls stand like sentinels, a testimony to the fact that Southerners will never yield!

I am requesting that you and Papa allow me to stay and graduate with my class of '67. Even though we are to be dismissed for the summer and if you cannot come for me, I can stay in Lexington and help rebuild the Institute as is the desire of Superintendent Smith.

I hope Papa will not be disappointed in me. I am suited for a soldier. I have also begun to see the need for Confederate independence and much admire the philosophies of John Locke and former Vice President John Calhoun, among them: states' rights, a limited federal government, free trade and the right of the concurrent majority.

Surely General Breckenridge will need our assistance in the Valley before the time the war is over. Afterward, I can apprentice in law as Papa wished, however, I would stay in Virginia and help strengthen our new Confederate government. I do not wish to disappoint Papa, but after reflection, I find myself conflicted on the issue of slavery. I believe that each man has the right to liberty and to make his own decisions. I believe as Papa did, that all men should be free to own property. But how can a black man be made suddenly free? How we would advocate for him in our society at this time, I do not know. What would become of him?

Mama, do you have any idea where Joe is that I might write to him? If you can get word to him, please tell him I need help with the binomial theorem. I know he could explain it to me so

*as to make sense of it. If there is anything of redemptive value
to be found in all of war, it would be the postponement of my
examinations. I fear I excel in gunnery and horsemanship more
so than in Latin.*

*Tell Mary Annie I have learned many new songs, some of which
I can teach her upon my return. You should not worry about my
religious education as General Smith instructs us in the Bible
daily, and we have prayers with "revelee" and before "taps". I
often attend the voluntary prayer meeting in the evening with
my friend, Saxby, unless I am worn out from drill and sleep
through the meeting. Please let Papa know I wish to speak to him
as soon as possible. Please write to me with news of the family.
May God protect all of you.*

*Your loving son,
Johnny
Cadet CPL, CSA*

Johnny could not have known that two of his closest cousins had fled
Virginia to Maryland's eastern shore to take up arms for the Union, devastating
his Aunt and Uncle. Julia McLane sold what was left of her ravaged home and
store for the price of a wagon and supplies, and with her few remaining worldly
goods, drove to Lexington for her son.

Sick of the songs, and sick of war, she left her 17-year-old daughter, Mary
Annie, in a grave next to a memorial stone erected to her husband, who had
been lost in the Battle of the Wilderness near the Rapidan River in Virginia--a
week before and only the distance of a day's ride from the Battle of New Market.
Worn and thin, Julia had given her last ounce of strength nursing Mary Annie
but had not been able to bring her back from the ravages of yellow fever. Her
eldest daughter, Rebecca Keaton, whose husband remained with General Lee,
had cried and begged her to stay; but Julia, brokenhearted, only wanted to
leave the devastation of Virginia and save her youngest son. She did not know
if Joseph was alive and could no longer hold her beloved John Robert, but in
her wounded heart, she held his dream for their future and headed westward
with Johnny.

"Before the South shall bow her head, before the tyrants harm us
I'll give my all to the Southern cause and die in the Southern army...
If I must die for my home and land, my spirit will not falter,
Oh, here's my heart and here's my hand, upon my Country's altar...
I'll place my knapsack on my back, my rifle on my shoulder
I'll march away to the firing line, and kill that Yankee soldier!"
(*The Southern Soldier*, Traditional Folk)

5

THE INTRIGUE

SNOW FELL AT a moderate pace, the wind whipping it into a frenzy. Traveller sidestepped and moved gingerly forward as Deputy Johnny McLane held him to a jog, both man and horse exhilarated by the chill, crisp Wyoming air.

"Easy, son. I know you're glad to be out," Johnny said, rubbing Traveller's muscular neck in a circular motion and calming the animal.

"I've had enough of this mess!" Johnny exclaimed, realizing freedom from the shackles of his recent disability and the laudanum. He gave Traveller his head in a gallop over the remainder of the two miles from Sideling to Mabel Baker's farm.

Marshal Brett and the temporarily deputized Jess Bryant had taken the 20-mile ride to the northeast of Sideling as reports of cattle rustling, numerous in the last month, had come from ranchers as far as Cheyenne to the east, and stretching all the way northward toward the town of Iron Mountain. Jess had taken time off from the stage relay to ride to Laramie City with Marshal Brett, and Johnny had sullenly watched them ride out earlier that morning.

Under orders from Doc, which were enforced by Sam Brett, Johnny had been placed on "light duty" after his head injury. After a week, he grew tired of keeping the office log and of Sam Brett's, "Oh no you don't!" rebuke at every attempt he made to break free of the jailhouse. Not happy to be left out of the hunt, but glad enough to be cut loose from the mop and broom detail, Johnny had grudgingly accepted the minor task of finding Widow Baker's missing heifer.

Hunting an errant cow was better than confinement, and he knew the Widow Baker had no one to help her since her husband had passed away shortly after Johnny had become deputy. Johnny had taken to helping her around the dilapidated farm even before Emory Baker passed at an advanced age.

Swinging down from the saddle, Johnny tied Traveller in the dilapidated barn. The snow had lightened to flurries and the sky began to clear. Doc had removed the sutures in his cheek, leaving an inch-long scar, and although Johnny was glad for the demise of his dizziness, he still sported a yellowing bruise to his left eye. The bone had been bruised and it was still tender when he smiled, although smiling hadn't been much of a problem in the past week.

He bound up the wooden steps, crossed the porch and knocked on the door of the small log cabin with his gloved fist.

In less than a minute he was inside the cozy cabin, mesmerized by the aroma of something baking in the oven and standing in the presence of Mabel Baker. She was a sprightly woman of 78 years with a face that crinkled with laughter and eyes that sparkled bright blue. She was a tiny thing, but had a fearsome hug for Johnny.

Looking up into his face she stopped short, "My stars, boy, what happened to you?" Before he could get a word in she added, "I hope you'll quit that job! You'd probably add another 20 years to your life!"

"No ma'am," Johnny laughed, and he followed her to the kitchen. "I suppose I'm too ornery to die young."

Mabel poured him a steaming cup of coffee, delighted to have his company. Warmly, she offered, "Sit your self down. I have some fresh bread; it's almost done." Opening the iron door of the cook stove oven, she peered inside. The aroma was excruciatingly overpowering, and he felt his stomach growl, wishing he had time to eat it now.

"I'll look for your cow first. She can't have wandered too far, there is not much to graze on this time of year, so I expect she'll be heading back to the barn from wherever she's got to. I don't want to lose daylight."

"You'll fix the fence then? I don't know where the break is but you know where the tools are in the barn," she said, facing him expectantly.

"I do know. I'll fix it, and be right back." He took another swallow of coffee, setting the cup on top of the warm stove. "Just keep it hot for me, please ma'am."

As he exited the back door, a rush of cold wind stung his face. Just as he had expected, old Bessie was making her way back across the field toward the barn. He and Traveller rode out to herd her through the broken fence and into the barn.

He broke the ice on the large wooden bucket, and the cow drank steadily. Tossing hay to Mabel's horse and the cow, Johnny used the pitchfork to muck out their stalls, replacing some of the soiled straw he had carried out to the manure pile with fresh straw. With a hammer and penny nails from the wooden box on the rickety table by the barn window, he repaired the fallen fence boards. For a moment, he surveyed the barnyard.

"Oh lord, what a mess," he said to the wind, returning the tools to the barn.

The bread was hot, and the butter melted instantly, sinking into the golden crust. Johnny and Mabel talked easily about the town and his job while they enjoyed the fare.

She shared the story of the man who had been the "love of her life". Her eyes glistened, and she dabbed at them with her handkerchief, unashamed of her emotion. "We were married almost sixty years," she concluded, and paused to study the young man before her.

"What about you Johnny? Do you ever consider having a family of your own? From what you told me, I gather there is nothing left of your birth family."

Johnny took a breath, pushing back from the table. He crossed one boot over his knee and attempted to broach the painful subject. He never allowed himself to dwell on it for long, and whenever it rose from his core threatening to undo him, he forced the thoughts down most masterfully.

"I do have a sister still living in Virginia. She wrote once, about a year ago, and I sent her a letter back a couple of months later. She and her husband have a small house in a town not far from where we were raised. Her husband, Jet Scott, went to work as a banker after the war, and they have a little girl, Julia, named after our mama."

He offered a brief smile. "Not much to tell."

"I hope you'll get to see her again, Virginia is so far off." Her eyes had regained the impish twinkle, and while folding her napkin, she grilled him.

"You didn't answer my question. A young man like you needs a family of his own." She eyed him with such genuine concern that it touched his heart. Others had asked the same question of him, mostly out of curiosity, but Mabel Baker had asked because she honestly cared. He knew her well enough to be sure of that.

He answered slowly. "Well, I hope for that...someday. Just don't know if I could ask any woman to share this kind of life."

Her countenance had brightened again, and he laughed. "Anyway, I don't know anyone who would have me."

"Pshaw, Johnny McLane! I know half a dozen girls who would be honored."

She rose to retrieve a second batch of bread from the oven, the huge red-checkered potholders dwarfing her small hands. Johnny stood and quickly opened the large oven door for her.

Noticing the nearly empty wood box beside the stove he offered, "I'll fetch some firewood from the shed while you get that out." He was out the back door before she could object and left his coat hanging on the back of the kitchen chair. Mabel shivered from the cold draft that rushed through the back door, and placing the last wood stick in the oven, she wrapped the shawl lightly around her shoulders.

"Aunt Mabel?" a voice called from the front of the cabin. "Are you home?"

"I am in the kitchen, child, come on in!"

Cassie Wilkerson appeared in the kitchen doorway, a basket hanging from her arm and big white snowflakes melting on her blue woolen scarf. "I'm so sorry to barge in like this," she said happily, "but I knocked, and you didn't answer."

She set the basket on the table, taking her scarf off and unbuttoning her woolen cloak. "It's snowing harder again. I thought it was clearing!" She gave Mabel Baker a smile and a warm hug.

"Cassie honey, I am sorry I didn't hear you when you first came in. I was just taking this bread from the oven."

A gleam pierced the corner of Cassie's eye, and startled, she looked about. She noticed the brown jacket hanging over the kitchen chair. The metal star upon it had deflected the firelight and cast the glint like a spark.

She stopped short, exclaiming, "Oh! You have company!"

"You come right on and sit down; it is just Sam Brett's deputy, Johnny, come to help me out." Mabel straightened, placing the fragrant bread on the iron trivet in the middle of the table. "We were about to enjoy some of this and I want you to join us; you can spare a few minutes, can't you?"

"Oh, well," Cassie said haltingly, "Ma sent me with some cheese and butter for you, but I am on my way to town to get more lace and ribbon."

Mabel Baker's home had been a second home, and Cassie had spent many a pleasant afternoon having tea and cookies with this good, kind lady, who had become her adopted "auntie" since childhood. Suddenly everything felt different. The familiar, now intruded upon by a disquieting presence, caused apprehension which morphed into an unfamiliar tension, warming Cassie, but not disagreeably so. She trembled, feeling foolish and not knowing how to respond.

"The ribbons aren't going anywhere, but I expect this loaf may after Johnny gets hold of it," Mabel said, laughing. "Just move that jacket over and have a seat. I'll put some hot water on for tea."

"Yes, ma'am," was all that came to Cassie's mind.

She stared at the brown coat a moment then reached out to touch it. It was of comfortable, well-worn brown leather, but the touch brought a rush from her fingertips to her toes...warmth unfamiliar, but not unwelcomed.

Mabel busied herself by cutting the loaf into thick slices, and Cassie found herself touching the metal star. Cold, hard, and powerfully mysterious, she allowed her fingers to linger on it briefly. As recently as this past spring, she had been among the schoolgirls who had watched the comings and goings of the coat's owner and his beautiful silver-gray horse. The man was as silent and nomadic as one who seemed to ride on an ethereal plain above the common terra of Sideling. Rumored to have been in the terrible war, he had magically found his way to their small town in the foothills of the Medicine Bow. She had seen him at church, where he would appear, then disappear. He smiled at her once, briefly, though she had not been brave enough to return the smile.

Now the mystery of the unknown had invaded the familiar, and she trembled again. He had knocked her off her feet and into the street and later lifted the heavy water bucket from her hands in the schoolyard. She knew of his strength and remembered his eyes.

"Just move the jacket to the chair by the door and rest yourself," Mabel instructed, turning from the oven.

Cassie took a halting breath and lifted the coat, replacing it on the appointed chair. She sat down under the weight of the new sensations, trying to sort out her feelings. 'Foolish! You are being foolish!' She silently chided herself.

The back door swung wide and with a gush of cold air, Johnny elbowed his way through it, arms bearing a load of split firewood, his hair and shoulders covered with snow. He shook his head, and the lacey flakes disappeared in the warm air.

"This time I took off my boots, they're pretty soggy," he exclaimed, dumping the firewood in the box by the stove. "I think this will get you through the..."

He froze in mid-sentence, his eyes having adjusted to the dimmer light of the kitchen. He hadn't noticed the girl sitting quietly across from where he stood, half of her face bathed in the lamplight which caught the gleam of her coppery curls.

"Oh Johnny, I believe you may know Miss Cassie, Dodge Wilkerson's oldest girl. Cassie, this is Deputy Johnny McLane." Mabel's merry eyes and gentility cloaked the formal introduction.

Cassie took in the details of his face and her heart caught in her chest. How different he appeared without the badge or the hat he usually wore tipped slightly forward, covering his brow.

The surprise which registered on his face was followed by a flicker of almost shy uncertainty. He recovered quickly, fixed her steadily with his fascinating blue-green eyes and suddenly seemed to remember his manners.

"Why hey, Miss Cassie! Yes, Miz Baker, we've bumped into each other a time or two," he replied, smiling at her. His left eyebrow arched over his injured eye in the teasing way she remembered.

Her raw nerves and his hesitation emboldened her. Demurely, she placed her folded hands on the table and straightened in the chair.

"Yes," she replied, trying to hide her flustered nerves, "I do believe it's true, and it looks as though you may have collided with something else recently, Deputy McLane. You didn't injure yourself... falling from your horse, I am sure." She gave him a bright smile but was unable to keep it from fleeing.

His hand involuntarily went to his cheek. "What? Fall? Why no...," he defended heartily, then catching the merriment in her eyes, knew instantly that she was playing with him.

"Only cowhands fall off horses, Miss Wilkerson" he replied calmly, "and at times, frail young ladies," he added, returning her smile.

"Well, sir, I can tell by your accent you don't hail from these parts, so I must advise you that there is nothing 'frail' about me...or any of the women in territorial Wyoming, or haven't you heard? We have had the right to vote, serve on juries and...own property, since December 10th of last year. Did it escape your notice that the first vote cast by a woman ever, in all of history, was two weeks ago on September 6th, in Laramie City? It took gumption for Mrs. Louisa Swain to cast her ballot, for there was much opposition to her doing so," she said, proud to be able to defend this subject, for it had become dear to her heart.

"Yes, Miss," he countered evenly, "and that right may well be a temporary state for the women's suffrage struggle here, for it's more than a rumor that the legislators may rescind the vote."

"You don't think women's rights to be a good thing?" Cassie asked, wondering if he approved of the rescinding. Even her own father thought that a poor idea.

Johnny answered her question without hesitation. "I am not saying it's not. Freedom is a God-given right and for all of mankind, but what about the Negroes? They fought in the war and are now free, and should be assured the vote first, don't you think? And what about the Chinese who worked so diligently on the railroad?"

"Well, if we are all free, under the law of God, as you say, then that right should not have to be earned, it has been granted and by a higher authority than man. Thus, it cannot... morally, be taken away." She saw that he was watching her with interest and somewhat surprised. This gave her courage. "Furthermore, your view on the Negro vote seems an unusual opinion for a Confederate to hold," she countered, and with the sudden undecipherable flicker crossing his eyes, she feared she may have overstepped the bounds of propriety.

"There were many reasons the war was fought, Miss Cassie," he replied factually, and his tone was neither condemning, nor self-righteous.

Cassie redirected the conversation to what she assumed was higher ground. "So you think that the Chinese and Negroes...the men...should have the vote before white women? Why even Councilman Bright thinks women should have voting rights and he's a Democrat," Cassie offered, with much conviction.

"He says that only because he wants to bring more settlers to the territory, not because he's an advocate for women's suffrage. There are about six men to every woman out here, and certainly no one's arguing that the numbers of women don't need to increase. It looks good for the Democrats if they push women's suffrage, even equal pay for women teachers, but these are the very men that oppose voting rights for anyone other than the white man, and they'd like to make Governor Campbell, a Republican, look weak. They thought he'd veto the vote in the long run. They were wrong. It's politics, Miss Wilkerson, and men play hard at them."

Did he mean that women were too frail and lacked the brains to play the "game"? Cassie strove to recall the debates they had held in class and her conversations with Pa, to put them forward in a logical discussion, while Johnny seemed content to instruct her.

"There was much conflict during the vote debate, and it was tough getting that bill to pass. Some legislators tried to attach amendments to it to make it unattractive. The squaw vote, for one. Yes, equal rights for all mankind need to come about one day, but they have to be legislated in correct order, and done methodically, then enforced, or we'll end up with the same confusions that rack the southern states."

Not certain of those issues, she became frustrated. He seemed confident in what he believed, and maybe it was good that he had not given her time to respond, but it seemed unfair.

"Don't get too anxious about the thing." he added honestly, watching her eyes and misunderstanding her thoughts. "You need to be twenty-one to vote, not age eighteen as first supposed. That amendment did pass, and it probably helped carry the suffrage bill. You have plenty of time before you need to consider these things seriously. Who knows what will happen before that time, or even when Wyoming actually applies for statehood? The whole women's suffrage debate may fly out the window just like it did when the Nebraska and Dakota territories tried to give rights to women years ago."

Did he think to pacify her with that statement? Cassie stared at him, wondering how he could be so nonchalant about such an important issue. As she watched him, she recalled something that she believed made a difference.

"Miss Davis says..." she began factually, but she paused when he shook his head, tightened his lips, and turned up one corner of his mouth.

"She says," Cassie re-emphasized, "that over 1,000 women may have gone to the polls to vote that day. Surely that proves women are qualified and serious about retaining their rights."

"On that day," he replied, simply, "but it still remains to be seen whether or not women's rights will stick until next election. The right to serve on juries doesn't seem to be holding up since the 'champion of the cause', Judge Howe, died and his successor isn't calling up any females as jurists."

The basic issue for him seemed to be whether or not women would be allowed, by men, to keep their rights. This piqued her senses. The issue for her was simple human dignity and God-given rights. Surely he could see this. "So, we can exercise our rights only when the men in charge grant them? This seems like a form of oppression to me."

Mabel had taken in their exchange, heard the last challenge Cassie raised, and with the wisdom of her advanced years, interrupted sweetly and rapidly. "I am sure I don't know, but I do think you two seem to have similar interests."

Mabel moved to pull out a chair. Still standing and seemingly unaffected by their debate, Johnny reached out to steady it for her as she sat down. Stymied, Cassie watched as he helped her settle, and then seated himself across from her, smiling contentedly.

"Thank you. Now let's eat this before it cools...Oh! Cassie, dear, your tea," Mabel cried, suddenly. Cassie placed a restraining hand gently on Mabel's forearm.

"No, thank you, Auntie. I'll just have some coffee along with both of you, and I'll take it black. Sit still. I'll get the cup."

She rose, and Johnny watched her move around the table and reach for the coffee cup and pot. She was certainly more than just a "girl", and he found her more than intriguing. After filling her cup, she came close, offering him more coffee but he declined.

Their eyes met, Cassie's cheeks colored slightly, and the heat within Johnny replaced his political assessments with less noble ones. He began to study the butter melting on the bread before him. Mabel Baker watched the two of them and smiled knowingly. Neither of them noticed her, noticing them.

Cassie took her seat, trying not to meet Johnny's eyes. With unsteady hands, she gathered her locks mechanically, twisted them loosely, and placed them over one shoulder, focusing her attention brightly on her auntie. "There!" she breathed, "I believe we are all set!"

"You had better get those boots before they fill with snow, Johnny," Mabel advised.

"Ma'am?" Johnny replied blankly, refocusing on Mabel.

"Your boots! You know, the ones you left on the back porch!"

"Oh," he rose quickly, opening the door to retrieve his snowy boots. He returned to the stove, boots in hand. "I'm sorry, but I'll have to get back to town. I'm afraid I stayed too long, and who knows what's happening back there."

"Well, that's fine, and take a loaf of bread with you!" Mabel smiled. Fixing her eyes on Cassie's surprised face, she advised, "Now, you can escort Cassie to town. She has to get supplies from Miss Halstead's shop and is expected home before dark."

"You both go along now. You don't want to get caught in a snowstorm." She rose, offering Cassie her coat, but Cassie sat still, numbly watching Johnny struggle into his wet boots.

Inspired by Mabel's fine idea, Johnny retrieved his coat and pushed aside the kitchen curtain.

"Looks like the snow has stopped again, but we only have about an hour of daylight left. I'll get Traveller and meet you around the front, Miss Cassie. Thanks for the loaf, Ms. Baker. I'll check in on you next week."

Placing his hat on his head and taking his gun and holster up, he gave Mabel a quick peck on the cheek and was out the door.

Cassie glared at Mabel. "What just happened, what did you just do?" she asked, confronting Mabel's sly smile.

"Now, you run along dear, and you'll remember to thank your ma for me, won't you?"

"Aunt Mabel, I ..." Cassie began, but Mabel, handed the empty basket to her.

"It's proper for a young woman to have an escort, especially this late in the day. Johnny's a fine deputy; he will take good care of you, so go along now. Don't keep him waiting in the snow for heaven's sake." Mabel smiled while her blue eyes snapped. She herded Cassie along, directing her toward the front door.

"Since when do I need an escort? You know I can take care of myself!" Cassie's pride chipped again, but this time she was confused. Aunt Mabel had always encouraged her to step out of the shadows and grasp her independence. Although Cassie felt like a novice in her political discussion with the deputy, she had survived and sensed he had taken an interest in her. Now, the tables had turned. She felt like a mere girl again, vulnerable, unsure, and thrown to the wolves by her own dear auntie.

"I know, dear, but you just go along now...you must get home before dark. You'll come back to see me real soon." Mabel opened the door, and Cassie found herself ushered out onto the porch. "Don't forget to button your cloak, dearest. I'll see you soon." Mabel closed the door, waving at them from the window.

Johnny waited with Traveller next to Cassie's mare, and as she descended the steps he handed the reins to her.

"Leg up?" he asked, with a quizzical gaze.

"Why, no thank you. I can manage just fine," she said demurely, cocking her head. She mounted in a flash and spun Lady around, almost knocking Johnny sideways.

Now back on grounds where she felt more than competent, she challenged him, calling over her shoulder, "Wanna race, or are you afraid you'll lose your hat?"

Lady danced in a wide circle, and Cassie was down the road before Johnny could swing up on Traveller's back.

"You're on, gal!" he hollered, as he spurred Traveller forward, and they galloped off with Lady ahead by lengths.

Mabel watched from her window, clapping her hands gleefully and laughing out loud. "That's the way to fix it, that's the way to get it done!" she exclaimed, taking her handkerchief to her eyes which had gone teary again, this time from laughter and expectation.

Less than a quarter mile down the road, Johnny slowed up, reining in. The ground was slippery under the blanket of snow, and with a slight lead now, Johnny motioned for Cassie to slow. Pressing his leg into Traveller's flank, he moved the horse into Lady's path.

Cassie slowed Lady to a jog and Johnny reined Traveller abreast of them, thankful that she wasn't angered by his having taken control of the potentially perilous situation, but seemed grateful for his quick assessment.

"Sorry Miss Cassie, I thought it was getting too slippery," Johnny said evenly. He gave her a rueful smile. "Guess we'll have to race in better weather."

He watched her, and her breath came quickly, her cheeks pink with excitement, colored from the sting of the wind and snow. Her blue shawl had fallen over her shoulders and her hair blew in the wind, a mass of auburn ringlets tumbling around her forehead and over her shoulders. She smiled, trying to keep her hair out of her face and replied invitingly, "Thank you, I'll take you up on that offer!"

Exhaling slowly, he thought she was the most desirable creature he had ever known. She topped them all, girl or not. "You're gonna be soaked through. Maybe you better wear my hat until we get to town. It'll keep the snow off your hair and out of your face, that is, if you'd like." He must tread cautiously. He did not wish to anger her or in any way diminish her receptive spirit, desiring only to talk with her and keep her by his side, just the two of them, even if it was only slogging over a snow-covered road. He had not noticed the cold; the evening was beautiful. Vibrant and alive, she rode quietly beside him, framed in a backdrop of white and gray, stunning in a green frock that reminded him of every forest which had ever lured him to explore its mysteries.

She laughed. "I couldn't take your hat," she protested.

He moved Traveller close, playfully plopping it on her head. It slid forward over her eyes, and she smiled shyly and set it in place.

Under the weight of his hat, she realized how wet her hair had become, aware of cold snowflakes melting and trickling down the sides of her face, her neck, and beneath her collar.

They jogged their mounts slowly along. She shivered, not from the cold, but from the strange sensation effected by the man in the jacket with the star riding beside her. Just the two of them, wrapped in the warmth of a magical blanket, with no one else on this wide expanse of prairie. She was exhilarated; this was freedom, and she felt totally happy.

As they jogged slowly toward town, Cassie was curious as to where Johnny was from. She inquired about that faraway state of Virginia, a place she had only read about in history books--books about great men who had changed thirteen British colonies into thirteen American states. They talked about life there, and Cassie asked what made it different from life in Wyoming.

"Like the difference between night and day," Johnny said chuckling, not taking time to explain his statement.

She asked his opinion on the outcome of the war. Did he come west because the South had been defeated, and why had he come so far? Johnny was surprised by her direct questioning and more surprised at his own reluctance to answer with little more than general comments regarding those years. He was relieved when she redirected their conversation to a book she had been reading and asked him if he enjoyed reading, pleased when he answered affirmatively. *Les Miserables* was her favorite to date.

Written about another revolution, Johnny found it far easier to discuss the rebellion that had taken place on French soil rather than that which had taken place on the clay and sandy terra of Dixie.

It seemed a very short two miles back to Sideling as they talked, and gradually he fell silent, peppered with thoughts of the town which he had left unprotected all afternoon. Concerned about the evening clouds that had thickened again in the darkening hour, Johnny realized it was too late for Cassie to get ribbons and whatever else she needed, before returning to her father's ranch four miles in the opposite direction. His eyes found hers, aware she had asked him a question which he had not heard and was waiting expectantly for his answer. His apparent distraction disappointed her.

They had passed the schoolhouse, and were rounding the bend when he offered, "After I check out the town, I could ride back to the ranch with you. It'll be dark."

Before she could respond, a buckboard appeared, coming rapidly toward them. Johnny was relieved and simultaneously disappointed.

Cassie waved, "Howdy, Pa!"

Dodge Wilkerson wasn't smiling as he pulled alongside of them. "Deputy," he greeted, "is everything alright?"

"Yes sir, everything is fine," Johnny replied, but Dodge had already turned his attentions on Cassie.

"Where have you been, daughter? I was worried. Your mother said you would be at Miss Halstead's, but Olivia said she hadn't seen you this afternoon."

Johnny thought to answer but Dodge continued, "Why were you not where you were supposed to be?" He studied Cassie questioningly.

Cassie was puzzled by his frank questioning. "I was just on my way from Aunt Mabel's. Ma sent me by to take cheese and butter, and we got to visiting. Guess I lost track of time. I thought I had time to get the ribbons before I came home."

Why was she made to defend herself like a wayward child, and why had her father drilled her before the deputy? It was not his habit to do so.

Unassured, Dodge's brow furrowed as he stared at her costume. Cassie snatched Johnny's hat from her head, shoving it at him with a weak, "Thank you."

"Mr. Wilkerson, this is my doing," Johnny explained. "I was at Miz Baker's, chasin' her wayward cow, and my appearance at the house caused Cassie's visit to become extended."

Dodge looked from his daughter to the deputy and back again. "It is not like you to ignore a potential storm, Cassie." The set of Dodge Wilkerson's jaw exposed his double entendre, at least to Johnny, and whether or not Cassie caught it, she glanced at Johnny, flushing.

"The deputy was kind enough to ride with me part of the way, so you see, I am fine. I'll get the ribbons, and return immediately."

Dodge considered her a moment, then dismissed her. "I need to talk to Deputy McLane about a different matter. Don't be long."

Cassie turned Lady toward Miss Halstead's and looking back over her shoulder, uttered a formal, "Thank you, Deputy, and goodbye."

Johnny watched them trot off until he realized Dodge was speaking to him.

"... the meeting tomorrow night. I've been looking for the marshal. Is he in town?"

"I am not sure." Johnny answered, refocusing. "He should be back by now. He went out on business this mornin'."

"I just want to make sure he's at the council meeting tomorrow night. Flynn and a few other cattlemen should be there. We need to get to the bottom of this rustling as soon as possible. We're losing profits."

"Many folks are concerned. Those rustlers may be holed out not far from here, we can't be sure. We're investigating, have been for the last few days. Marshal Brett won't forget that meeting, you can be sure of that, sir."

Traveller stamped impatiently, and Johnny shifted in the saddle.

"Good." Dodge looked indecisive for a moment. "We will see you tomorrow night, unless the snow piles up so that no one can get anywhere."

Johnny looked to the sky. Clouds scudded across the darkening heavens. "I think it's gonna clear, the air doesn't feel like a storm."

"Hope you are right," he replied. "I appreciate that you were concerned for my daughter."

"My pleasure, sir," Johnny responded matter-of-factly, tipping his hat. He turned Traveller and headed for the office. Dodge Wilkerson's buckboard groaned and rumbled as it made way toward Olivia's cabin.

Perhaps Johnny had misunderstood the man. There were more pressing issues to be dealt with than a harmless ride in the evening, along a public road. Besides the wagon and the crunch of horses' hooves on snow and ice, there were very few sounds from the town.

Johnny dismounted, tied Traveller to the hitching post, and walked to the office door. Still locked and dark inside, he retrieved his keys from his gunbelt and entered. Lighting the lamp, he threw wood into the potbelly stove, added paper and blew on it until it leapt into flames, sparked by the live coals buried deep under the ashes. He would have to clean it out tomorrow, he thought. Finding no note on the desk he walked back out onto the porch, closing the door. He gazed up and down the street. Few people had ventured out this night, and the glow from the saloon across the way reflected on the snowy road. A loud burst of laughter broke the silence. Soft lamplight shone from the buildings along Main Street, but there were no signs of trouble, and no note tacked to the communication board outside of the doorway.

From the corner of the porch, he glanced toward the cabin which housed the "millinery". All but a single lamp appeared to be out, and Mr. Wilkerson's buckboard, along with Cassie and Lady, were gone. Johnny shivered and drew his coat collar up around his neck. The cold, soggy damp of it chilled him, and he put it back down.

As he led Traveller to the livery, he shivered again. Entering the darkened stable, the loneliness, when it came, was suffocating. A mild ache plagued his right temple; he was hungry and tired, but he wanted Cassie's company more than sleep or food.

Although Dodge Wilkerson had seemed to give them the benefit of the doubt, Johnny wondered how sincere the man had been in expressing his appreciation for Johnny's "concern" for his young daughter when finding her disheveled, decked out in his hat, and improperly accompanied so late in the evening. Sam Brett should be returning soon, and Johnny knew he needed to concentrate on the matters at hand. Although he quit speculating, he could not get Cassie out of his mind.

6

THE QUEST

THE OFFICE WARMED quickly and as Johnny was opening a can of pork and beans, Marshal Brett stomped through the doorway, shaking snow off his hat.

"Well, you're back, how did it go?" Johnny asked, dumping the contents of the can into a pot.

"Alright, but we didn't find anything. Rode up near Cheyenne and met Marshal Riddick from Iron Mountain way. He and his deputy gave chase to two men they thought were a couple of rustlers two days ago, but it turned out they were just some ole boys herding steers to a ranch up north. Had the bill of sale, so they let 'em go." Sam Brett took off his damp coat and hung it on the rail near the stove.

"Had they seen anything strange or noticed signs of a large herd being moved anywhere?" Johnny asked, stirring the pot of beans.

"No, we got no leads. Jess thinks he may know where the rustlers could be holed up, though. Said it may be the same canyon you and he camped in when you went hunting in July. Do you remember it?"

"Yeah, I was thinking about that earlier...want some of this?" Johnny lifted the pot from the stove with a bandana.

"No thanks, I think I'll go to the saloon and get a steak," Sam replied warming his hands by the stove. "So what about that canyon?"

"It sure would be a good place to hole up, if you were hoping not to get caught." The mention of the canyon sent Johnny's thoughts racing as he realized the possibilities, and he faced Sam. "It's quite a ways off the beaten track."

Massaging the stubble on his chin, Sam eyed Johnny for a moment, then changed the subject. "Did you find Miss Mabel's Cow?"

"What? Oh, yeah," Johnny replied dismissively, wanting to get back to the details of the search.

"And the dizziness...is it gone?"

"Well, yeah, I didn't have any problem with it today or yesterday...or the day before, either," Johnny answered tersely, wondering why Sam had resurrected the topic now. Sam took notice.

"Alright, you're cut loose. Consider yourself fully reinstated to active duty."

Sam yawned and stretched. "I'm plum worn out from that ride. About that canyon, you were saying...?"

"Mr. Brett, I have a hunch I could find those rustlers." Johnny pulled up a chair in front of the marshal, threw a leg over the seat, sat backwards, and rested his elbows along the top of the chair. Sam found it telling that Johnny didn't mention his reprieve.

"I'd like to leave tomorrow, say late afternoon," Johnny said enthusiastically. "I'll make my way up the mountain and search from the rim above the canyon--see if I can find their camp. They can't be too far into the rocks. Sound carries further at night, and I can pick up their voices, draw a bead on them, and find out how many there are. Then I'll figure the best route possible to get at them."

"You plan to take Jess Bryant with you?" Sam asked, tapping a pencil on the desktop.

"No, too much noise with the two of us movin' through those rocks. We might end up bein' spotted. Just gettin' myself up there quietly in the dark will take some ingenuity. No, sir, I can track, and I shouldn't have a problem."

Sam Brett leaned back in the chair. "So you plan to do this alone, at night?" He waited for Johnny's reply.

Johnny stood to pace slowly back and forth, contemplating his next words. "I've scouted often at night, Mr. Brett. Trackin' Yanks and beaver in the swamps of Virginia seems a lot more dangerous to me."

"Beaver don't carry guns, Johnny." Sam shook his head and pursed his lips, waiting for a reply.

"Yeah, but there is sucking sand, moccasins, and a tangle of thorn branches that will rip your clothing right off of you, and you've got to go through it quietly or you catch nothin'," Johnny replied, halting in front of the marshal.

Sam saw the hope and expectation on Johnny's face, the excitement in his eyes. Silently he thought of himself. How long had it been since he felt that passionate about a chase? He couldn't remember.

Standing before him, Sam beheld the young man, confident and sometimes foolhardy, with a courage most likely born of that great and terrible war. A year ago he seemed little more than a boy, though a good marksman to be sure. He had protected Johnny and had tried to keep the riskier assignments for himself when possible. Now he realized that he had to let go. The boy was a man, young though he might be. Sam needed him now as much as Johnny had needed Sam. This town, this territory, demanded the man Johnny had become.

Sam exhaled, "Well then, I reckon I'll keep the meeting of the cattlemen in check by myself tomorrow night. Just be sure no one finds out that you are leaving town, or where you are headed. There are too many curious eyes and hot heads around town already. The less anyone knows, the more successful you're likely to be."

"I got it, Marshal. Thanks, sir." With a tight lip smile, Johnny agreed. He turned and walked toward the backroom.

"Yeah," Sam murmured softly to himself, "I hope you live to thank me." He threw the pencil down on the desk, stood and stretched.

"I'm gonna go get that steak," he called through the office. "You make the rounds."

Later that night, Johnny lay on the cot in the backroom. Other than a few inebriated cowhands, whom Johnny had sent packing, Sideling had been quiet. His thoughts kept returning to Cassie, and try as he might, he couldn't make himself focus. He needed to be sure that he had remembered everything he would need for tomorrow's hunt. Food, extra layers of warm clothing, and his map. There would be no fire to warm him; he needed to be close to the canyon before dark closed in. He would have to keep moving throughout the night. Those mountains were cold enough to freeze a man, and he knew that the weather was unpredictable as it blew in from the northwest. The plains could be cold and dry, but those mountains were something else again. The wind would howl through them like the sound of a freight train, like the wail of a dying man...or a rebel yell.

As Cassie came to mind again, he marveled at her inquisitive nature. She made him feel wise, had even challenged him at Miss Baker's, and again as he answered her questions on the ride into town. He had experienced so much more of life, although he was only four years her senior. And there it was again.

He was a man, she still a girl. Not in her physical appearance, no, not at all. But there was a vulnerable, innocent quality about her, as though she was untouched by the hard things of life. He groaned, sat up and put his head in his hands, resting his elbows on his knees. He was crazy to think her father would allow him to court her, crazy to think any more about this. Yet, she seemed to enjoy being with him at least until her father had come on the scene this afternoon. She had suddenly become distant; she must have known her father would not approve and, well, who would? Their lives were at different places, and that was that.

In the chill of the room, he placed his bare feet upon the floor, yawned, stretched, and lit the lamp at his bedside. He entered the office, added wood-sticks to the glowing embers in the stove, then sat on the chair and glanced about him. Even though he had just stoked the fire, he considered tamping it down and removing the ashes, for that chore was long overdue. Motivation, like sleep, evaded him, so he returned to the backroom, taking his Bible from the small shelf next to his bed.

Remembering that he usually grew drowsy reading, he thought it might just be what he needed and flipped it open. From the summary title of Chapter 102 in the book of Psalms, he read: "A prayer for the afflicted, when he is overwhelmed and pours out his complaint before the Lord."

He laughed softly. "Well, that is me alright," and he sat on the bed to read.

"I watch and am as a sparrow alone upon the house top."

With his back supported against the wall at one side of the bed, he reread the verse and closed his eyes. 'That will be me up in those mountains,' he thought.

"Hide not thy face from me in the day when I am in trouble, incline Thine ear unto me in that day when I call, answer me speedily."

'Of course,' Johnny thought, 'God always listened to David. But who am I that the God who rules the earth would really see me or care about me?' Instantly he felt guilty for those thoughts and grew contemplative. He knew that God could see him anywhere, and he knew that the wicked would eventually be punished, but would he be able to thank God in a day or two, or in a week from now?

'This is my job,' he thought, 'and regardless, I'll find these men and bring them before the law. I reckon I'm the one 'in the middle'. I represent the law but am not the law. If God is the lawgiver and the judge of all things, will God support my cause as He did David's?'

God had not forwarded the Confederate Cause, even though many had believed He would champion it. Men had lifted high the Southern Cross and marched forward to destruction. Who could understand the ways of the Lord? Mama had said, "Just trust." Papa had said, "Be courageous and stand firm, Johnny, you know who you are." He wondered again if he really did know.

He read on. "For he hath looked down from the height of his sanctuary: from heaven did the Lord behold the earth: To hear the groaning of prisoners, to loose those that are appointed to death..."

'Ah, the groanings of prisoners.' It seemed to Johnny that all men were prisoners of a sort, then slowly the words, "To loose those that are appointed to death," gave him pause. He thought of Mama and Mary Annie and as he read, sorrow permeated his heart. He remembered Joe and Papa, so long ago, the cricket chorus, the smell of tobacco so rich and poignant in the still air, with a longing so fierce he ached.

Papa had talked of a loosening, a restoration, liberty and a move toward freedom. But was there really freedom anywhere? They had fought for it and many had died struggling for it. Freedom seemed elusive, something to strive for but hardly ever attained, and if found, not easily held. Maybe it did originate with God, and maybe only He could grant it.

But death was not elusive. It was final, yet he had heard that freedom was obtained in it, a paradox for certain. He grew weary, closed the Bible, and pondered. Men who lived for their own interests alone never seemed to be free. They took freedom, along with the lives and possessions of others, always trying to evade the law. In their striving to be free of the law, hadn't they chosen bondage instead? Hunted, imprisoned or put to death, they brought bondage on themselves, and he knew it was his job to deal with them.

Skeptically, Johnny considered the 12th verse in the Psalm. "But thou, O Lord, shalt endure forever; and Thy remembrance unto all generations." He placed his closed Bible on the small bedside table.

As he blew the lamplight out, fairly certain that God would endure for all time, he couldn't help but wonder if it was possible that his could be the one generation that God had forgotten. Weary and disillusioned, he searched his heart.

Papa had said there was One who could set captives free. One who had the power to loose and break the chains of those bound. Staring into the darkness, he tried to recapture the assurance he had known then, and from a faraway place, the refrains of a childhood song came to mind. Quietly he let the words flow through him.

"Jesus loves me, this I know, for the Bible tells me so."

'This I know, this I know...' Exhaustion overcame him, and with the repetition of the literal verse, tension eased from his gut and his muscles.

"This I know," he whispered. So simple to recite, yet in its simplicity, so hard to believe.

He left Sideling earlier than he had expected, taking advantage of the stir in the town created by cattlemen and citizens in anticipation of the meeting to be held that night. The townsfolk and the few surrounding homesteaders wanted solutions, and they wanted them yesterday. Johnny was glad to be out, glad for the opportunity to do something tangible. He had a plan, and it did not include placating angry men with words and promises that he and the marshal may or may not be able to keep.

By early afternoon, Johnny reached the mountain range in which he knew the canyon to be located. He found an out-of-the-way place to tether Traveller among the cottonwood and scrub bushes in an aperture formed by a large red rock.

As he navigated the large boulders, the sunlight on his shoulders provided a false sense of warmth. Sweating, he took off his jacket, wrapping it around his waist as he climbed. He figured he would ascend the mountain for about a mile to its ridge, then make the gradual descent for another half-mile before reaching the final canyon ridge. If he stayed on the east of the mountainside as much as possible, he could decrease the impact of the northwest wind.

The climb took him out of the sun as the afternoon waned. The air was cold and crisp. As long as he climbed, he stayed warm without his coat. Sweat meant damp skin and clothes which could freeze a man when the temperature dropped. The climbing was slow going and at some points, the snow had blown away from the smooth rock within the boulder maze. He forced himself to drink from the canteen and placed into his haversack to keep it from clanking against the rock. He had to remove his haversack and rifle to crawl through a narrow passage, pulling them through behind him. In the unlikely event that a scout may be watching from the canyon rim, he tried to stay out of sight but knew he would have to trust his luck on that point.

Twilight came on. The wind rose as he neared the highest ridge. Resting against a rock, he ate a sourdough biscuit and jerky and consumed a small amount of water. He glanced out over the rocks which fell away for about one hundred yards before rising sharply again. It was almost dark, and with about a quarter of a mile to travel, he would have to watch his step. He could see stars begin their nightward climb through the sky and was thankful for clear weather. The half-moon would provide some light, but the deep pits formed by the rocks became black holes which could prove treacherous.

He walked until he could no longer see where to place his feet and then found shelter between two large boulders. Pulling off his boots, he changed his woolen socks then leaned against the cold rock wall swaddled in an army blanket. He thought of Cassie, picturing her beside a warm fire. What would she be doing? Working on flowers for hats or maybe reading quietly? He had never pictured her in quite that way, but he could imagine himself with her.

The Wilkerson ranch was the closest ranch to the mountain range, and it lay to the southwest of Sideling, four miles from the town. Johnny knew the rustlers would need supplies from the town, and suspected they had been customers of the mercantile and saloon in the last few months. Not fools, they most likely came to town alone or in pairs. He wondered if the saloon's proprietor, Leafy Misner, had an inkling as to who the strangers were who lifted a glass at his bar, now and then, and availed themselves of some other "sport" offered in his establishment. Suppose they encountered Cassie alone on the ride to or from town? Growing increasingly colder, he closed his eyes, anxious for first light and anticipating the distant lowing of cattle borne on the whining wind.

Unaware of the passage of time, the distant howl of wolves gradually dragged him back to consciousness. The sharp retort of a rifle startled him, its echo ricocheting off the rock canyon walls. So they were out there, and most likely, confident that no one else knew it.

The cold, hard rock had stiffened his muscles, and he stood to get his bearings, taking up his rifle. The moon was high, and the stars shimmered brightly in the black velvet sky. Fingers aching, he could hardly feel the boulders as he passed his hands along them, using both arms to steady himself. The darkness could cloak his progress from human eyes, but not from canine senses, and if he encountered that pack of wolves, he could not afford a shot.

The North Star provided direction. He struck a match to check his compass, then chuckled wryly at his caution. Many things in this universe could fall from the skies or deviate in their pathways, but the North Star was not likely to change course. He watched it glimmer brightly at the farthest point of the constellation.

What had ole Moses and Jim called that formation of stars? He searched his recollections, back to his boyhood days. They had called it "The Drinking Gourd", but Johnny had learned that it was the Big Dipper, and that men had been using those glowing sentinels to plot their course since the beginning of recorded time.

He thought of the shepherds watching the ancient sky, naming the heavenly bodies. He remembered reading, "A man could plan his ways, but the Lord directed his steps," or something similar, somewhere in the Bible.

His foot slipped, dumping him into a narrow crevasse. With a clatter, his rifle caught horizontally at the mouth of the pit. Unscathed, but angry with himself for not concentrating, he wedged his feet and hands against opposite sides of the boulders and climbed up. He retrieved his rifle, and managed to pull himself out, regained his footing and moved forward.

The dark sky paled as he reached the last ridge of boulders. Quietly, he struck a slight westward course. As the pale sky pinked to the east, a flock of birds flew from the northeast, descending as they soared on the currents. He knew he had reached the canyon, for birds always looked for water in the morning, then flew away in the evening to roost. The stream, he remembered, flowed into the canyon through a very narrow pass from the northeast.

Twenty feet further, light filtered through the narrow cracks of the wide boulders. He caught the sound of cattle lowing and an occasional distant clang of metal against metal. He crouched, then crawled on his belly toward the canyon rim where the contour of the ridge fell away dramatically, to a depth of over 200 feet.

Cattle milled about in a rough camp stretched out below. He counted at least eight men, and noted a cavvy of horses strung out near the stream. Quickly and quietly, he turned and made his way back.

The sun was high in the sky when he returned to the base of the mountain. Unable to find any sign of the cottonwood stand, he moved eastward along the base of the rock for a quarter of a mile, then spotted the trees. Traveller nickered as Johnny approached. Building a small fire well away from the road, and between the rocks, Johnny melted the frozen water in his canteen, drinking and then filling his hat for Traveller.

"Sorry for the long delay," he said, rubbing the horse between his ears. Traveller drank deeply as his ears twitched in opposition. Suddenly, he pushed his muzzle forward, flipping the hat and the remaining water onto Johnny. It rolled off his coat, quickly soaking his pants which began to stiffen in the cold. Admonishing his horse, Johnny attempted to dry by the small fire, but the damage was done. He quickly mounted Traveller, removing the tin star from his jacket and placing it in a pocket. No one would suspect a lone horseman along this well-traveled road.

———————◦———————

Without the protection of the mountain range, the wind was harsh and frigid. He kept Traveller moving at a lope. The day was waning, and he did not relish another night spent out in this weather. As he neared the Wilkerson ranch he decided to take the trail splitting off along the back line to the north end of the spread. Not the most direct route into town, he reasoned, but he could search for further signs of rustling. From a herd of almost one thousand cattle, Dodge Wilkerson had lost fifty head at last count, including a fine longhorned bull.

The wind slacked off and the late afternoon clouded over. Heading south, he could see the roofline of the Wilkerson's barn just over the rise. The trail sloped to the southeast, becoming broader and flat. Weariness began to overtake him, and his hands and feet were numb. The cold and lack of sleep, along with the rocking motion of the canter, had him almost asleep in the saddle. Hunger kept him conscious, but just barely. The whinny of a horse snapped him out of his lethargy, and he observed a rider coming northwest, from the direction of the Wilkerson barn.

Cassie recognized the gray horse immediately and slowed to meet the rider.

"Howdy," she greeted, smiling at Johnny, reining in and pulling aside Traveller. She took in the haggard look of his eyes, the brown stubble of his beard, and realized he had not come from town. Dirt streaked his clothing, and Traveller's legs were clumped with frozen mud.

At the same time, he searched her winsome face, surprised by her appearing alone so late in the evening.

"You look a little worse for wear, Deputy" she appraised honestly, then softening her tone asked, "What are you doing out here?" Lady pranced in circles, and Cassie stroked the mare's neck to calm her, holding Johnny with an intense gaze.

"I'm on my way back to town. I should be asking why you're out so late. It's gonna be dark in no time." His exigent reply caught her off guard.

She heard the reprimand in his tone, and the animation left her face. She stared at him as disappointment swept through her. 'Not this again...not from him,' she thought dispiritedly. Her defensive pride, which had been piqued no more than an hour earlier, flared again.

She could not hide her dismay.

"I am perfectly able to take care of myself," she answered, more caustically than she had intended.

He frowned. "You may be able to now, but it is going to be dark in no time, and it is not safe to be out alone. Does your pa know you're out here?"

Unknowingly, he had fanned the flame and seared her with his words. A torrent of unbidden emotion rushed to her lips.

"He does, and why do you question me? I can't seem to do a thing without someone always questioning me! Where I go, what I do! I can shoot as straight, ride as fast, and probably out-think any two men in this territory, and all at the same time!"

He was stunned by the onslaught of her words, then angered. "Well, unless you have a pistol buried beneath your skirts, I think it'd be rather hard to defend yourself!" he retorted.

She flushed, caught off guard. He was sorry for his tone, simultaneously wanting to take her in his arms, for behind the fire of her attack, tears glistened in the red-tinged rims of her eyes, and he realized that she had been crying.

He shook his head, and tried to rein in his emotion, not quite sure of what had happened to precipitate her reaction. He was used to defusing tense situations, but this one was different.

"These are dangerous times, Cassie. You don't realize how bad the rustling situation is, how dangerous the rustlers are, how unsafe it is for a girl to be..." He searched for words, and she blasted him.

"I am not just a girl! I am a competent woman, and you and Pa need to realize this! I can take care of myself! I make good decisions and..."

With the situation escalating rapidly, and too worn to spar, he interrupted her harshly. "Well, the decision you are makin' now is a poor one! You could be apprehended, held for ransom, endangerin' the whole town, or much worse!"

"Really? I don't see what could be worse than that, sir," she retorted. He knew the exchange was out of control, and he forced himself to speak reasonably.

"Cassie, you're so... you are very..." He lowered his gaze and found himself unable to express what he meant. Raising his eyes, he saw the tears escape down her cheeks. She wiped at them angrily.

"I wish people could see me for who I am!" she cried, still defiant.

"I am seein' you for who you are, just like any man would, and that is the problem!" He thought she would follow his reasoning. Surely, she would understand what he meant with so direct a statement, but her anger hung in the air. He forced himself to continue.

"Any man would want... well, you must realize how..." And he ran out of words, dumbfounded at his inability to communicate. He was used to speaking his mind, but he couldn't put into words the thoughts which overwhelmed him now.

Angrily, she waited for him to finish what she perceived would be his condescending assessment of her frail abilities. When he failed to, she glared at him and turned Lady quickly, riding away in the direction from which she had come.

He spurred Traveller to her side and grabbed the reins, halting both of them. "Cassie, I can't let you leave like this," he said, searching her face.

There was something in his eyes that defused her, a kind of weary sincerity, matched by the tender way in which he now spoke.

"Let me ride back to the house with you," he offered.

She had set out an hour earlier in anger and defiance against her father's wishes. The habitual gallop across the range that usually freed her soul and cleared her mind was now to become an unrealized exercise. She sat on her mare, clothed in the twilight of evening, halted in her tracks by this man.

He held her gaze intently. Shadows brushed under his eyes and in the softening of his features she noticed how worn he looked. It occurred to her that he must have been out on the trail for quite some time. As she considered him, her restlessness began to drain away. Instead of feeling constrained, she became conscious of his person as his leg pressed against her skirts, and he skillfully held both jostling horses as one.

"I can ride back by myself, you know," she murmured, trying to summon up self-protective defiance and not succeeding.

"I know you can," Johnny answered, releasing her reins. "I want to ride with you," he replied simply.

The unnerving warmth swept through her again. Protection-but not like the burden of her pa's protection, so suffocating lately and constantly weighing on her. She was inclined to accept this restraint from the deputy.

But how did he see her? Did he consider her a child? She realized he most likely thought of himself as looking out for her the way an older brother would; the way Robert would have had he not died. How could she discern his thoughts? Somehow, he drew her to him, but she felt the need to push him away at the same time.

"Truce?" He asked finally, after her long silence. She breathed deeply, discarding the remnants of her resistance. She was unable to clearly see the details of his face. Twilight had deepened into gray.

They trotted side-by-side. He was the next to speak. "So...do you accept my white flag?" She glanced at him, but could not read his expression.

"Well," she contemplated softly, "maybe a truce... but what would you give me as a token of peace?"

'My life,' Johnny thought without pause, but answered lightly. "I'll have to think on that one," and he chuckled.

They arrived at the barnyard just as the curtain of darkness fell. The huge barn stood silent in the gloaming. "I'll take you to the door," Johnny offered, as Cassie halted her mare.

"No," Cassie answered quickly, uncertain of how to behave in the intimacy of the moment. "I have my barn chores, and I am late getting started."

"Then I'll light the lamp for you," Johnny said, dismounting quickly and walking to Lady's side. Cassie looked down at him and trembled.

"You may think yourself a knight, rescuing me from those you believe to be the evil doers of the kingdom," she teased bravely, "however, your shining armor is kind of tarnished, sir," and she feigned contempt at his appearance. "I can light my own way, Galahad; you may go...take a bath!"

Relieved by her playful spirit, he joined her with his own. "Yes, my Lady, but first I must see you safely off your steed and into the castle."

He offered his hands to assist her as she dismounted, placing them gently at her waist, slowing her descent and placing her feet on the ground. He turned her slowly to face him, trying to read her face in the darkness, and found himself struggling to resist the tremendous urge to draw her closer. She tilted her head back, searching his eyes innocently, and took a step closer.

'Oh, God,' he prayed silently. Releasing her, he stepped back quickly. "I've gotta get back to town; I've been gone too long already."

He vaulted onto Traveller, tipped his hat, and with a brief nod, wheeled his horse and cantered off into the night.

Suddenly, she was aware of the frigid air, the deep shadows of the looming barn, and the large expanse of the prairie. The sense of being turned out from an incredibly warm shelter chilled her. She stood in the cold, small and alone, and missed him terribly. He hadn't said a word as they had stood so close in the darkness for that brief moment, hadn't lingered as he held her, or even tried to kiss her. She had been correct in her earlier assessments. To him she must seem like a kid sister and nothing more. Anger at her own foolishness coursed through her. She stamped her foot, opened the barn door, lit the lamp, and tried in vain to focus as she did her chores.

Dodge Wilkerson looked out the kitchen window. He had been working on his finances when called to supper, and had not noticed the darkness creeping in from the east. The glow of lamplight from the open barn door diminished his aggravation. She must be there.

His earlier words with Cassie had been couched in strong terms as they had argued. The girl must settle down, and it was his responsibility to see that she did. So easy going as she grew, she had now become contemptuous, even of his most genuine requests.

"It's getting dark. Just get your chores done, and go help your ma in the kitchen," he had instructed just hours before. Cassie challenged him on that. She had always ridden out in the late evening. Why not now? He was "being unreasonable", she had argued. He disliked her questioning, and feeling that her tone bordered on impudence, he had allowed his anger to get away from him. He had been gruff with her; then she had disobeyed him.

With a twinge of guilt, he knew he was responsible for her unrestrained attitude. She was no longer a little girl; he could see that, but she didn't seem to realize that becoming a woman would naturally limit her participation in some of the activities she held so dear.

Freedom to ride off day or night could not be tolerated. With rampant greed and disregard for the law, these were increasingly dangerous times. There was always rustling, contention, and unrest between the homesteaders who settled on the free range and the cattlemen who did not want them there. Although the Sioux, Cheyenne, and Arapahoe had not struck hard in the area for the last eight years, had he not lost a nephew in an Indian attack on the cavalry at Medicine Bow earlier in the summer? But to lose a daughter?

He had to make her understand. Maybe Kate could make her understand. The girl, as brave and as competent as she was, was not equal to the times. Life had changed for all of them, and he was certain of it.

Although ragged out from scouting, Johnny had taken the time to meticulously explain the canyon situation to Sam, and they had spoken of it in great detail in the dimly lit office. Conferring until the early morning hours, Johnny had stressed the importance of a quick siege of the men in the canyon. At the break of dawn, Sam Brett watched Johnny pace the floor, waiting for the telegraph office to open. The stove had been stoked up to the point that Sam was actually sweating, although Johnny sat drinking hot coffee, trying to warm his hands and feet and throw off the deep chill in his bones.

"Well, we need to wake Sherm up!" Johnny responded bluntly to Sam's statement that the telegraph office would not open for another hour. Sam reminded him that even if it did open, there would be no one at the other end of the wire to receive the message.

Although Sam understood the importance of a rapid exchange of information, he knew that this morning, lack of sleep had dulled Johnny's ability to think through the whole scenario. Sam also had an uneasy hunch that there might be something else in play here.

Johnny's apparent agitation was not characteristic, as the deputy usually grew less intense after formulating a plan he thought might solve the problem at hand. Sam tried to tell himself that maybe it was just fatigue that had Johnny so edgy, but could not quite buy that.

"Sit down son, you're wearing me out," he commented, trying to bring some levity to the drama. Johnny did, but was up again in a minute, looking out the window to check the weather.

"Gonna be a sunny day. It's a dang shame we can't get started…" Johnny trailed off, raking his hands through his hair.

Sam responded easily. "It will probably be two days before we can get the posse together, you know that. Organizing something this big takes time."

"Yeah, time we don't have," Johnny stated flatly, as he opened the office door, looked up and down the street, abruptly pulling it shut again.

"Bring me a cup of coffee, will you?"

Mechanically, Johnny did as Sam asked. As he handed the hot cup to Sam, Sam looked him straight in the eye.

"I want you to sit down. I could send you on rounds, but I want you to tell me something."

"What?" Johnny asked distractedly, heading for the window once again.

The marshal frowned. "Well, sit!"

Johnny pulled the chair around, and sitting upon it backwards, faced the marshal who sat at his desk. He glanced up at the wall clock. "Six-fifteen," he muttered shaking his head.

Sam studied him. "What else happened when you were out there?"

The pointed question threw Johnny. He had not expected it, and he was puzzled.

"What? I told you everything," he replied.

"I don't think so. You seem on edge, not yourself," Sam replied, holding the deputy's eyes with a steady gaze.

Adamantly, Johnny responded. "Well, it is a volatile situation, at best and I… I think it is hard not to take it seriously," Sam's gaze never veered.

Arrested, Johnny finally bogged down in a swamp of jumbled thoughts, none which he knew how to put into words. He dropped his gaze, folded his arms along the back of the chair and shook his head. Exhaustion got the best of him and he didn't answer. Sam watched patiently.

When Johnny raised his eyes, he looked into the face of the man who knew him better than anyone else: a man who had studied him for the past year, had given him a second look, and had taken a chance on him. It had not been an easy road. Sam was blunt and firm, but Johnny sensed the marshal was motivated by the potential worth he thought he saw in his deputy and maybe, even a slight affinity for him.

But under such intense scrutiny, Johnny felt exposed. Sometimes, something hidden deep within him would suddenly slip to the surface, bobbing like a cork on water, the hidden becoming the obvious. Sam had a way of reeling the thing in and examining it. This seemed like one of those times.

Johnny sighed deeply, then answered. "Last evening as I was returning, I rode the line north of the Wilkerson ranch. It was almost twilight when I noticed a rider coming at a gallop. I slowed and realized it was Cassie Wilkerson." Johnny paused to look at Sam expectantly.

"And?" Sam asked.

"Well, it was getting dark, and I wondered why she was riding away from the barn," Johnny replied bluntly.

"Did you ask her?"

"Ask her what?" Johnny questioned, feeling the heat of scrutiny.

"Ask her why she was riding on her ranch, away from the barn?" Sam repeated patiently.

"Well, no, I didn't ask her to give me a reason. I told her it was too late to be going out, it wasn't safe for her to be there, it would be dark soon, and that she should turn around and go home."

"You told her to go home? How did she respond to that?" The marshal picked up his pencil, tapping the end of it slowly and rhythmically on the desk top.

"She got mad... unduly mad, I'd say, telling me no one respected her judgment, and that she could take care of herself. Can you believe that? A girl like that, out in the wilderness, all alone in the dead of night?"

"Didn't you just say it was almost twilight and that she was on her father's ranch?"

Tap, tap, tap, went the pencil. Johnny looked at Sam incredulously, decided the marshal hadn't heard him correctly, and continued with the facts.

"Then, because it was so late, I had to escort her home. At first she argued with me. She didn't want to go, but I convinced her it was not safe and that a girl like her should never be riding alone in this territory, at any time, especially in the dark."

The pencil tapped away as Sam considered the man before him. Johnny's eyebrows were bunched and his face troubled, and he appeared vaguely confused. But there was more to this story, and Sam concluded that his deputy was passionate about the subject at hand.

Then Sam remembered. It was in the churchyard after Sunday service. Sam had asked Johnny a simple question which had seemed to stump the young man, until Sam realized that Johnny had not heard him. He remembered the spark in Johnny's eyes as Cassie Wilkerson passed. Johnny had tipped his hat, following her with his gaze. Sam had not thought much of it at the time, dismissing the scene as nothing out of the ordinary. Sam thought a moment, then spoke.

"It seems that you did the right thing in taking her home, Johnny, although you might have expressed your concerns differently. She is a very pretty young girl," Sam reflected, accompanied by the methodical beat of the pencil.

"Young girl? Why she's a... She probably doesn't realize the danger to her, maybe has no idea that men would consider her... Or take advantage of her, that is," Johnny dropped his gaze. "She's not that young, Mr. Brett."

"You like her, don't you, son?" Sam asked casually.

Caught off guard again, Johnny became overly defensive. "Well, yeah. I like her just fine. Everyone likes Cassie Wilkerson." He looked away.

Tap, tap, tap, went the pencil. "You really care for her, don't you?" the marshal asked quietly. A long moment passed.

Suddenly, Johnny wearied of the struggle, unsure what to do with the feelings he had stored up over the past month.

"She's just a kid, Mr. Brett," Johnny confessed to his hands, "But, maybe...I do."

"Well, obviously not that much of a kid," Sam replied, tapping away. "She must be seventeen or near to it."

Johnny rolled his eyes. "Jess says she might be 16, maybe even 15. At least that is what he thinks."

"Jess, huh?" Sam Brett gave Johnny a wry smile. "You're just twenty-one yourself. She's helping to teach school now, and is already working for Olivia in her little business venture."

The pencil tapped--a call for advancement on the battlefield of the unknown.

"It is not so much her age, that's only part of the problem. It's this job. My life, my experiences are so different from hers." He watched the marshal, waiting for confirmation of his assessment.

"You live in the same town, don't you? Go to some of the same social events, at least when you can, don't you?

"I get the point," Johnny replied, "but I can't see her pa wanting her to have anything to do with me."

"Did you ask him?" Sam queried, as his pencil rallied the facts.

"No, I've tried to think if I should or how I could, a dozen times at least. I can never quite come up with an answer," Johnny said plaintively.

Tap, tap, tap...

Sam saw the quandary, offered no further solution, and threw the ball back to Johnny concluding, "You sell yourself short, boy. Wilkerson knows you are a good man. I have heard him say so myself."

He paused to let his words sink in. "If you want something bad enough, you'll go after it."

He looked up at the clock. "It is almost seven, let's go send those telegrams."

He rose, tossed the pencil on the desk, stretched, and walked toward the door. He was gone before Johnny could respond.

(Proverbs 3:1-6)

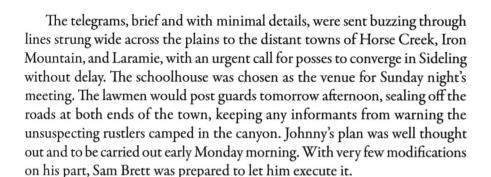

The telegrams, brief and with minimal details, were sent buzzing through lines strung wide across the plains to the distant towns of Horse Creek, Iron Mountain, and Laramie, with an urgent call for posses to converge in Sideling without delay. The schoolhouse was chosen as the venue for Sunday night's meeting. The lawmen would post guards tomorrow afternoon, sealing off the roads at both ends of the town, keeping any informants from warning the unsuspecting rustlers camped in the canyon. Johnny's plan was well thought out and to be carried out early Monday morning. With very few modifications on his part, Sam Brett was prepared to let him execute it.

Marshal Brett had worked enough of this territory to know how easy it was for settlers or businessmen to fall prey to "get rich" schemes such as rustling. If there was anything Sam hated, it was men who used other men for their own selfish gain.

Sam and Johnny had been resistant to the idea of federal troops assisting in the operation. As a borderline garrison town, Sideling would be overrun with officers from Fort Sanders near Laramie, each having a better idea of how to handle the situation, then taking too long to plan and mobilize. Johnny and Sam had knowledge of the people and the countryside and generally felt that the men of the territory could handle their own affairs more efficiently. Let the Blue Coats deal with the Indians and the railroads.

Johnny hung around the telegraph office just long enough to intercept the replies. He threatened the operator, Sherm McNeil, with his life if he dared utter a word to anyone as to the message he had been obliged to tap off the minute he unlocked the door to the telegraph office at 7:00 a.m. With each returned tap, each letter forming a word, Johnny felt hopeful that their plans would be realized expeditiously.

Earlier, after the messages were sent, Johnny had relinquished command, relented, and made a short run to the café to fetch coffee for the frazzled young telegrapher. The after effects of Sherm's Friday night carousing demanded the brew long before Sherm was able to obtain it. Johnny needed it more. A dull ache had formed behind his eyes, and his throat hurt when he swallowed. Maybe hot liquid would make him feel better. Time dragged on, and it seemed that many days had past since he had encountered Cassie along the trail.

He returned to the office with the responses for Marshal Brett, gazing toward Miss Halstead's cabin as he came, but he did not see Cassie. It was barely 9:00 a.m. on Saturday morning. Sideling was coming to life just as he wished he could go back to bed.

After his noon rounds, Johnny and Sam went over the strategy for deploying the posse. "It's a lot like a set piece battle, boy, and we've got to know that it will be executed correctly," Sam stated, as he pushed back his chair.

Johnny had drawn up the plan on paper and arranged the timing as best he could calculate. He stood, rubbing his aching temples. A thousand thoughts and visions assaulted him, and he stared off silently.

Sam noticed and was silent for a moment. "I know you were really young. I can't exactly understand why they sent you boys into a battle like that one. I was Union cavalry, but can never recall using kids, except for buglers or for drummers," he reflected.

"Maybe that's what a military institute is for," Johnny answered thoughtfully. "At least in times of war. Your side had more men, more money. I think Colonel Breckenridge was desperate to accomplish a miracle for old Marse Robert." Sam recognized Johnny's reference to General Lee, and smiled wryly as Johnny continued.

"Everyone loved that man and would do anything he asked, at least up to the end. I saw him once: a big man--and his horse." Johnny paused, remembering. "Well, that's why I gave Traveller his name. After Mama died and I was taken to Montana to live and work with the Ord family, I took a fancy to a gray colt. His coat shone silvery-white in the sunlight, and I took one look at him and knew what I would name him if he were mine. Same color as Lee's horse, same spirit." Sam Brett nodded.

"I trained him, and Mr. Ord gave him to me," Johnny said reflectively.

"That battle you fought. How was it for you that day, son?"

Johnny blinked. "I try not to think about it. I put it out of my mind as much as I can." He was vaguely uncomfortable, and knew from experience that the marshal's question actually held two questions and required two separate responses. The first he had answered as noncommittally as he could. The second question, as he understood it, put him on edge and brought a slight defensive tone to his response.

"If you are askin' me if I can face a conflict without losin' my wits, yeah, I can," he replied, bluntly.

Sam did not comment and continued to gaze at him evenly. In a moment he spoke again.

"I don't think there was one battle fought where I didn't feel fear. It's natural, it heightens your senses-can even make you see the danger before you more clearly. It's nerve that keeps a man going, and can bust through the wall that blocks your senses, propelling you forward. Fear makes you cautious, but nerve keeps you moving. You need both." He let his words hang in the air, hoping they would settle on Johnny and diffuse the defensiveness, which seemed to have cropped up.

Johnny had never spent much time questioning the marshal, always listening to his advice, weighing his words, and trying to incorporate them in his duties as a lawman. Suddenly he was overwhelmed with the need to have Sam Brett see him on equal terms. He knew the marshal cared about him, and realized this question was as much about Sam's need to be assured that Johnny could react appropriately, as it was to prompt Johnny to think through the situation at hand.

Johnny slowly exhaled, holding Sam's gaze intently. "Mr. Brett, I know I can do this because it has to be done--for this town, for this territory. We can't allow men who are thieves and liars to take advantage of others who want to be free to live their lives, raise their families, and make an honest living. I hate the fear, and I hate the feeling of being trapped. It is like war. It's causin' us to have to close down the whole entire town. No, I'm not wantin' a battle. I just know there will be one. Whatever happens to us, we're doin' what we're paid to do, the right thing and at the right time."

Johnny stood and walked toward the window, peering out into the day. "I want to live here; this is my home. Our way of life needs defending. I lost everything on the other side of this country, and I'll be hanged if I will see it happen again."

He turned to face Sam Brett, who studied Johnny's passionate response, and nodded in agreement.

"And if you don't need me right now, I'll ride out to see just why Jess hasn't bothered to respond to the telegram we sent," Johnny finished.

"If you give him the same speech you just gave me, he'll come along," Sam replied, a slight smile playing along his firm lip line.

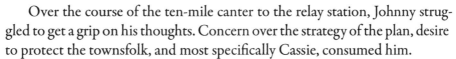

Over the course of the ten-mile canter to the relay station, Johnny struggled to get a grip on his thoughts. Concern over the strategy of the plan, desire to protect the townsfolk, and most specifically Cassie, consumed him.

He was just plain irked that Jess had not responded. It was in times like these that Johnny felt like taking Jess' easy-going nature and kicking it a country mile, but reason told him that although Jess could be nonchalant, he would never let them down. It was his way.

From a distance, Johnny spotted Jess by the corral and immediately knew why he had not been at the telegraph receiver. Johnny cantered toward him.

"Evenin', Jess."

"Well, howdy, Johnny, you're just in time!" Jess greeted expressively, then raised a quizzical brow. "What brings you out this way?"

"I'm here to repossess that telegraph key and wire you don't need," Johnny answered, caustically. "Why'd you bother to install that contraption if you're never gonna use it?" Traveller danced beneath him.

"Been out here all mornin', and never got your message, so how could I?" Jess replied, grinning and rewinding his lariat.

The combination of his master's aggravation and the scent of the mares in the corral sent Traveller sidestepping beneath Johnny.

"You can pure suck the joy out of livin' with that grumpy nature of yours, McLane," Jess harped, taking in his friend's scruffy appearance, and realizing he hadn't come to discuss telegraph lines. "We're going to the canyon to take 'em; that's what all of this fuss is about, ain't it?"

"We meet at the schoolhouse tomorrow evening at six. Be on time, we're closin' the road in and out of town after that--except to lawmen. We'll pull out after first light Monday mornin'. I'll explain the rest later."

"I'll be there," Jess confirmed, nodding. "Oh say, before you go, I need a little favor."

Johnny caught the familiar glimmer in Jess' eye and swung his gaze toward the corral. "No...no, I can't. I'm tired and hungry and I got to get back to town."

"Oh, come on McLane! How is it that you can ask me to risk my life for you and you don't even help me out with a couple of docile mares?"

Indecisively, Johnny perused the horses and Jess saw his interest pique as a fancy paint paced around the corral, flicking her tail excitedly.

"When was she ridden last?" he asked.

"Oh, last spring some time. She's been out on the range all summer."

Whereas Jess could confess his own weakness lay in cavorting with the fair sex of the human variety, he would bet everything he owned that Johnny's weakness was a good horse-the more difficult, the faster, the better. He knew he almost had him but also knew his friend took his marshaling job seriously, and if that was the case, he decided he would need to sweeten the pot.

"Wanna make a little wager?"

Any bet concerning a horse was too much temptation, and Johnny asked, "What wager?"

"I bet you my best lariat that that ole gal can make you cuss." Indicating the fancy mare, he paused, "Yes you, John Scott...cuss a blue streak!" he challenged wickedly.

"That so? I doubt it," replied Johnny cockily, swinging off Traveller and tying him to the nearest rail.

Jess taunted him further. "She ain't like one of them high steppin' thoroughbreds you raced through the Virginia countryside trying to impress those hothouse southern lilies, no sir. She's a real horse. Let's just see if you can hang on to a thrashin' bronc, son."

"Well, I reckon I have the minute it will take to do this," Johnny replied, shooting Jess an arrogant glare, then opening the corral gate. He lifted the bridle from the fence.

"This the right one?" Slowly he walked toward the skittish paint, crouching down a few yards in front of her, perfectly still.

"Oh, for the love of money, just get on with it," Jess hollered, and spat in the dirt.

Johnny remained quiet and still as a stone. In time, the mare found him interesting enough to come forward. She stood before him, lowering her head with nostrils flaring as she sniffed his face and shoulders. Murmuring gently, he stroked her muzzle. She snorted softly, tossed her head once, then lowered it to sniff him again.

He stood slowly, just brushing her side with his, crooning softly, his hand on her jaw as he caressed her and slid his hand along her sleek neck. He held the bridle against her neck and placed the reins over her mane, gently manipulating the bit into her mouth. Leading her to the corral rail, he lifted the saddle off the railing. She shied but did not rear. He placed the saddle on the ground and soothed the mare, letting her sniff the leather.

"Ya just have to treat her like a lady, Jess...but maybe you don't know how that goes," Johnny chided evenly, still stroking the horse. "She has a nice round eye, she'll do just fine."

"You better listen and learn, Jess Bryant!"

A female voice interrupted, laughing softly. Johnny glanced over his shoulder.

"Oh hey, Sodie," Johnny replied, smiling at the young brunette who had joined Jess by the fence.

She waved and the mare threw her head, backed up suddenly, and almost pulled Johnny off his feet. Fitting the saddle and cinching it as they circled in place, he calmed her once again.

"Alright, let's see what you can do, buckaroo!" Jess exclaimed.

Johnny placed his foot in the stirrup and swung into the saddle. Two quick hops forward, two outright bucks and a half-hearted rear later, Johnny remained in the saddle and brought the mare to the corral railing, holding her to a jerky canter, then loping in circles and figure eights until the mare was winded. He walked her to the fence where Jess and Sodie sat watching.

"Oooh, oooh, Johnny," Sodie cooed coyly, batting her eyelids. She climbed off the rail and stood by the mare. "What are you doing later tonight?"

"Depends on what you have in mind," Johnny responded roguishly. "Looks like Jess will be busy attempting to break that other nag far into the evenin'." He laughed, winking at Sodie.

"Excuse me, you two, but I think the lady already has plans." Amiably, Jess dropped down from his perch on the railing and draped an arm over Sodie's shoulders.

"Still frying up that chicken, sweetheart? I'm a hungry man!"

"Sorry Johnny," Sodie pouted, "guess we'll have to make it another time. Stay for dinner? We have plenty." She flashed a genuine smile.

"That would be great, but I got to get back to town. Still have business to take care of."

Sodie paused with hands on hips, eyeing Johnny suspiciously. "I hope that business doesn't include hauling Jess off again."

"Just a few days is all, Sodie, then you can have him back," Johnny replied, winking at her again.

"You may be easy to look at, Johnny McLane, but you always leave trouble in your wake!" She had chanced the subtle caution on the unlikely event that Jess might be persuaded to take heed.

"Seems like it, don't it?" Johnny chuckled.

Jess began a vague explanation, but Johnny cut him short. "See you tomorrow, Jess," intentionally bailing out of the conversation in light of Sodie's concerns. Jess nodded knowingly.

Sodie drew her coat around her neck and trembled. "Well, I am freezing, and I know I will get no answers now, so I am going back inside."

"Hey! Don't you want to watch me break the next one?" Jess asked, striving to revive her interest.

"You can break your fool neck without me, sir, and I'll not be coming to your funeral!"

She flashed a smile at Johnny who watched with some amusement. "Bye for now. Good to see you Johnny... regardless," she quipped.

"Likewise, Sodie, and say 'hey' to that brother of yours."

He mounted Traveller, tipping his hat cordially. "And tell him to stop by the office as soon as he can, if you please, ma'am."

I'll let Skep know you asked after him," she replied with misgivings, adding, "Now don't go dragging my brother into this mess, Johnny!"

She shook her head at the men who studied her innocently, then stood on tiptoe, giving Jess a peck on the cheek. Turning with a sigh, she retreated for the warmth of the relay station.

"She's a great girl--just showed up this afternoon with biscuits and chickens to fry for the boys," Jess exclaimed, as they watched her leave.

"She deserves better," Johnny replied, laughing.

"Yeah, but she loves me," Jess joked. "Seriously," he added, "I'll be there tomorrow. Let's get this mess over. You and I can lead that posse. We're the only ones who know where we're goin'."

"Thanks, Jess. We'll talk tomorrow. I better get out of here."

Jess swatted Traveller's rump, and the horse moved forward. Johnny turned him toward Sideling.

The sun was still high in the western sky, and Johnny calculated the time to be about 3:30 p.m. Entering the marshal's office, he glanced at the wall clock, and found his assumption to be correct. Though certainly warmer than the cold borne on the northwest wind, the chilly office indicated that the marshal had been out most of the afternoon.

Johnny removed his gloves, and touched the potbelly stove. Finding it still warm, he placed the short fat sticks into the yawning cavity, and blew the ash away from the glowing embers until a spark blazed to life. He pulled off his boots, and placed his numb stockinged feet as close as he dared.

Cold to the bone, his head throbbed. Slowly, the air warmed around him. Removing his outer garments, he sat, elongating until his head rested against the back of the chair, and his elevated feet could soak up the warmth from the stove. His eyelids fought the weight of the day's trials, and succumbing, he fell asleep.

When Sam entered the office an hour later, the wind caught the heavy door, flinging it wide and slamming it into the wall. In an instant he found himself sheltering behind the corner of his desk, held at gunpoint by his bleary-eyed, confused deputy, whom he reprimanded harshly.

"If you stay in this condition, if you can't think straight and don't know what you're doing, how will you function tomorrow? Now," he commanded, "get some food and get some sleep, and in that order, boy!" Aggravated, Sam turned and walked out, slamming the door behind him.

Bewildered and sick at the thought of what could have transpired, Johnny donned his coat, hat, and boots, and walked through the cold toward the café. The icy wind, like a welcome friend, assaulted him, cooling the burning inside. He thought there was not much left in life that could really terrify him, but finding himself out of control and becoming his own worst enemy had come mighty close.

He tried to put two plus two together, but it came out oddly. Little self-control with too much pressure and the words emerged from the recesses of his mind, "friendly fire"--the curse of fighting in situations where there was no clarity. "Wake up! Know what you're doing!" Sam's reprimand and the northwind howled through the restiveness within him.

Around 4:30 p.m., after a much-needed meal of stew and sourdough biscuits, eaten in solitude and with a dose of introspection in the back corner of Frances Kelly's café, Johnny returned to the office.

Sam rose from behind the desk. "I'm going over to the Watering Hole Saloon. Cy Riddick and his posse just rode in from Iron Mountain."

"Good!" Johnny exclaimed, "How many men did he have with him?"

"Besides himself, I believe there are three," Sam responded.

Johnny quickly calculated the logistics and number of men available. "We'll send Marshal Riddick and his men toward the western pass; they number enough to hold the flank of the canyon," he said, glad to be able to plug real numbers into what had previously been only figures in a sketchily-formulated plan.

"You eat yet?" Sam asked.

"Yeah, I did." Johnny replied absently, as he scanned a roughly drawn map of the Medicine Bow Range.

"I'm amending my earlier order. No sleep yet. Make rounds and drop by the schoolhouse. I noticed her rig over there as I rode in. Just want to make sure that Myra Davis understands we have need of the building tomorrow evening. Then, you get some sleep."

Johnny grunted and nodded, still studying the map. At the door, the marshal turned.

"You find Jess?"

"I did," Johnny answered. "He was where we thought he'd be. As usual, nowhere near the telegraph key."

Johnny turned up his collar against the icy blast as he made the rounds in the dark. All went well until he touched the doorknob of Clancy Miller's Flour and Grain establishment. The knob turned under his hand, and the right side of the large wooden double door swung open immediately, caught with a gust of the wind. Johnny held his lantern high while examining the lock, positioning himself against the wind to keep the flame alive. The lock had been tampered with and broken. Slipping his gun from the holster, he unlocked the safety and cocked the hammer, setting the lantern on the porch. He stepped through the door and backed up against the darkened inside wall.

As his eyes adjusted to the dark, he scanned the room's interior and found nothing unusual. He retrieved the lantern from the porch. Once back inside, he moved through the shadows, examining the room by the glow of lamplight. He walked the length of the counter and backed along the remaining shelves, until he came to the doorway of the rear room.

Resting the lantern on the floor, he aimed his gun and moved quickly through the doorway, keeping his back to the wall. There was no one about and the room was silent, except for the rattle and creak of the window sashes disturbed by an occasional gust of wind. He found the back door unlocked, but the lock appeared undamaged.

Finally able to arouse Mrs. Abigail Miller from a deep sleep after pounding upon the front door of her upstairs apartment, Johnny faced the bleary-eyed, indignant matron, who explained that her husband, Clancy, would not be home until tomorrow afternoon. He had gone to visit his brother in Iron Mountain.

"No," she had not heard a sound and did not care to check for missing items at this "ungodly hour". "No," there was no one else in charge except the boy, Lester, whom Clancy had left to mind the store in his absence.

But the inconvenienced woman's countenance abruptly changed as she seemed to remember something, and as the harsh wrinkles in her face appeared to melt away in the lantern's glow, she smiled beguilingly.

"Fix the lock...tonight," she suggested. "If not, you are welcome to stand guard over the establishment until dawn, that is, if it would make things easier for you."

Johnny stared at the woman incredulously. Quickly, Mrs. Miller thanked him kindly, closing the door in his face.

Forty-five minutes later the lock was repaired using the supplies from the closet in the backroom of the office. Long ago, the marshal had determined to alleviate such nocturnal traipsing about and cached hardware items in the backroom closet, easily accessible for midnight repairs. Johnny tested the door and the lock held.

He shoved his icy fingers into his gloves, thought about his next venture, and mumbled an expletive. He rode toward the schoolhouse, and from a distance, noted lamplight glowing steadily through the panes.

He dismounted and reached the top of the steps just as all but one of the interior lamps extinguished. Opening the door, he collided abruptly with Myra Davis.

"Johnny!" Myra exclaimed, clearly surprised. "What brings you here at this hour?"

She laughed softly, regarding him curiously and took his arm to pull him out of the wind. Facing him, she leaned against the closed door and looked up expectantly.

"You're here alone?" Johnny asked disapprovingly, noting the darkened classroom beyond the threshold.

"I was just closing up. Two of the older boys were working on a platform rise for our poetry presentation, but they left a while ago. I thought I'd use the quiet to grade a few papers, but you are a nice surprise," she said pleasantly, as mild interest played in her brown eyes.

Uncomfortably aware of the dimly-lit interior, Johnny removed his hat and stated his mission. "I came to make sure you understood that we will be holding our parley with the lawmen here, tomorrow night, at 6:00 p.m."

Uneasily, he rested his hat against his thigh, tapping it imperceptibly, awaiting her response.

The air was close and she searched his face. He straightened, feeling the need to leave, but she rested easily against the door, blocking his retreat.

Conceding, he placed his foot casually on the low bench and hooked his thumb over his gunbelt, realizing she would hold him there until she spoke her mind. As he did so, she relinquished her lean upon the door and straightened, stepping toward him.

"You are always so businesslike nowadays, no time for fun, I imagine," she said softly, searching his eyes.

He recognized her tactic and thought of a slow dance. They had done this before, most often without touching, just sidestepping, moving forward and backward but never in the same direction, and never at the same time. This time the distance between them was not only defined by space. She continued to gaze at him.

"We used to talk more frequently, Johnny. Now I hardly ever see you."

Johnny fixed her with his eyes. "You see me, Myra, at church, at the schoolhouse, and sometimes around the town."

She interrupted softly, "But, you never speak to me."

"Usually," he said directly, "your attentions are engaged elsewhere, and I don't think those fellows you're focused on would welcome my interruption."

Always mindful of the appearance of propriety and the need for singular morality before the matrons of the town, Myra guarded her nocturnal activities zealously. Though a rumble from the schoolboard surfaced now and again, most were content with her handling of the town's offspring. While the older men watched her with a detached fascination, the younger men kept silent regarding their part in her dalliances, the exception being when they shared stories of their leisure activities over libations in the gaming places.

"Well, let's see," she said, her voice engaging his accusation and her eyes narrowing slightly. "Maybe there wouldn't be any other fellows if you ever took the time to ask for me."

Johnny straightened. "Come on, Myra, let's be honest. Who was it who always took a step backward every time I moved forward? The line of gents occupyin' your time was hard to step over," he said, weariness edging his tone.

"A girl likes to be pursued, you know. It would be nice if just once you showed some resentment toward the others," she said stiffly, "or let me know that you wanted me. You really never did."

"I just don't have time for games or even the time you require, Myra. Look, it's Saturday night and I'm working. That's all I've done for the last month or so. And how would I even know what you want? You never said one word. I had no idea you ever thought about..."

She interrupted. "But, I did. Maybe not with words. I stopped by the office to see you several times--not that you were ever there!"

"That dog won't hunt, Myra, and you know it. We always get to the same place, in this same conversation, over and over."

He had not meant to speak so sharply, and immediately, iron clamped over her features.

"So I see. That is it!" She exclaimed, cold with anger. "That's really it, isn't it?"

"What's 'it'?" Johnny asked, not understanding and not really caring if he didn't. "What are you talkin' about?"

Having been dragged into this discourse unwillingly, he forced himself to abate his surging anger.

"You don't want to have this conversation with me, and I know why. It must be true then. I see the way you look at Cassie Wilkerson. Oh, yes, and you've got her looking right back at you! She is just a child, Johnny!"

Dumbfounded, Johnny stood mute, and Myra continued her slow, seething ambush.

"Do you think I don't know this? How could I not? I spend a good part of most days with her, you know, and I have seen the change in her. I see it every time someone mentions your name or you come along."

"Hold it, Myra, that's plain crazy," Johnny protested. Heat rose in his face, and he was glad for the dimly-lit room. "I don't just 'come along' toward anyone in particular, certainly not near her, not even near you."

He couldn't think of any further defense and no way to tread the tide of her ridiculous accusations.

Myra was not through. "Not so! She's a young girl, Johnny, a kid, but she is so wonderstruck that every time she's in your presence she seems to lose her senses. And you, you…well, gravitate toward her. I see you on Sunday mornings, that is, when you bother to stay around until church lets out!"

"Now just wait a minute!" Johnny began, unable to dodge the rampage she had unleashed against him. "I don't need…"

She interrupted him, verbally reloading and firing angrily. "Oh, you have no idea what you need, Johnny!" and to his amazement, her eyes were misty in the flicker of the lamplight.

"You need someone who understands you! You need a woman who can tolerate your way of life. Not a girl, especially one who doesn't know what sacrifice is. Look at her! She goes without nothing; she doesn't have to."

Johnny threw his palms up. "Hold it! Let me get this straight! You're willing to 'sacrifice' your life to be with me, is that what you are sayin'? To sacrifice all your happiness for a man like me? And, oh yeah, let's not forget my lowly station in life. Thanks, but I don't need that, and I don't need a wife if that's what you are gettin' at!"

She fired back, "Oh, you don't know what you need! You have the same needs as any other man! Don't say it is not true, and if you lie, well, there is no honor in what you say!" She glared at him, the mist in her eyes now replaced with flint.

He glared back at her. "All I have to say to your unfathomable and unreasonable attack is, if you meant all those words you just hammered me with, I would make you miserable in about one week's time. Where is the love in that?"

Frustrated and angry, Myra groaned and turned quickly, snatched her coat and bonnet off the wall peg, yanked the heavy door open, and fled down the steps.

She stopped on the bottom step and turned to yell up at him. "You turn out the lamp! You lock the door! See that it's done! It's your job!"

She stormed to the rig, unhitched the horse, and drove off into the dark.

Johnny stood in the gloom watching her leave, and wondered what he could have possibly done to deserve such an attack. Why did she seem to care about him now, and worst of all, how had he become so transparent? Self-condemnation and confusion burned within, flamed by her perceptions and stinging words.

He turned to lock the door, grateful that the day was mercifully over, then turned to face the swirling wind. He welcomed the cold, gusty air and pressed on, descending the steps and tamping down the internal chaos.

"What circumstances might those be?" asked Marshal Brett, curiously observing the young rancher.

"I've spoken with Jess, sir, and I am here to offer my services. I know the need to conceal this mission, and understand the importance of it. If those rustlers set their sights on our horses, Uncle Willie and I are finished. No horses, no profit," Skep Duane explained seriously.

"I am not sure where Johnny is, but he's certain to show up anytime now."

Sam gazed at the clock on the office wall. It was already 8:30 a.m. Consumed with the planning, Sam was disinclined toward pleasantries even though he had not seen the young rancher in quite a while. He knew Skep must figure somehow in the puzzle.

"I'll be around town," Skep advised, as he left the office. "Would you let Johnny know I'm here?"

Sam Brett needed coffee. Though it had never been verbalized, he now knew how the plan would unfold. Johnny, Jess Bryant, and Skep Duane would be the ones to go over the rocks, using the same route Johnny had taken a few days before. It made sense. They had the stamina, knew the territory, and more importantly, worked well together. For the past year they had done what young men usually did with what little free time they had: fished and hunted together. This time, with a lot of luck, they would bag their prey again.

Just one day to get it all together...where was his deputy anyway?

"I am sure I do not know Mr. Miller's inventory, so I do not know what that thief might have stolen!" Abigail Miller snapped. "And, no, it could not have been Lester Bolton! He's a trustworthy boy, not given to such. I'll just have to stay closed until my husband returns. You know we don't open of a Sunday anyway, except in special circumstances!"

She clearly did not like dealing with her husband's affairs. She was so frustrated at having been awakened early, then asked about her husband and the business, that Johnny wondered if she liked dealing with Clancy Miller in any fashion.

"I did my best to make sure everything is locked tight this morning, Miz Abigail, so I think you're alright for now."

"No need to tell me, Deputy. Clancy will be back late this afternoon and as I said, you can deal with him directly," Abigail snapped.

Johnny tipped his hat to the small, rotund woman. "Good mornin'," he said retreating, glad to be on his way.

His head throbbed uncomfortably, and he had found it difficult to breathe during the night. The tightness in his chest and coughing continued throughout the morning. Coffee helped, and standing upright enabled him to catch his breath.

Crossing Center Street, which ran perpendicular to High Street and between the Livery and the Flour and Grain, he glanced up the road toward the church. A few rigs and horses appeared in anticipation of the Sunday morning service. Children ran in circles and he noticed a knot of young people talking and laughing in the open air.

Johnny realized the juxtaposition of his circumstance. Most folks had no idea what this day could mean to their community. The heavy weight of responsibility burdened him, and he felt old. His eyes searched for her, but found only the pleasant faces of other congregants.

Beau Brenner stood slightly off to one side, leaning against the white picket fence. Johnny saw that his attention was fixed, not on the young people, but on the town's streets. There were an unusual number of horses tied to the hitching posts. Maybe, Johnny thought idly, that was what attracted Beau's attention.

But the more he considered Beau, the more he doubted it. He turned toward the boy, but just as he did, Beau turned and walked off.

Johnny would have to question Lester Bolton and Beau later. For now, it would be enough to keep this evening's operation under wraps, and he needed to keep his attention focused on the comings and goings of the population before the roads were closed.

He walked toward the office, inhaling deeply to clear his thoughts. The vengeful cough caught him again, and he leaned against a barrel until it passed.

Sam Brett exited the office as Johnny stepped onto the porch. "I was wondering where you were. The town's filling up slowly, and all the posses are here. You sleep any?" he asked in his usual clipped tone.

Johnny gave a vague nod and related his earlier interaction with Mrs. Miller. The marshal was thoughtful. The unspoken question which had occurred to Johnny was evident in Sam's expression.

"I don't see any real connection between the break-in and the rustling yet, but I am keeping my eyes open," Johnny replied, his voice becoming gravelly.

Sam narrowed his eyes and questioned him. "You sick?"

"Just a cold."

"Get a shot of whiskey from the desk drawer. It'll help. I'm meeting with Charlie Tilghman. He came in just an hour ago from Horse Creek with his men. Eli Tucker and his men from Laramie are already here. Oh, and Skep Duane wants to see you. Don't know where he went, but he is around town." He put his hand on Johnny's shoulder and in an unusual gesture, gave it a firm squeeze, and then walked off.

Johnny entered the office and sat down intending to write a report on the incident at the Miller's store. He pulled the lower desk drawer open. The half-empty bottle of Old Crow sat corked. Its contents, used in the office only for medicinal purposes, was seldom a temptation to the deputy. But the way he felt at this particular moment might just justify that slug.

He picked up the bottle and the crimson-hued liquid sloshed within its confines. He uncorked it and sniffed for the familiar sweet corn scent, but with his olfactory senses being severely diminished, felt no desire for it. He could tolerate whiskey made with corn, but the cheaper, more popular American rye blend always made him sick. Both made him sleepy, no matter which grain they contained, so he corked it and replaced the bottle, closing the drawer with a shove of his boot.

"Better drink when I need to sleep, not now," he muttered to himself. He made his way to the bathhouse, thinking a hot soaking might do him some good.

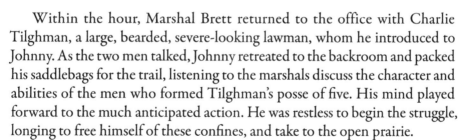

Within the hour, Marshal Brett returned to the office with Charlie Tilghman, a large, bearded, severe-looking lawman, whom he introduced to Johnny. As the two men talked, Johnny retreated to the backroom and packed his saddlebags for the trail, listening to the marshals discuss the character and abilities of the men who formed Tilghman's posse of five. His mind played forward to the much anticipated action. He was restless to begin the struggle, longing to free himself of these confines, and take to the open prairie.

Cassie came to mind, rising in his thoughts like the distant whistle of a train on the far horizon, coming for him in a blast of rising steam with clanging bell that heralds the arrival of the stroking engine. 'I have to see her,' and from the corner of his mind came the more subtle thought, 'Maybe even for the last time.' He knew his desire was irrational, but realized he was unable to push it away.

"I'm gonna check on a few things, Mr. Brett, I'll be back directly. A pleasure to meet you, sir." He nodded toward Marshal Tilghman as he strode through the office, not waiting for a response from either man.

As Sam Brett checked the ammunition chambers in the rifles on the back wall and watched through the window, Johnny mounted Traveller and cantered off.

The hours between late morning and early afternoon brought no sign of further trouble and no other arrival of telegrams. Earlier, the church service had commenced, then wound down quickly as few men had been in attendance. Sam knew the word must have gotten out, and that there would be no shortage of Sideling's men when the call to form a posse was broadcast this evening.

The challenge would be gleaning the few really competent ones. No hot heads or inquisitive joy riders would wear the badge and take the oath tonight. He would not win any popularity contests, but he was used to that.

If he had to guess, he would bet that Johnny had left the office to ride off some tension. The waiting game strung nerves tighter than banjo strings.

Johnny spurred Traveller to a gallop, then slowed to a jog in the cool afternoon sunshine. The change in wind direction and decrease in its intensity brought unusual warmth to the late October plains. Briefly, Johnny reflected upon that good fortune, for if conditions held, it would make the thing more tolerable tomorrow--no ice, no snowstorm. He glanced up at the cloudless blue sky, calm and brilliant, stretching out until it collided with the huge distant snow-capped mountains, which continued in their vast expanse, rolling on seemingly forever.

The odd paradox came to him. He had sensed this long ago in battle. Confusion had rained down upon the earth, blackening, burning, tearing and gnashing while the heavens remained beautiful and calm. It seemed as though the two had no connection, existing apart from one another. He knew not many hours would pass before the same situation might hold true again.

He had not been completely truthful with Sam Brett, and it bothered him. Cassie had been his goal. He had not yet thought beyond just being with her. If she wasn't at Miss Mabel's then what would be his recourse? Would he continue on to her father's ranch? What reason would he give for his actions? He pushed away any attempt to make sense of this and continued on.

The rig in the shade of the large oak tree in front of Mabel Baker's cabin was unfamiliar to him. He saw no sign of Cassie's horse and disappointed, he rode alongside the rig and dismounted. Voices from within the house wafted on the breeze, and just then the screen door flung wide as Kate Wilkerson exited, holding boxes and a patterned valise. His eyes met hers and it was hard to distinguish which one of them was most surprised.

Johnny bounded up the steps, taking the valise and one large box from her hands, smiling. "Hey Miz Wilkerson, let me help you."

"Why thank you, Deputy, what brings you out this way? I thought you and the marshal would be out hunting cows since they seem to have trouble staying put!" she said lightly. Noting the expression on his face she added, "I am sorry, I didn't mean to make light of the situation. It is serious, and I just can't seem to comprehend such men and their way of reasoning. What belongs to others, they just take any way they see fit. This affects all of us, ruins our businesses, leaves us vulnerable, and it's most unfortunate that you must deal with them."

"We've studied on this and have come to a few conclusions. I thought I would check on Miss Mabel before..." he paused and, thinking quickly, finished, "before we may have to take some kind of action, sooner rather than later."

Kate studied Johnny thoughtfully and her heart ached for him. She perceived his hesitation to give details and knew that eventually he and Sam Brett would have to make a sacrifice for the wrongdoings of a few thieves. He was so young, probably the age her Robert would have been had he not....she blocked the thought and focused on the man before her.

She had never taken much notice of him as their paths had never intimately crossed. She had seen Johnny in church talking with Myra Davis at times, and had even supposed as the rumors indicated, that they were sweethearts.

In the midst of her reflection, she vaguely heard the question which he was now repeating. "Would you like these boxes in the rig, ma'am?"

As she smiled and nodded, he stood holding the cumbersome items and asked another question. "Is Miss Mabel about?"

"Oh no," Kate replied quickly. "I am sorry. She is going to be staying in town with Mrs. Winkler for a spell. She became ill and unable to be by herself and, yes, you may put those things in the wagon."

"Mabel did request that we let you know of her whereabouts, and she told us that you had been so kind in helping her."

This time it was Johnny who did not hear Kate Wilkerson's words, for he was distracted as Cassie came from within, and then stopped in the doorway behind her mother. Her eyes sparkled, and her auburn hair hung in waves over her shoulders.

Noting that his attention had shifted, Kate Wilkerson was momentarily puzzled at the change in Johnny's expression. She turned to find Cassie behind her and was struck at the look upon her daughter's face.

"Well," she said, interrupting what had become a very long pause, "Cassie, I was just telling the deputy about our dear Aunt Mabel."

Cassie came to life and tore her gaze from Johnny, stepping onto the porch with more awkward items. A lamp, and a few books of different sizes were cradled in her arms, the books barely remaining in her grasp.

"Hold it," Johnny said animatedly, rapidly descending the steps and placing the boxes and the valise into the rig. Mrs. Wilkerson returned to the house for the last of Mabel's possessions. Cassie had descended to the middle step by the time Johnny reached her side.

"Better not try to take anything from me, Deputy," she laughed, "or I'll likely drop the whole kit and caboodle!"

He placed a hand at her elbow to steady her as they cleared the last of the steps, then steered her toward the rig. He took the lamp from her carefully, wedging it into a small place between the boxes.

She leaned over the side of the rig and shoved the books under the front bench, turning to face Johnny as she brushed the dust from her palms. "Well, that does it," she said brightly.

He stepped closer; she caught her breath. Taking in his expression and his blue-green eyes...or were they hazel...she was drawn into their depths: captivating pools of color, intense in the sunlight.

What did this mean? She caught the look she thought she had seen once before. He had gazed at her in similar fashion the evening she had agreed to let him accompany her home in the twilight. She remembered her sense of loss and confusion that evening, after he had ridden so quickly away.

This time, he did not turn away. He held her with an expression so intense she found herself searching for an entrance into his thoughts.

He put his hand lightly at the small of her back, barely touching her, but in the warmth he invoked, she spoke breathlessly. "The cows and chickens are at our ranch, Johnny, you don't have to..." losing her words completely, she silenced.

He spoke her name, gently. "Cassie, I need to ask you a question. I've thought a lot about this. I know you have no idea, but I must ask you now." He paused, searching for words.

Transfixed by his gaze, she whispered, "Yes, Johnny?"

That very moment, Kate Wilkerson entered the front room, just passing the window at the porch with a few more items in her hand. She stopped short at the scene below her. Stunned at what she observed, suddenly everything fell into place. Her daughter's tears and conflicts of late, the elated giddiness and the melancholy must be the result of this. How could she have missed it? Why had she not known? This was no schoolgirl crush her daughter carried, and she could see it clearly. Suddenly she was afraid for her.

"This can not be," she murmured, and raw concern prompted her to snatch the door open wide.

"My goodness!" she said brightly, stepping onto the porch and feigning exhaustion. "I am glad we are finished! Cassie, we need to get to town to deliver these things to Mrs. Winkler's as soon as we can, dear. I am sure the deputy has much to do and would like to check out the property. Will you lock up for us please?"

She did not wait for the young man's reply or consider the reaction of her daughter. She descended the steps briskly, watching the placement of each foot lest she slip and fall, then placed the remaining items into the rig. With a great sigh, she turned and looked up pointedly, forcing a smile. Johnny and Cassie had stepped apart, but only slightly. He looked uncomfortable and she, stricken and embarrassed.

"I hope you will visit Mrs. Baker soon, Deputy. She will be looking for you. I will surely keep you in my prayers...sincerely, for your safety in the matters at hand. Come along, Cassie," she ordered, hoisting herself into the rig and picking up the reins.

Johnny took Cassie's hand and helped her up onto the seat. She flushed, and he squeezed her hand gently before reluctantly releasing it.

"Farewell," Cassie responded haltingly, as the wagon lurched forward.

As he watched the wagon disappear in the distance, he realized with clarity why Mrs. Wilkerson had left so abruptly. He did not dwell on that fact, however, because even without the time or ability to express all he had desired, Cassie seemed to understand and had wordlessly returned his sentiment. Had he not seen this in her expression and in the depths of her eyes?

Johnny stood for a while, awash in swirling thoughts, waiting for the sediment of insignificance to settle. When it did, it became clear that he would lay down his life for this girl. He would fight to make the territory a place where she could have a decent life, regardless of when or if she could ever be his.

This conflict he faced would be different. There was no gray area here; this conflict would be won and the property restored to the rightful owners, bringing hope for the future, or they would die trying. He whispered the absolutes instilled from his youth, "Life, liberty, and the pursuit of happiness," dictums he had memorized long ago, "and to secure those rights, governments are instituted among men, deriving their just powers from the consent of the governed."

The governed were the folks. In the town, he was responsible to see that this happened; in this new frontier he had the privilege to stand on the side of justice. A deeper awareness settled on him of the sacrifices men had made in the past, why they had made them, and what would be required to hold those freedoms. He desired to be a man like those who had come before. Now, he had more reason than ever to take that stand.

As Cassie and her mother drove away from Mabel Baker's farm, leaving Johnny standing in the road, the wagon rumbled over the rugged ruts but Cassie took no notice. Her thoughts were far off, in an unfamiliar place. It was a place of ice and heat, like the cold sip of sweetened iced tea, heavy with the tange of lemon on a hot summer's day.

One hand remained tightly gripped on the edge of the wagon bed, while the hand Johnny had grasped lay motionless in her lap. She focused, realizing she had not moved it, and everything around her faded except for the sensation of his touch. She remembered that just moments before, she was standing unconventionally in the sunlight before him. She had not worn gloves or a bonnet, neither was her hair braided or pinned up neatly, yet just before she was whisked away, his hand had lingered on hers longer than was necessary, and his gaze had penetrated hers as though he knew her completely.

By 6:00 p.m. the schoolhouse resounded with boisterous talk and spurts of laughter as the posses from Albany and Laramie counties gathered. The roads had been closed by the marshal's order, and the town was effectively sealed off. Boasting was evident in the overcrowded classroom, but most conversations dealt with the facts at hand. The territorial citizens demanded the cessation of rustling and demanded strong action be taken against the perpetrators of the crimes. Two men were dead; their efforts to stop the thieves and defend their property lay as cold and as silent as the victims. Two families were left with no providers. The brutal cold and snow of the high plains winter was about to descend from the storehouses of the heavens, threatening to tear the life from every unprotected living thing.

Marshal Brett faced the assembly of lawmen. After expressing appreciation for their convening, he concluded his introduction. "Men, I'll turn the particulars over to my deputy, Johnny McLane."

The young man stepped forward, coughed violently into his sleeve, and due to the night air, proceeded in a raspy voice. Jess and Skep stood to one side of Sam.

As Johnny explained the strategy, using the map posted on the blackboard, a churlish, bearded man leaned over to his neighbor and complained gruffly, "Heard he was young; why he's nothin' but a snot-nosed kid, and a Reb to boot!"

More than one man noticed Sam Brett lay a firm hand on Jess' shoulder, staying him. Jess shot the burly man a hard look but remained silent. Marshal Riddick cast a harsh glare at his dissenting comrade, but found no reason to intervene. Unaffected, Johnny continued explaining the posses' responsibilities, the timing, and the result he hoped to obtain.

"We bring them in, alive if possible, to be tried under law by a judge and a jury of their peers. Is that clear? Any questions?"

There were a few as to the timing of the siege. The question of most concern was how each posse could be sure the others were in proper position.

"It's impossible to know exactly. We can only estimate the time it'll take for the Iron Mountain and Laramie men to reach and cover the northern entrance, theirs being the longest ride. Each man must move quickly and efficiently. The Horse Creek posse should reach the canyon's creek passage on the eastern side at about the same time, if the times we allotted for travel are kept. No one can predict the unknown influences of weather, which looks good for now, or of injury, but we have to take that chance. Marshal Brett and Tilghman's men will fill in where needed. Mr. Bryant, Mr. Duane and I know our way over the rocks to the south. We'll hold off any rustlers who try to escape from our vantage point on the rim, overlooking the lower range of the canyon." As he spoke, he indicated their positions on the map. Prisoners would be taken to the nearest towns.

"We'll sort it out from that point. Remember, we want prisoners, not corpses, when possible." Johnny paused to drink the water Skep had provided and Sam took over.

"We'll move out at first light. Horses should be fed and ready by 5:00 a.m. Any further questions can be directed to your marshals. There will be no drinking or carousing in the town tonight. The bar is closed as of 8:00 p.m. Godspeed."

Johnny raised a hand. "Where is Reverend Stoner?" The men stopped milling and turned toward him.

"Don't see him," a voice from the rear replied.

"Alright, I'll offer up a petition to God," Johnny volunteered. Some of the men followed his lead, some just stared. At the conclusion, a hearty "amen" was sounded and the men slowly began to disperse.

The heavy-set deputy, whose coment on Johnny's abilities had riled Jess, was about to exit. Marshal Brett moved quickly to his side, took a handful of the front of his jacket and pinned him to the wall. "That rebel kid is the reason we even know where those thieves are. He spent the night freezing in those hills to scout for us, and you'd be damned lucky to ride beside him, which you won't. We've gotta act as one unit. He is the commander, got it?" With that, he released the man's jacket.

"Yeah, I got it," the surly man murmured, walking off.

In the lamplight of the office that night, Johnny, Jess, and Skep sat for a long time by the woodstove, discussing their strategy and how best to signal one another from their positions in the rocks. They would move along the canyon range in a grid, in search and rescue fashion, stretching out over the roughly half mile length of the southern rim of the canyon. With rifles slung across their backs and six guns loaded with extra cartridge belts, they would scale the rocks, reaching the highest point to hold a line against any rustlers attempting to escape from the canyon below. Johnny knew the rocks would look like an escape route, but the 200-foot rim above the canyon floor would give the deputies an excellent vantage point.

"You still got that old Whitworth rifle, Johnny?" Jess asked, nursing his steaming coffee.

Jess and Skep slouched in chairs and Johnny sat with his stockinged feet propped up on the railing.

"Yeah I do and I'm keepin' it--won it from a Confederate sharpshooter in a poker game."

Skep stretched and yawned. "I hear it shoots about 2000 yards, a pretty fair distance I'd say. However, being its muzzle loaded you only get two to three rounds per minute, which slows a body down."

"Maybe someday I'll have it converted, but it only has an effective range of about, oh, maybe 1000 feet, so maybe it ain't worth the effort. It's lightweight but sometimes hard to sight and has a definite recoil."

They continued on, fond of discussing arms and ammunition, easily dropping their command of language for the casual slang they preferred when alone. When Jess declared that he favored the old Enfield rifle, Johnny challenged him.

"Give me my .44 caliber Henry repeater any day of the week," Johnny replied smartly. "We used 'em some in the war. I think they were stolen from the union troops. We were never sure where anythin' came from. Fifteen cartridges and it fires as fast as it takes to work the lever and squeeze the trigger. I wouldn't take a pretty penny for it."

Jess scoffed, "Well I think you boys could 'a had all the rifles you wanted, but you sure ran out of ammunition, didn't ya, son?"

"Yeah, they had us cadets scoutin' through those mountains looking for bat guano to get the nitre to make saltpeter. We got so desperate we got nitre from anywhere we could find it."

"Yeah," Skep added, with a gleam in his eye, "and I heard ole John Harrelson, head of the Nitre and Mining Bureau in Alabama, or was it South Carolina, came up with a pretty good plan for obtaining nitre! Got those fair southern belles involved, right enough! I can just see those wagons going through the city early of a mornin'...excuse me ma'am, you got a little somethin' for me? Oh, come on now, sweetheart...surrender that chamber pot!"

Johnny laughed, "Nasty business, collectin' all that urine. Guess I won't be forgettin' that poem about it either. Saxby and I got an extra week on night guard for settin' that poem to song."

"Let's hear it then," Jess insisted, adding another stick of wood to the stove.

"Quit!" Skep complained, "You're gonna run us out of here if you keep crankin' up the temperature!"

"I think I got it, if you can stop bickerin' long enough to let me sing it," Johnny chided, dredging up the long dormant tune and beginning his lively rendition of the quirky poem.

"John Harrelson, John Harrelson
Could you not in the event a meter Or some less immodest mode Of making our salt Peter?
The thing it is so queer you know Gunpowder, like the crankey That when a lady lifts her shift She kills a bloody Yankee!"

"Lord have mercy," Skep muttered with an almost envious inflection, "Those times must have been something else."

"Yeah, they were somethin' alright, but not what you think."

They sat sipping coffee until Johnny spoke again. "Skep, why'd you decide to come with us?"

"What are you gettin' at?" Skep asked, pushing his shaggy brown forelock to one side and fixing his brown eyes on Johnny.

"Well, I guess I was wonderin' what Beck had to say about all of this and with you two so close to marryin', I reckon she's concerned."

As he spoke, Johnny wondered what Cassie might think and wondered if, due to the excitement in town, she knew that something was about to transpire.

"We talked about it. She doesn't like that I am goin', but I think I made her understand."

In a twist of fate, Skep and Beck had grown up in the same household. Because of the deaths of both sets of parents and because they were distant cousins, Beck lived with Skep, Sodie, their older brother, Jase, and a younger brother, Skeet. They were raised by their Uncle Willie and Aunt Nancy on a small ranch in Colorado where Will Duane bred and trained horses for the US Cavalry. After moving to Wyoming, claiming land in the Homestead Act, and purchasing more land, the years passed well enough for them until the fifteenth birthdays of Beck and Skep, five years ago.

Skep's Uncle Willie found the two cousins alone in the barn kissing, and after many a plea for clemency and much deliberation, Beck had been sent to Laramie to help tend the children of a widow woman. They were to be married soon, after having waited for Skep to finish his apprenticeship to a well-known horse breeder just outside of Cheyenne.

Johnny raised his eyebrows. "You asked me to stand up with you at your weddin'. I want to be sure I am not gonna be standin' there all alone after this altercation." The clock on the wall ticked away in the silence.

After a long moment, Jess broke through their contemplations. "No problem there, John Scott. If Skep don't survive, you can marry the forlorn girl yourself. That way there'll still be a weddin' and everyone goes home happy."

Skep chucked the wood stick he had been whittling, catching Jess on the shoulder. "Not funny, son."

"Whatever happens, happens, boys," Jess said easily. "You worry like a bunch of girls. The ladies can survive without us if they have to. I had a similar conversation with Sodie."

Johnny laughed. "What good would it do for her to say anything? You always do what you wanna do anyway."

"Oh, fine, and this statement from a feller who loves his horse more than he has ever loved a woman or anything else for that matter," Jess chided.

"Well, at least I know how to be faithful," Johnny defended, chucking a stick of stove wood. Jess caught it and tossed it to the floor.

Jess rose and stepped over Skep, making his way to the desk. He pulled the drawer open and removed the bottle of whiskey, uncorking it, and taking a long pull. Johnny eyed him warningly. Jess ignored him, poured a slug into the remainder of his coffee, and then replaced the bottle, returning to his chair.

Skep broke the momentary silence. "Just remember, Jess, Sodie is my sister. I won't take it kindly if she gets hurt. I don't know what she sees in you, anyway. I tried to warn her, but she won't listen," Skep replied, not altogether lightly.

"All right boys, I think our conversation flows better when we stick to death and guns," Johnny interrupted grimly, coughing raggedly into his sleeve.

An hour later, Johnny arose from the cot and went to the large oak desk. He opened the bottom drawer and took a slug of the Old Crow. It would either cure him or make him sick. 'Can't feel much worse,' he thought. Stepping over the sleeping forms of his buddies, he returned to the backroom.

That night, Sam Brett slept in the hotel room reserved for the lawman. Sam and Johnny took turns sleeping in the small second-story room at the end of the hall to the rear of the hotel. Imagining their presence to be a deterrent to crime, Hyrum Brown supplied the room gratis, and it came in handy when one or the other needed a good night's rest away from the jailhouse.

Tonight, two marshals occupied the space: Sam and Charlie Tilghman. Neither slept much and they talked long into the night, reviewing possible scenarios for the upcoming siege in the canyon. They exchanged the latest information on Big Nose George Parrot and Jesse James. Sam raised the question as to whether or not the outlaw, Judd Barrow, who was wreaking havoc on the plains around Cheyenne and Laramie, could be connected to the rustling situation.

Charlie mentioned he had been impressed by Sam's young deputy. He thought him to be an excellent communicator and Sam briefly explained Johnny's military history. Charlie noticed, but did not comment on the fact that Sam seemed to take pride in his deputy.

7

THE RECKONING

BY 4:30 A.M. both Sam and Johnny were at the livery with a dozen other men, feeding and tacking up the horses. Johnny examined Traveller's legs and picked his hooves, checking for small stones or anything that would impede the ride forward.

The posses left town at their appointed times, the first, just as purple streaked across the darkened sky. The roads to Sideling were now opened. Johnny, Jess, and Skep were the last to leave, riding four miles southwest toward the Wilkerson ranch, intending to take the trail which ran along the northern property line toward the mountains. Johnny could see the top of the Wilkerson's barn just over the rise.

As the purple sky gave way to early morning, he wondered if Cassie was awake, or maybe already in the barn. An image of auburn hair, spread across a pillow, played with his mind. He had fallen slightly behind and gave more leg to Traveller as the horse quickly caught up with the two other riders. Jess shot him a knowing glance and Johnny scowled in return.

They rode on through the cold, dry air, the sun's pale, yellow light adding little warmth to the day. They reached the canyon by early morning and took some time finding the aperture where Johnny had left Traveller on his last reconnaissance. They strung a cavvy for their horses and the two extra mounts they had commandeered from the grouchy proprietor at the livery.

Beginning their climb through the rocks, they took little more than ammunition, their rifles, and sourdough biscuits. As they fanned out, using the plaintive call of a hawk, they signaled each other on a regular basis, checking their proximity until they reached the high ridge of boulders. It overlooked the lower and final ridgeline that loomed above the canyon floor. From the higher ridge, they could not see into the depths of the canyon, but had an excellent view of the lower ridge. They stopped, waiting silently.

Johnny checked his pocket watch. It was 10:00 a.m. They would have to depend on sound traveling up from the canyon, and Johnny prayed that the posses' arrivals would coordinate with the planned times. He knew they may have an hour or more to wait and watched as the sun climbed higher in the sky.

Buzzards circled high in the sky to the northeast, soaring and dipping with the currents, free from the confines of the earth. Johnny leaned back against the smooth rock, his rifle now resting on his knees. He closed his eyes, listening intently, thankful that the wind had calmed. In the distance, the cry of a hawk alerted him. Then in answer, a closer cry. He turned his face to the sky, cupped his hands and like a trumpeter, returned the call.

Shielded by round, smooth boulders, the men stood like sentinels, watching the rocks and the rim of the canyon below.

"Cassie, Cassie!" With the front of her skirts bunched in one hand and the rest trailing wildly behind her, Millie Beale ran over the boardwalk and crossed the street to the cabin, flinging wide the door and almost knocking Olivia Halsted to the floor.

"What on earth!" Olivia exclaimed angrily. "Slow down, you look an absolute fright!"

"I'm sorry, excuse me, Miss Halstead," Millie said, gathering herself together enough to make the slightest of curtsies before the dismayed woman.

She rushed on, "Have you seen Cassie this morning? She is not at school, and I thought she may be here."

"Well she isn't, and you need to start acting like a proper young lady, not tearing around town like a child! What would your mother have to say?"

Through the window, Millie caught sight of Cassie, riding down the street, coming for the cabin.

"I'm sure she would be disappointed, ma'am. I'll certainly try to behave more appropriately. Excuse me," she babbled, her face a picture of sincerity. She backed through the doorway, shutting the door on Miss Halstead's disapproving glare. Wheeling around, she hoisted her skirts and ran toward Cassie.

"Cassie!" she panted excitedly, as she grabbed at Lady's rein and the horse danced sideways. "Have you heard? Did you know what happened last night... and what's happening even at this very moment?"

Puzzled by the frenzy, Cassie stared into Millie's large bright eyes. "I don't know what you are talking about," Cassie exclaimed. She dismounted and led Lady the few remaining yards toward the hitching post. Millie slipped her arm confidentially through Cassie's free arm.

"They're all gone to a canyon somewhere up north. The outlaws are there--the ones who have been rustling!" she exclaimed breathlessly.

Cassie took in Millie's flushed face. "I know there was a meeting at the schoolhouse last night. Pa seem to worry all day, and he and Ma talked a long time after supper. I thought it odd that they stopped when we girls came 'round."

Millie's cheeks brightened with excitement. "Well, none of the boys from school got to go, you can bet, but the marshal got together posses from three different towns and took off at first light! I watched them leave!"

"You mean our marshal...and the deputy, also?"

"I'm certain of it!"

Numb and smothering under the news, Cassie disengaged her arm from Millie's and she mounted her mare, responding in a flat, wooden tone. "I need to go, Millie. You'll be late for school; you go on now."

"Cassie, what's wrong? Where are you going?"

Cassie caught Millie's anxious gaze. "I'll see you later."

Cassie wheeled Lady around, riding out of town the way she had come. Just shy of the schoolyard, she realized there was no reason to go home. What excuse would she give her mother...what would be her mother's response?

She thought of Aunt Mabel and her heart leapt but caught instantly. She realized there was no solace to be had there either, for the little cabin stood vacant. She pulled Lady up, circling in the road. "I'll go to her in town..."

Turning back, she took the uphill trail that branched off from the southern most entrance to Sideling. She continued across the rise behind the cemetery, until the trail desended and narrowed. Having skirted the town as intended, she was well out of sight of the business establishments and inquisitive eyes.

Bertha Winkler's sat house nestled within a picket-fenced yard. Arriving at the gate, Cassie sat still in the saddle for a moment, attempting to settle her emotions. She knew she must think logically, and not upset Mabel with idiotic confusions. What would she say? "I must think of her," she whispered.

She wiped the frozen tears with the sleeve of her coat, dismounted, and tied Lady to the post by the front gate. Steam rose from the muscular arch of Lady's neck and placing her cheek against its warmth, Cassie murmured softly, "What shall I do?"

Inhaling the comforting scent of the horse, she called out to God for courage. Bunching her skirts, she turned and mounted the steps, gaining the width of the porch and rapping upon the rough, wooden door.

A moment later, Mrs. Winkler answered and with a welcoming smile, held the door open. "Why Cassie, come in! What brings you back so soon?"

Cassie stepped into the parlor. "Is Mrs. Baker resting, or may I see her?"

"She just finished a little breakfast and is sipping tea, I'll show you to her room. I know she'll be delighted that you've returned so soon." Although her tone was merry, concern touched Berta Winkler's brow, causing Cassie to be painfully conscious of her disheveled appearance.

"Would you care for some hot tea?" Berta added thoughtfully.

When Cassie declined, Berta did not insist and led her down the short, narrow hallway. Through a partially-opened door, Cassie saw Mabel sitting in a rocker, a frilly blue wrap over her shoulders.

"I heard your voice, Cassie, come in, sit down!" Mabel said affectionately. Cassie sat on the side of the bed next to the rocker as Mabel took her cold hands in her warm, weathered ones.

"Goodness, mercy, you are freezing! You must have been out a long while. What brings you here so early?"

Cassie removed her bonnet, and tendrils of her hair fringed her face. Her eyes glistened and she tried to speak, then shook her head hopelessly, dropping her gaze. Mabel sat quietly, allowing Cassie time to collect her emotions. Finally, the young woman spoke.

"I don't know...I'm afraid. I had to talk to you; you're the only one who can help me. I think..." She paused as tears escaped, slipping down her cheeks.

"What makes you afraid, child?" Mabel asked simply.

"It is, well...my ma, this town, the rustlers. Aunt Mabel, the lawmen are up in a canyon to the north, intent on apprehending the rustlers. I am so afraid, I don't want...suppose they're injured? Suppose someone is killed?"

"I suppose that could happen. There's always risk when there is conflict."

Mabel took up Cassie's hand and held it tenderly to her wrinkled cheek. "I know you have a tender heart; you care deeply about those you love. I think you may need to identify your real concern. It is for something...or someone specifically?" Cassie looked at the kindly face and answered truthfully.

"You know, don't you? You knew before I did, didn't you?" Cassie asked, remembering the distant day and her encounter with Johnny in Mabel's kitchen. Fear began to subside as she searched Mabel's face.

Mabel smiled slightly and nodded. "Tell me Cassie, have you spoken with your ma?"

"I can't, she won't give me a chance!" Cassie said incredulously.

"Tell me what has happened."

Cassie related the events of the day before. "I know Ma saw us by the wagon. She didn't even look at Johnny. We drove off and left him standing there. Ma was short with him--told him to lock up the house and be sure the barn was closed, or something to that effect! She hurried me away in the rig saying, 'Cassie you don't know what you're doing.'"

"How did you respond?" Mabel asked.

"I said nothing. There was nothing to say! Johnny never had a chance to say much, really. He had begun to ask me something. I am not even sure what he was going to ask. He was intense, as though he needed to say something important. Then Ma came out and started flinging orders about. Then she whisked me away in the rig! On the way home she talked about Pa, and how she met him, and how he planned for their future, saved money, bought the land and built a house! I knew all of that already, but she seemed to need to tell me again to make some kind of a point. After she told me that I didn't realize what I was doing, she didn't say anymore and neither did I. What could I say?"

"Cassie, all this has come about so suddenly, and neither of you have had the time to properly sort out the events of the last day. It has only been a day, you know."

"But I am afraid." Fresh tears slipped down Cassie's cheeks, and she whispered. "Afraid for Johnny."

Mabel studied the girl. "Cassie," she asked firmly. "Who owns the cattle on a thousand hills?"

Surprised, Cassie repeated the question slowly. "The cattle on a thousand hills...Oh, I see what you mean."

Mabel continued, "If Johnny should be harmed or even die, he belongs to God first, not to us." Her words met Cassie's fears.

"Oh, but Aunt Mabel, how do you know that?" she implored.

"I know Johnny. I have talked with him many times out at the farm. I know God has His hand on that boy. Why do you think I would have thought him a suitable match for you if I didn't believe it to be true?" Confident, the old mischievous twinkle returned to her eyes.

Cassie offered a slight smile, gently squeezing Mabel's hand. "I am so confused, I don't know how he feels. I think he cares, but I don't know for sure. The only thing I do know is...I care for him. I can't tell anyone, not even Millie. Oh, I'm a child. He is a grown man. What could he possibly want with me?"

Mabel nodded knowingly, tilting her head in question. "How old do you think 'that man' is?"

"Why, I don't know. Maybe 22 or 23. I know he must be, as he is the marshal's deputy, and has been so for a year now." Cassie fell introspectively silent.

"He has only recently turned 21," Mabel continued. "But he has had a life very different from yours, it's true. Come clear across this country after that horrible war, lived with different families after he lost his own. That, my dear, can grow a boy into a man quickly."

Cassie removed a lace handkerchief from her sleeve and dabbed at her nose.

"Why don't you give your fears to the Lord? I know it's hard when you are so very young; it's hard to trust through difficult times. But you wait, pray, and watch, Cassie dear. You watch for the man, the one God has for you, whomever he may be. Can he build a home? Not with wood and tin, but with the strength of Christ as the cornerstone? Is he a watchman, guarding the hearts and minds of the people entrusted to him? And is he a warrior? Will he fight to protect those he loves from evil and injustice? All these things God will reveal to you in due time. But for now, my dear, you are to delight yourself in the Lord while you wait. Then, he will give you the desires of your heart. He has promised that."

Cassie studied her Aunt Mabel, and through the frailty, saw the strength of her dear, sweet soul. How wonderfully wise she was, but how difficult this was to process.

"Let us pray together, Cassie."

As Mabel's words rose to the God of heaven, the stricture around Cassie's young heart began to loosen, and she felt the stirrings of new hope in a place deep within her. A place of peace, if only for this moment. She did not understand it, but thought that if she remained very still, she would be able to return to the place for peace and answers to the questions and concerns that haunted her. Cassie rose to hug Mabel, and as the old woman smiled and returned the hug, she put her hands on Cassie's shoulders, searching her eyes intentionally.

"I know you must go now. Please let me know how things are for you. I love you, child. I know the Lord brought me here to this home to rest for a reason. Maybe to rest from the temporal cares of this world and to focus on prayer for you and the town in such chaotic times as these."

(James 1:2-8)

8

THE CANYON

THE FIRST SHOTS echoed through the canyon and the men on the ridge were unable to distinguish the ricochet of bullets from the actual barrage of gunfire. Rifle ready, Johnny strained to see any movement among the boulders stretching out one hundred yards below him. If the rustlers fled from the canyon below the last ridge, it would be soon. The deputies remained alert, the element of surprise being crucial so as not to drive the outlaws back into the crevices of the boulder field below.

Rising up from the canyon, the blasts from rifles and six guns were continuous. A sharp, golden glint caught Johnny's eyes, and he ducked behind the boulder. With his shoulder against the rock and edging around its breadth, he took aim, steadying his rifle against the side of the rock.

A lone gunman made his way forward, coming around and through the boulders below, disappearing momentarily and reemerging, unaware that he was being observed.

Only fifty yards distant now, Johnny drew a bead on the man and followed his progress through the sights of his weapon. At twenty yards out, Johnny prayed no shot would ring out along the ridge, having no idea if Jess or Skep saw this man or any other, and not wanting his prey to shelter. The hunted man was now no more than fifteen yards before him, perfectly exposed and dead in the center of Johnny's rifle sights. The deputy shouted a warning.

"This is the law! Throw down your weapon, put those hands over your head, or I'll shoot!"

Stunned, the man stopped. Boxed in by huge boulders to his left and a crevice dropping 15 feet on his right, he faced the barrel of a rifle with no obvious path of escape. He surrendered and dropped his weapon. It clattered loudly and fell beyond his reach, bumping and sliding down the rock face.

Johnny drew his pistol and slung his rifle over his shoulder, instructing his captive to come forward. Using the advantage of his elevation, Johnny kept him in his sights and moved toward the man, removing his cuffs from his belt.

As commanded, the sweating, exhausted thief moved forward until he stood just below Johnny. A shot rang out to Johnny's left, followed immediately by returning gunfire. Keeping his eyes on the man directly below him, Johnny positioned himself so he could see horizontally across the boulder field to the west. He waited, listening to the ragged breathing of the cowhand.

"I need water," he moaned, not bothering to look up.

"Too bad, there is none," Johnny answered gruffly.

To their detriment, the deputies had left their water with the horses below, fearful of the clanking of metal against the metal of guns, rifles, and ammunition. It had been a split-second decision, and Johnny knew it was a foolish one, for without water, the arid atmosphere could suck away life quickly if circumstances kept a man in the high elevation long enough.

Time hung suspended and neither man spoke. Then Jess and Skep appeared in the distance, manipulating another disabled rustler through the boulder field.

Johnny yelled, "Over here, Jess," and was greeted by his friend's raised arm as he called back, "Got us a live one, Johnny!"

As the men approached, Johnny saw the blood-stained chaps of the apprehended man whose left arm oozed under the makeshift bandage from his torn shirt. His hands were cuffed before him. Pale and worn, he struggled to keep his footing.

Few words were exchanged as the five men cautiously made their way back down the steep decline to the horses waiting below.

Reaching the aperture, Johnny grimaced. "You're bleedin', Skep." In the struggle down the slippery rock, he had failed to notice the wan look on his friend's face.

"Yeah, they winged me, ripped up my jacket, too," Skep replied, failing to maintain the bravado he hoped to feign.

"It's just a flesh wound. I'm alright. You may need to worry about that one, Johnny." Skep indicated the rapidly paling face of the injured outlaw just yards from where they stood.

Bunched tightly in his hand, Jess held the man by the scruff of his jacket collar. He gave the thin man a rough shake, then allowed him to crumple onto the ground.

"Water," moaned the man. Jess retrieved the canteens slung over horns of the saddles, and Johnny built a small fire to thaw the frozen contents.

The injured man coughed and sputtered, as the offered water caught in his throat. He fell back, closing his eyes as he gasped and struggled to regain his breath.

"Where are you takin' us," bellowed the suddenly verbose captive, who sat near the spot where his accomplice had fallen.

"To jail, that is if I don't plug your thievin' hide first!" Jess growled, his rifle barrel pressed hard against the man's chest.

"You can't prove nothin'," the defiant man challenged, raising his burly, bearded form.

"You boys been travelin' down the wrong road," Jess growled, "We're here to mend your fractious ways. Take care, or you'll end up on the other side of this dirt." He shoved the man hard with the toe of his boot.

Skep, who was silently observing, staggered to a nearby rock, sitting heavily upon the flat surface. With elbows on his knees, he lowered his head into his hands.

"You alright?" Johnny asked, approaching him to offer the last of the canteen. Skep drained it, wiping his mouth on his intact sleeve.

"Yeah, just a little lightheaded, I guess."

Johnny held out a hand, beckoning for Skep's coat. Unbuttoning it with his good hand, Skep protested flatly, without much conviction. Helping him slip the coat off his shoulder, Johnny could see the torn, powder and blood-stained fabric of the shirt and ripped the cloth further to examine the wound. Skep flinched.

"Hope you didn't plan on this one for your weddin' shirt," Johnny muttered as he retrieved a small flask of whiskey and a few strips of clean cloth from his saddlebag.

"This is a little more than a graze," he reprimanded, pouring the whiskey over the oozing wound then dabbing it with a cloth. The muscles in Skep's jaw tightened, but he made no comment. Johnny dressed the wound then proceeded to help the thin rustler who had wriggled closer to the warmth of the fire. Whining, the man held his forearm, shielding a gaping wound. Johnny bathed the wound with whiskey, and wrapped it tightly. "Bullet passed right through. You're lucky."

Jess had been leaning against the boulder parapet, with his right boot heel hooked into a small crevice, and had rested his rifle diagonally across one knee. Leaning menacingly toward the injured man, he stepped forward.

"Don't know about that, John. Saving him for a hangin' don't seem like luck to me."

"Lay off, Jess." The weariness of the last days drew impatience into Johnny's tone. "Our job isn't to judge him, just to deliver him to the judge and jury; let them take care of the rest. Sometimes you gotta show some mercy."

Jess spat on the ground, "Yeah, just like he would have shown if he had gotten the drop on us. What is bad is bad...and it produces only bad.

Thorns don't come from grapevines, you know." Ignoring his sarcasm, Johnny didn't respond.

(Luke 6:43-45)

After burning the blood-soaked cloth in the fire, Johnny walked toward Traveller, who nickered and dug the ground with his hoof. Removing his glove, he stroked the horse's muscular neck and replaced the flask in his saddlebag. With his chest against the saddle fender, Johnny placed his forearms horizontally across the seat, and rested his forehead on them.

The slow, steady rhythm of Traveller's respirations helped to quiet him. He figured mercy had been shown to all of them this day. They were still alive, but what about Sam?'

The thought carried him home to the safety of his childhood, and for a moment, he sat upon his father's knee.

"Seek justice, love mercy, Johnny. Walk humbly with the Lord. Our God commands it."

He closed his eyes and wondered if God's realm still included him, for those words were veiled by his doubts, and the passage of time.

The pit of his stomach tightened. 'I can't clearly see him now. I can hardly recall my papa's face. There is so much I would like to ask him. He would have the answers. How is it possible to guard the path of justice in the face of evil or show mercy to the merciless? Why do I lack Papa's wisdom?'

The old familiar doubts crept in, leaving him hollow. Willfully, he slammed the door shut on those thoughts.

(Micah 6:8, 1 Peter 3:3-9)

Jess was calling to him. "Let's get out of here before it gets dark, we don't know where the others are and Skep needs the Doc."

Jess had extinguished the fire and with their joint effort, the captives were placed on the waiting mounts, hands cuffed before them and tied to the saddle horns.

The party trailed off to the southeast as deepening purple consumed the torch-lit sky; each man quietly alone with his private thoughts, each ministered to by unseen angels, or tormented by private demons. With the cold wind at their backs, some thought of their comrades' struggles to the north or of loved ones waiting anxiously on the wide expanse of the darkening plains.

———————◆———————

'Cold'. Johnny's first conscious thought was of ice water. 'Gotta get out!' He swam to the surface through the fog in his brain, and jerking awake, remembered where he was. The embers of a fire glowed dimly, and he could make out a dark form leaning against the rock, rifle across his bent knee.

Jess noticed Johnny's movement. "I'm freezing here, John Scott, think you could throw a little wood on the fire?"

"Yeah," Johnny said standing unsteadily, stomping his feet to bring feeling back to them. His head was heavy; his eyes ached. He coughed and spit into the darkness.

"How's Skep," he asked, stretching and slapping his arms to warm himself.

"He moves now and then so I know he ain't dead."

The night had become as black as pitch. With no moon or stars to guide them and further encumbered by exhaustion, they had been forced to camp along the trail. Johnny built up the fire then awakened Skep, who warmed his hands and feet, as the orange flames leapt and danced-a tiny warmth in the darkness.

Skep was coherent; there were no further signs of bleeding from his wound. Johnny thanked God that he did not have to return to Sideling to tell Beck that the man she had loved since childhood was dead. His thoughts drifted to the first time he met her, shortly after he met Jess, when he had first become Sideling's deputy.

He was struck first by the dark-haired girl's green eyes and then by the way she looked at Skep. It seemed as though she needed nothing else in this world. They were natural together and so comfortable with each other that Johnny succumbed to the cold loneliness so familiar to him.

He stared into the fire, warming his hands as Cassie's face formed and danced in the flames, her fiery curls swirling with the flickering light. He longed for her. Did she think about him or even know that this day could hold tragedy or resolution? In the silence, Johnny found himself fighting off the misery of the cold and the fear he felt for Marshal Brett and the posse. As the unknown loomed, first light split the sky.

9

THE BOOTJACK

THERE WAS NO apparent sign of the other lawmen as they approached the marshal's office two hours later, and although Johnny had not expected to find the others there, he clung to a thread of hope that they might have arrived first. Hope faded with the rising of the sun for the odds of all returning alive were doubtful. When he dismounted at the hitching post before the office, it was still early morning. He unhooked the keys from his gunbelt and unlocked the door.

Jess held the captives at rifle point, and Johnny rejoined them in the street.

"You hold 'em Johnny. I'll get this one over to Doc."

Jess pulled the wounded man from the saddle, still cuffed. Hardly able to stand, the thin man staggered so Skep dismounted, helping to support the captive with his good arm. Both captives remained at rifle point.

"Have Doc take a look at you, Skep," Johnny ordered, observing his friend's pasty coloring.

The burly, heavy set, bearded man had refused to identify himself and had cursed and taunted the lawmen for most of the morning's ride into town. He didn't speak now, but stood glaring at Johnny, arrogance and disgust sharpening his rugged features.

Drawn by the sight of the deputized men and their surly captives, the townsfolk trickled into the streets. Circling, they began to congratulate the lawmen on their seeming success, at the same time questioning them pointedly and demanding to know the fate of the absentee posse.

As he wrestled the belligerent captive through the office doorway, Johnny answered them with terse phrases, then closed the door solidly on the growing throng.

Excited voices filtered in from outside the office, and a few women entered, clamoring to find out the fate of their men. Frustrated and still clutching his captive, Johnny turned as the heavy door opened for the third time, only to find Beck, wide-eyed and breathless.

"Oh Johnny! You're alright, thank God! Where is Skep?"

Refocusing his attention on the hostile captive, Johnny pinned the man against the outside of the cell, with pointed gun and angry eyes.

He answered her over his shoulder. "He's injured but alright--over at Doc's."

Without comment, she fled from the office, slamming the door behind her.

Jess entered moments later. "Doc will let us know when he's done, and we can fetch the injured felon. Skep is comfortable, but Beck near about ran me over tryin' to get at him!"

Still in hand, Johnny's captive slouched against the bars of the cell, and Johnny yanked him up fiercely.

"Get those wanted posters off the desk, Jess, let's see if this man's picture is decoratin' any of 'em."

A corner of the sullen captive's mustached lip drew up as he mocked Johnny with his eyes.

"You won't find me on none of 'em," he boasted.

Johnny pressed his gun to the man's chest. "It's time you tell us who you are." His words were exact but dulled by fatigue.

"You tell me, boy...where ya from? The Carolinas? Virginia 'mebbe?" He smirked and his eyes narrowed. "Just know this, ya little coot, I ain't givin' no reb the time of day."

In a split second, Johnny slammed his left arm across the man's chest, forcing him upward and pinning him against the iron bars. He shoved the barrel of his gun hard up under the outlaw's jawbone, placing the butt of the .44 flat against the pulsing artery at the man's neck.

With jaw clinched, Johnny growled, "I'll tell you what time it is you murdering thief. It's the eleventh hour and fifty-ninth minute of your miserable life, and you better start talkin' before I blow your damned head off your shoulders!"

Johnny's other arm pressed hard against the surprised man's chest, sliding up to his Adam's apple. As the man gasped for breath, Jess heard Johnny cock the hammer. In two strides, Jess was on Johnny, pulling his arm from the gasping man's throat.

"Johnny! Take it easy, man, you're gonna kill him!"

Johnny's face was just inches from the strangling man and he inhaled the stench of old tobacco, stale whiskey, and sweat.

"He ain't worth it, Johnny! Let 'em go. Put the gun down!" Jess barked. "I got him."

Johnny swore and pushed off, holstered his gun, and spun the choking man around, forcing his face onto the iron bars. Jess opened the cell door and

Johnny wrestled him inside, shoving him onto the hard cot as the gagging man caught his breath in ragged gulps.

Jess pulled Johnny from the cell, slamming the door then locking it.

"Ya need some fresh air, John. Take a minute. Get out of here."

He grabbed Johnny's jacket and turned him toward the backroom, directing him toward the rear door with a shove.

Glaring, Johnny removed his hat and wiped the sweat from his forehead. But he turned without comment, retreating quickly through the back door and out into the glare of the bright sunlight. His eyes stung, wet with frustration, and although he pulled the brim of his hat low, shielding his eyes, he saw clearly how easily he had been pushed beyond his limits. Foolish anger, taunting words, were all it had taken, and he had responded in kind. He chastised himself severely.

'I let that fool get to me! If I can't control myself, I leave this town vulnerable, like a city without walls. When I crumble, men will know it, and I'll stand for nothing.' Vexed, he took a deep breath of cold air, and his chest tightened. He coughed fitfully.

(Proverbs 25:28)

Crossing High Street toward the hotel, he broke the ice on the closest watering trough with the butt of his gun handle and splashed the frigid water on his face. Wiping it away with his coat sleeve, he continued to condemn himself.

"I need to get a grip. I have to get back in there," he murmured, shaking his head. As he turned for the office, he caught the action across the way.

Standing on the porch by the front door and against the wall of the Flour and Grain, he spotted Cassie. Leaning in with his arm braced against the wall next to her upturned face, a man stood hovering over her.

Johnny recognized the burly form of Beau Brenner. He could not make out their expressions, but their conversation seemed intense. Johnny tensed. Why would Beau be confronting Cassie? His stance seemed menacing as he cornered her there.

The door of the establishment swung open and a tall man appeared who paused a moment, taking in the scene with apparent interest. Johnny watched as the man stepped toward Cassie and encircled her waist with his arm. Drawing her to him, he guided the girl around Beau, and walked away, his arm still firmly at her waist. She was looking up at him, and Johnny saw that her coppery hair hung in a loose braid down her back.

His mind numbed and his heart turned to stone as he moved woodenly, reentering the office through the rear door. Clamor and gruff voices sounded through the backroom, and he quickened his steps toward the cells.

Marshal Brett was hauling a thin, lanky, dark man through the doorway, followed by Marshal Tilghman who was limping and covered with sweat and dirt.

Sam Brett's weary eyes met Johnny's and relief flooded his face. He jailed the man as Johnny crossed the room, then turned to place a dirty hand on Johnny's shoulder "You boys alright?"

"Yes sir, we are. How did you fare?" Johnny asked, greatly relieved.

Sam only grunted, then nodded toward the cell, indicating the ruffian who raised his shaggy head at the commotion. "That yours?"

Johnny's captive rose to a sitting position on the side of the cot.

"Yes sir," Jess answered, "And there's another, shot up pretty good, at Doc's. Skep is with him and was wounded, but he'll be fine."

"Do you know who they are, where they're from?" Sam Brett continued to eye Johnny's captive who seemed to have lost most of his swagger and stared stupidly at the lawmen.

"No, can't get it out of him, but Skep is workin' on the other one over at Doc's."

As Johnny spoke, Sodie Duane burst through the doorway, froze in her tracks, caught sight of Jess and burst into tears.

"Lord a'might, woman, I am alright." Jess reached her side and scooped her into his arms. As Sodie buried her head into Jess' coat, he gently stroked her hair, kissing her face.

The gesture, tender but intense, caused Johnny to look away. He had never witnessed this type of emotion in his friend, for Jess seemed to be able to breeze through most situations, taking them manfully in stride. 'He loves her, he really does,' he thought. The intimate scene prompted Johnny to busy himself with the wanted posters.

Speaking softly, Jess walked Sodie to the door and in a few moments, Johnny overheard him say, "See you in a bit." Sodie stepped away from Jess and departed the office.

Replacing his rifle in the case after checking for ammunition and propping the other rifles against the far wall, Sam Brett had watched the scene play out.

"Where's Marshal Riddick?" Johnny asked Sam, removing his hat and sitting on the chair by the desk.

"We left 'em a ways back; they split off and took the road toward Laramie City with three outlaws trussed up in tow, and two more dead, slung over their saddles. Besides the scrawny one, we brought back another and left him with the undertaker.

"So we got eight of them all told, I reckon," Johnny calculated.

"Yeah, they're all we found."

Marshal Tilghman sat on a chair by the desk, wearily rubbing his sore feet and emptying stones from his boots, seemingly oblivious to the preceding conversations until he finally rallied and spoke. "And by the count you gave us, that should be the whole lot of 'em. Good work, son. It's cold in here."

"Sorry sir, didn't think of it. I'll fire up the stove." Johnny moved to get the wood.

Sam's heavily-bearded captive paced the secluded cell to the rear while Johnny's unnamed, belligerent detainee leered at them from the forward cell.

Exhausted and desiring to get things settled, Sam suggested, "Charlie, let's head over to Doc's and see if we can identify that other man. You boys alright here?"

"Couldn't be better, sir, "Jess replied and Johnny nodded, cleaning the soot from his hands.

As the marshals left for Doc's, Johnny picked up the wanted posters on the desk. He turned to stare at his nemesis, who glared back at him obstinately.

"Hey Jess, does this feller look familiar to you?"

Jess viewed the picture in Johnny's hand, then caught the mischief in Johnny's cool eye.

"Oh, you mean the one in this picture here--the one wanted for murder and bank robbery? Yes, he does at that, John. Yeah, that's him alright," Jess answered decidedly.

"Dirty him up a little and this picture is a dead ringer for him," Johnny commented, continuing to eye the burly outlaw in the cell before him. Determinedly, he thumped the wooden desk top with a fist. "Think we got our man, Jess."

Alert now, the captive spoke. "Now, wait a minute. I ain't no bank robber and I certainly never killed no man," he protested loudly. "That ain't me."

Jess overruled him. "Well, we say it is, and I guess we are the ones with the guns and badges, now ain't we?"

"You can't..." the caged man protested loudly. But Johnny stepped to the cell and stopped him.

"We can and we will, and by the time you get to the town of Diamond, they probably won't care who you are. Sheriff Wade's a tough man and known for takin' the law into his own hands on occasion. He likes to rid the territory of criminals and doesn't really care how he does it. Sometimes to trial, but most often he communicates justice on a telegraph pole-at the end of a rope."

"Yeah, John Scott, and I hear he is known for quick burials, too," Jess added, thumbing his way through the rest of the posters quite casually.

"I'll wire Diamond, Jess," Johnny decided, replacing his hat and coat and making a quick exit onto the porch.

The wind whipped through the streets, but the icy sensation had vanished. The sun shone brightly, though there was little warmth to it. He would leave Jess with the captives to glean information in any way his deputized friend deemed best, for suddenly Johnny was too tired to care.

He walked aimlessly up the boardwalk and back again, perversely entreating the crisp air to dull his senses and whisk away the vision of Cassie and the stranger. Entering the office again, he found Jess taking down the town address of the subdued captive. He didn't ask what else Jess had said or done to extract the information; the captive was still breathing and beyond that, he didn't really need to know.

Jess stood and stretched. "Alright, John Scott, I've done my duty here. Now if you'll excuse me, I need some food, a bath, and another kiss from my lady."

Jess wiped a sleeve over his worn and tired face and plopped his hat onto his matted hair. "You might want to try that for yourself," he advised, giving Johnny a roguish wink, "or haven't you tiptoed down that crooked path yet?"

Jess chuckled, slapping Johnny on the back. He did not wait for an answer and sauntered toward the door. "I'll be back before I leave for the stage depot, Johnny. Thanks for my life, son," he added in his usual nonchalant tone, but Johnny caught the sincerity in his eyes.

10

THE VOLITION

THE SUN BROKE through the clouds over the cold mountains, and after a night of filling their bellies and washing down the trail dust, Tilghman's haggard crew left Sideling early the next morning with Sam's bound captive.

The body of the man taken to the undertaker remained to be claimed, or not, by whichever kinsman or acquaintance could be found.

Up on the hill along the ridge, just behind the white steeple church, and partially shaded by the spreading branches of a lone black oak, a row of crude wooden crosses, each marking the internment of a forgotten one, stood like sentinels in a lonely land. Only God knew the names of those who had returned to the dirt upon which they had struggled.

Earlier that morning, Johnny and Marshal Brett had taken turns at soap and water; steak, eggs and potatoes; and finally a few hours of sleep. Later, when Johnny went to the livery to fetch his horse, he had encountered old man Sublette at the side of the barn. Sublette implored Johnny to come along with him to the churchyard.

"My wife is missin', Johnny. She goes to church sometimes of an afternoon, just to take the early evenin' air. You got to help me find her!"

Johnny had tried to dissuade the red-rimmed, bleary-eyed man, but knew there would be no end to it unless he accompanied Lucas Sublette on the search. Finding nothing of the old woman, Johnny gently reminded Lucas that his Sally had died the year before.

Old Lucas cried as Johnny patiently assured the mumbling man that his Sally was "in the arms of the Lord".

After thanking Johnny profusely for his time and encouragement, Sublette made his way home again as he had so many times before. This was Sublette's pattern and would probably continue once or twice weekly until the old man followed his Sally "home".

For the last few hours, the telegraph lines buzzed with information transmitted first to the west toward the Green River, then northward through South Pass, coursing eastward through high plains towns: a conduit linking the distant towns of Medicine Bow's snow-capped range that some called 'Leviathan'.

Crackling and humming through the valley and contiguous plains, the stories of crimes that entangled the remaining two outlaws came to light.

The cattle rustlers' layers of dirt, scruffy beards, and lies had not disguised the darkness of their evil bent, and they were alleged to have performed almost any criminal act that could turn a profit. Robbery of a Wells Fargo owned stage line near South Pass City, and hold up and attempted murder of a miner near Grand Encampment, were the acts that would send them back over the mountains to the settlement at Fort Steele where they would be held until it was determined where they would be tried by jury.

That one man could take so much from others in an attempt to increase his own gain yet risk ending up with less than he had begun with puzzled Johnny. He contemplated this as he walked along the white picket fence line which enclosed the well-tended family plots in the small graveyard beside the church.

He picked up a stone. It was hard and rough in his hand and he stood a moment before chucking it at the trunk of a stubby tree. Walking around to the back of the church, he rested upon a rock.

Old Lucas Sublette could not wait to join his wife in the arms of the Lord. Most people seemed to be trying to flee from God, as far as Johnny could tell, and if they were not outright fleeing, they were subtly backing away. Would those "arms" of the Lord really bear up a man or was it all a myth? Maybe God just wanted something no one could give.

He watched the sun as it glinted off the minute fragments of granite and quartz at his feet, and stirred them around with the heel of his boot. He searched the mountains and took a deep breath. Bits and pieces, bound by time and forged under extreme pressure, formed that beautifully strong, white-capped mountain range.

In his childhood, Johnny had never experienced anything like them. The flat swamps of eastern Virginia boasted only of decaying logs and soft rich peat. He contemplated the contrast and recalled his father's words from long ago. "Hold fast to the solid rock, son."

His eyes ached, and he closed them. Dizzy from exhaustion, he knew the rock beneath him, hard and cold, held him firmly. Although he knew there was no chance of it, the sensation of sinking sand and the sucking mud of the swamps, as though he were being drawn downward, mired in the decomposition of disseminated things and unable to breathe, seemed real.

He hated the feelings of weakness and vulnerability and remembered that Papa had told him time and time again, "The solid rock is God."

This was his father's truth and now, Johnny couldn't pull it together for himself. For so long, nothing had seemed "solid".

'Why do I encourage ole Sublette that his Sally is with God? Because it means so much to him to hear it? He believes it, he always did...' He rested his head in his hands and whispered, "God, I'm so worn."

He saw himself as a child, seated between Mama and Papa in the little Buckhorn Church, not far from the mill pond. A warm and safe place, it was full of light and peace...until it had become a place for stitching during that tumultuous fall nine years before...of butternut fabric, with a yellow stripe stitched along the length of the pant-leg, fashioned for young men who would soon face the battle.

'Maybe that idealistic place is a place for children only. But Papa had been a grown man then, not a child; a man who would never have betrayed his ideals, family or homeland. What does it take to be a valiant man, without regrets--a good man, like Papa, who would never have...' Sickened under the burdensome weight, he wearied of the thoughts.

'I'm grown now. I'm a man and the sum of my life experiences. I'll play from the hand I have been dealt in life.'

He could do this, he had done it and gotten through tragedy and war. Nothing, he reckoned, could be that terrible again. He forced himself to refocus on the next thing at hand.

(Proverbs 4; Isaiah 40:1-11)

Deciding to ask Jess to accompany him with the two captives over the mountain to Fort Steele had been an easy decision. Deciding the best way to navigate the wildlife, Indian, and miners' trails would not be so easy; he knew he needed Jess' scouting skills to navigate the mountain pass while guarding the captives.

Jess seemed fit for the life of a lawman and Johnny wondered idly why Jess had never rangered for Texas. He supposed it was easier to play at enforcing the law on occasion than to endure the day-to-day drain of the job. Still, Johnny would not trade his work for any other he could think of, unless, perhaps... The image of a young, auburn-haired girl caught at his heart.

Immediately dismissing the thought, he propelled himself toward the livery, planning his next move as he walked.

On the way to recruit Jess, he would have to pass by Mrs. Winkler's cottage and Cassie would be there, visiting Mabel Baker. She had to be there. Remembering the tall young man who had whisked her away from Beau on the porch of the Flour and Grain, he felt compelled to find out just who that man was. Johnny wanted to make sure Cassie understood how much he cared for her. He looked to the northwest and the high mountains, resolving to end his torment over this before another day dawned and he must cross that imposing range, known as the "Great Leviathan".

Delayed at the office while the marshal checked out another apparent break-in at Miller's Flour and Grain, Johnny restlessly awaited Sam's return. While the captives slept the afternoon hours away, emitting psoriatic snores and grunts from the cells, he swept the office, cleaned his gun, and tried to think of what to say to Cassie.

Sam returned after finally interviewing the nervous boy, Lester Bolton, and had come to the same conclusion that Johnny had reached previously. Lester Bolton was innocent, and Beau Brenner was nowhere to be found. Sam also observed that his deputy seemed distracted and anxious to leave the discussion and the office, attributing this to what he thought was Johnny's desire to set plans for tomorrow in motion.

"Go on boy, the town is quiet enough for now. Just make rounds first," Sam said, sitting down behind the large desk, hot coffee and a stack of sandwiches before him.

"Want one?" he asked, as Johnny made for the door.

Gratefully, Johnny relieved the marshal of a thick slab of beef between two slices of sourdough bread. He took a bite and with a mock salute and a crooked smile, exited the office.

He stood in the chill at Traveller's side and ate all but the last quarter of his sandwich, which he offered to his friend. The horse pushed at his hand, ate the sandwich and then nudged Johnny hard, searching for more.

"Come on hog, we're on a mission." Mounting, Johnny turned the dappled gray horse to the cottage at the north end of Main Street.

Cassie's horse was not in front of the Winkler's cottage nor was the Wilkerson rig. Undaunted, Johnny spurred Traveller on toward the stage depot, swearing, "I'll find her as soon as I get Jess' commitment. Even if I have to go to her father's ranch to find her, I will."

Jess was glad for an opportunity to leave the stage depot. With wagon wheels repaired and new ones in stock, business was running smoothly. Always happy to live on the "edge", he was restless when treading calm water and did not think twice about leaving the relay with a small crew.

"Yeah, I'll be over to the office tonight, and we can get that early start. You and me, hittin' the perilous trail again."

"The good times just keep a rollin', don't they?" Johnny replied, not even bothering to dismount. He turned Traveller to leave.

"Hold up! How's Skep doin'?" Jess called out to his retreating friend. Johnny pivoted Traveller around to face him.

"I don't know. I think either Beck took him back to their Uncle Willy's place or he took himself. I haven't seen either of them. Everyone seemed to disappear at once, yesterday afternoon."

Satisfied with the response, Jess' typical mischievous grin plastered itself across his face. "By the way, I am not lettin' Sodie know where I'm goin' this time; she worries too much. I'll let her know where I've been when I get back. By then she will be so glad to see me, she'll forget how mad she is with me for not tellin' her."

"I'd sure hate to be the one in love with you, son," Johnny mocked, "and it makes no difference to me what you do along those lines. Just don't be late tonight. We gotta be up at first light."

Jess tossed a careless salute and turned back for the relay.

Cantering off, Johnny ruminated on Jess' response. 'He doesn't have a clue how lucky he is; he just takes her love for granted.'

Needing to find Cassie more than ever, he picked up his pace back toward the town.

Gaining ground toward his goal of the Wilkerson ranch and fighting his inclination to bypass the office as he reached the north end of Main Street, Johnny suppressed his desires and surrendered to obligation. Upon entering the office, Marshal Brett drew him up short.

"Glad you're back, Johnny. These two need something to eat about now." The captives milled about the cell, emitting terse testimonies to the fact.

Sam continued, "I need to get some sleep, I'm not feeling too sharp."

Within the pale cast of Sam's complexion, dark circles shadowed under his eyes and spoke plainly, attesting his fatigue and canceling Johnny's best hope of finding Cassie.

With all the civility he could muster, Johnny rallied. "I'll cover this, sir," adding as sincerely as he could, "and I hope you feel better. Maybe a couple hours of sleep'll help."

Johnny had to admit had never seen the marshal look so worn. Nevertheless, the disappointment of his thwarted plans smoldered like coals in his belly. Taking a cleansing breath, he added a few sticks of wood to the stove and took off his coat. Without further comment, Sam Brett left the office, grateful for the solace of the hotel room.

11

THE LIAISON

CASSIE SAT IN the spacious kitchen of the Wilkerson's two-story cabin with baby Emma upon her knees. Warmth and light surrounded her. The fresh aromas of baked pie, warm bread, and having her family around the rectangular oak table always brought great contentment. So many happy times had passed in this manner and had been all she had ever desired.

She loved her mother's younger brother, Alden Perryman, and two years ago when he had taken the young widow, Odessa, to wife, the family had rejoiced. It was Alden's first marriage and the blonde, curly-headed, laughing Emma, had been the welcome product of their first year of marriage. The baby had taken to all five Wilkerson girls but especially to Cassie.

Emma grabbed and tugged at Cassie's auburn hair, pulling hard with her stubby fingers and dragging Cassie back from her reverie.

"Ouch! Emma, don't hurt cousin Cassie!" She smiled down at the child and pursed her lips in an expression of mock sadness. The baby burst into laughter and tugged at Cassie's hair again. Both giggled and Cassie snuggled Emma to her breast, then stood and whirled around and around until Emma squealed with delight.

Fourteen-year-old Mary came dashing into the kitchen, her light brown hair bobbing under a big blue ribbon. "Mama says you're to give Emma to me now, Cassie, she needs her nap."

Mary held out her hands to Emma who frowned and clung to Cassie.

Seeing the hurt on Mary's face, Cassie said softly, "It's fine Emma. Go to Mary, she'll take you to see your mama, won't you, Mary?"

Cassie placed a hand lightly on her sister's arm and smiled. The baby's gaze fixed on the shiny gold cross at Mary's throat, and she reached for it. Mary brightened and laughed as Emma came into her arms and clutched the gold cross in her chubby fingers.

"Let's go little Emma, Mama's waiting!" Emma squealed as Mary ran from the room, delighted with the additional jostling and attention.

In the quiet of the kitchen, Alden, who had been sitting on the opposite side of the table sipping coffee, watched Cassie admiringly as she returned to her seat on the bench.

"She's so precious, Aldie, I'm glad you brought her to visit."

Cassie used the pet name she had given him when she was not much older than Emma. He had been twelve at the time and had considered Cassie his little shadow. No matter what Alden did or where he went, Cassie followed him. He reveled in teaching her everything he knew. Now, as they sat alone at the table he considered her solemnly.

"So, we haven't had much time to visit, you and I, but you look fit and have become a beautiful young woman, missy," he said, gently.

She screwed up her face and laughed. "You always did tease me so!"

"Well, I am not teasing you now," he replied lightly, and his comical expression faded. "How are things with you?"

"I am fine, did you think otherwise?" She tried to read through his question and knew him well enough to know there was concern for her behind it.

"You've seemed a little distracted since we arrived, and I wonder if it has anything to do with that young man we encountered at the grain merchant yesterday. Is he someone special to you?"

Cassie shook her head as he continued. "I thought your conversation to be intense when I came onto the porch and saw him with you."

Alden's expression grew mysterious behind his slight smile, and he tilted his head as though he might have uncovered her secret.

"You mean Beau?" Surprised at his assumption, she rushed to assure him. "Oh, no! We're actually just classmates, and not good friends at that."

"Oh, I see."

But Cassie saw that she had not convinced Alden.

"He seemed very, well, very engrossed in you, Cassie. Are you sure he doesn't think more highly of you than you know?"

Cassie remembered Beau's words, which had pinned her to the wall. Uncomfortable now, she blushed under Alden's gaze and tried to think of a proper response.

"He just had a question about a class assignment, that's all." It was a lame response and they both knew it. Cassie studied the last drops of coffee in her saucer.

Her mind fled to the safety of her childhood. She wished she could commune with Aldie as she had in those days of innocence when they sat under the trees sharing their hopes and dreams.

But now, there was only confusion. How could she begin to tell anyone the little she really understood about Beau or explain the cryptic message she thought to be buried beneath his disturbing words? And, there was Johnny. How to put those feelings into words without sounding like a lovesick calf, she didn't know.

She was relieved that he had returned safely and was desperate to see Johnny again. She tired of pretending that it didn't matter what happened to him and that everything was fine and wearied of Mama watching for her reactions but never specifically commenting. How could she express these things to Aldie, and would he even understand? The tears that always seemed to be just behind her eyes clouded her vision, and she could not meet his steady gaze.

Alden rose and came to sit by her side, putting an arm about her shoulders. She turned to him and rested her cheek against his chest. He sat quietly and after a moment she lifted her head, blinking back tears and sniffed, but still could not look him in the eyes.

"It's all right, Cassie, if you want to talk about it I'm here. If that boy has hurt you…"

"No, Aldie." She dabbed her eyes with a handkerchief she had tucked in her sleeve at the wrist. "He hasn't hurt me. He's just a foolish schoolboy. I have a lot of things on my mind; that's really all there is to this."

"Well, I'd say those things are sinking you a mite low, don't you think?"

She did not respond, and he hugged her again. He tickled her nose with his finger, reaching her wounded heart as only he could. She smiled in spite of herself.

"I am glad all of you are here, Aldie, I really have missed you."

Alden leaned close to her ear. "Hey, I'll let you in on a little secret if you promise not to tell, that is. It might just cheer you up."

His eyes twinkled merrily and briefly she was caught up in the old game they used to play.

"Alright, I promise. Tell me, tell me true!"

"Well…" He dragged the word out mysteriously. "Odessa is going to have a baby," he whispered. Cassie threw up her hands and hugged him tightly.

"Oh, Aldie, I am so happy for you! Oh, that's why Odessa has been napping so frequently and hasn't felt well. Do Ma and Pa know?"

"I told you it was a secret!" he warned, placing his finger to her lips then laughing. "Odessa will tell them when she is ready, but I reckon your Ma's figured it out by now. I am glad you're excited for us."

Cassie took his hands in hers. "I am truly glad you found one another and found such wonderful love, Aldie."

"One day you will also, Cassie. You still have plenty of time, sweet one. Don't let anyone force you into anything. Take your time. You've much to offer the right man."

They sat in the warmth of the kitchen and she snuggled childlike in the safety of his embrace.

But Cassie's aching heart sought Johnny's face, 'The right man.' Cassie repeated silently, 'The right man...'

In a moment, Alden kissed her cheek and excused himself to see if he was needed by Odessa. Early evening was upon them and Cassie rallied to start her chores. From the peg on the wall by the kitchen's back door, she removed her bonnet, then donning her old coat and gloves, stepped out in the chill.

"The right man...." she murmured, as she walked through the side yard toward the barn. A verse from Proverbs came to mind.

"As iron sharpeneth iron; so a man sharpeneth the countenance of his friend." Easily, another verse followed. "As in water face answereth to face, so the heart of man to man."

She leaned against the barn door and watched the shadows lengthen from the house and outbuildings, stretching out across the prairie to join the dusk which faded the mountains beyond. Her sight turned inward, again recalling Johnny's face, ruggedly handsome, whose eyes had drowned her in their depths until she found herself reflected in the gathering concern there. Suddenly brushed with something more, the reflection had disappeared so quickly, she had not been able to fathom the meaning of it-a man who had earned the respect of the townsfolk and her father in particular. Pa had said he was a fine man, and that the marshal could trust and depend on him. 'Iron sharpening iron', that was what the marshal and his deputy did for one another.

"The right man..." Aunt Mabel had stated. "He is a good man, Cassie. The Lord's hand is upon that man."

(Proverbs 27:17 Proverbs 27:19)

Cassie's gaze fell on her gloved hand. She could still feel his strength, recalling the day he had helped her up into the wagon when he had come to Aunt Mabel's cabin. Ma had whisked her away quickly, but not before she had found herself again reflected in his eyes. His strength not only lay in his hands and arms, but in his character. But would he ever choose to love her as Aldie had chosen Odessa?

'I am just a girl,' she thought dejectedly. 'How will he ever find me?'

Hadn't he found her that evening by the barn in the dusk, when after having helped her from the saddle he had held her briefly? Leaving her in a pool of unexpected warmth, he had stepped back quickly and left her so suddenly; what had it meant? But she remembered the urgency in his grasp and longed for it again.

Bewildered, she turned to open the barn door. The wind had a different feel tonight, for it blew from the south. Mingled with minute particles of dust, there was a hint of warmth which drove away the stinging chill. Another verse came to mind. Having been instructed carefully from the Proverbs at home and in school, she had copied the letters meticulously, studying the form and sound of each. Eventually letters became words, and words became concepts, opening up new worlds of understanding.

"The upright shall inherit the land and men of integrity will remain in it."

"Oh Johnny, when will I see you again? If I could but explain my feelings and understand yours. Thank you for being brave and...."

She couldn't finish. There was too much to be said and only the wind to hear her. It would bring no answers as it carelessly carried her words away, dispersing them into the ever-changing atmosphere, and confirming her sense of being insignificant to his world. Wiping away the tears of confusion, she set her face to the frivolous wind and, like a true child of the prairie, breathed in deeply, capturing what it could provide. But the clarity and determination for which she hoped would be fleeting, for the restless wind would bring about a challenge greater than any she had ever known.

Even though the chill wind blew steadily down Main Street, Johnny had chosen the chair on the porch. The stars twinkled brightly, and the quarter moon hung high in the sky. Feeling himself to be the prisoner, he could not tolerate the scurrility of the captives another minute. Glad for the fresh air, he pulled his hat down over his eyes, tilted the chair back against the outside office wall, and attempted to enjoy the momentary quiet. Jess came, just as dark covered the town.

Johnny's hat hurled from his head in a sideways trajectory, hitting the office window just as Jess' hat smacked him in the side of his head.

"Sleepin' on the job again, I see!"

"Dang it!" Johnny cursed, "You scared me senseless!"

"Well, now, that don't take much doin'." Jess laughed and offered his hand in greeting. Johnny took it and Jess pulled him onto his feet.

Striking like lightning, Johnny clamped an arm around Jess' shoulder and slung him off the porch and into the dirt.

Wiping the dust from his pants, Jess cursed. "Hey! You almost pitched me in the trough!" Johnny scowled and offered a hand to pull Jess back onto the porch. "Quit messin' around, we've serious business to attend to!"

But their eyes met, sparking a challenge and in that second, both men knew the die was cast. Jess had clasped Johnny's outstretched hand and although Johnny expected it and braced himself, Jess yanked hard. With gravity and leverage against him, Johnny found himself on the ground with his hat in the dirt next to him.

"Hey, you made me step on my hat!" Johnny complained, awkwardly getting to his feet. "It's squashed!"

"Here, take mine," Jess replied, and dusting the dirt off his hat, flung it toward Johnny, watching as it landed cockeyed on Johnny's head.

Straightening it, Johnny tamped it down possessively on his head. Then he picked up his own hat, dusted it off with a few smacks to his thigh, and reshaped it expertly.

"Oh no you don't! Give me back my hat," Jess ordered, taking a menacing step toward his friend. Johnny backed up.

"Just hold still a second, Jess."

Raising his arm with his hat clutched firmly in his fist, Johnny quickly assessed the distance between them and tossed it in an arc. It sailed into the air, illuminated by the dim lantern light and landed on the crown of Jess' head, sliding lopsided over his left ear.

"Ha!" Johnny crowed.

Jess caught the hat before it slipped to the ground. Obligingly, Johnny removed Jess' hat from his own head and Jess met the test, returning Johnny's hat in the same manner, arcing it through the air. Landing lopsided on Johnny's head, the hat slid down over his eyes, and his nose stopped the brim's descent. The hat remained lopsided, but still on his head.

"Two for two, John Scott, guess I got ya!" Jess bragged.

Adjusting the hat on his head, Johnny jumped up on the rim of the watering trough. Unsteady and moving his feet gingerly to maintain his balance like a man on a tightwire, he barely managed to stop his fall.

He looked down at Jess. "Back up! You're too close."

Jess took four exaggerated paces backward. Johnny whipped the hat off his head and in a precise and studied motion, let it sail, landing it squarely atop Jess' head. Johnny let loose an elated whoop.

"Ya just got lucky!" Jess cried, "Bet you can't do that again!"

From behind the office and around the corner Sam Brett had come, and now stood silently in the shadows. Inclined to question Johnny as to who was watching the captives, he held his tongue and watched for a moment. The past few days had proceeded severely, one after another, allowing no time for anything except constant observation and planning. Anticipation of the unknown had rolled in like a wave, ebbing away their strength and setting raw nerves on edge. Now, there was release and Sam envied the young men at their game. Like the boys they were, they pushed aside responsibility briefly and just simply played.

He scuffed his boots along the ground, spurs jingling, and the young men turned quickly, Johnny almost falling into the trough.

"Nice night, isn't it?" the marshal observed, stopping before them. Tickled by the look on his deputy's face, he held his expression stoically and tilted his head toward the closed office door. "You boys know if our captives have yanked the bars off the cell window and fled through the back, or do you think they're still in there?" he asked casually.

Having bolted from the rim of the trough and over the hitching post, Johnny was on the porch in a flash. "We been out here just long enough to catch a breath of air..." but he dried up in mid-sentence. Marshal Brett was already in the office.

12

THE CRUX

THE TWO CAPTIVES' hands were bound to their saddle horns as before. With rifles, side pieces, and ammunition, Johnny and Jess mounted their horses and rode up Main Street about 8:00 a.m. the following morning, flanking the captives on either side.

Unable to get themselves up at first light, they had not awakened until dawn had driven the darkness completely behind the western range. The day promised to be unusually warm for mid-October. Before departing, they breakfasted thoroughly. Sam Brett did not comment on finding them still at the office with much of the morning spent, for they had been up late the night before, readying themselves for the morning and drawing up a crude map to indicate their proposed route across the Medicine Bow Range. At the last moment, Johnny remembered the map and handed it to the marshal.

"Almost forgot, sir, in case we turn up missing."

"Those mountains can be treacherous. I know you're both aware of it, just be sure you're watching the skies as well as those two. I don't trust this weather," he cautioned.

"Don't worry Mr. Brett, I'll take care of this young 'un."

In return for his comment, Johnny shoved the butt of his rifle into Jess' ribs.

Sam Brett shook his head. Jess was twenty-two, worldly-wise, and as smart as they came, but for all the world, he sometimes appeared to Sam as an overgrown kid. Still, Sam was confident in both of the men's abilities, and he watched silently as they departed.

As they turned to leave, Johnny glanced toward the Halstead cabin, for Cassie was never more than a breath's pause from his mind. As if on cue, the door opened and a matron appeared at the threshold, but there was no sign of Cassie. Undeterred, he held onto the hope of finding her when they passed her father's ranch. Even if only for a moment, to see her would put his mind to rest, for she had unsettled his dreams in the night. Although he had restlessly pursued her in vain, by dawn, he had mercifully fallen asleep.

They traveled the main road, accompanied by the clank and jangle of their weaponry, interrupted occasionally by a colorful invective hurled at them from the surly, bearded man. The sullen twig of an outlaw was slumped in the saddle, at odds with the rhythm of his horse. Johnny spotted a rig in the distance approaching at a good pace. He studied it intently and as it drew closer, recognized the gleam of coppery hair spilling out from under a wide-brimmed bonnet.

Cassie drove with her sister, Mary, beside her and was headed straight for them.

Johnny left his position at right flank, dropped back, then spurred Traveller up alongside Jess on the left flank.

"Can you hold them here Jess, just for a minute?" Johnny asked.

Jess perused the approaching rig and fixing his friend with a salacious grin, agreed. "Yeah, do what you got to do, only don't take all day."

Jess forced the captives to halt and with his shotgun trained on them, rode tight circles around their horses. Glaring at their unkempt forms, he spat.

"Just give me an excuse, boys, just one!"

Johnny spurred Traveller forward and crossing the path of the oncoming rig, caused Cassie to sharply rein in her horse and wagon. Her surprise was obvious, but before she could comment, Johnny greeted her.

"Hey, Miss Cassie!"

Time hung suspended and he sat tense in his saddle while Traveller danced sideways, sensing his emotion. Johnny reined him side to side with a quick hand, attempting to hold him straight on.

From over the back of the wagon seat and bunched together like a litter of kittens, the three little sisters peered out from between the older girls, staring at the deputy through wide, round eyes. Remembering his manners, Johnny acknowledged them with a nod and a touch of his hand to the brim of his hat.

"Ladies," he said, more calmly than he felt.

Cassie found her voice and asked too brightly, "Howdy, Deputy McLane. What brings you out this way?" Immediately realizing how nonsensical her question was, she flushed. His mission was obvious and her question juvenile. But she kept her gaze on his face, which was exactly as she had remembered.

"Jess Bryant and I are taking these captives over the mountain to Fort Steele," he answered quickly, glad that she had given him a topic for conversation.

Unable to think of how to express all that he needed say, especially in the presence of the innocence which surrounded her and peered up at him, but feeling the need to clarify his actions, he detained them. But his mind remained numb as he gazed at Cassie, and he tried desperately to separate logic from emotion.

From under her bonnet brim, a minutely freckled, upturned nose, and deep blue eyes confronted him expectantly. Her lips parted slightly as though she would speak, but Cassie issued no sound.

"Are those the criminals, Deputy McLane? Are you taking them to prison?" It was Mary who spoke, so Johnny tore his gaze from Cassie's and addressed her.

"Yes, Miss Mary, they're the ones. We are taking them over the mountain so they can stand trial for their string of crimes, but they'll go to prison only if the judge and jury say so," he added, again glad for the conversation.

Mary appraised him sweepingly, but he had refocused his attention on Cassie who stared at her sister sternly.

"I am sorry, Deputy," Cassie apologized, cutting her eyes sidelong at Mary. "We should not interfere with your business."

Returning her attention to Johnny, Cassie collected her emotions, needing to end the momentary awkward silence.

"Did you stop us to tell us that something is wrong in town or...?" Under his incomprehensible stare, she pinked, waiting for his response.

It dawned on Johnny that he and Jess must appear to be headed for battle. His rifle rested diagonally across his back, its barrel protruding above one shoulder. A large sheathed knife hung from one hip, and his gun was holstered on the other. An extra belt of ammunition crossed his chest. Coiled rope hung from his saddle, and saddlebags crammed with supplies rested across Traveller's rump. With Jess similarly outfitted, he knew they gave the impression of a moving, armed fortress.

The contrast between his entourage and the three young girls, with neat, blue-ribboned pigtails, and curls framing their sweet rosy-cheeked faces, peeking wide-eyed out from under frilly bonnet brims, suddenly struck him as humorous; he smiled in spite of the tension.

Still holding Cassie's eyes intentionally, he replied with a simple, "Yes," and then chuckled wryly at the absurdity of the situation.

As Cassie watched him intently, she thought, 'There it is again.' That vexing expression, his one eyebrow raised and that crooked grin which she found so perplexing. She frowned in confusion.

"Pardon me?"

Noting the change in her expression, he quickly corrected himself and his humor faded. He grew serious, remembering he needed to answer her question.

"Well, no. I mean that...no." and he faltered, trying unsuccessfully to gather his thoughts.

Truly wishing to understand, Cassie asked, "I am sorry; what do you mean?"

She had to rein him in. She wanted him to say something, anything that would revive the surety he seemed to have expressed at their last encounter, and hoped it to be the reason he detained them now. But he stared intently into her eyes with an expression she had trouble comprehending. Then she watched as he formed the words.

"I have to talk to you, Cassie," he said haltingly, "I mean, with you, if you will agree to meet me."

He rushed on, "I'll be gone for a couple of days, but when I get back, I will look for you."

Cassie nodded, managing a tentative smile and was horrified when Mary piped up, nudging her hard with an elbow.

"I'm sure Cassie would be delighted to meet with you, Deputy McLane!"

Mary glared at Cassie, indicating that Cassie should make an immediate verbal response.

Cassie flushed, wanting to shake her sister, but found herself mute as she dumbly watched the deputy's horse dance in place beneath him.

Suddenly Jess was moving toward them, circling the captives as he would a herd of cattle. "Let's go, Johnny!" he called impatiently.

"Have a nice afternoon, ladies," Jess drawled, saluting the rig and shooting Johnny a 'let's git' warning.

Jess tipped his hat to the girls, and with his shotgun pointed menacingly, proceeded to herd the horses and the two bound captives, who turned to leer at the rig full of girls, as they moved down the road. Immediately, Johnny regretted having exposed them to the embodiment of evil. As the departing men looked on, and aware of running out of time, he drew Traveller to Cassie's side, partially obstructing their view. "I am sorry Cassie. I'll see you soon… don't forget."

He wheeled Traveller around, touched the brim of his hat in salute to the girls, and cantered off to take up the right flank position as the men moved further down the road. Dismayed, Cassie sat still and watched him leave.

Then she unleashed her frustrations. "Mary, how could you? How could you embarrass me in that way?" Tears stung her eyes and she struggled to keep them back.

Stunned, Mary faced her sister. Her voice was shrill and her face incredulous.

"Me? Why I helped you out! You didn't answer him, Cassie! I thought you liked him! He was asking you to see him, for mercy sakes!"

"You don't know that for certain!" Cassie retorted, "Neither of us could possibly know why he asked to see me! Just mind your own business, Mary, and stay out of mine! You're a mettlesome...little girl!"

Focusing ahead, Cassie smacked the reins hard on the horse's rump, causing the rig to lurch forward, unaware of the tears on Mary's shocked face.

The girls fell as silent as tombs. Cassie could only speculate, her mind in a turmoil. Did he stop her to finish the conversation they had begun when last they spoke? That had to be why. He had not had an opportunity to complete his question that day, and if she was honest, there had been more of a perception on her part as to what he had intended. What was the last thing he had said? What had he said today? She tried to remember. He said he was sorry, but why? Was it because he had stopped her on her way to town or because he had not been able to finish his interview?

Uneasiness fringed her anger as the hidden memory portentously arose. This must have something to do with Beau, but why would she think of him now? Cassie knew he had been a thread in the fabric of concerns blanketing the townsfolk lately--but he was just a dumb school boy! No one would take him seriously. Why would they? Not used to jumping at shadows in the dark, she certainly would not allow him to trouble her further.

Johnny must have discovered that she had encountered Beau that distant morning...how could he know? There was no one else present at daybreak that day, or was there? She searched her memory for details and found only the uncertainties of that experience. Beau's dominating, arrogant persona, infelicitous on that lovely spring morning, had captured her full attention. She had shut up the memory of the confrontation and his foul words. Now it angered her to think he had the power to overwhelm her in that fashion...for she secretly feared him but could not admit it.

If Johnny's motive for stopping them had been in reference to Beau, why had he not gone to her father first? Why had he not questioned her when her mother was present at Mabel's cabin? She wasn't of age and would not be seventeen for another month and a half; surely he wouldn't interview her on the matter without Pa's knowledge.

She believed that Johnny cared for her, but today he had not made that clear. Hadn't he laughed at her again? For the few moments he had held her with his eyes, she remembered being held in his arms. But the intensity he seemed to display moments ago had quickly turned to that exasperating expression, almost as though he was toying with her, and she could not fathom why. Had it not been for Mary's rude interruption and Mr. Bryant's insistent calling,

Johnny might have clarified further. It seemed to her that all they ever did was part, separated by the circumstances of their different lives.

"I will come for you."

She remembered those had been among his parting words. The crux of the matter loomed frustratingly, and she shook off the chilling thought passing through her. A man with a demanding job; questions unasked and unanswered; and a schoolgirl, yet one with a woman's budding heart.

13

THE LOSS

JESS ATTEMPTED CONVERSATION, but Johnny was not in the conversing mood. As they moved up the Laramie Valley, northwest toward the well-timbered mountains, following old cart tracks and crossing remains of corduroy roads, the captive's complaints and grumblings interfered with most of Jess' comments. For a while, he kept his words at a minimum.

Johnny tried to get past the confusion that had marred his brief encounter with Cassie. He placated himself with the fact that he had met his two goals for the day. He had seen her and asked to meet with her.

If he was honest with himself, and he vacillated on this point, he'd have to admit it had not gone well. He hadn't spoken to her as he had hoped to, hadn't seen any spark of admiration for him, or even a glimmer of desire. But what could he expect, having accosted her in broad daylight, looking like a bandolero with a gang of thugs in tow?

Worst of all, he couldn't say for sure that she had consented to see him upon his return. She might have, but Mary's outburst had taken everyone by surprise and had seemed to anger Cassie. So whether Cassie was angry at Mary for her outburst or at him for the incident, he could not be sure. He was miserable and yet, he had seen her again.

"Why don't you play us a tune on that gadget of yours, Johnny?" Jess asked, breaking the monotony of the trek.

The day remained cool, but the warmth of a season past held it fast. The air was calm, except for an occasional slight breeze which stirred the dust and rustled the needles of the scrubby pines growing sparsely among the rocky terrain.

Johnny extracted his harmonica from the pocket of his jacket which lay across the cantle of his saddle. He blew "Ole Zip Coon", hoping to revive his spirits, but even that lively tune left him flat. Traveller's ears twitched forward and sideways, and his gait quickened with the melody.

> "Ole Zip Coon was a learned scholar
> Ole Zip Coon was a learned scholar
> Ole Zip coon was a learned scholar

Singin' possum up the gum tree, coonie in the holler."
(*Zip Coon*, Bob Farrell, George Nickols, 1834)

They fell silent upon entering the forested mountains and all went well enough until out of sheer boredom, Jess requested another tune.

Johnny piped, "Carry me back to old Virginny", and the rebel-hating captive exploded with expletives that made even Jess and the emaciated captive cringe. There was nothing left with which to quell the swarthy outlaw's outbursts except Jess' old standby--immediate death and decapitation.

Irritated by the sour moods prevailing, and on edge from the contradictory events of the day, Johnny divisively finished his performance with the tune of "The Battle Hymn of the Republic".

He informed the angry hater in no uncertain terms that he was actually playing a dirge in remembrance of John Brown's body which lay "a moulderin' in the grave", as payment for Brown's various perpetrations against the South's most upright and law-abiding citizens in the state of Missouri, but most notably, the noble citizens in the state of Virginia.

The deputy then indicated a similar fate might await any criminal in any state or territory who dared besmirch the name of a Virginian. This precipitated an argument between Johnny and Jess over whether or not Virginia could claim Harper's Ferry or John Brown's body as her own. Had not that area become the state of West Virginia by 1859? Johnny chose to ignore Jess' "chronological and geographical exactitudes" by impatiently proclaiming that his own assessments were "close enough".

Jess would not let it rest and continued. "Fools like you, John Scott, are the very kind that keep notions in this territory boiling as to where the exact boundary between Albany and Carbon counties lie, so much so that the same mining ventures are filed by nervous miners in both Laramie City and in Rawlins Springs--just so miners can be sure they cover themselves. I say those county seats are a mighty fair distance apart, so make the decision to accept the surveyor's damned chain, and get on with things!"

The hater had fallen mute and Johnny reckoned that even he wished for peace and quiet. But in the silence, beyond the aggravation, Johnny found himself unsettled. By having callously maligned John Brown and his raid, he had whole-heartedly defended the Southern Cause. Although violent and radical, Brown's actions had stemmed from a desire to free the oppressed. Left in the continuing double-bind and feeling guilty, Johnny pushed the contentions away.

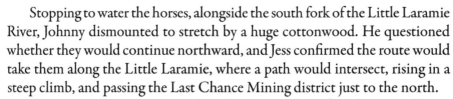

Stopping to water the horses, alongside the south fork of the Little Laramie River, Johnny dismounted to stretch by a huge cottonwood. He questioned whether they would continue northward, and Jess confirmed the route would take them along the Little Laramie, where a path would intersect, rising in a steep climb, and passing the Last Chance Mining district just to the north.

"Atop that mountain is Cinnabar City. Miners have found some gold, but not much I hear. Don't think there is much else up there, a few cabins, and hardy prospectors is all. Hear they applied for a post office, but I'm not sure anything has come of it. Anyway, there are no women and the mining season is short due to harsh conditions. Snow was really deep last year."

Johnny acknowledged Jess with a grunt, and then replied, "I read about the Ute attack, last July, in *The Laramie Sentinel*. The miners were said to have fled into Laramie City and missed most of the season. Maybe we should start prospectin'. Might be an interestin' change."

Jess returned a grunt, and Johnny checked his compass. Single file, they followed the rushing waters, then forded the shallows successfully, following the trail upward as the afternoon dragged on. The horses' respirations grew labored. Their coats were layered in dust, which mingled with sweat and ran in minute rivulets over their chests, down their flanks and legs. The deputies wished for relief from the saddle.

From the rear position and nearing the top of a high rise, Johnny yelled, "I say we're stoppin'!"

Jess halted the procession and the men stood among the outcropings taking in their surroundings. Scrub weed was prominent and the forest of the lower elevations had fallen away. They had entered a high, rolling plain where brown prairie grasses, sporadically dotted with sprinklings of Parry Gentian, bent low with the fickled winds. The remains of blue-tinted alpine phlox, with moss-like leaves, sheltered among the rocky places along the obscure trail.

Visible through the clumping stands of fir that lined the depressions to the distant southwest, the heraldic shimmer of an azure lake gleamed in the sunlight. The plains rolled off and continued similarly until meeting a line of pale blue-hued mountains. Immediately off to the north, the salient peaks loomed above the grandeur.

Awestruck, Johnny whispered, "All this beauty...like a prairie in the sky."

Jess turned in his saddle to study the surroundings and scan the horizon. "I know we're on the correct trail, but things don't look like I thought they would."

"When did you come this way last?" Johnny asked.

"I reckon a month or so ago, huntin'. I've only been on this plain once--never saw anyone other than a few miners and a few peaceable Oglala Sioux who disappeared into a pass somewhere over in that direction. It's said to cut through the mountains, but until today, I've had no particular reason to scout it further."

They dismounted, and Jess picked up a small stone and slung it haplessly. Extending his arm straight out and before him, he sighted the western range. Squinting into the sun above the mountains, he bent his wrist horizontally and resting his fingers atop each other with his index finger marking the bottom of the sun and his little finger marking the top of the mountain range, he calculated the remaining daylight, with each finger width representing fifteen minutes.

"We have about one hour before sunset, even more if we can find the pass and get on the other side of those mountains. We better rest and quick," he exclaimed.

The lawmen pulled the two captives from their horses and watered the thirsty equines. They pried the tops from two air-tights containing tomatoes and sardines and shared the contents with the outlaws.

Johnny bent to assess Traveller's right front leg, using his pocket knife to remove a small stone which had lodged between the shoe and the frog of the hoof. Traveller shoved him with a soft nicker.

"You're welcome." Johnny dropped the hoof and straightened.

Jess appeared in the distance, standing atop a mound of boulders, surveying the high mountain range.

The outlaws, with hands cuffed before them, were hobbled among the scrabble rock with their feet bound together. Johnny turned, flattened himself against a nearby boulder, hoisted the rifle atop, and climbed to sit next to it. Dangling his feet over the edge of the rough rock face, he took in the landscape.

The sky stretched out like a deep blue canvas, unbroken except for a dark gray, thin line, which lay along the mountain peak to the northwest.

"Hey, Jess!" Johnny hollered, his cry echoing off a distant wall of rock. There was no answer, and he hollered again, hailed only by his returning echo. Unconcerned, he grew lethargic in the warmth of the sun, finding it difficult to keep an eye on the captives. The loud clang of metal on rock below startled him, and he shouldered his rifle, finding Jess directly in his rifle sights.

"Announce yourself before you sneak up on a body!" Johnny reprimanded gruffly, grabbing a loose stone and bouncing it off Jess' hat.

"I might worry if I thought you could hit anything with that, son," Jess replied, but Johnny was not in the mood to spar.

"I'm thinkin' we should go straight over those rocks." Jess pointed northward and to the west of the high peak. "The pass is in that direction and I'm told it's the shortest route. But there seems to be a split off. Could be an elk or antelope trail, or maybe Ute or Arapaho, but I'm bettin' the split off leads back to the Cherokee Trail, too far to the south. Nevertheless, it would still take us along the North Platte River and up to the fort." he concluded, eyeing Johnny questionably.

"Well, are you askin' me or tellin' me? What's your best opinion, before I give you mine?"

Johnny knew there could be no half-hearted decision. He trusted Jess' senses, knowing him to be an excellent tracker, for he was "good in the wood", as the saying went, and had taken them through the wilderness many times.

"I'm tellin' you I think we should take the shortcut." Jess' expression was mild, and his words confident. "When we get to Fort Steel, we'll hand these ole boys over. I heard J.W. Hugus opened a store at the fort, and I'd like to check out his line of hardware. After that, we can ride south to the place where the warm springs are and soak our weary bones in the hot pools. Then, we'll follow the Platte south to Douglas Creek, then up the mountain and head for home. Sound good?"

Johnny thought a moment, then nodded. "If the Indians still consider those springs neutral territory, and the soldiers still use the pools, I say we do it. We'll need to check at the fort first."

Jess realized his friend's response seemed to lack his usual enthusiasm for sport, and when Johnny spoke again, Jess followed his troubled gaze toward the west.

"Did you notice the sky?" The black line snaking along the mountain ridge had thickened only slightly.

"Yeah, we've got time before that gets here, if it does, and hopefully we can find shelter further up the mountain.

"Great place to be in a storm," Johnny replied, studying the mountain ridge and eyeing Jess skeptically.

"Look, if we head back down the trail, or take the split off, we'll lose half a day and maybe even have to take up this same trail again."

Jess removed his hat, scratching his head. "It could have been a rockslide that closed the obvious gap that passes near the peak of this mountain. I just expected to be going through that pass by now, not having to go higher. Seems to me that it was at a lower elevation than this."

The two captives who had been keeping to themselves and relatively quiet, had begun to listen intentionally. The Reb-hater spoke.

"So you don't know where we are, right? Me and him," and he tipped his head toward his now alert compadre, "we can get us outta here."

Johnny and Jess exchanged glances. Jess shifted his position, lifted one foot to rest upon smaller rock and positioned his shotgun across his thigh, leaning back against the boulder. He was the first to answer.

"I'll bet you can. I'll bet you know a great way to get through these mountains and I'll wager further, in fact, I'll put money on the table--that you'll have a big party for us with all your friends invited, waiting just on the other side."

The hater cursed and spit toward Jess' boot. Jess took a quick step forward and Johnny grabbed his arm. "Let it be, Jess. Like you said, he's not worth the effort. We're wastin' light and if we're goin', let's git."

Picking up the last of the air-tights and drinking the remainder of the tomato juice, Johnny tossed the can to the rocks below.

They mounted, riding in column toward the northwest. Jess led the first captive's horse and Johnny, rifle ready, held the drag position behind the Reb-hater.

As they climbed, the paling light of the sun dimmed under billowing black clouds along the rim of the mountain range, and the temperature dropped. It became obvious that they were traversing a pass of some sort, although nothing was familiar. The trail narrowed as the pass emptied into a steep draw and hugged the side of a high rock wall to the right.

A ravine fell away to the west and Johnny estimated its drop to be about 100 feet with boulders interspersed throughout the scrabble rock below. The rock held very little soil and no plants or trees grew anywhere. Dark clouds blew in from the southwest on a maelstrom of wind, and thunder resounded up and down the mountain range, rumbling along like a cannon volley, but there was nowhere to shelter.

The sky directly above them turned pewter-gray, heavy with clouds, then blackened as the clouds scudded low. The wind whipped wildly, blowing and sucking as it collided with the narrow canyon walls, forcing the men to hug the rock wall, and fight to steady the horses as the narrow trail took a turn northward. As a wicked finger of lightning bolted from the sky, a strong wall of wind slammed them head on. In terror the horses reared, whirling in different directions, refusing to move forward against the wind.

The Reb-hater, riding in front of Traveller and Johnny with his hands still cuffed and tied to the saddle horn, lost control of his big bay gelding. The horse spun around, eyes wide with fear, and charged toward Traveller, colliding violently at an angle at the edge of the ravine.

Traveller's hind leg slid on the loose rock and as his rear quarters began to slide down the grade, Johnny reined him hard to the right, standing in the stirrups and leaning forward in a desperate attempt to spur the struggling horse upward and forward. He felt the horse lose ground beneath him and slide backwards. Johnny threw his body to the right, grabbing at the mane of the outlaw's bay to keep from falling with Traveller.

The bay spun in panic, dragging Johnny up onto the trail. The captive clung to the saddle horn, holding himself in the saddle and cursing wildly. In seconds, Johnny's hands slid from the wet mane and he landed in a heap on the trail, while the bay side-stepped the body under his feet. Johnny's rifle slid to the rocks below. In a wild gallop, the frightened bay and bound rider continued back down the trail until the horse tripped, rolling onto his rider in the pelting rain.

The second captive's horse, fleeing after the bay, jumped over Johnny in an effort to keep from stepping on him. Colliding with a boulder, the horse threw the rider, who had managed to free his hands from the saddle horn. The outlaw vaulted over the head of his mount and disappeared into the dark ravine, while his frantic horse continued back down the trail.

In the fury of the wind and the crackling of lightning and thunder, Johnny lay on the edge of the ravine. Terrified shrieks from Traveller, who lay awkwardly across a large boulder about 20 feet down the grade, rose from below.

The horse thrashed and groaned, trying to rise. His right foreleg dangled oddly, and frothy blood bubbled from his nostrils. Jess staggered toward Johnny, trying to pull him to his feet. Johnny attempted to stand but his legs would not support him. Kneeling, he frantically clutched Jess' jacket.

"I've got to get to him Jess, I have to get down there!" Johnny pleaded, as Jess knelt in the mud with his arms around Johnny's chest to hold him firmly.

"It's too late. I'll have to use my rifle, Johnny!" Jess hollered through the storm. The agonized cries from the pitiful horse below drove Johnny to struggle to free himself from Jess' bear hold.

"Oh God, no! He's all I have left!" he cried, trying to tear himself away from Jess and get over the edge of the ravine.

"You can't save him, Johnny, it's too late! He's too far gone!"

Johnny struggled to get a foot under him and pulling away from Jess in rage, swung a fist at him blindly. "No! Damn it, no! Give me the rifle then; give it to me!"

"I'll do it, Johnny!"

"No, Jess," he bellowed, "He's my horse! It's for me to do! Give me the rifle!"

Jess took in his friend's contorted, rain-soaked features. A mixture of mud, blood, and what he knew to be tears, dripped from his partner's nose and streamed down his face; Jess removed the rifle strapped across his back and handed it to Johnny.

Johnny yanked it from Jess' hands and rolled sideways, pulling with his elbows in a crawl to the edge of the ravine. Jess grabbed at Johnny legs, steadying him as Johnny lay flat and lowered his shoulders and the rifle over the edge of the grade. Wiping his eyes, he placed the injured horse in the sights of the cold, metal barrel.

Forcing himself to focus through rain and his tears, Johnny watched as Traveller lifted his noble head in one last vain attempt to pull himself up. He steadied the rifle, held his breath, cocked the hammer and slowly flexed his forefinger, squeezing, and engaging the trigger. The hammer slammed and the bullet propelled forward, blasting through the violence of the storm with a resounding crack, joining the rumbling echo in the canyon like the firestorm of battle.

The white horse jerked as the bullet struck his head. Johnny fired again and Traveller lay still. The rain fell on the white animal, mixing with the blood from his mortal head wound and washing down the face of the boulder.

With an anguished cry, Johnny drew back his arm and hurled the rifle down the ravine, his head dropping into the mud and the rock, his shoulders heaving with great sobs.

On his knees now, Jess grabbed Johnny's gunbelt, then dug his heels into the rock and pulled Johnny's chest and arms off the grade and up onto the trail. Exhausted, he fell on the limp form of his friend with an arm around his shoulders and his head next to Johnny's.

Unmoving, they remained inert while the wind and rain pelted them, until the only light left in the fearsome sky slashed vertically and horizontally through the rolling clouds. In moments the rain changed to ice, pelting them from above.

Jess forced himself to stand, tugged at Johnny's coat, then staggered alone toward the rock wall. Johnny drew up on his hands and knees at the edge of the ravine, trying to get his feet under him. The lightning lit the sky, and Jess moved his hands along the rock wall, searching for any recess that might provide shelter. Finding an overhang, he yelled for Johnny to follow, but the hammering of the stinging hailstones drove his cries away.

A low rumble shook the mountain and Jess ducked, crouching under the rock shelter as rock began to slide from above. It rained down on Johnny, and he covered his head with his arms to shield himself.

"Johnny!" screamed Jess, "The wall! Come toward me, it's a slide!"

It came in an avalanche, the force of the rock pushing Johnny over the edge onto the steep grade, downward toward the ravine. He forced his legs forward and bent his knees, grasping at the rock in a vain attempt to slow his descent, but the crushing rock propelled him onward, into the choking mayhem. A blinding white bolt of lightning lit the sky causing Johnny to turn his head away, and through the dust and debris he came face to face with the bloody mass of Traveller's head, hanging lifelessly over the edge of the boulder. He grabbed desperately for Traveller's bridle and his right hand caught the bit and slid down the leather rein. He flung himself on his side and grabbed the leather with both hands, struggling to wind it around his wrists.

Holding the leather fiercely, the force of the descending rock strained his shoulders and arm muscles until he thought he would tear apart. As the tonnage of rock began to fill the space under the boulder, it carried his body along. He clung to the rein wrapped around his wrists. The weight of the dead horse, the length of the rein, and the strength of his arms stopped his descent. Dust and rock particles clogged his nose and mouth. He choked and spat, coughing and gagging on the debris. Digging hard with his heels, then freeing one hand, he grasped a hand- hold beneath the rock and fought his way under the overhang, digging in and pulling with one boot and pushing against the slide with the other. Still clinging to the rein with his right hand,

his left foot caught in a small crevasse and he was able to drag himself onto the ledge of a lower boulder. Rising to his knees, he crouched in the small space with his back against jagged rocks and rewarapped his wrists with the rein. The roar became increasingly intolerable as the slide rained down around the boulder.

He held fast to the lifeline of the rein connected to the dead horse immediately above him. Pulling his bandana from around his neck, he covered his nose and mouth. His chest ached with his effort to breathe. Closing his eyes to keep out the debris, he lost perspective and seemed to be tumbling through a black void. The terrifying sensation forced him to reopen his eyes, and he tried to steady himself. Flashes of light illuminated the rocks beneath his feet and in despair, he watched the falling rock rise like the tide, encroaching into the space under the overhang.

Crushing weight, like a vice, pressed against his legs and rose to his thighs. There was little air as he crouched there and no room to back up. The leather strap binding both wrists mercilessly began to drag him forward. He released his grip on the rein, frantically trying to untwist the leather from his wrists and fighting the fierce drag. The strap cut into his flesh, tearing skin away as it pulled his hands downward. With heels jammed into a fissure in the rock, he leaned back, fighting the drag and pressing hard against the jagged rock behind him. As he resisted the pull forward, the stressed muscles in his thighs and arms sent fire shooting through inflamed nerves.

Suddenly, the leather rein snapped, flinging his shoulders back against the rock. His head whiplashed, striking a jagged rock. A flash of white light shot from behind his eyes as searing pain coursed through his head. He covered his head with his arms.

"Jess!" He gasped. "I can't...!"

Entombed in cold, eternal darkness, he called out in desperation. "This is death! Oh God, this is hell! Before the black void swallowed him completely, he cried out to Jesus.

14

THE MIRROR

North Carolina, Outer Banks
August, 1859

DEAFENING ROAR, TUMULTUOUS spinning, and young Johnny's small body slammed hard upon the sandy depths; shells tearing away flesh, and ingesting great gulps of water. Now forced to the surface, eyes stinging, mouth open, lungs sucking at air, then water and salt. Dragged back under, tossed, somersaulting wildly, foam and bubbles, and stinging spray, senses assaulted in the terrible roar.

Hands raised overhead and arms pulling hard, forward; legs aching, burning, kicking harder, sucked backward, then bright white glare, forced underneath again, a massive crush to the hard sand of the bottom, then, tumbling once more.

"Johnny, Johnny! Take my hand! Over here, Johnny!"

Strong hands grip his hair, pulling hard, then grasping his skinny forearm, tugging, dragging the child through the waves and onto the sand. Coughing, sputtering, until legs meet the sky, held by those same hands, pounding, pounding; then laid across a knee, more pounding, hard, against bare skin. Thump, thump, until water pours from his mouth, salty and acidic, coughing and vomiting.

"Johnny, Johnny! Open your eyes! Look at me!"

His eyes fluttered, opening to the brilliant white light and were forced to close from grit and pain. Shaking, shuddering, and shivering, he was laid upon the cool, wet sand.

"He's breathing, Joe, you are gonna kill him! Stop pounding him!"

Marcus grabbed Joe's arm and pushed him backward. Joe McLane was up in an instant, kneeling beside Johnny as Marcus rolled the boy onto his side.

Johnny stirred, trying to speak. "Ohhhh," he moaned. "I can't..." He coughed violently, expectorating water and mucus.

Joe stood and picked Johnny up, cradling him in his arms. He ran with him toward the dune, over the white sand, through the tall sea oats and grasses, following the sandy path toward their camp which lay tucked in a pine thicket away from pounding surf and incessant wind.

Marcus ran ahead and grabbed a blanket he found carelessly tossed over the stump of a pine, shook the sand from it, and laid it on the ground. Joe placed Johnny on the blanket, and crouching next to him, took another small blanket and roughly massaged Johnny's chilled body.

The fire had gone to ashes, so Marcus rekindled it. The orange flame lept to life, warming the chilly, early evening air. Joe raised Johnny's head and gave him a sip of water from a canteen. Pouring water onto the corner of the small blanket, he rubbed the dried salt and sand from Johnny's face, arms, and legs.

"Oww, Joey! That hurts...stop!" Johnny cried weakly, attempting to push his brother's hands away.

"Stupid little kid, you could have died! Why were you still out there? You knew the tide was comin' in! You're just lucky I turned around when I did!" Joe gave Johnny an angry shake.

"I didn't see it," Johnny answered with a stubborn sob, knowing his defense was simple and poor at best.

"Oh, so you couldn't see that the sand bar had started to cover with water? You stood right there and never felt those waves lickin' at your ankles! Guess you didn't know how far it was to shore either, ya little fool!"

Marcus came and plopped down on the blanket alongside of Johnny, sitting crossed legged. Joe continued to rail at the boy.

"You should know the ways of the ocean by now! It's dangerous and unpredictable, you got to keep your eyes open! You watch the waves, know what time of day it is. Everything has a rhythm, Johnny, a time. It's not stormy, you know better, and there is no excuse!"

Joe stared at Johnny, becoming aware of the mess that he was. Scratches and red, patchy scrapes marred his young face, his brow, and chest, contrasting with the dark tone of his tanned skin.

"I don't know what in blazes possessed me to even think of bringing you here!" Joe snapped.

The light in Johnny's eyes clouded as the contention and look of wounded pride became one of remorse. Joe saw tears form in the reddened rims, but they did not slip down Johnny's cheeks as the boy turned his gaze away.

Rising from a crouch, Joe sighed deeply and settled next to Johnny. With his arms across his raised knees, Joe lowered his forehead upon them, and stared down at the sand.

'This is all my fault. I promised I'd watch him, take care of him, keep him safe,' he thought silently. The full knowledge of what could have happened, what their lives would have become had it happened and the weight of responsibility for the boy settled heavily on his heart.

It had been a pure chore convincing Mama to agree that ten-year-old Johnny should accompany Joe and Marcus to the wild oceanic coast of the islands off northeastern North Carolina. Joe, like Papa, was an adventurous man, pushing the boundaries of the world he knew from Southampton County, Virginia, to more distant places.

Rivers, islands, and wilderness drew him like a magnet. Papa knew Joe's heart, knew the love the brothers shared for one another, and was glad for it. He trusted Joe, and after a long walk under a full, bright summer's moon, Papa had convinced Julia McLane to allow her youngest child the adventure of his life. Julia had always been fearful of water and did not swim, so the idea of Johnny near the ocean terrified her.

"Boys must become men, Julia dear, and how better to teach the unpredictability of life and nature than this?" John Robert had said, trumping her objections with his masculine logic.

She had never given her approval, just did not deny it, and held her fears in her mother's heart. But Joe had seen the look in her eyes the morning they had left and felt guilty until Johnny, bursting onto the scene in the ecstasy of anticipation, had driven those doubts away. He would show Johnny everything, and teach him all he knew about survival. Joe knew Johnny had always idolized him and would be no problem at all.

Joe's mind drifted back in time and he wondered what Papa would say if he had known all the risks Johnny had been subjected to on Joe's behalf. The boy was quick, agile, and compliant. For the past year Joe had Johnny exercising his thoroughbred throughout the countryside in Southampton County, challenging Joe's friends and their fastest mounts in pick- up races along the dirt roads, and through the fields, and swamp lands. Johnny was a natural horseman, light and fearless, even beyond the point of good sense.

Joe had also introduced his brother to his experimentation with plum wine quite by accident, mostly due to the fact that Johnny had followed him unbeknownst one Saturday. Shotguns and large Bowie knives had been Joe's training tools. So if Mama ever knew the reckless things to which he'd exposed Johnny, she would have had a fit.

This afternoon had been an eye-opener, and Joe realized that his influence on Johnny was more powerful than the boy's ability to recognize the consequences inherent in his involvement in Joe's escapades. Joe and Marcus had been cleaning fish on the beach, throwing the fish heads into the air and laughing as the seagulls dove for them, talking about the usual: classes they took at the College of William and Mary, fair maidens, secession and looming war. The boys did not see eye-to-eye on the last two issues, which always made for lively debate. Joe had not noticed the turn of the tide and had forgotten his brother who searched for shells and shark teeth on a sandbar built up by the mighty force of the ocean nearly twenty-five feet offshore.

'I am eighteen, he is ten...my fault.'

Marcus' voice cut through Joe's silent castigations. Seated on the child's opposite side, Marcus attempted to lighten the moment. Johnny moved stiffly, sitting up between the two young men. The blue bruise on Johnny's cheekbone was difficult to discern due to his sun-browned skin. The knot it had produced was not.

"Good thing the sun has turned you into a towhead or we'd be in danger of our lives, accused of harboring a runaway darky! The sun's got you lookin' like a brown berry. Your mama won't recognize you or claim you for that matter!" Marcus said, giving Johnny a knuckle rub on the top of his sun-bleached, blond head.

"Ouch," Johnny cried, but the corners of his mouth turned upward at Marcus' laughing face.

Marcus leapt up and ran over the dune for the beach, hollering back over his shoulder at the two remaining on the blanket.

"I'm gonna get those fish before the seagulls steal our supper! Keep that fire goin'!"

Joe moved closer and draped an arm around Johnny's shoulders. Johnny grabbed Joe's large hand with his small one which was swallowed in the grip of his hero.

"Sorry, Joey." Johnny tilted his face upward, meeting his big brother's gaze.

"Me too, bud. I should have watched you better."

They sat still, watching the sunset to the west and Joe began his tall tales--tales of Lewis and Clark, the Louisiana Purchase, and the great expanse of land to the west called the Frontier. Joe aimed to go to that distant land to practice law on the prairie as soon as he finished his schooling. One day he intended to become a famous judge.

"You'll send for me, won't ya?" Johnny asked.

"Sure, I'll need a good assistant. You can do research for me and together we'll tame the frontier."

After Joe explained what "research" would entail, they fell silent, just watching purple fall like a curtain upon the western sky. Johnny loved to hear the stories, never tiring of them as long as Joe's lively imagination spun fact and fiction into a far-off place, filled with incredible people and events. Joe pointed to the low-flying geese, honking as they moved into the marshes to settle for the night.

"You know, Johnny, it's true. I mean about the rhythm of life. Just like the waves have a rhythm, God created times and seasons. All the heavens tell the glory of God and the firmament proclaims his handiwork. Day to day pours forth speech and night to night declares his knowledge. Everything points to Him."

(Psalm 19)

Johnny murmured sleepily, "Did Papa tell you that, Joey?"

"Yeah...well not exactly. God told it to Papa in the Word, in the Psalms, then Papa told me." Joe looked down at Johnny who was fast falling asleep with his head resting against Joe's chest.

"We can go there...out west... together, right Joey?" Johnny murmured, almost imperceptibly. Joe eased him down onto the blanket and covered him. He kissed the sleeping boy's forehead.

"We'll go there together...I promise. I love you, buddy."

Cassie sensed, or had she actually heard and felt the low rumble from the mountains to the west? The groan and quake of the earth seemed to be borne on the wind as it tore across the plain, slamming the barn, filling her with awe and dread. She gripped the barn door to hold herself steady against the wind and hail which stung her face and pelted her body. She scanned the western range and cried to the skies.

"Oh, God, You can't be as cruel as to take them in this! You are mighty and they are nothing before You. We are but dust and ashes!"

The words of Job assaulted her memory. 'We live on the earth in days of misery and fear and they fly by like a weaver's shuttle without a pattern! How are we to comprehend so terrible a thing?' Job's lament preceded her own as her fears increased with the storm, and she raised her burdens heavenward.

"I can't rest! I can't make sense of this! I am full of anxiety, tossed and turned; this day seems so very long. I am frightened with visions, terrified of things I don't understand. You overturn the mountains, and move them in Your anger. What have we done? Have we displeased You?" She sobbed. "If my ways and thoughts have displeased You, God, then I will change! Just don't... please don't!"

(Job 7)

Hardly daring, yet driven to boldness by fears, she remembered and proclaimed the ancient words toward the darkened sky.

"Who are we that You should set Your mind on us? That You test us all of the time? I try to do Your will, I try to serve and love. But what have I done? I am suddenly fearful...please, God, please rescue us! Give us safety, give us hope, oh, give us a future! God, let him live! Bring them home, make me brave, help me, Lord...help us!"

(Job 14; James 1:5)

His eyes opened, not to darkness but to cold, gray light. The wind whipped upward, commanding his body to functions he could not think to perform. His nostrils flared and he inhaled deeply, coughing violently, expectorating dirt and mucus through his mouth and nose. He choked and gagged again and again until exhausted, fell back against the jagged rock wall with his lungs inflamed and tight. But as oxygen filled his lungs, his mind began to clear; kinetic energy moved his arms and legs, and reality returned slowly.

Light and wind ballooned through a narrow passage just yards below his feet. He tried to focus but his eyes burned and watered from grit. Dizzy and wracked with pain, he inched off the small boulder beneath the huge rock overhang, pushing with his feet. Digging at rock until his hands bloodied, he entered into the cold world and blinding light of the silent mountains.

Sensing the need to move away from the boulder but lacking a sense of direction, he took a few unsteady steps and collapsed upon the scrabble, blinking until his eyes adjusted and he could focus. The sky was motionless, and the white of the sun shone down, blinding him with its intensity.

The sun was directly overhead, but he could not remember the significance of this. Abstract thoughts gathered themselves but took no form. He looked senselessly about him, conscious that something was lacking. Reaching out, he groped at the pebbles and rock-strewn surface around him, unsure of why or for what he sought. Mercifully, his eyes closed and his desire faded to nothing.

The moaning of the wind through rock roused him again, and he struggled to sit up. In the sunlight his shadow lay before him, short and wide, and he remembered. 'Midday...I must move on.'

Although his eyes watered continually, his sight began to clear. He took in more of his surroundings. The mountain loomed to his left, and the rocky terrain descended gradually to his right.

With a rasping whisper, he called out for Jess. "I have to find him. I'll get Traveller and we'll go."

He tried to stand and coming up on one knee, looked around desperately--nothing but the silence of boulders and an ocean of rock, rising like a wave against the base of the sharp mountain. Remembering, he clutched the sides of his head, trying to obliterate the memory, but the visions came relentlessly. "Oh no, Traveller...oh, God, no!"

Wracked with sobs and in anguish, he dragged himself forward, desperate to leave the horror. Moving upward, only to lose ground on the loose rock, he was overcome by exhaustion and collapsed into oblivion.

Hunger gripped his belly, and he awakened with a parched tongue. Searching the deep pockets of his coat, he recovered two strips of jerky. Consumption of half of a gritty piece increased his thirst, and he drew his knife from the sheath on his hip and chipped weakly at the ice that had formed in the divots of a worn boulder. He sucked on it until it dissolved. As the sun began its slow, systematic descent, he began his faltering, wretched struggle upward.

He tried to close his mind to every fearful thought and to the pain then prayed to God to find Jess. The wounds on his wrists, head, and hands stung and throbbed. The cold and the pain labored his breathing, stealing away the remnants of his energy.

When he tried to rest his eyes, the vivid images were worse. He remembered the white horse upon the boulders, the bullet splattering blood and shattering bone, then Jess above him disappearing from sight as rocks rained down.

He struggled to stand, as if the action could remove him from the prison of hurt, but he collapsed in agony. He willed himself forward again, crawling and moving tortoise-like along the rocks, slowly, methodically, upward. The dusk drew the light from the mountains and Johnny strained to see ahead. He caught movement in the rocks about fifty feet distant and stopped abruptly.

Weakened prey, defending instinctively against bear or wolf, he reflexively felt for the handle of his knife. Withdrawing it, he gripped the cold metal and his hand cramped, then froze with a spasm. He dropped the knife, watching as the shadowy figure moved, concealed partially by a boulder. The cramp lessened, and he reached stiffly to retrieve the knife.

A hand appeared atop the distant rock, slipped back and reappeared. Johnny called out hoarsely, but the hacking cough vengefully returned. A man's head appeared alongside the hand.

"Johnny! My God! Is that you?" The man struggled to right himself.

Johnny rose and stumbled toward Jess, adrenaline quickening his pace.

"I'm here! Over here!" Jess cried. Johnny staggered to the rock and slumped to his knees beside Jess.

"I can't believe you're here! How did you get out?" Jess held the ragged shoulder of Johnny's coat with one fist.

Breathless, Johnny couldn't speak and stared at Jess through glazed eyes.

"How did you get out of that slide?" Jess repeated, amazed. "Saw you go down... thought you were dead," he gasped. Jess gripped Johnny's shoulder, squeezing firmly and staring into the face of his friend.

"Do I look as bad as you?" Jess choked with emotion, still holding firm to assure himself of the reality of the miracle.

Johnny nodded and eased down next to Jess, leaning against the boulder.

"Hard to breathe," he panted, "I think...." but a coughing fit seized him. He slumped, angled against the rock, and Jess saw the blood tinged sputum on Johnny's ragged coat sleeve.

"Those rocks got you good." Jess shook his head to clear his thoughts. "I can't believe we're alive!"

Johnny's whisper was barely audible. "Are we?"

His chest heaved as he struggled for air. He stared at Jess' swollen leg and croaked, "You walk?"

"Don't try to talk; I'll talk, you nod."

Jess continued, "I can't walk on it, I know it's broken, and it hurts like fire. I think my boot is splinting the bone. My right arm is broken also. I can't move it and my hand's gone numb. Got nothing for a splint, but I have some jerky in my pocket...my knife, gun and ammunition. You?"

Johnny's eyes were closed. Wordlessly, he produced his jerky and fumbled for his knife. Jess took note of his holstered gun, but it was Johnny's ghostly pale face and blue-tinged lips that concerned Jess the most. Although they had escaped the rockslide, Jess knew they might both be facing a slow, agonizing death. They needed to get out of the pass and up over the next ridge. If they couldn't, there was little hope that they could be seen, and less that they would be rescued.

Johnny fell motionless, so still that Jess placed his hand to Johnny's neck to check for a pulse. Johnny's eyes flickered, then opened and he struggled to sit. Johnny removed his suspenders with great difficulty as Jess watched. He unsheathed his knife and handed it to Jess, crawling carefully around Jess' injured leg. Exhausted from the effort, he rested against the rock for a moment, then took the knife, slitting Jess' coat sleeve and shirt, examining his deformed forearm.

Though bluish purple and swollen tight, the skin was not broken. Johnny lay the long blade of his knife flat against the underside of Jess' forearm. Clenching his jaw and gritting his teeth, Jess sweated in the cold as he helped hold the knife in place. Johnny wrapped his suspenders firmly along the length of the knife, binding it as a splint to the arm.

Fumbling awkwardly, Johnny cut and tore Jess' shirt sleeves into strips, using them to secure the metal and suspenders in place along the arm, and tying the last remaining cloth strip over the replaced coat sleeve to cover the splint as best he could. He collapsed against the rock and struggled to breathe.

"Let's get out of here, we're headed east," Jess said weakly, but neither moved and they lay still, blanketed in the twilight.

As the ravine grew dim, Johnny struggled to his feet, took a step and staggered, catching himself against a boulder. With a groan, he extended his hand to Jess who also managed to stand with the help of the boulder. Johnny silently helped to bear Jess' weight as they moved forward. They were forced to stop and rest every few feet to relieve the strain of aching muscles and shooting pains. The night closed in, the stars and the full moon filled the sky. Resting only briefly, they inched forward keeping the light of the North Star to their left. At the moon's zenith, they rested. Jess ate jerky and sucked on ice chips, feeding the chips to Johnny, who ate little, then fell into a restless sleep.

The screech of a falcon awakened Jess to aching cold as the first gray streaks of dawn appeared over the ridge before them. He propped himself up with his left arm. His head swam, and he fought nausea as pain from his broken extremities shot through his body. When the sensation abated, he turned to look at Johnny.

Propped against a rock, Johnny's face was ashen and beaded with sweat, retaining its bluish cast. Jess prodded Johnny's boot with his good leg.

"Johnny, wake up, we got to move on." He kept prodding and kicking until Johnny opened his eyes.

"I can't, Jess," he answered through clattering teeth. Trembling violently, he coughed and was unable to rise.

"You gotta," Jess implored. "I can't walk without you and I am not leavin' you; now, come on!" He kicked Johnny's boot again. "Come on, son, don't give up. Get up!"

"Come on Johnny!" Jess pleaded again, "Help me out now!" Johnny's face portrayed no line of response. Desperate, Jess tried a lyric, delivering the well-known tune weakly;

> "...the ole log raked the boat aft and fo'...
> I thought it wouldn't do for to give it up so...
> 'It'll never do to gib it up so, Mr. Brown...
> it will never do to give it up so!'"

> (*T'will Neber Do Gib It Up So*, 1843,
> Minstrel River Song, Daniel Emmett)

"Come on, John Scott, help me out here. Think of all those pretty lil' gals just waitin' on us. Come on..." but the pain leached away his efforts and he lay next to Johnny, nudging him sporadically with his boot.

After a long moment, Johnny roused and struggled to his feet. The hours wore away as they progressed, arm to arm, shoulder to shoulder, resting when one or the other could not bear up. With less than forty yards remaining to the crest of the ridge, Johnny collapsed.

Jess implored him to continue, pulling and tugging feebly. When he could not rouse him further, he left Johnny, barely breathing and propped against a boulder, and pulled himself upward to the top of the ridge.

Spilling out from the base of the high ridge, the flats below him rolled off into the distance. With the last of his strength, Jess drew Johnny's Colt from the gunbelt he had taken from his friend and fired three deliberate shots into the air, then collapsed against a boulder and crumpled onto the rocky surface. Moments later, he emptied the chamber, firing another three shots rapidly into the cold, clear-blue sky.

The creak of the rocker halted abruptly at the same time both front legs of the cane-backed, pine chair plunked down upon the front porch boards of the old cabin.

"You hear that?" Jeremiah Rudd spoke around the pipe he held clenched between his sparse teeth.

"I did." Lycurgus straightened and placed the iron ore he had been examining onto the porch railing, then turned toward the direction of the distant shots. He tugged at the length of his ancient beard.

"Three shots; mebbe trouble-an' from the same direction of that devil quake two nights hence. I lay you odds on it. Let's take a look see."

"I'm 'a put the fire out, you fetch the mules and wagon, some water n' blankets, Curk," Jeremiah mumbled. "I'll meet ya by th' barn."

Twenty minutes later the brothers left the cabin yard, heading out of the valley toward the ridge to the southwest. Traces jangled and dried boards creaked as the dilapidated wagon drawn by the sure-footed mule team, moved upward along the rocky, rutted trail.

Jess kept his eyes fixed on the plains below, straining for any sign of a horseman. He reloaded the revolver, ready to fire another signal if necessary. Over the western edge of the ridge, he could see Johnny lying dormant, and strained his eyes for any movement or change in his position. He prayed to God that someone would find them and that he and Johnny would still be alive at the end of this interminable day. Jess had not consumed more than the last strip of jerky and a trace of water for some hours, and he knew Johnny had none.

At first he had been able to hear Johnny's wracking cough, but the deputy had been still for some time now. Jess thought about his own life, about Sodie, and about what he would give just to see her again.

"Please, God, don't let me die before I even get another chance to tell her I love her." Everything else that had mattered before seemed like a pittance in the face of this desolation.

He thought about Johnny and thought it miraculous that they had found each other after the nightmare of wind, rock, and hail. He remembered that the end of the 'age' was supposed to be similar, being so horrific in that day, that people would beg mountains to fall upon them. Jess never wanted to live through horror like this again.

"We're laid out here with nothin', on a ridge, stretched out like an offerin' before you, God. Like some kind of sacrifice. I am not worthy to be any kind of sacrifice," he lamented to the winds, and turned his gaze on his friend.

"What about him, God? He is a good man, still a kid, really, but in his life he lost all he's ever had. Don't let us die before we get a chance to live! If you're there, God, have mercy," he pleaded, and groaned with the pain of his shattered limbs.

From a distance, the crack of a rifle split the silence, and he turned his head to the east to squint at the horizon. A brown dot moved in the distance on the prairie below, coming toward the ridge. Jess reloaded and fired three shots into the sky. A rifle answered the echo of his signal. He yelled back over his shoulder and down the slope of the ridge.

"Johnny! They found us, someone knows we're up here!"

Johnny did not hear Jess. As his chest rose heavily, each inhaled, burning breath and the sharp pain in his head brought only the roar of the falling rock. Over and over again, it pounded his senses, becoming the rage of the wild ocean, sucking away life and breath. The visions returned, horrific and violent. A beautiful silver-gray horse, powerful muscles straining, strong legs pulling, digging hard against the sliding rock in a vain attempt to save them both.

"Traveller, Traveller," he whispered. Though the sun shone hard upon him, he shook with wracking chills. "Oh, God, help me...help me, or let me die."

Over the roar of rock and ocean, in a strange paradox, a soft voice called distinctly.

"Johnny." He tried to lift his head, to listen, to catch the voice again, but he could not. Then it came again, faintly. "Johnny...Johnny...take my hand."

'Joe?' His thoughts churned, and colors whirled like pinwheels behind his eyes. "Joey?" he whispered faintly. His head pounded as he strained to hear, then hopelessly, he closed his eyes.

"Johnny."

The voice came again, distant and persistent, but he lacked the ability to search for the source. Slowly and persistently, words rose in his confusion... refuge...strength...time of trouble...though mountains tremble...seas roar... we will not fear.... though the earth should change. I Am...a very present help. I Am.

(Psalm 45, Psalm 46)

15

THE ADVOCATE

THE SMELL OF soap and fresh linen was a welcome relief to Talitha.

"Yes, Mrs. Cullins, I can do all the sheets today. What happened over there?"

"Doc has been busy, Maldonado...with surgery and the like. Talitha Cullins lay her weary hands on the counter.

"Be sure to use good, strong lye soap. I want the stains out as much as possible."

"Si, Senora." The young Mexican tipped his head respectfully, acknowledging the large framed, rosy-cheeked woman.

"Doc and I'll be needing them back directly."

"Oh, si, Senora, es posible," he agreed, lapsing into his native tongue and smiling. Taking the large basket, he disappeared behind the curtain in his small laundry, situated at the edge of town along a low bank on the Laramie River.

Jess Bryant's surgery had taken a long time, but Doc had successfully repaired the tendon and set the bone in his left leg, carefully cleaning the area while the ether did its magic. Jess' arm had been reset and infection might yet be a problem, but that remained to be seen.

Johnny McLane was another matter. Deep in thought, Talitha pulled the buggy up to the surgery, disembarked and paused beside the door to straighten Doc's shingle before entering the small office.

"How is Jess Bryant this morning, Doc? The wounds looking better?"

"Red and oozing, but for the most part, alright. He is ornery enough to live, I think--young and strong, which accounts for a lot."

Talitha's eyes clouded, and she cocked her graying head slightly in the direction of the hotel. "And Johnny?"

Doc shrugged tiredly. "Alright for now. Left him there with Sam just long enough to come check on Jess, but I'll be needing to get back over to the hotel. Marshal's got work to do." Clarence Cullins sighed deeply. "Jess believes that the captives lost their lives in the accident. We would be hard pressed to do for those two as well. What I wouldn't do for a hospital, Tilly. We are so far removed from everything, and I could use more space, better equipment, and another good man."

He looked around and shook his head. "I'll be going now. You come as soon as you settle Jess. One of us needs to stay with the deputy."

"Yes. Every time his fever breaks, he's drenched in sweat. Then it spikes again. It cycled like that all night," Talitha replied, wiping her eyes wearily.

"You need some sleep. Won't do if you get down, m' love." Doc squeezed her arm and left.

Entering the rear door of the hotel, Doc climbed the backstairs leading to the second-floor landing, slowing at the first room to the right. As he entered the bright room, Sam Brett looked up.

"Glad you are back," he commented flatly. "He's restless and doesn't seem to know where he is. Sometimes he doesn't seem to be breathing at all. When he does breathe, it's a sickening, sucking sound--like he's pulling air through a straw."

Sam sat on a chair at the bedside, his hand resting on Johnny's shoulder. Doc had never seen either of them look worse.

"He is, sort of, Sam. His lungs are full of mucus, dirt, and dust from the rockslide. It causes the bronchial tubes to swell inside, and it narrows the passage for air exchange. Usually those tubes are like the trunk of a hollow tree but they're now, like you say, as narrow as a straw."

Doc walked to the opposite side of the bed and felt the pulse at Johnny's wrist. "Heart's beating rapidly; that's probably due to the fever. I turn him every now and again, pound on his back and some of that mucus gets released. He gets laudanum for his muscle spasms--the result of straining to lift all that rock to get free. Mrs. Cullins has been giving him sips of white willow bark tea when he arouses. It seems to relieve the internal swelling, as does the salicylic acid. I think that should bring down the fever also. But he's a mess, Sam, you need to know that. We'll try to get the fever down, ice will help, but I don't know. Respiratory issues are a real problem. He is young, which is in his favor, but I don't know if he even fully recovered from that illness he caught up on the mountain a couple of weeks ago. He has lost some weight and that's not good. Gotta have something to fight with."

Sam Brett did not speak. Doc dipped a cloth in the cool water and busied himself with trying to cool down Johnny's fevered body.

"Thanks for what you are doing, Doc. I'll be back later." Sam Brett wiped his forearm across his brow and stood, took up his hat and coat, then quickly left the room.

Doc continued bathing Johnny with cool water, talking quietly to him and assessing his respirations. He reflected on his own life.

'If this boy was my son,' he thought tiredly, 'I'd send him as far away from this place as I could. Maybe to study law in New England. Some place civilized, some place where a man can walk the streets and not be afraid for his life-- where mountains don't fall on people, and there are real hospitals for the sick.'

He placed a hand on Johnny's hot arm. He prayed for God to give him the ability to keep the young man alive and recall what he knew about pneumonia and consumption.

Cleaning wounds, stitching gashes, setting broken bones and delivering babies--those were the ordinary, everyday things he felt comfortable treating. Measles, mumps, and chickenpox, even cholera could be seen outwardly and dealt with.

It was the internal things, those things that lay hidden, that bothered him the most. The things that may or may not display symptoms, and could take a life before it was too late to do anything. There was not much on Johnny's body that was not affected by the crushing weight of falling rock. Bruises outside likely meant bruising inside. Doc hoped there was no internal bleeding.

He passed his hands along Johnny's extremities, wondering what might be fractured under the purple welts. Expertly, he moved them slowly along either side of Johnny's rib cage. Doc closed his eyes to focus on the anatomy, visualizing it with his mind's eye as it would appear on the pages of his medical text. He continued the examination laterally over the hip and pelvic bones assessing for any differences. He felt the firmness of the bladder and he knew that the semiconscious boy would need his immediate help to keep the bladder from rupturing.

He stood, walked to the dresser and opened his medical bag, taking from it a black, narrow, rectangular box and unlatching the minute hook, lifted the lid. The rigid silver catheter gleamed against the black velvet lining. He lifted it from the box, checking the wax tip to make sure it was intact. He hoped that Talitha would soon be coming. He would need someone to help hold the boy steady.

That afternoon Talitha sat with Johnny, bathing him with cold water much as Doc had done throughout the morning, changing his clothing and sheets frequently as the fever broke and drenched him in sweat, then climbed dangerously again. When the spasms clinched his muscles and he involuntarily stiffened, Talitha massaged his arms and legs.

Doc attended to Jess, encouraging him to rest which was not a problem as the ether was slow to leave his lungs and the laudanum furthered his drowsy state. Between the waking and sleeping Jess found his voice. Having overheard the marshal and Doc talking, Jess motioned Doc to his side.

"Go get the girl," Jess murmured hoarsely.

"What's that?" Doc bent closer, smelling the remains of the ether on his breath. "Say again?"

"You and the marshal say Johnny's not good...get the girl, it will help him if you do." Jess groaned and lifted his head. "She is the only thing he truly loves, other than...that horse of his." Jess moaned, retched, and vomited.

Doc Cullins injected him with morphine and he slept again. Considering Jess' comment, Doc wondered if it was precipitated by confusion and the result of anesthesia and medication. "Get the girl". It seemed an odd request. Jess must be referring to Myra Davis. But surely Myra had heard of the accident by now and would come of her own accord. Doc was not one to meddle much in the affairs of men's hearts. He had learned that lesson long ago.

"Please Mrs. Cullins, just for a moment. I promise I won't stay long; please just let me see him," Cassie entreated.

She had come early to town, before Miss Halstead opened her shop, on the pretense of helping Millie with an overdue synopsis for poetry class. Instead, she had run up the back steps of the hotel, skirts bunched in her hand.

Talitha Cullins faced the distraught girl whose sudden appearance, on the landing outside of the deputy's room, had taken her by complete surprise. Cloaked and bonneted, Cassie was flushed and out of breath.

"What are you doing here, Cassie?" Taking the girl's cold hands in her large warm ones, Talitha did not give Cassie a chance to repy. With an accusatory tone, she questioned her further.

"Why do you ask to see him? What reason could you possibly have for this? You must know I can't let you in there. He is very ill, and Doc would not approve."

Overhearing the monologue, Doc took the last two steps rapidly, reaching the landing. Cassie stood to the right of Talitha, her slender frame erect, contrasting sharply with Talitha's plump figure.

"I must see him, he...."

"Cassie," Talitha spoke firmly, "It's not proper. Why, I could not..."

Calmly, Doc interrupted. "It's all right Tilly, I'll see to this now." He stood between them and focused on Cassie. Talitha dropped Cassie's hands and stood with her own folded against her apron. Her face was etched with concern.

"Just why have you come here, Cassie? Why is this so important to you?" Doc asked gently. He studied her bright eyes which glistened with unshed tears.

"I must see him," Cassie repeated.

Doc was struck by the way she held herself. Unlike the girl he knew so well, she stood before him with an almost slight arrogance, her slender body a portrait of resolve. She managed to hold back the tears which had welled in her eyes again.

Doc considered her thoughtfully and continued. "I can relay a message to the deputy if you would like." Still studying her, he added intuitively, "Have you come here with your father's permission?"

"No, sir. You don't understand. I must see him," she repeated, trembling slightly, "...for myself." Cassie's auburn hair cascaded down her back, but copper tendrils had escaped from the sides of her bonnet and now curled loosely under the bonnet's brim.

Doc considered her for another moment, unsure of what to say and found it difficult to imagine why this young girl should have such need to see the deputy.

Cassie watched him intently. The blush of her cheeks and the bright searching of her eyes cued him, and it was then that he remembered.

"Get the girl," Jess had said, "the one he loves." Incredibly, the pieces began to fall in place. Could it be that Cassie was Johnny's girl?

Against his better judgment and more for Johnny's good than for Cassie's sake, Doc allowed Cassie's request. He brought her to Johnny's side with Talitha following closely behind them. He instructed Cassie to speak his name, to let him know she was there, but forbade her to touch him.

Cassie studied the face before her, flushed with fever and battered, contrasting markedly with the stark white pillow case. His eyes were closed. She tried to remember the depth of the blue-green, but lost the vision in the purple welts that marked his face. Scrapes and cuts in angles streaked his cheek, neck, and shoulders and, at times, he struggled to breathe. She called his name. His eyelids flickered, but did not open. His lips moved slightly, unintelligibly.

Tears slid down her cheeks, but she made no sound. Doc placed an arm at her waist and turned her gently.

"Let's let him sleep, Cassie. I think he knows you're here. It was both brave... and foolish of you to come."

Cassie freed herself from Doc's embrace, and bending close, whispered in Johnny's ear.

"Johnny, remember! 'He drew me up from the desolate pit, out of the miry bog and set my feet upon a rock, making my steps secure. He put a new song in my mouth, a song of praise to our God.' Remember Johnny, please, please, remember!" And very softly, Doc thought he heard her whisper, "I love you too."

She straightened and turned toward Doc and taking a ragged breath, dabbed her sleeve at her nose. Doc took her arm and escorted her to the doorway where Cassie glanced back over her shoulder. She could see that Talitha attended to Johnny now, then could see no more. Doc closed the door softly as he turned to face her.

(Psalm 40)

"He'll be alright, Doc, I know it." The depth of her hope and expectation shook Doc, who was ever aware of his many limitations in his "practice" of medicine, for practice was surely what he did. It weighed heavily on his shoulders.

"Cassie," Doc confessed, "only God knows, child. You can pray for him. I think you better give him a few days before attempting to see him again. Let his fever turn and we will see." Doc's kindly eyes met Cassie's. "One other thing, Cassie. Let your ma and pa know that you were here."

Cassie raised a stricken face, studied her clasped hands, but did not reply. Doc had seen that same tragic look many times before.

Lifting her gaze, she thanked him. "Thank you, sir. Thank you for taking care of him." She turned quickly, leaving as she had come.

Doc returned to Johnny's bedside. Talitha looked up and whispered urgently. "I can't imagine this!" Her eyes bored into Doc's. "She is a schoolgirl! Whatever made her come here? Even if she cares for him, even if she thinks she loves him, this is an awful place for a young girl to come! She should know better."

She waited for Doc to agree, and a frown creased her brow as her capable hands placed a cool cloth upon Johnny's forehead.

Doc studied her. Understanding of her concern etched his tired face. He nodded slowly.

"I can't begin to understand it. I guess love, whatever else it may be, takes courage. It is something you do...something you do for someone else."

Friday dawned cloudy and gray. Cassie moved through her day like a marionette whose strings were manipulated by monotonous routine. She displayed no creativity at the shop that morning and left Olivia Halsted wondering if the girl was coming down with an illness. By 3:00 p.m., Cassie stood up from her desk, shoving papers into her poetry book. The classroom had emptied out rapidly and only the two girls remained.

Millie Beale caught her by the arm as Cassie passed her desk. Millie's face twisted in a questioning grimace, her dark eyes flashing anger.

"Wait! Aren't you coming to supper and to spend the night? Did you forget? I thought friends shared things, Cassie, and that they didn't hide secrets from one another. You have been avoiding me! Something is wrong, don't try to deny it."

Cassie plunked the book she held down upon the desk and slipped into the chair behind Millie's. She stared silently at her friend and her eyes filled with tears. Millie's face softened, and she placed a hand on Cassie's forearm.

"Oh Cassie, is someone sick at your house? What? Tell me."

Cassie shook her head, "No, no one is sick at the house. I just have a lot on my mind, a lot to think through."

"Well, what? You've been acting queer for a month now. What could be so awful? The trouble in town?" Millie paused thoughtfully. "You're not unwell, are you?"

Cassie shook her head and wiped her eyes with her sleeve. "No, I'm alright. Listen, Millie, I can't talk about it now. I promise I will tell you soon, just not right now."

Millie studied her friend's worn face. "It must be pretty bad if you can't even share it with me. Is it..."

"Please don't ask, Millie, I can't say anything yet. Please believe me; you're my best friend! I will tell you as... well, as soon as I can."

Millie thought for a moment then cocked her head, tightening her lips. "This doesn't have to do with Beau Brenner does it?"

Cassie's stomach jumped, and heat surged through her. "What do you mean? Why do you say that?"

"Eric Flynn said that Beau asked you to the dance Saturday night and that you agreed to accompany him. Eric was angry and later, I heard Beau say that you would do anything he wanted you to do. Of course, I called him a liar, and told him that you would never in a million years agree to go with him. He is such a braggart! I am right, aren't I?" The confidence in her tone had changed to caution as her statement became a question.

A chill ran up Cassie's spine, and she trembled visibly, then reached up to straighten her thick braid, hoping to hide her reaction. "That's just ridiculous! You're right; you know I'd never go with him. In fact, I'm not going at all! Those dumb boys must sit around trying to think of ways to torment us!"

Cassie tried to laugh, but the effort fell flat.

Millie searched her with questioning eyes. "Maybe there won't be a dance. It doesn't seem right, anyway, with the trouble in town. Nothing seems right. Have you heard how the deputy and Mr. Bryant fare? No one seems to know exactly what happened. Certainly my pa doesn't; he says the marshal isn't saying much except that the prisoners were lost. Doc won't talk about it... guess he can't. Miss Davis is low, but I suppose that's to be expected also. I mean, the way she feels about the deputy and everything. It's so tragic, Cassie."

Cassie closed her eyes tightly and silently shot an arrow prayer toward heaven for strength and for God to take this from them.

She shook her head and said wearily, "I'll be at your house tonight, Millie. I need to deliver something for one of Miss Halsted's customers, then I will be over. Ma sent some sourdough bread and jam, and I'll bring it when I come. We'll talk...about the dance."

Cassie hugged Millie quickly and rushed out into the cold air taking in great gulps, hoping to quell the rising nausea. 'I can't speak of this, not now,' she thought desperately.

She had not noticed Myra Davis ascending the stairs, carrying a bag of clean blackboard erasers, and almost ran her teacher down. "Excuse me, Miss Davis, I..." but she did not finish.

One look at Cassie's face confirmed the suspicion Myra carried in her own heavy heart.

'It's true,' she thought, and could not respond to her student with more than a simple, "Are you alright?" The words rang hollow in her own ears, and she could not bring herself to care.

Cassie managed to choke out, "I think I just need some fresh air, good-night, Miss Davis." Hiking up her skirts, Cassie dodged Myra and ran down the stairs.

Myra watched Cassie untie Lady, mount, and ride off toward town. Alone at the top of the stairs, Myra's mind flashed back to another night which now seemed far removed, although it was not. Myra had been the one fleeing then, down those same stairs on that cold evening, running away from Johnny in anger, her pride wounded from the truth she had not wanted to face. Now jealous regrets pricked her heart.

'She is just a girl. How can this be?' With a sinking feeling, she knew that Cassie's flight, like her own that night, was compelled by the truth now confirmed. The girl loved the deputy who lay wounded, and it stung Myra's heart to know that Johnny loved Cassie in return.

Supper at Millie's was another draining affair, and Cassie endured it with strained civility sprinkled with false attempts at gaiety. As the Beales talked of the lawmens' accident and speculated on the ramifications of it, Cassie had to force herself to eat, each bite sticking in her throat, each sentence slicing at her heart.

"And that poor Jess Bryant, at least he's on the mend, I hear. If the deputy doesn't survive, Mr. Beale, do you think this town can tolerate having just one law officer?" Mrs. Beale's lovely mouth turned down at the corners.

"I met Almon Baird and Clancy Miller outside the Flour and Grain. They seem to know some of the particulars of the accident." Millie's father paused in thought, then continued. "Seems a lot of speculation as to what actually happened, but maybe Baird found out what can be known due to the fact he's a lawyer. That poor young deputy. He's been such an asset, but what a risky thing--taking prisoners over the mountain and not around it."

Cassie felt Millie's eyes upon her. Did she know? She seemed to sense Cassie's discomfort. Lightheaded, Cassie felt suspended in time, caught in a space that had nothing to do with the reality surrounding her. She was at the core of the horror, they were on the periphery, and no one except Doc suspected it.

She could stand no more talk. She excused herself from the table, asking permission to use the "necessary", with one thought in mind. 'I have to get to him.'

Moving quickly through the kitchen's backdoor, she sheltered for a moment under the cover of Mr. Beale's shed roof, leaning against the warmth of the blacksmith forge, but grateful for the cleansing chill of the night air.

She hated her next thoughts, but rationalized. 'I have no other recourse.'

Ten minutes later, she was on the street, supposedly headed in the direction of Mrs. Winkler's, feigning the need to deliver a message for Mabel Baker from her mother. It had been difficult to keep Millie from accompanying her, but Cassie's explanation of Mabel's ill health and frailty dissuaded her friend.

Mrs. Beale's fear of the impropriety of a young woman alone on the streets at twilight had been assuaged when Cassie stated confidently, "Please don't worry, I shall be right back, and it is not quite dark. I'll hurry."

As she rushed down the windy Main Street, she pleaded, "Please God, forgive me," and turned for the Sideling Hotel.

Cassie entered the quiet lobby and passed through the hallway to the back staircase. She ascended rapidly, surprised to find no one on the landing of the second floor. Tentatively, she approached the door to Johnny's room.

The door was pulled to but not shut. Silently, she froze, held her breath, and closed her eyes to listen. Hearing nothing except the hammering of her pulse in her ears, she hurried to the other end of the hallway, and peered out over the banister into the front lobby below. She did not see Doc or anyone else and jumped when a bearded, middle-aged man came up behind her.

"Please excuse me, miss," he said, passing to her left and descending the stairs.

"Where is everyone?" she whispered, immediate dread chilling her. "He's gone! They are all gone!" she cried softly, as she ran back to the room.

She placed a hand on the doorknob then hesitated, listening intently for any sound. The squeak of the bed frame and a deep raspy cough strengthened her resolve. Releasing the doorknob she tapped lightly upon the door. No one answered, but the door swung slightly open.

She took a step inside. From the left corner of the room a lamp glowed brightly, casting its light just to the bed. No one was about. Trepidation made her hesitate.

'Where was Doc? Why had they left Johnny alone?' Only silence met her anxious thoughts.

From the bed in the corner, Johnny took a great raspy breath, and quickly, Cassie crossed the room to his side. Lamplight from the dresser barely touched his face. His eyes were closed and sweat glistened on his feverish brow. She tried to take in every feature of his face, but her gaze was drawn to his bare chest, scraped, bruised and shining from the sweat of fever. His breathing came raggedly and he moaned, moving restlessly beneath the covering of the thin, white sheet at his waist.

Fear for him, disquieting anxiety, and guilt for having entered the room alone, unchaperoned, and without the permission Doc had required from her parents, set her on edge. Discomforted by the close atmosphere and unsettled in the thought that she looked upon him in an intimate, vulnerable state and he could not know it, alarmed her. The situation demanded that she should step away, but she was drawn to the bedside and could not make herself turn to leave. He was alone, and she must help him. Determined, she picked up the cloth on the edge of the washbasin and dipped it into the cold water.

The air in the room was very warm, and she found it difficult to concentrate. The scent of herbs and medicines, vaguely familiar but unnamed, filled her senses and cast her thoughts backward to a small room much like this one. Ma had held her hand as she stared down at her older brother's ashen face, so boyish and thin, framed in the depth of the large, white pillow. She had been thirteen, and it was the last time she had seen him alive.

"Oh, Robert," she moaned softly, remembering as the tears and memories clouded her senses. Reeling, she caught her breath and blinked, refocusing on the man before her.

"No, no!" Death could not call again to steal yet another whom she loved. She bunched up the cloth and pressing the water out with her fists, straightened and stepped closer. She called his name softly. He did not appear to hear but his lips moved, and he murmured words she couldn't quite comprehend.

Damp, tousled hair curled slightly at the temples above his flushed face. His features drew taut with the spasm of pain, then released into an unconscious expression. His helpless state whirled Cassie's heart in turmoil, touching her deeply and releasing the tears that welled in her eyes.

Restlessly, he raised his left arm, opened his hand to clutch at the air, and froze in pain. With his right arm he pushed the sheet away from his sweating body, arching his back and lifting his hips as another spasm hit his core.

Cassie froze in dismay, then involuntarily stepped backward. The flannel of his under drawers, soaked from sweat, clung to his form. She stared in awe, terrified and captivated, unable to move. As if to rid his body of fever, Johnny arched his back and slid his right hand from his chest down over his arched belly, trying to push away the offending, soaked garment.

Jolted to reality, Cassie willed herself to move, grabbing and tugging the sheet upward, covering his body as best she could. She did not flee, but with heart racing, grabbed up the cloth she had dropped on the floor, dipped it into the cool water, and willed herself to concentrate as she stroked his flushed face.

His eyes fluttered, opened briefly, and then closed again.

"Mary...an...Mary," he whispered. Cassie strained to hear him and watched as his lips formed the question, "Mary?"

"Johnny," she implored, "Johnny, it is Cassie...it's me, Johnny, I'm here. Please, Johnny, wake up! Please open your eyes."

His brow raised as he struggled to lift his eyelids, but he could not. "Cassie?" he whispered weakly, then slipped away.

"What on earth?!" exclaimed Talitha Cullins. She came through the doorway with a stack of fresh, folded sheets in her arms.

With a harsh whisper, she scolded sternly. "What are you doing in this room, young lady? This is no place for you! I left for a minute," she admonished, "and what do I find?"

Cassie turned to face her defiantly, "You should not have left him alone! He is so ill! No one was here and he was all alone! I looked for you and Doc, but no one was about and the door was open!" Cassie cried out. "I couldn't just leave him with no one to help!"

Talitha lay the sheets on a chair by the bed and stared hard at the young woman. "You know this is not proper, don't you, Cassie?" It was not a question and she continued, "A young girl in a sick room! You can see how ill he is and disturbing him will not help. Not only that, you know how people in this town talk. If folks knew you were here alone with this man, no matter what the circumstances, it would be shameful. What were you thinking? You cannot just come and go as you please. It is wrong and certainly won't do him any good!" Although Talitha had managed to control her tone, her eyes snapped furiously.

The frustrations and the frenzy of the last few moments snapped Cassie's emotions. She fled to the window and threw the sash upward. Whirling around, she raised her hands in despair.

"This room is all wrong, it is stuffy and dead! Johnny wouldn't like this! He likes the fresh air, he needs to be outside in the wind! He'll die in here, it's like a prison--like a cell!" Tears streamed down her anguished face. "He can't breathe!"

Talitha met Cassie at the foot of the bed and took her by the shoulders. "Cassie, listen to me," she commanded the sobbing girl. She took Cassie into her ample arms and Cassie could not control her anquish or tears. Talitha held her upright, stroking her hair, and softly whispering softly.

"There, there, child. He can breathe and we are caring for him. I know you are thinking of Robert. I understand, I do. This is not like before."

Talitha remembered Robert's death and spoke tenderly to the girl of that dark time. She knew well the horrors of accidents and illnesses which tore children from parents and parents from the lives of their progeny in this unforgiving land. It always broke her heart.

She held Cassie's tense body until it eased. "You mustn't fear, child. It will be alright."

She led Cassie to the chair at the head of the bedside, directing her to sit. She dipped the cloth into the cold water, pressing it to Cassie's forehead and handing it to her.

"Just a moment more. Rest and collect yourself, and then you must go."

She crossed the room, closing the window against the cold. Five minutes later, Cassie left Johnny's side.

Talitha's parting words stung at Cassie's heart.

"Remember what I said, Cassie. Remember for your sake as well as his. Doc and I will take care, good care of him. His fever has broken and may not return. I will make him comfortable. Pray for him, that's the best and most you can do. Time will tell, but it is dark now, and you must return to Millie's."

As Cassie left the room, she closed the door quietly behind her. She was spent. Her legs trembled, and she stopped to regain her strength, leaning against the wall outside of the room. She closed her eyes and haunting visions of Robert drifting away, diminishing until there was nothing left of him, filled her mind. Squeezing her eyes tightly shut to rid herself of that sorrowful time, she forced herself to breathe evenly, knowing she must compose herself and leave.

Unbidden, statues of the ancient Greeks as they had appeared in her textbooks moved slowly across her mind's eye: the Shepherd, the Hunter, the Warrior--all carved from fine marble, masculine and strong. She had never imagined they could be more than fanciful works of art and thought them only an artist's conception that would not ring true.

But she had been wrong. They were models of man, like the man she loved in the room she had just left. The thought pricked her senses, causing the numbness to flee as those visions brought about the strange, unfamiliar longings which increasingly welled up in her of late. She had witnessed truth tonight and now she knew for certain. Johnny was as the Bible described--a man formed and intricately wrought in the depths of the earth. A man knit together and wonderfully made by God.

(Psalm 139:15)

Later that night, Millie slept peacefully while Cassie found that sleep eluded her. She lay in the darkness long after the house and the streets of the town had quieted. Shadows in the room dispelled, except from the darkest corners, and moonlight glowed through the lace curtains, casting soft patterns like a spider's web upon the bed, lending fantasy to the night. Over and over again, visions of Johnny and Greek heroes carved from marble appeared, and the truths repeated and flooded her with anticipation. "Fearfully and wonderfully made...his fever has broken, pray for him...the most, the best you can do."

She gave thanks to God for Johnny's life and prayed that God would see him through. "Heal him Lord, sustain him."

She remembered a favorite Psalm. 'How precious to me are thy thoughts, oh God! How great is the sum of them! If I should count them, they are more in number than the sand: when I awake, I am still with thee.'

She contemplated this truth and prayed that for both of them, it would be so. In the beauty of the moonlight she fell asleep, dreaming of a handsome knight, who rode with the wind over the prairie on a beautiful, silver-white horse.

(Psalm 139:17)

16

THE SEDULITY

ANOTHER 48 HOURS of feverish, dry, flushed semi-consciousness, interspersed with intermittent drenching sweats and lucid periods, passed before Johnny was finally able to sleep. But sleep lasted only a short while, for the wracking cough and spasms remained, along with a persistent low-grade fever. Throughout the ordeal either Doc or Talitha remained faithfully by his bedside, offering laudanum at appropriate intervals, which he refused as his lucid moments increased.

"Laudanum...like taking a trip to hell," he whispered with as much resistance as he could muster, precipitating another coughing spell followed by relentless, accompanying muscle spasms.

Holding the cup of willow bark tea, a tired Talitha confronted the young man in exasperation. She had forced as much of the substance down his throat as he would tolerate.

"I'm drownin' in that stuff," he whispered.

"It'll keep you more comfortable, since you refuse the laudanum--now drink!"

There was a rap on the door and it opened. "Can I come in?"

"Surely! Come on in, Marshal. He's awake and judging from his poor attitude, I'd say he's recovering," Talitha imparted, sitting the cup of tea next to the bed and smiling gratefully at Sam Brett.

"I'll take a break. Maybe you can get him to be sensible and toe the mark."

Sam pulled a wry grin, removed his hat, and sat beside Johnny. "What's up, son? You giving that saint a hard time?" he asked, placing a hand on Johnny's shoulder.

"Hey," whispered Johnny, grimacing in pain as an explosive cough precipitated another spasm in his leg.

"You don't need to talk much, just listen," Sam said, placing his hat on the floor by the chair. "You feel like listenin', son?"

Johnny nodded and closed his eyes.

"We are both lawmen; I've been one a long time and I know the way things are, so I want you to hear me out. Before you get to lying there thinking yourself into a mire of quicksand, I am gonna tell you what usually happens when situations like this occur. You ready?" Sam asked, focusing intently on Johnny, who kept his eyes closed and nodded his head.

"Number one. You're going to spend a lot of time second-guessing yourself as to why you did what you did, what you could have done differently, and wondering how you can unscrew the mess you think you've made. The answer to this is simple. You are not God; you made a wrong choice. It could have been the right choice, it turned out not to be, but you had no way of knowing that for sure. You can't do anything to rectify it now. You can't bring those two thieves back to justice.

You probably did the territory a favor. Both are most likely dead; you saved money and time that would have been wasted to defend them. If they weren't guilty of a train robbery, they sure as hell were guilty of rustling." Sam took a breath and looked at the boy to see if he was listening.

"Number two. You're gonna wonder what the people of this town think of you. I can answer that also. The women will bring pies and cakes to the office--many have already. Then, they snivel into their handkerchiefs. They want to visit, to see if you are comfortable. Lucky for you, Doc kept most of them away. Their husbands, on the other hand, spend time debating what would have been the best thing you boys could have done to get those criminals to justice, refining and improving their plans as the days go by. Then once you are back on your feet, they will give you the pleasure of their wisdom, tellin' you what would have been the best way to have handled the situation.

Then, there is the mayor and the city council which brings up my third point--the tough one. They are gonna debate whether you should keep your job or not. Will you be able to hunt, ride, shoot, fight and kill as effectively as you used to? They'll bring it up, talk about it til everyone's opinion is exhausted and so are they, then they'll stop. They'll check on you, see how you are doing; ask some downright embarrassing questions, then, talk about firing you if you don't come back to life quick enough to suit them. Furthermore, they'll leave you hanging on the fence while they debate the issue for a time. While you are wondering what is to become of you and how you are going to make a living, they'll be deciding to give you another chance, on probation of course, all the while knowing damn well no one else can do the job as good as you do, or even wants the thankless job for that matter. Is this clear to you, son?"

Sam fixed Johnny with his stoic expression then finished. "It's not a pretty picture I paint for you boy, but it's the way of things."

Johnny nodded then whispered, "Suppose I..."

Sam stopped him. "Don't think of quitting Johnny, you're a lawman. Don't dwell on the things you can't change."

Johnny opened his eyes. "I got nothing left, sir." His voice was ragged and hoarse.

Sam leaned forward, forearms braced against his knees, his hands clasped together. "You've got the man you are. The mountain can shake you, make you question your life, even that faith of yours, but not the man you are. You survived for a reason, boy."

"For what reason? Why?" Johnny whispered coarsely, trying to catch his breath. Sam straightened up and placed his hand on Johnny's forearm.

"That's a question only you can figure out. You and God. One man can't decide for another, son. But if you need to talk it through, I'll listen--anytime."

Johnny eyes had closed and remained closed. He nodded silently. Sam Brett sat pensively, another matter weighing heavily on his mind. He was a man of decision and did not second-guess himself often. The subject before him was one he would lose his arm to, rather than broach, especially now. He was uncomfortable in the knowledge that the thing would not just go away or that the passage of time would not make it less of an issue. Being a direct man, he knew only one way to begin.

"Johnny, I am sorry about Traveller. I know nothing I could say will help."

Johnny's squeezed his eyes tightly and knit his brow. Sam covered one of Johnny's clenched fists with his own hand. He watched Johnny struggle with his pain. Sam knew this one would be a long time healing.

He said quietly, "I just want you to know that Horse Handler has a saddle and bridle waiting for you at the livery when you need it...when you're ready."

Fleeing trouble was not what Sam Brett did often, but now he came as close to it as he had in a long time. Outside of the room he paused and pounded his fist into his open hand. What good could possibly come from this, what was the purpose? How could he help Johnny understand something he could not? He closed his eyes and took in a deep breath.

Doc climbed up the last step onto the landing as Sam refocused.

"Howdy, Sam, you coming or going?" He aimed for joviality but missed the mark and asked tiredly, "How is our boy tonight?"

Sam shook his head. "I'm at a loss for words, Doc. He seems better, but he's discouraged and rightfully so. You know," he rushed on, "if we could bring that horse back and rid the world of most people, life would be a whole lot easier now."

Doc chuckled, "Yeah, then you and I could spend our lives fishing. How bad could that be?"

Sam smiled ruefully, then sobered. "Do you think he'll be able to work? I mean, just an estimate, how soon would you say? I need some ammo for when the mayor comes callin'."

"Don't know, Sam, and don't worry about having to ask the question. I know what that kid means to you and to this town also, whether or not they realize it. Let's see--pneumonia. About three to four weeks, and muscle tears and strains--probably about the same." Sam nodded but did not reply.

"One other thing is important, I think." Doc had Sam's attention. "You'll need to let him work as soon as he wants to. Knowing Johnny that would be tomorrow, if he was able to drag himself out of that bed--which I don't believe he is. It's the issue of his youth--and that horse. We don't need him lying around thinking about his pain and Traveller. Sooner he's up, the better he'll do in that department."

Doc thumped Sam on the back. "Gotta get to the patient. Got some quinine I think will help his muscles." Doc held up the clear bottle of white liquid.

Sam chuckled softly. "And here I thought you might be intending to ease your own pain this evening."

"No, it wouldn't do for me to stagger around town. As tired as I am, alcohol woul just knock me for a loop...but I reckon we could all use a little more shut-eye."

Doc was wrong about Johnny. When Talitha entered the room at 7:00 a.m. the next morning, she found Johnny sitting on the edge of the mattress at the foot of the bed, one arm wrapped around the bedpost, the other hugging his abdomen. He looked up as she entered and attempted to cover himself with the sheet and blanket which had loosened from their moorings and were dragging on the floor.

"Well, howdy! I am surprised! I didn't expect to find you up and from the looks of it, you could use some help. Maybe back to bed?" With a broad smile, she walked toward him, lifting the blanket which now covered only his feet.

"Is Doc around?" He asked flatly, obviously uncomfortable.

"No, I am afraid he's out on a call. He is over to Martha Blount's, I believe. She has two sick children--measles, I think."

She stepped closer, placing her wrist against his forehead. "No fever it would seem and that's a good bit of news. Here," she said, genuinely pleased to see him feeling better but concerned that he might be pushing himself before he was able, "let me help you lie back. You're still very weak."

She moved as if to help and he winced. "I'm alright, I'll stay put...but when do you think Doc will be back?"

His face was drawn, and his blue-green eyes as flat as his voice. She drew up to her full height, took a quick assessment, pursed her lips and locked him with a perceptive eye.

Talitha Cullins did not understand surgical procedures, could not properly set a broken bone, nor did she understand the intricate inner workings of a man's body as Doc did. But she could perceive the cerebrations of men well enough. Years of attending to traumatized cowboys, men whose methods of persuasion included knives, fists, and guns, and even those "crazies" who enjoyed being tossed off the back of thrashing bulls, had enlightened her.

She found, generally speaking, that men took the presence of bodily functions in stride. Expelling gas, belching and the like, came naturally to them and left them as unaffected as the breaking of the dawn on a cloudy day.

There was, however, one problem men did not deal with well, and Talitha expected this to be the dilemma Johnny now experienced. Fortunately for him, she knew how to bridge this delicate topic so as not to mortify his sense of propriety, thereby leaving his masculine dignity intact.

She began. "You have been through a lot of trauma. I don't need to tell you about muscle spasms. However, have you considered that your bladder is a muscle, and when it spasms the result is what you are now experiencing? Am I correct?"

To her, this was a matter of fact and she required no response. His nod was almost imperceptible and she continued. "I've taken care of you, Johnny, with the help of the Doc for past few days and if you recall, even as recently as last month. As long as you persist in this profession, cheating death every month or so, I will continue to care for you when you cannot do it for yourself. So, shall we say, I am already intimately acquainted with you. Now..."

Johnny opened his mouth to protest but Talitha held up her palm, facing him square on. "Hear me out, young man. Doc is not here, and I don't know when he'll return. If you can't handle this matter by yourself, I will have to help you."

She walked to the dresser and held up the slender silver tube. It caught the morning sun, sending its gleam toward the dismayed deputy, who sat silently, still clutching the bedpost with one hand and his abdomen with the other.

"What?" Johnny asked dumbly. When she did not respond, he began to understand the correlation between the instrument she held and his own pending fate.

"This is a catheter. You are familiar with it although I doubt you remember. It is inserted into the bladder and drains the urine if one cannot perform that function on one's own. So, son, I would suggest you do as I say."

Johnny's expression left no doubt as to his intentions, and she continued to address him.

"I am perfectly serious. Yes, I have done this many times before and, no, I will not allow any foolish notions on your part, for they would ultimately result in bladder rupture and your demise. Before Doc returns, we will take care of this."

Having delivered the shock as the first step in the plan which usually brought about resolve in the hearts and minds of most men, the ones who were at least semiconscious and able to move one or more of their extremities, she quickly delivered the second part of her dissertation, which usually brought the desired result. "Now, what you need to do is to stand upright as best you can. Gravity works wonders in this matter."

Talitha was just finishing her impartation as Doc entered the room. Johnny took a grateful breath and repositioned himself uncomfortably. "She's not serious is she?"

"Yes, son, I am afraid she is," Doc replied taking in the scene succinctly. "But you, my boy, are an amazing miracle! I never expected to see you up, even though you are clinging to that bedpost for all you are worth."

Pleased and relieved, Doc came to Johnny's side. "Although you look like the last scrap the cat dragged in, let's see if you have the strength to stand. I'll give you 30 minutes to get the thing done on your own. If not, we'll have to help you out. Here now, take your time. I'll help you; lean on me and you'll get it done. Stand up now...no, no, don't look down at the floor or we'll both most likely find ourselves upon it. Just keep your eyes up, straight ahead." Johnny did as directed and watched as Talitha let herself quietly out of the room.

Half an hour later, Doc joined Talitha in the hallway as she folded a stack of clean cloths and towels. "Well," she smiled confidently, "It worked didn't it? It usually does...almost every time."

Doc took her hands, cradling them in his. He nodded and smiled, gazing into her gentle face. "Those healing hands, Mrs. Cullins," he praised, "are amazing hands," he added, lifting them to his lips and tenderly kissing them.

Johnny slept for the rest of the morning, but the afternoon found him moving slowly about the room. Talitha had provided a tub with hot water and soap, and he had taken advantage of it, declining her offer to assist him, then attempting to remain awake in the warmth of the therapeutic heat. It had been a chore and had left him as weak as a kitten.

He dressed with difficulty, managing to pull on his pants. The woolen socks slipped on easily enough, but he could not maneuver his boots over his heels without sending spasms through his upper arms, legs, and the lateral muscles in his back. He left the boots off. Shaving had been another near disaster when his right hand spastically nicked the skin under his chin.

Arriving at the office before the marshal made evening rounds had been his plan, but it had been thwarted by incapacity. Sullenly, he eased himself into the rocker by the window, trying to squelch the rising frustration.

"Dang it! I can't even be a proper old man," he grumbled, as he attempted to set the rocker in motion and pain shot up his left leg. Careful to move his body as one unit, he raised the shade and appeased himself by watching the people appear and pass across his narrow window view.

The evening appeared to be cold and the few trees he could see moved only slightly, their bare branches resistant to the wind.

"The trees are like me," he mused, "stiff and half dead." The few pines in his view stood at the grove near the livery and moved more gracefully with the wind. He closed his eyes and tried to remember the whisper of pine needles. It was a sound he cherished, a sound he had heard almost every night in another small room long ago, far across the plains and mountains.

He opened his eyes. "I've got to get out of here! I can't stay inside another day. I'll lose my mind!" Though the window was just standard-sized, suddenly it seemed to be his portal to the outside world, and he stared intently through it.

Directly below him, a slim, bonneted woman crossed High Street. The figure stopped, and the face under the bonnet brim turned upward to look at the window.

"Cassie," he rasped, "Cassie!" He forced himself out of the rocker, stumbled and grabbed the window sill, breaking his fall, then twisted agonizingly to face the window. With muscles aflame, he groaned then pushed the window sash upward.

"Cassie!" His words caught in his throat, and he coughed violently.

She stood still, watching intently as he motioned to her and called through the partially-raised sash. "Cassie, don't go...meet me at the bottom...the backstairs."

He struggled to his feet and made his way haltingly to the door. Hoping she had understood, he reached the landing and looked down the daunting staircase. Taking the banister with both hands, he sidestepped down the first few stairs, paused, then turned and stumbled, catching himself as the fire shot from his feet to his groin; he forced himself downward.

As he stood on the bottom step, Cassie came through the back door. He held out his hand and she took it. He wavered and she came up under his arm. He stepped to the floor and pulled her to him. Her strength, warmth, and the scent of her hair filled his senses and he thought it strange that suddenly he did not feel pain. The hallway before him faded to white-wash pale, and he lowered himself to sit on the bottom step with Cassie following his descent.

"Put your head down, Johnny!" she ordered, placing her hand on the back of his head and forcing it between his bent knees. "Do it now, before you pass out!"

She pressed firmly. "Are you alright? How in the world did you get out of bed, let alone get down the steps?"

When he finally lifted his head, the walls regained their colors. He turned to look at Cassie. Her hair had loosed from its braid, and her deep blue eyes were wide beneath a concerned brow.

"I said I would come for you," he rasped, and coughed violently into his sleeve.

Unsure she understood what he had said, she moved her hand to his shoulder. "I was passing by...and I saw you..." she confessed tentatively.

He shook his head. "This... is not what I had intended, Cassie," he choked hoarsely, trying to catch his breath.

Arrested by his words, she dropped her hands into her lap, intertwining her fingers, afraid she must have been too presumptuous. She shuddered, unnerved, and staring down at the folds of her woolen coat asked carefully, "What did you intend?"

Impulsively, he took her hands in his. "I'm sorry, Cassie. That's not what I meant to say."

She met his gaze woefully. She was so very tired, tired from the questioning conversations she had had to endure, her raw emotions, and the deceptions of the past three days. She wanted to be with him with all of her heart, to understand what he had meant, and his motive for what he had said to her when last they had spoken.

How long ago had it been? A few days? A week? It felt like a lifetime. She looked into the blue-green pools of his eyes, trying to interpret the truth they held, and her heart skipped like a pebble across a pond. His features, his nose and mouth, though scraped and bruised, she found to be perfect.

She became uncomfortably unsettled beside this man who drew her so totally into his existence. She blushed deeply, and embarrassed for having revealed such emotion, withdrew her hands from under his and spontaneously pushed her stifling, confining bonnet backward. Tugging at one end of the tie, she loosened it and removed it quickly. In an attempt to collect her swirling thoughts, she took a deep breath and found that her embarrassment had emboldened her.

"Just what did you intend then, Johnny?" she asked again. "You never told me why you wanted to come for me, so please tell me now. What did you mean to say to me?" She steeled herself against his reply.

Johnny noticed the withdrawal of her warmth and immediately missed the press of her against him, feeling only the edge of her words. He would not lose her again and was desperate to keep her beside him, even if this moment was all he could ever have.

He would answer her now as he had promised, but could no longer speak his heart. He would tell her the truth as he knew it, as it had become, not as he wished it were. He needed to do this.

"I've wanted to ask you something...but I don't have any right to ask now. Things are different; things have changed." His mouth went dry, but his eyes held hers intensely, needing her to understand.

"What has changed? Changed from what to what? Tell me...I don't understand!" Her eyes glistened and his heart ached. Uncharacteristically, he dropped his gaze.

"I have nothing left, Cassie, nothing to offer you, no way to care for you. I had little before, but now..."

Cassie touched his face and turned it, drawing his eyes to hers. "Circumstances don't change what is in a heart, so tell me honestly, just this once, what you meant to say."

He put his arm about her waist and drew her to him. "I love you, I do! I have ever since that day on Main Street when I knocked you over. No, before that, from the day I saw you in the schoolyard. I know it doesn't make sense, it doesn't to me. I've tried to keep from it, but I can't. I've wrestled with myself every day, but I can't keep you from my mind and now that I can tell you, I shouldn't. These circumstances..."

She stopped him.

"Nothing that has happened changes one thing! I love you, too, Johnny. That night by the barn I knew it, but I thought that you would never be interested in me, a schoolgirl. You left so suddenly but I thought I felt it...do you remember that night? You laughed and called me 'my Lady,' remember? I knew then...that you were my knight."

"I remember," Johnny confessed. "It took all I had not to take you in my arms when I helped you from your horse. But now...this is no medieval fairy tale, Cassie. This is life, hard and ugly, and real. I may not have a job to go back to, I don't know the future. I can't even imagine what it will hold. Every day is a battle. I fight to move, I fight to breathe. I am worn out from fighting." He took his arm from her waist and leaned forward, elbows on his knees.

Sensing his vulnerability, she did not move away, but slipped her arm through his, resting her hand on his forearm. She continued persuasively.

"When I imagine the future, Johnny, I see us. I see this town, this territory. I need you and this place needs us, not separately but together. I've wondered about this, and I have prayed. I feel it so strongly. I prayed you off that mountain Johnny, and not just me, but the good people in this town, especially Mabel Baker. Aunt Mabel told me about you, about what kind of man you are, how you care about true things. She encouraged me to wait for what God would bring about in you and for us. I've seen the way you care for her and her home. I've listened to what people have to say about you, even my pa. They are good things and they will say those good things again."

As though he doubted what she said, he shook his head slowly and feeling this might be her only chance, she continued adamantly. "Listen to me. I was at home by the barn when the wind shook the mountain and tore across the prairie that night. I felt the earth shake and knew that you and Jess were on that mountain. I don't know how I knew it, but I did. It seemed that God called to me. I felt His presence and His great power, and I knew that if He brought you back it would be because you have a purpose. Oh Johnny! Are we to accept the good things from his hand and not the hard things?"

As she pleaded, he turned to search her face. Moisture glistened on her brow and tears filled the rims of her eyes, spilling silently down her cheeks. He raised his hands to wipe them tenderly from her flushed face. The heat of her skin caused him to loosen the tie at her throat, to relieve the burden of the heavy woolen coat. It parted and eased at her shoulders. Suddenly aware of his impropriety, he stopped.

She held his eyes with hers and shrugged the burdensome garment from her shoulders. He touched a curling strand of copper at her temple and pushed it from her dampened brow.

She whispered softly, "What happened that night on the mountain? Tell me Johnny; how did you survive?"

Intently, she awaited his reply and watched as he searched her eyes and struggled to answer.

Her face floated before him, soft and radiant. Desiring the warmth of her lips, he cared for nothing more, except that she was with him and in this moment, belonged only to him.

But she urged him to remember. "Tell me what happened that night. Can you recall?"

He struggled against his need, muscles aching, and core on fire. He made himself concentrate on her request, trying to remember, and willed himself from the brink of the pit.

'Remember...' he reprimanded silently, 'before you lose this chance forever.' He traced his memories backward, to that virulent day and groaned as the rocks, hail, dust and dirt rained down on him so heavily that he clenched his fists and closed his eyes tightly. Forcing himself from the cleft of the overhang and out from the dark suffocation, he took a tremulous breath, and she took his hand.

"There was something then," she murmured softly.

"Yes," he began, "but it was not in the dark...I thought I'd die there." He paused to catch his breath, "When I did not, I made my way up the ravine and found Jess. It was a miracle; I don't remember much, except pain and thirst. I remember lying in the open upon the rock, baking, then freezing in the brilliant white light, fading in and out of nightmarish darkness, stretched out under the sky."

"Oddly, someone called to me from a distance. It was a familiar voice. I thought it was my brother, then my papa, but it called gently, and I was unable to discern whose voice it was. But it was a voice...without sound, a touch... without sensation."

He paused, still searching his memory. "It was distant, but distinct. 'I am'; I know that's what it said. I haven't remembered this until now. It was... a perception. 'I am'. I believe I felt it more than heard it. It must have been...God, for what man could utter those words?"

Through misty eyes, she studied him in wonder. For a long moment, she contemplated his words. "So you fought to hear...to remember. You say you fought to live, you fought and God delivered you."

He did not look into her eyes until she grasped his arm firmly.

"Please Johnny...fight again. Fight for strength, for courage to get well. Fight to know God's calling, and fight for us. Don't fight against your feelings for me, fight for them...fight for me!"

This time there was no embarrassment, only steady resolve. She tried to read his eyes and through them, she hoped to understand and share in what he had experienced.

How could he make her see the truth? She was innocent, brave, untouched by harsh reality, and though he desperately wanted to believe she was right, he needed to protect her against what life with him would certainly bring.

"Cassie, you must understand..." he began, but she cut him short.

"You're a good and honest man, Johnny. I know it with my heart...and this is what I understand! We are to be together. Where you go, I want to follow, and what you do, I'll do with all of my heart." Impulsively, she drew close and brushed his lips with hers, gently, almost imperceptibly, then pulled away slowly.

Admitting a frigid gust, the rear door of the hotel opened halfway, dispelling the warmth and allowing its manipulator entrance. Doc stopped short, surprise flickering across his face, then his features grew solemn. In an instant, Johnny drew back, aware of how the scene must appear.

In stockinged feet, with shirt half buttoned, Johnny held the hands of a young woman, and he knew instantly that the term 'young woman' would likely be one for considerable debate amongst the fine citizens of Sideling. Her bonnet lay upon the floor, her coat cascaded over the steps, and her hair hung in abandoned disarray. No one spoke. With an innate ability for quick assessment, Doc watched Cassie's face pale, then rapidly set with rosy determination. Eyes that had first held dismay, now sparked.

Doc raised his eyebrows and pursed his lips. "Well, it's a good thing it is I coming through this door upon such a scene, Deputy, or there would likely be hell to pay. You appeared to have...let me rephrase. Miss Wilkerson, I have warned you against further visitation without permission from your parents who, by the way, are legally responsible for the 'minor' that you are."

The import of his censure was not lost as Doc faced them full on with a decisive frown. "Get home, Miss Wilkerson, or wherever it is you belong at this particular time. It is not here for certain," he warned, drilling her with his eyes.

(1 Corinthians 11:31-32)

Johnny rose with difficulty, awkwardly taking Cassie's hand as she stood. He lifted the coat from the steps, placing it about her shoulders, and as she fastened it, he picked up her bonnet from the floor, handing it to her. She stepped away, and he grasped her hand.

"I'll talk to your pa...when I can ride." Johnny said, and Doc overheard her answer softly.

"Please...soon." Stepping nobly past Doc, she let herself out of the door.

Shaking his head in disbelief, Doc faced Johnny square on.

"You don't know what happened here," Johnny protested. "Whatever you're thinking, it is not as it appears."

Doc considered him a moment, nodding thoughtfully. "Well, Deputy McLane," he said, "It seems you have tangled with just about the strongest-willed, most determined child that I have ever known--and I do mean child, for she is substantially under age. As for appearances, you need to get a few things straight."

Confused and cornered, Johnny began a defense, but Doc stopped him.

"Just let me advise you in case she failed to, which I hope for your sake is the case; she has no permission from her father for this visit or for any of the late afternoon excursions she made to your bedside. Given your level of consciousness at the time, you may be unaware of the reason for my concern. From what I just observed, you may still be mildly unconscious and unaware of the perceptions I gleaned, specifically when having found the two of you alone, in the corner of a stairwell, in the back of a hotel."

Blindsided, Johnny winced and stared at Doc angrily. "Wait," he protested, "what visits? What are you talking about? Permission? To do what? She and I were talkin', for Pete's sake."

"I am not the one making the mistake here, son," Doc replied, silencing as a couple came from the lobby to ambulate the staircase. The gentleman nodded at the two men engaged in lively discussion, while the lady lowered her eyes demurely.

"I suggest perhaps we go upstairs to finish this conversation. There are a few things you need to know."

Doc assisted Johnny in the climb and they entered the room at the top of the stairs. Johnny lowered himself onto the bed and clung to the bedpost, exhausted from the escapade.

Doc faced him, his expression lacking sympathy. "How in the world did you manage to get down the stairs without killing yourself? Did you have help?"

"Now wait a minute, sir. Cassie has not come into this room, in any shape or fashion, with me, ever!" As weary as Johnny was, the implication infuriated him. "This is the first time I've seen her since the accident and the longest conversation I ever had with her...alone, in my entire life! She is not that kind of gir...woman, and I won't have anyone say otherwise."

He coughed violently and struggled to regain control of himself. Doc started to speak and Johnny held up a hand, signaling for him to stop. He gasped for breath and tried to continue but was unable.

Doc pulled up a chair and sat facing him. "Clearly, you don't know what has been going on in the last day or so, son, so let me speak. I know that Cassie fancies herself to be in love with you. I know that she is a smart, intelligent, lovely and yes, a proper young lady and you must think these things of her as well. But how is it that she champions your cause, and how is it possible for her to know you well enough to think she is in love with you if you've never spent time with her? A young girl's infatuation? She is not the type. Some things don't add up here. And to confuse me further, if you don't know her well, how is it that you were so intimately engaged, conversing as you were on the back steps of the hotel?"

Johnny stared at him. "I don't believe this, Doc! You're giving me the third degree over a...a conversation! I guess it could have looked like something else, but believe me, it was not."

He coughed violently, breathed raggedly and began again, forcing himself to speak calmly. "Am I on trial for somethin'? Have I been accused of somethin'?"

"I am certainly not a judge and this is no trial, son, and what you do on your own time is your business. But you need to know..." And Doc related the story of the past two days' occurrences, which completely silenced Johnny.

"Oh, no," he breathed softly, but as the murky facts cleared in the light of day, Doc could see an odd mixture of disbelief akin to admiration in Johnny's expression.

Doc finished with, "It was foolish, I'll grant, but it took guts and determination on her part. I could see she believed in everything she said and did, and by the look on her face as she left here this evening, she's not finished yet." He chuckled wryly.

"Oh," Doc continued as an afterthought, "one other thing gave credence to her story, for me at least. Jess said, 'Go get the girl; the one he loves.' I thought he meant Myra at the time. Cassie changed my mind on that assumption."

Johnny sat silently as his mind returned to his intense and intimate conversation with Cassie. 'She believes in me, in us,' he thought. Cassie, Doc and even Jess seemed to grasp the depth of her feelings for him before Johnny had understood it or been able to put his own feelings into words. Admiration for her fire and independence had been what had initially drawn him to her. Need for her had been the greatest part of what he had felt recently, and passion had overshadowed his admiration for the kind of woman she was becoming.

"Whew, Doc," Johnny sighed, silenced in the face of the swirling milieu.

Doc replied evenly, "I don't want you to forget something. In all this agrestal passion lies a truth. Your moral ground can be easily off-centered. It can happen to any of us. You, especially, I think, because you seem to move in a rhythm born of a different culture. In this vast wilderness, rests this very small town and a few people in it have small minds to match so you must tread lightly. You've seen that life out here is different. It's quick, it's hard, and young men tend to grasp wildly at its fleeting shirttails; the women do the same. There is much injury, disease, and suffering, and when some snatch at life so passionately, they fail to realize it takes time to build a decent future. The land from which you hail has, or had, a slow, gentle cadence. I don't know, but I think that may be part of your struggle. When you passed through that bloody war, you were still a kid.

(Proverbs 10:8-9)

"That was one kind of struggle...this is another. Doc, you have no idea, and I am not likin' the man I've become. It's hard to explain what I mean, but these things that come out of nowhere to plague my mind, seem to have the force to change the things I do...or wish I did not do. Cassie makes me lose my senses. Thoughts of her...well, are like a bullet that flies out of nowhere when you least expect it. It strikes so fast and hits you so hard that you don't feel a thing until the heat and burning spread through you and the pain becomes intolerable. The bullet stays, tearing and burning, and there is no way to rid yourself of it," he said, despairingly. "Do you know what I mean?"

Doc did, and the remembrance caused him to nod in agreement. How well he remembered.

"So how does a man stand against this? How did you do it? How does anyone?" Johnny asked earnestly.

"Ahhh Johnny," Doc said contemplatively, leaning back in the chair. He took an exaggerated breath. "The desire to love is a beautiful thing, but that perspective usually only comes with age as you reflect upon it. I believe it's described in the Bible as one of those things men find too wonderful to comprehend, along with 'the way of an eagle in the air or the way of a ship in the midst of a sea.' It's... the 'way of a man with a maiden.'"

(Proverbs 30:18-19)

"Wonderful, aye? Then why do I feel like a walking contradiction?" Johnny rasped.

"The quality of a gentleman, which I believe to be part of your affliction, can be sorely lacking in these parts, for it's a new territory and folks have come from all walks of life. But don't get me wrong, propriety and a gentle nature are good things and needed things for a decent civilization. If desire for this gir...woman, is truly your first sincere encounter of this kind, then more the better for humanity and you are to be admired. How to get through this? I have no idea, my boy. I can treat the symptoms, got some ideas for that, but as far as a cure for the desire itself? Short of time, matrimony or immorality, I don't think there is a cure."

As they talked, Johnny alternated between standing and sitting, attempting to stretch his limbs, then suffering the spasms caused by the effort. After pacing briefly, he finally stretched out on the bed, and he and Doc talked late into the evening.

Doc was a skilled physician and as such, admired by many in the town of Sideling. A few citizens of the teachable variety, when they availed themselves of it, also experienced another of Doc's God-given talents. He was skilled in the art of listening, a gift not appreciated by many independent, headstrong men in a town struggling to find its way.

The events of the afternoon qualified the deputy as a recipient of his wisdom and out of pure self-preservation, Johnny immersed himself in it. They talked about the inconsistencies of life and when Doc brought up the war, Johnny could only say that both he, and his papa, had been caught up in a fight against a cause they actually believed in, but that they seemed to have little choice in the matter.

"Like the scum on the pond, we were in the mill trace and over the water-wheel before it seemed we knew what was happening. Don't know, sir. Now I sometimes wonder if we didn't purchase a ticket to hell on a train of regret. I was thirteen when I was sent to the military institute. I never really thought to ask Papa what his position on fighting for the Confederacy really was. For me, at the time, it seemed a grand thing. There are so many things I'd ask him now...so many things."

In the ensuing silence, Doc studied him. "That war took much from a lot of folks, son, even in Sideling. Beau's pa, Chester Brenner, seems to have suffered abysmally, though no one seems to know exactly how. But the effects on his kin, well..."

Listening, but not hearing, Johnny's thoughts were far from the peace and comfort of the room. It was the most Johnny had ever confessed, and in fear of his rising emotions, he pulled the plug on them. It would be all he was willing to say about the war for a long time.

Doc recognized his struggle and it became necessary to allow him to return to the issues at hand. Johnny expressed his concerns about Cassie and her father, and for the first time ever, was able to confess his confusions relating to the abstruse events following his mother's death on that dark and sultry night five years before.

Quietly and solemnly, Doc considered the incident and was in the midst of co-piloting Johnny through the sketchily-charted, turbulent waters surrounding women, propriety, and lawlessness, when a light tapping on the door ended their explorations. The door swung open.

"There you are Doc! Good evening Johnny. Am I disturbing you?" Talitha bore a tray in her hands and as she crossed the room, left a tantalizing aroma in her wake.

Doc graciously set her mind at ease. "No, you are welcome, Mrs. Cullins."

"Brought some chicken stew, Johnny. I hope you feel like eating this evening. See that you eat all of it--you need to get your strength back," she advised, smiling at the deputy. "There is some bread and willow bark tea, also."

"Thank you, ma'am, the stew smells great." Struggling to sit, he realized his appetite had returned.

Doc watched him. "Come along, Miz Broody Hen," Doc said jovially, placing a hand to the small of Talitha's back and guiding her toward the door.

"Get some sleep, son. I'll see you tomorrow. Be sure to stay put now," he ordered, with a raised brow and a wink, "and rest those muscles! Good night."

Out in the hallway, before descending the steps, Talitha turned to Doc. "How is he doing, Doc? Has he been out of that bed much? You know he will stay weak if he languishes in the bed for too long," she offered with the authority she sometimes borrowed from her husband.

Doc gave her a kiss on her soft, round cheek, taking her hand in his. "Don't concern yourself, my delight. At his age and in this particular environment, I think muscle stimulation and strengthening won't be much of a problem."

Talitha nodded, reassured. She sometimes floundered in the depths of Doc's medical knowledge, but her confidence in him never flagged. Doc was so wise.

Illuminated by the light from the bedside lamp, Cassie's face was aglow with an aura steeped in empyrean mystery. As she confided the events of the evening, Millie stared unbelievingly, her eyes round and her mouth agape.

"What? To whom? Stop fibbing!" she clamored as she sat bolt upright. Cassie rose quickly, covering the astonished girl's mouth with her outstretched hand.

"Shussh!" Cassie whispered loudly, "I don't need any more trouble than I already have!"

They lounged on Millie's bed as the night blanketed Sideling.

"Cassie, you are serious! But you can't be! Johnny? The law–Johnny McLane? That Johnny? It can't be! How do you know him personally? And he wants what?"

Impulsively, Millie grabbed at Cassie's arm and did not allow her friend to answer. "I had no idea, not one! How could I not know this?"

Cassie remained mum, but there was a twinkle in her eyes. Intrigued, Millie grew solemn. "Oh Cassie...what about Miss Davis? Why, it's just like a steamy dime novel!"

"Stop, Millie. I will explain, if you let me! Now lie back down, you are making me dizzy." Taking her friend's hand, she pulled her down. They lay side-by-side in the soft glow of the lamp, as Cassie recounted the events of the last week.

Millie's disbelief was assuaged momentarily but only slightly, and she begged for more details of the saga. Cassie continued for as long as she was able and finally overcome by exhaustion, could no longer concentrate. She fell asleep, and Millie's unbridled speculations fell on deaf ears. When her questions failed to brook a response, Millie plumped her pillow and with thoughts awhirl, lay down.

'Johnny McLane.' She could not fathom it. Each of her friends had wondered at and talked about this man--deputy marshal of Sideling, upon a gallant, silvery horse. Handsome, quiet, mysterious, the very defender of their very lives, he was in a clandestine relationship with their schoolmarm.

But Cassie? Her Cassie? Cassie loved reading, drawing, and never cared a flip about boys! Everyone had assumed that Cassie would marry Eric Flynn someday, although Cassie had never owned to it, and as long as Millie had known her, Cassie had never bothered to stand in the customary cluster of chattering girls. Nonsensical gossip irritated her.

Poetry, horses, her pa's ranch, and the never-ending array of baby, orphaned animals to care for, rescued from the prairie or saved from the harsh realities of the survival of the fittest inherent to ranching...those were the things that filled Cassie's days. Sometimes she played "kick the can" with the boys, but the deputy? When had she found the opportunity? Shoot a gun, make a dress...all in one day, that was Cassie. Perplexed, Millie snuffed out the light, weary from the evening's speculations, but anxious for the dawn's early light.

When lawyer Almon Baird had suggested paying Beau Brenner a pittance to tamper with the Flour and Grain and other locks on the business establishments in Sideling as a means of distracting the lawmen from the issue of rustling, Clancy Miller had thought the idea unwise. Brenner was untrustworthy and wild, and had proven Clancy's suspicions by the actual theft of a few items.

Now, it seemed that Sam's deputy was likely to recover. When Clancy had returned to Sideling on the evening of the break-in at the Flour and Grain following a visit to his brother, Vistor, in Iron Mountain, he knew there was a larger problem. Clancy had been able to evade Deputy McLane in the few days before the young man had been injured on the mountain, and Clancy's fears had been briefly quelled. The fact that the Brenner boy had alluded Johnny's questioning as well, appeared to have bought Clancy some time.

After the first break in at his Flour and Grain and having received an earful delivered like a firestorm by his unsuspecting, agitated wife, Abigail, Clancy was rattled. The news of the theft of a harness from the store followed shortly and precipitated constant needling from Abigail for answers as to who was responsible. In addition, Vistor's weekly communications and his pressuring for details concerning the deputy's recuperation, and what the town council thought of the whole situation had unnerved Clancy further. He questioned why Vistor seemed overly concerned.

Now, Clancy was sorry he had acquiesced to the lawyer's proposition, for although Almon was knowledgeable about loopholes in the law and an influential member of the town council, Clancy was not sure he could hide out in his shadow.

As for Clancy's own part in the shady dealings, he hoped no one would be the wiser if he "laid low" and played his part by continuing to provide information to Marshal Riddick's informant, ole Leafy Misner, down at the saloon. A bar, like a barbershop, or a Flour and Grain, was a good place to eke out facts from cowhands concerning the number of beeves, the quality of the herds, or the timing of the cattle drives east to market. It had seemed simple enough, for Clancy's friends were the cattlemen who frequented his business and no one would think to point a finger, but was it even worth the modest profit he and Leafy received from Riddick?

Now, the deceptions seemed more ominous and the plan appeared broader in scope than he had originally imagined. Lately, Almon Baird treated him coolly and Clancy could only surmise that Vistor's new interest in the health of Johnny McLane must involve Marshal Riddick and the man's insatiable greed. But why should Riddick worry about the young and relatively inexperienced deputy, when the real force of the law in Sideling rested with Marshal Sam Brett?

17

THE SPIRAL

A FRONT ROW seat in laudanum hell was decidedly a better place to go than the battleground of gripping muscle spasms that seized Johnny every time his body drifted toward the edge of sleep. It was the path he had chosen by midnight, and through the early morning hours he slept, as abstract dreams of Cassie came and went.

The sun was high in the sky before he awoke, and he struggled from the bed trying to fight through the fog in his brain. He dressed in agony, managed to pull on his boots and dizzily navigated the stairs. Oddly, he found that walking helped relieve the pain, but exertion brought about an aggravated assault from coughing, so as long as he did not have to move rapidly, he could get around.

He made it to the office by mid-afternoon. Sam Brett looked up as he entered.

"Well, Mr. Brett," Johnny quipped weakly, "I never thought this place could look so good." He hobbled to the corner, picking up the broom.

"Welcome back, you sure you are up to this?" Marshal Brett stood and offered his hand in greeting.

Johnny smiled and took it. "I guess there must be something I can do around here, besides just lookin' good."

Sam chuckled, "If those looks of yours are what you're countin' on, you'd best take up that mop as well." Johnny's purple welts and bruises were fast becoming a sickly yellow; he also needed a haircut and a few extra pounds.

"Why don't you go on over to the mercantile and see Bradford Jones? It's too cold to walk around half naked." Sam reached into the top drawer and pulled out a badge. "Here--took it off what was left of your old coat. You'll be needin' it. I cleaned it up some."

The metal had been polished until the dented star winked in the daylight flooding through the windowpane. It seemed like a warm, living thing as Johnny held it in his palm. At a loss for words, he closed his fingers around it, while Sam studied the paper on the desk before him.

The marshal explained the events of the last week, and Johnny swept as much as he could of the floor, struggled over to the mercantile, bought a coat, then spent the remainder of the afternoon seated by the wood stove. Sideling had been quiet for days now; cold weather and harsh winds dampened the cowmen's enthusiasm for the pleasures which awaited them in town. Troubled by reports of cattle rustling, Sam had decided on a trip to Cheyenne. There was a stir over the whiskey tax also, and he would combine those pieces of business with a little pleasure for himself. Skep Duane had agreed, for modest pay, to marshal with Johnny for a few days in Sideling.

The truth was, Sam needed a break, and he knew Johnny was not likely to throw off the weight of his trial so easily. Skep just may be able to reach him on a level that Sam could not.

Two evenings after Sam's departure, Johnny made rounds slowly and methodically. The burn and pain in his muscles tended to dull his senses. Uneasy, he prayed nothing would require any quick reaction on his part. Nothing did, until rounding the corner of the livery, he collided with Skep.

Johnny groaned as Skep apologized profusely, steadying him. "Guess you don't bounce so well! Maybe you'd better sing when you walk in the dark so's a body knows you're comin'! I am really sorry, Johnny," Skep said, adding, "When you didn't return, I thought I'd check to see if you were alright. I'll join you if you don't mind."

Johnny had said little during the time Skep had spent with him. Johnny had not mentioned Traveller and had ridden briefly only once--on a horse borrowed from the livery. He had not commented on the venture, so Skep reckoned it had not gone well.

They turned and walked along the storefronts, testing the doors already locked and speaking briefly with the proprietors still closing up for the night. For the "umpteenth" time that day, Johnny thought about Cassie. He knew it was too late to catch a glimpse of her as she left Miss Halstead's, and kept his thoughts to himself. What was the point of bringing it up? Until he talked with her father, there was really nothing to say.

When the businessmen greeted him with, "Nice to see you; glad you are up and about," he wondered what they really thought. To minimize the pain, he splinted his ribs with an arm as he and Skep crossed High Street.

"Good thing they can't know how I feel inside," he commented, as they talked randomly about the town and how the next couple of days might play out.

"You haven't said much about yourself, Johnny," Skep observed thoughtfully. He waited for a response.

"What can I say? I dropped a bag of coffee beans; it scattered all over the floor. Then I dropped a bag of silver coins on my way into the bank--all from my right hand. I shoot with that hand, Skep." Johnny's inflection was flat.

"So what does Doc say?" Skep asked.

Restlessly, Johnny stretched and rubbed his right arm. "Skep, what matters is now, today, tomorrow, not three or four weeks from now. If you weren't here, this town would be up for grabs. You know that, Marshal Brett knows it, and so do I. I got no answers."

The wind blew snowflakes in swirls across the back street. Skep leveled his gaze at Johnny. "Seems to me you need to work with what you do have. You can pick up things with that hand. Maybe all you need is to strengthen it, use it more. Practice shooting or something. Just don't give up, Johnny."

"Does this look like giving up to you?" Anger had flared in his tone. "I am here, aren't I? Out in the streets doing my job."

"Yeah...yeah you are."

They stopped in the road at the rear of the office. Skep paused and placed a hand on Johnny's shoulder. "I've got something else to say. Somethin' I need to ask of you. Want to go inside first? I'm about to freeze out here." He dropped his hand from Johnny's shoulder.

"No Skep, you go ahead."

Johnny struggled with his desire to escape. He knew he was being irrational, but couldn't stop himself. "I'll be there in a bit. I need the cold and the wind right now," he confessed. "I'm clamped in a tomb and it seems like I can't breathe. Sometimes being outside helps. If I stand out here long enough, the wind might just tear something loose or clear something out...something trapped inside of me. I can't explain it."

He sat on the steps outside the back door, and Skep followed suit. "So you want me to suffer in this weather with you, right?" Skep chuckled softly, drawing up his coat collar.

"Yeah, maybe."

Skep caught the despair in Johnny's tone. The thought of delaying the pressing matter occurred to Skep, but only briefly, and he pushed it aside. He knew he had to get to the business at hand.

"I'd like to help you with this, Johnny. I am sorry about Traveller. I understand what he meant to you, and I know you don't want to deal with it now, but..."

Johnny broke in caustically. "I deal with it alright. Every second I think about this job, I deal with it. In the day and in dreams at night, so don't tell me I don't deal with it! I just can't make myself do anything about it."

Skep attempted to qualify his statement, but Johnny let go with a torrent of pent up words. "I can't explain what he meant to me...he was more than my horse, and I don't seem to be able to string any rational thoughts together as to why I can't just move on--except one. A man without a horse is a shop-keeper, Skep, not a lawman."

Johnny shook his head, took two steps as if to bolt, then turned to face Skep. "I didn't think anything could be worse than what I experienced in the war or on that mountain. But those things happened to me; I got through them because I had to. This thing...well, it is me. It's me not being able to take a step toward anything, to fix anything. I've always been able to find a way through bad times, but this..."

His voice broke, his eyes misted, and he turned away.

"Listen, Johnny, I got a solution. It, well, I need help with this. It's a horse." Skep continued haltingly, "He's a good horse, Johnny. He is young, just three years old. I got him green broke and he knows the basics. I just don't have time to work with him. You would be good with him. You know a man trains a horse each time he rides, and you're the best rider I know. Would you do this for me?"

He took a breath and continued encouragingly. "The beauty part of this is that we both win. You need a horse, I need a horse trained. If you don't like him, if he is not a good fit, I'll take him back. What do you say?"

Johnny rubbed his eyes and breathed deeply, coughing. Weary of the struggle of mind and emotions, he stood silently for a moment and Skep waited.

"My hope is wearing thin. I've got to do this, Skep. I don't care how I feel about it, just... make me do it. I've got to be able to ride and shoot."

Relieved, Skep delivered the rest of his plan. "Tomorrow we'll get a nag from Horse Handler and ride out to Uncle Willy's ranch so you can check the horse out. The town can survive a few hours without us." Johnny did not comment.

"Look, I know this is a struggle for you. You're still fighting your way off that mountain. I don't know how else to help you." Skep said. He rose, tapped Johnny's shoulder and entered the office.

'The mountain, the struggle,' Johnny thought, and closed his eyes against the wind and the world. Cassie had used the term "fight", just as Skep had, and Johnny wondered if just trying to put one foot in front of the other to drag himself forward each day constituted any kind of a fight. He prayed it did because that is all he knew to do and all the strength he could summons went into it.

The ride to Willy Duane's farm was easier than the last ride had been, but still far from comfortable. Johnny walked through Willy's barn trying to ease his burning limbs. Placing a leg on the second board of the corral fence and his hands on the top rail, he carefully stretched his muscles, alternating legs.

The chestnut gelding was a handsome one. Only a hand shorter than Traveller, he had three white socks and a white snip on his face. Johnny watched as Skep paraded him back and forth across the paddock. The chestnut had a kind eye, good ground manners and moved well, pleasing Johnny.

"What do you call him?" Johnny asked, as he mounted stiffly.

"Cody," Skep replied, smiling easily. "Named him for the man who sold him to me. It's easier to keep track of where I get the horses from if I do, and I reckon I'm just plain lazy."

Cody was truly only green-broke, but Johnny liked him well enough. He was fast, but stoppable, and would easily learn to respond to the leg. Johnny tried his best not to compare this horse to Traveller. Traveller...who sensed when a change in direction was indicated and responded to any minute shift of Johnny's posture. With just the turn of his head, Johnny could change the horse's direction. Quick to sense the tides of Johnny's emotion, Traveller could take off in a second and outrun a fleeing miscreant. Hadn't he danced nervously before Cassie as Johnny's mind and body struggled that day on the trail? His friend, his transport, his lifeline, always accepting and trusting. Since Johnny was sixteen, Traveller had always been there for him, but no more.

Johnny ached as he silently brought the horse to a halt before Skep.

"You can shoot a rifle while riding him, Johnny. I swear he's that dependable," Skep promised, grinning up at him.

"Alright. Got yourself a deal," Johnny agreed, trying to sound enthusiastic.

Later, they rode for Sideling in uncharacteristic silence as Horse Handler's nag, on a lead line, trailed obediently behind them.

Marshal Brett returned the following day. Cattle rustling had picked up again, this time proximal to the ranches provisioned by Cheyenne's merchants. Sam discovered the reason taxes on whiskey had become problematic, finding that government agents had turned a blind eye to a certain percentage of the distillate for cash. In return, the proprietor would have their tax payment reduced by almost half. Nothing seemed untouched by corruption. Sam would keep a sharp eye out, but for now, as far as he knew, the whiskey tax scheme remained a problem only for the larger city of Cheyenne.

Johnny's acquisition of a horse relieved Sam greatly, measured minimally by the relaxing of Sam's brow, jaw lines and a terse comment. "I see you got yourself a mount; looks like you made a good choice."

The following afternoon, having been cut loose from the tedium of office duties, Johnny headed for the relay and found Jess working slowly, but effectively, to fit a wooden felloe to a wagon wheel rim.

While Johnny helped him, they spoke of their recent recuperation under the watchful eye of the Doc and Mrs. Cullins, agreeing that Doc had saved their lives, but not without the help of Talitha's formidable, albeit, capable hands. Johnny asked if Jess had had an encounter with the catheterization process. Jess promptly denied ever seeing the offending instrument and informed his friend that due to its use upon Johnny's person, he was sorry to inform him that all of Johnny's progeny should he now be capable of siring any, would be born both naked and bald. Johnny promptly informed Jess where he could spend the rest of eternity, pleasing Jess exceedingly.

Nevertheless, it was good to see his friend and better to find him able to work. Neither man spoke of their personal losses and owing to the spirit of comradery, few words passed between them concerning the venture, for they had accepted the consequences of their decision. Out of loyalty, Jess briefly brought up the loss of the captives.

"Are they giving you a bad time over it? I'll be glad to go before the town council with you if it comes to that."

"The council meets next week, but I don't need help. I'll tell them the way it happened, and they'll deal with it, or not," Johnny replied flatly.

Well known were the various opinions amongst the town council, and neither man knew or cared to speculate on the decision concerning the fate of the deputy. Without further contemplation, Jess changed the subject.

"If I am right, I believe you had a visit or two from that girl of yours. How is it going for ya?"

By the quizzical expression on Jess' face Johnny knew there was no escaping until he gave some sort of answer, but Johnny hesitated, and Jess continued glibly.

"You did talk to her, didn't you? You know I helped you out from ma' deathbed. Hope you took advantage of my efforts." Johnny could not suppress a smile.

"She got ya out of that bed right quick, didn't she?" Jess added smugly.

"Yeah, I don't know how I'd get through life without you, Jess. You sure have a way about ya--fosterin' mayhem one minute and matrimony the next."

Jess smiled. "No one here is speakin' of the latter, especially not me, so quit trying to dodge my question, son."

"I'm gonna ask her father if I can see her. In fact, I am going to do it as soon as I leave here. I am fairly certain I already know the answer, but I promised her, and I can't wait any longer."

"Dang it, John, you sound like someone's twistin' your arm! Those rocks damage your brain, or did you just change what little's left of your mind?" Jess shook his head, "You beat all, ya know."

Irritated, Johnny fired back, "I just don't want Dodge Wilkerson telling me 'no'. He's got every reason to say it, and you know it as well as I do. And tell me, what do I do when he denies my request? Argue with him?"

"No, you bide your time. She won't be sixteen forever. She'll make up her own mind one day," Jess said evenly.

"Well, that's great. Just wait it out. I am sure that will go well, I know I can hardly stand the waitin' now." There was so much misery on Johnny's face that, contrary to his nature, Jess tried to think of something helpful to say, but he could not.

He resorted to his odd sense of humor. "Well, you got the town down on you and soon, possibly, Dodge Wilkerson. Why worry about one thing when you can agonize over two, I always say. Just confront the issues, John Scott, get it over all at once and then see where you stand. Better to do somethin' than nothin'."

Johnny stared at Jess and shook his head. "Lord, I know I'm in trouble when you began to make sense," he grumbled, turning to go.

"Yeah, just let me know how it goes, Romeo."

In the time-honored concession of sorts, Johnny grunted, nodded, and mounted Cody.

"Good lookin' animal," Jess called, casting a careless salute as Johnny turned back down the road.

Jess never made mention of Traveller. There were no words to describe the totality of the tragedy that had bound the men together. It would do no good to dwell on it, but Johnny knew the event would haunt both of them for a long, long time.

18

THE PICKET

THE FOURTEEN-MILE RIDE between the Plains Stage Relay and the Wilkerson ranch had to be broken up by several stops, the last one being in Sideling. Riding Cody had taken much effort. Johnny had always found riding to be as natural as breathing. Now he labored to do both.

A slight shift in the saddle as a subtle command and a nudge of his leg against the flank took concentrated effort. He found himself weighing the consequence of movement against the consequence of pain. He fought frustration and pushed on. To diminish the burning ache, walking became a necessity. Entering Sideling from the northeast, he dismounted at the far end of the hotel and made his way behind the business establishments on Main Street, leading Cody along High Street, past the livery and the Flour and Grain. The town was quiet and as he glanced across to Olivia Halstead's place, he did not see Cassie's horse. Remounting Cody, he continued to the southwest, toward the Wilkerson ranch.

Eat, sleep, breathe and push onward as one day melted into another.

As he rode, he vacillated between reality and supposition, but when remembrance of the moment came, it came through his restlessness like wildfire, awakening, inspiring, and rallying him. Her eyes had searched his on that day for the hope of a promise to be found and kept, imprinting in an instant with a plea from her heart and the brush of her lips against his.

"Fight for me, Johnny, for us...for this territory. God delivered you...a reason and a purpose..."

The consummate, life altering whisper..."I am", and then unbelievable deliverance from where he lay injured in helpless despair.

He reined in his horse and in the lengthening shadows of the afternoon, sat still in the saddle. Suddenly the answer became clear. Why hadn't he realized this before? He turned Cody with resolve, heading back toward Sideling to amend his backward plan.

At the end of the boardwalk on Main Street, Johnny took the side stairs up to the mayor's office. The ten by ten room sat above the Land Assay Office next to the saloon. With a stack of papers tucked under his arm, the mayor encountered Johnny in the doorway. He appeared to be leaving for the evening and stopped short, obviously surprised.

"Good afternoon, sir, could I have a word with you?"

"I was about to leave, but I reckon I have a moment. Come in and sit down." The mayor's obligatory tone and reluctant demeanor did not thwart the deputy. Had it been another time, Johnny may have acquiesced to the late hour and withdrawn his request. He did not.

"Well boy, how are you feeling? You look better than expected." The mayor perched on the edge of his desk.

Melbourne Vaiden was a tall, thin man, shrewd, blunt, and usually honest. He was, however, conscious of the precarious position he was in, this being an election year. Johnny knew Vaiden's opinion would be heavily swayed by the folks in Sideling. As Sam Brett had forewarned, honesty and justice seemed to take second place for most politicians. But Johnny's sudden need to gain a sense of what he might be facing politically, drove his inquisition.

"Physically, sir, I'm riding and able to do what is required of me. I'd like to address any concerns you may have, and I'd like to do it today. I have some decisions to make, and before I do, I'd like to know where this community stands regarding my continued employment."

Taken aback and at a momentary loss for words the mayor remained silent, and hid his surprise behind a pacifying smile.

"You know the town council doesn't meet until next week. I am not sure I understand why you would question me now, Deputy. Do you feel that your job is in peril? Or might you be seeking some sort of change for yourself?"

Discerning the mayor's tactic, Johnny simply asked his question again. Melbourne Vaiden looked up over the rim of his glasses.

"I don't know what you may have heard. Folks do have a lot to say about the incident, but I don't believe any one man can agree with another on what they would have done had they been in your shoes. Hindsight is always the clearest, but in this case, confusion is universal. If you are asking if anyone is calling for your immediate resignation, anyone who has influence that is, the answer is 'no'. That is my opinion at this time anyway."

"Thank you, sir, I appreciate your honesty. It helps to clarify some things. It's always easier to make decisions when you have facts to work with."

"Just one question for you, Deputy McLane. You seem to have a sense of urgency about this, and I find myself wondering why." He looked squarely at

Johnny. "Are you thinking about leaving Sideling for employment elsewhere? Is that what this is about?"

"This territory is growing and changing, sir. There are opportunities everywhere, for all of us. I'm sure you are aware of that." With a definitive nod and a thoughtful eye, Johnny stood and offered the mayor his hand.

"Thank you for your time, sir. I appreciate it."

The mayor rose and shaking Johnny's hand, found that he needed the last word on the subject.

"This town appreciates good men, McLane, and I count you as one of them."

"Thank you, sir. I'll consider that. Good evening." And with that, Johnny turned and walked from the room, leaving the mayor to ponder speculatively.

The deputy stood on the landing a moment. His eyes swept over the town of Sideling. For now he was still deputy marshal, and it seemed likely he would remain so. It also appeared he may even have a choice in the matter. For the first time in a while, he experienced a potent sense of quiet control, having left the mayor to wonder. His mind was steady, but his legs trembled as he descended the steps to the boardwalk below.

"Great day in the mornin'; how did I accomplish that?"

Mayor Vaiden was struck by the decisive action of the young deputy, who had not waited to be summoned by the council. This was the same young man who had scouted out the canyon on his own, assembled a band of men, and led the advance that enabled the arrest of the rustlers. He now held the respect and even the admiration of several of the territorial lawmen. Vaiden speculated as to which lawman had offered him a job or which town might have need to find a good candidate to run for marshal this election year.

'I can't lose a good man. If need be, I'll find a way to sway the council on this one,' he determined.

Respectfully requesting the permission of Dodge Wilkerson was one of the most unaccommodating conversations Johnny had ever had. His words did not flow easily as they had with the mayor. As he stood before the man who held his immediate future in his hands, Johnny realized it would take the intervention of God Almighty Himself to make his case for him.

Dodge Wilkerson had been as calm and cool as a dead fish and as unpliable as taffy in January. Johnny could not remember all of what was said, but the "it is not in her best interest" part resounded in his ears, retaining clarity and removing the potency of the earlier conversation in the trying day. The four-mile ride back to Sideling passed in a blur of fury, fueled by self-condemnation.

"What's hardest is that I was stupid enough to think he might agree." Johnny said despondently.

Sam had seen the answer on Johnny's face as soon as he entered the office but had forced the question anyway.

"I can't say I wouldn't have said the very same thing if she was my daughter," Sam advised calmly. "She is only sixteen."

Johnny tossed his hat onto the table, and slumped in the chair by the desk. "Almost seventeen, but that's not the problem entirely. He loves her, Mr. Brett. I know he wants what he thinks is best for her. I understand and I know I should want that also. Everything he said made sense. And there I stood, defending my position with a slew of desires--telling him what every man would have told him. That I care for her, I'd respect her, and that I want the best for her, all the while knowing what I said wouldn't make one bit of difference to him."

Stymied, Johnny stared at the marshal. "I had to try. What else could I have said to make him give me a chance?"

"I don't know, Johnny. Dodge knows you fairly well; he knows you are a good man, and good at what you do."

"A good man, huh? You mean my character, my ability to do a good job? Yeah, he said all of that too." Johnny laughed sarcastically. "Those things must count for a whole lot! If I stay away from his daughter and do my job, he likes me just fine. Everyone does. But I got a funny feelin' that every father in this town would have the same thing to say. 'Why here comes that fine fellow, ole Deputy McLane. Just let him pass, daughters, he's on his way, headed straight for Boot Hill!'"

Sam Brett considered Johnny for a long moment then shoved his chair back from the desk and rose. He picked up his hat and coat, gazing levelly at his deputy. As usual, his features were stoic, but his eyes held a strange mixture of anger and regret.

"I'm goin' for dinner if you care to join me." He stopped in the doorway and turned to face the deputy. "You've got two choices on the matter of Cassie. You can feel sorry for yourself, or you can realize that this is a battle you and she have already won. One day she'll be eighteen and will decide for herself. I know you don't see it, but time passes quickly. If you love her, you'll wait--just wait. Not sayin' it's easy, but the day will come. Now, are you comin' with me?"

With eyes downcast Johnny shook his head, not trusting himself to comment. The marshal's words, "just wait", resounded in his ears like a funeral dirge. His stare bored holes in the pine floor, as he bemoaned his fate.

"I have little strength for breathin' and none for waitin'. I don't know how to move forward, and I can't retreat. I'm standing in a well with a six-inch rope and I can't get out."

Looking up, he realized that he was talking to himself. The marshal was gone. He stood stiffly, pulled off his coat, and slung it across the room in the direction of the chair by the desk. Hobbling across the floor, he lowered himself into the swivel chair behind the large oak desk. He yanked the bottom desk drawer open and pulled out the bottle of Old Kentucky. He uncorked it, took a gulp, recorked it then shoved it back into the drawer. With the toe of his boot and his spur scraping the wooden floor, he slammed the drawer shut. He hated the taste of the stuff. It burned his throat and warmed his chest, but did not pacify him as it slid down smoothly. He shivered. Drawing his sleeve across his mouth, he stood awkwardly and grumbled, "I ache like I'm 100 years old."

Forcefully, he caught the empty water pail with the toe of his boot, sending it flying, and thumping across the floor and into the backroom. Turning, he grabbed a rifle from the rack, then came about, gripped with shooting pain. A spasm locked his hand and he almost dropped the gun.

Trudging through the backroom, he kicked the errant bucket partially blocking his path with the heel of his boot, sending it careening backward into the office. He stomped out the back door, checking the rifle chamber as he went and finding it fully loaded. Burning muscles prevented an all-out run, so he jogged haltingly across the back street, having to slow and catch his breath frequently.

A lone figure stepped off the porch into the deep shadows of the Flour and Grain building and watched the curious sight with interest. Johnny jogged upward, along Center Street, then veered up the path to the rise beyond the white-picket fenced graveyard. Watchful eyes followed his progress toward the stand of pine and aspen trees just to the east of the last wooden cross which rested along the low ridge.

Panting, Johnny ran into the stand of trees, stopping at the old, barren ash tree. Huge, withered, and weathered gray, it stood like a sentinel, towering in the grove.

Johnny coughed violently and spat. When his eyes cleared, he raised the rifle high, aimed and fired, blowing bark and splintered wood fragments into the air, firing again and again into the heart of the ancient tree.

When the chamber emptied, he reloaded and repeated the assault until there was nothing left of his anger. He stood a moment, spent and suspended in the dismal gloom, and the mournful baying of a dog in the distance broke the dead silence. Shouldering his rifle, he turned and walked back toward town, hardly cognizant of the cold until icy sleet stung at his face and dampened his shirt, numbing his body. From the shadows, the watcher pulled up the collar of the heavy coat until it reached the brim of the large felt hat.

19

THE CONCESSION

THERE WERE FEW thick stone or brick walls in Cassie's territorial pale--few things that could not be broken by the hard swing of a hammer or sharp blade of a saw. What she faced at this time, squarely and straight on, could not be amended by any physical object or mental calculation and she knew it.

The steel of his eyes and flint in his voice stopped her cold and she stared in confusion and disbelief. "There will be no further discussion concerning this. I will not change my mind. This is for your good, because I am your father and I know the heartache and the odds against the kind of life he proposes. I won't allow this. You are a girl; you don't yet know your own mind."

Cassie shook her head, trying to comprehend, not able to speak and angry that she could not hold back her tears. How could he do this and say these things? This was her life, her dreams and not his, which had been wiped away with a single word. Could he not take time to consider this, to pray about it? Did her thoughts and desires count for nothing?

They had been so close, and she thought she pleased her father, and that he trusted her judgment. Occasionally, he asked her opinion on matters concerning the ranch. But this! He was being hateful, and it cut her to the core.

And what about Johnny? What would he think of her father now? What horrible things had he been forced to hear?

Earlier in the day, Cassie heard the knock on the front door as she sat attempting to read by the window above the porch. For three days she had waited for this. She knew he would come, he had promised..."when I can ride". She had watched as he rode for the barn, watched him dismount, and as he had entered she thanked God. Dashing to her room, Cassie had taken up her brush, freed her hair, and had brushed it briskly until it gleamed. She had searched her face in the mirror, frowned at her freckled nose, and pinched color into her cheeks, waiting, waiting, until Johnny would come to speak with her.

At the window once again, she had watched with heart racing as he exited the barn, mounted, then sat for a moment upon the chestnut horse. In her joy, she fled down the steps to meet him at the door, but he had not come toward the house for her. When she flung it wide, he was gone.

Kate Wilkerson stretched out on Cassie's bed beside her daughter. She smoothed back the curls from Cassie warm, damp face. "Remember when you were little and all we girls would pile onto the bed at night and tell silly stories? Sometimes we laughed until we cried." Cassie did not answer, only turned her face to the wall.

"Cassie, I could not allow you to fly off on Lady like some wild squaw after Johnny left this afternoon. Please try to understand. It was growing dark; you are not a child anymore."

Cassie flinched. Kate regretted her words, for Cassie had boldly proclaimed that point to her unrelenting father just hours ago.

"You must think things through before you act. Where would you have gone? What was the purpose, besides just running away from your problems, away from your father?"

Cassie sat up. She held a soggy handkerchief to her reddened nose. Her face was blotched with pink, and her curls were jumbled and fled from order in all directions.

"Your father and I don't seem to be able to reason with you lately. Your heart seems always to be in the way. Look at me, Cassie," Kate declared, taking her daughter's hand.

"Doc Cullins has squelched some of the town's murmurings about you and Johnny at the hotel. Most people still link Johnny with Myra, so for the most part the rumor mill has been hushed. I wish you had confided in me, daughter. Maybe I could have helped."

"How, Ma, just how could you have helped?" Cassie cried in frustration. "Even now it seems that all you care about is what people think! The last time you and I had talked about anything meaningful was the day we took Aunt Mabel's things to Mrs. Winkler's, remember? You wouldn't talk to me or to Johnny. We left him standing in front of Aunt Mabel's house. We just...drove off," Cassie exclaimed, clutching her handkerchief. "I never understood that."

Kate sat up on the bedside. "I care because a reputation can be ruined so easily by shallow-minded people. I guess I did not handle that day well. You are so young, the idea of you and the deputy together was unthinkable to me. Cassie, think! What a hard life you would have. Many times you won't know where he is, how he is, or if, God forbid, he will ever come home again. What a lonely life!

"He is handsome, a gentleman, I think, and I can understand the attraction he holds for you. But you are a cattleman's daughter. That is what you know, the life you could succeed in. There are young men who would, even now, want to build a life with you-Eric Flynn for one. Our families have talked of it since they came west two years ago. Your father and I have prayed and planned for that kind of life for you. In spite of this, your father has been so kind as to allow your exploration of other talents. He allowed you to work with Miss Halstead, for example, when he could have kept you here to help out. That seemed quite fair to me. Oh, my dear! This is a hard land, a difficult place. Why compound those problems?"

"I understand how you and Pa feel about the ranch. I know you have given me every advantage, but ranching is not all there is. I feel I am being called in a different direction. I can't explain it other than to say I believe I am called to stand alongside Johnny, to help him change the town; to make it an honest, decent place where people can build lives, grow businesses, raise families and not be afraid of violence and corruption. The people of Sideling seem to have changed, don't you see it?" Cassie added thoughtfully. "The joy and goodness seem to be lacking. Remember the quilting bees and the hoedowns? Things are not as they were. I think that Sideling could be a most favorable town again and one day, part of a great state. Ma, that's what God is calling me to."

"I don't understand how you think you are called to be a part of the life of a man you don't know. Your lives are so different! You haven't had the opportunity to be with him long enough to know what he wants out of life. None of this makes sense to me, I'm sorry, it just doesn't."

As Kate and Cassie talked late into the evening, Cassie told her mother of her chance encounters with Johnny along the trail, and of what Aunt Mabel had said about the kind of man Johnny was. Kate's heart trembled at the flash in her daughter's eyes and the passion in her voice as she spoke. Cassie told Kate of time spent with Johnny at Mabel's cabin, and their ride home through the snow. Then softly, Cassie spoke of her revelation during the violent storm, how she had begun to believe that God was speaking to her, and finally, of Johnny's experience on the mountaintop.

Kate had listened with the intention of helping her daughter distinguish between emotion and fact, but found she needed to comment only sparingly. As she listened, she was impressed with the amount of thought and prayer Cassie had given to this relationship, and surprised by Cassie's maturity.

When Kate delicately questioned Cassie about the night by the barn--the night when Johnny had ridden home with her after the argument with her father--Cassie seemed anxious to talk about it. Though Kate did not suspect so, she concluded that her daughter had no cause for embarrassment. Most importantly, the young deputy had done nothing to cause her daughter to be held in the particular emotional bondage often experienced by a young woman after having unintentionally, yet fully, surrendered herself.

Bare feet pattered over the wooden floorboards as Juney and Martha, accompanied by two scraggly cloth dolls, headed for the bed, dragging a brightly-patterned quilt behind them.

"We havin' a party?" Martha asked, rubbing sleepy eyes with her free fist.

"Party on the bed, party on the bed!" Juney squealed, throwing herself onto the high, stuffed mattress.

"No, no, girls!" Kate exclaimed, "Not tonight." She stood and smoothed her skirts.

"Are you unwell, Cassie? You look awful," Martha said, caressing Cassie's face with her soft hand.

"Oh, sweet, not very. Just a little unsettled," Cassie said, cuddling her sister.

Kate spoke, herding the young ones gently. "Come on girls, to bed now."

Simultaneously, the protesting girls hugged their older sister and Cassie smiled, even as tears escaped down her cheeks. "Go now, sillies, and good night. I'll see you tomorrow morning bright."

Later, as they lay side by side, Kate could not console her husband on the matter. He was incredulous that she would even consider Cassie's point of view, and even though Kate agreed with Dodge overall, she felt compelled to explain Cassie's position.

"She's given her heart, Dodge, and I doubt we'll ever get it back," she said finally, as she snuffed out the light. Dodge had turned his back to her.

Pungent thoughts became a silent, penitent prayer. "How do I garner fault in all of this? Why do they turn away from me as though these things were my fault? I could have done differently, I know, but dear Lord, I don't know how to help either of them." Bewildered, she lay in the dark, until finally sleep came.

On his first attempt to visit Mabel Baker after the accident, Johnny had been thwarted by an unfortunate misunderstanding resulting in the death of a drifter who had passed through Sideling in his attempt to leave the "god forsakenness" of the high plains winter. The sojourner had lost his miniscule fortune at the bar and poker table during the late evening hours of the previous night and then felt the need to recoup his losses from the dealer around midmorning. Sober he was not, and the indisputable mismatch had gone to the dealer who himself was new to the Sideling community and not a welcomed addition.

By the time Johnny and Sam sorted through the facts, it was time for rounds, and the task fell to Johnny. Sam faced his deputy who had not spoken more than two words, excluding those he had managed to expel as he bluntly interrogated the shooter.

"You're a dark and stormy piece of humanity this morning, Johnny. The thunder rolls every time you come my way. There is enough tragedy in this town without you adding to it, so fix it, boy!" Sam snapped, in a non-negotiable tone as he exited the office.

Johnny found misery a hard thing to hide, for it clashed with his usual sanguine nature. Picking up the broom, he pushed it idly back and forth without song, another element that seemed lost to him of late. Accumulating little debris, he swept the evidence of his sorry attempt under the marshal's desk and propped the broom against the wall.

Contemplating his woes, he walked out onto the porch and nearly collided with Sherm McNeil as the excited man rushed from the telegraph office next door.

"Where are you headed in such a hurry, Sherm?" Johnny asked, steadying his friend who had lost his balance.

"I'm trying to compose a succinct message for miserly ole Miz Brown, but first I've got to deliver this one to Reverend Stoner," Sherm piped hurriedly, straightening the visor which had slipped down over his eyes.

"I'll take it for you, Sherm," Johnny replied easily.

"That's mighty thoughty of ya, Deputy." He shoved the paper into Johnny's hand, and like a lizard darting for cover, the wiry young man disappeared back into the disorganization of paper, pencil and transmitting key.

Glad for the menial distraction, Johnny quelled his thoughts, descended the porch steps and rounded the outside corner of the office, headed for the church. Halted dead in his tracks once again, he faced Cassie Wilkerson.

Tragic eyes found his own, framed by reddened rims that haunted a face paler than he had remembered. She did not speak. He grasped her shoulders, focused, and held her off even though she attempted to come to him.

"I am sorry, Cassie. Your father wouldn't allow me to speak with you. But what he said doesn't change how I feel, not one iota."

She tried to step toward him again, but he held her shoulders firmly.

"Johnny..." she breathed.

"I have to respect your father's wishes, you know that. We will have to wait, I can't think of any way around it."

She stared at him, her eyes wide. "So that's it? That's all you can say?" The disbelieving look on her face raised his volition and he implored her understanding.

"I tried to reason with him, believe me, I tried."

"So, to you, this means we go back to how we were? We can't be together unless we encounter one another on the trail or at church? It is not enough, I want to be with you."

She spoke softly and did not cry, was not contrary, nor did she raise her voice. As her eyes searched his, the confidence in her level gaze shook him with the realization that she had no doubt he would resolve this matter quickly.

He knew he could not, and also knew he would not lose her, even if he lost everything else. Not wanting to release her now that she stood before him, with the reality of her presence much more than he could have anticipated, he answered. "Cassie, listen to me. We'll get through this. There is a right way and a wrong way to do it. Your father...he loves you. He is not an unreasonable man, and if I don't respect his wishes, then I am not respecting you or any life we could have together."

Her eyes grew misty. "I'm trying to understand, but I don't understand my father. He is being intolerant, and he is wrong. There must be some way he can be made to understand. He knows me well, knows he can trust me, and he thinks highly of you and your character," she reasoned, watching him intently.

Impulsively he pulled her to him, lifting her and holding her close as he turned. Then, he stood her on the ground, and immediately took a step backward. Her hair caught on his badge and he freed it.

"I will never stop loving you, girl. You have my heart. Go now, and do your best at what you have to do. I'll do the same. And while I'm doing my job, it will be for us...for you."

She seemed to search for words which, when found, tumbled out desperately. "Please, Johnny, promise me one thing. Promise you'll never pass me by on the street without seeing me, without speaking, no matter what the circumstances. Promise you'll always love me, and if you quit for some reason, promise you'll tell me so."

She searched the deep blue-green mirrors of his eyes, seeking the reflection of his heart. Opening her mouth as if to say something more, she stopped when he tapped her lips gently with a gloved finger, and nodded in the direction of the millinery.

"Cassie, please go now; I promise, but you must go before I do somethin' I'll regret."

Standing tall and drawing her heavy coat about her, and without another word, she turned and hurried away.

(Exodus 20:12, Mark 9:42)

Telegram in hand, he walked toward the church. The chance encounter with Cassie had blindsided him, sending him careening off course. He was thankful he had not anticipated it. Had he had time to try to formulate his thoughts he most likely would have been at a loss for words, but somehow on the spur of the moment, words had come. "How do people do this? How do I find words to sustain this relationship?" He could not answer the questions he posed. Unexpected, brief interludes were all he and Cassie had ever shared.

As he walked, he wondered. He had never read literature of a romantic nature and never even contemplated being a participant in this kind of affair. He walked now, over uncharted terrain, and as it had been in battle, explosions seemed to come from all directions. In these new encounters he had become the captain, and in the skirmishes, he would be the one to make decisions to keep what little he and Cassie had from being annihilated. He tried to remember interactions between his own parents. He had never cared then and had only enjoyed the effects of their strategies, never dreaming he would have to come up with his own. With each step, he looked down the path of disillusionment, and by the time he entered the church, he knew he needed help.

Reverend Stoner was worrying the fire with a long poker as Johnny let himself into the small sanctuary and walked toward the clergyman. The heat of the stove was welcomed after the wind and cold of the streets.

"Hey, Reverend Stoner," Johnny greeted as the portly man straightened, raising his arm to hail his congregant.

Johnny held the telegram high to which the minister replied, "Ah, let's see what God hath wrought!"

He extended his hand, shaking Johnny's. Pleased to see the deputy up and about, Reverend Stoner commented on the fact.

"You are much improved since our last encounter. Feeling fit, are you?"

"Tolerable, I guess," Johnny replied, smiling and helping himself to the fresh coffee offered from the tin pot.

"Let me see," quipped the Reverend, "just who from where needs what!" He read the yellow page as Johnny sipped the hot brew, glancing around the quiet sanctuary.

It had a different feel about it in the twilight of the afternoon, serene and still, without the Sunday morning bustle. Clear, gothic windows flanked the sidewalls, but Johnny's eyes were drawn to the one stained-glass master-piece over the pulpit. The colors, vivid, bright, and illuminated from without by the western sky, depicted Jesus as He struggled under the burden of the rugged cross.

"Sit awhile, if you have the time, son. I could use the company." Reverend Stoner folded the yellow paper he held, placing it in his pocket.

Johnny inquired as to whether there had been troublesome news in the telegram, which the minister denied. "It's actually good news. My daughter will be visiting in a week, arriving on the stage from Denver. You remember Barbara, don't you? Seems to me you shared a picnic lunch with her one Sunday last spring."

It was just an ordinary statement, with no intent to spur any inquisition or hint as to future design, so Johnny relaxed, remembering the day well. It had been an unusually peaceful day, and he had not had to rush off. He found Barbara Stoner to be a very pleasant companion for the brief time they had conversed that afternoon, but now he found himself wondering where Cassie had been on that day. He couldn't recall having seen her and had she been there, how could he not have noticed? Had she shared her lunch basket with another? He intentionally drew his thoughts back to the minister who had paused as though waiting for a response, or at least an acknowledgement.

"It was a good day, spent with a lovely lady," Johnny replied, conflicted and not managing to expound on his simple statement.

Reverend Stoner seemed not to mind and intuitively changed the subject. "I am sorry about your horse, Johnny. Out here a horse is a man's right hand, and good ones like yours are especially valued."

Johnny came to sit next to the warmth of the stove, on the pew behind the minister. They talked briefly about Cody and the trials of training with an injured body, then Reverend Stoner rose to add wood to the fire.

"You have a few healthy scars left from the accident...and I suppose it's a good thing."

Johnny touched the scars on his wrists, where the skin had torn as he had struggled to loose himself from the strangling rein on that terrible day. He responded with a wry laugh.

"The good thing is that the pain is gone, but other than that, I don't follow you."

Reverend Stoner smiled in return, then slipped back into the pew, settled himself, and proceded thoughtfully. "Well, scars are a kind of symbol as to where you've been, a type of marker for your life's journey." He fell silent, quietly regarding the deputy.

Conscious of the weariness within himself, Johnny did not reply, considering that if he sat still and just listened, perhaps this man of God could explain his life to him. He knew where he had been but suddenly needed someone to explain why--why so many hard places and questions without answers?

Gideon Stoner was a good judge of men. Years of practice had made him a fairly reliable reader of men's thoughts, and he found most men not difficult to understand. Most did not wish to expose their deepest uncertainties, and it seemed hard for them to be honest with each other. In Johnny, he perceived something different. His eyes bore the look of a man not unwilling to speak, but of a young man who truly did not know what to say.

With a little prodding, Johnny began to tell of his ordeal and of the strange voice on the mountain. "I remember the words. They came like a whisper...'I am'. I heard it twice."

Reverend Stoner was silent for a long moment, his kind eyes intense as he considered the man before him. He leaned over and drew his Bible to him from across the pew, opening it.

"What does it mean? Besides 'I am God?' And why would I have heard it? I guess I'm asking what meaning it could hold for me?" Johnny asked.

Reverend Stoner opened his Bible to Exodus, the third chapter. "When God chose Moses to lead the Israelites out of Egypt and bring His law to them, Moses asked God, 'Who shall I say sent me?' God revealed His personal name. 'I AM THAT I AM.' Names meant much to the Jews in those days. Moses' name meant 'drawn forth' and truly he was, drawn forth from the bulrushes as a Hebrew baby. Protected by God and raised by the Egyptian Pharaoh's daughter, he became Israel's great deliverer, and led the Israelites out of 400 years of bondage in Egypt. God told Moses that 'I AM THAT I AM' would be His name; the name by which He would be remembered from generation to generation.

"The same name means, 'I will be what I will be.' I recall through the fuzziness of time, from my distant theology class, that Jesus used the name 'I Am' for Himself also, when He declared Himself to be God. Two syllables, YHWH, are archaic forms of the ancient verb hwh... I believe it is now pronounced Yaweh and means, 'He who causes to be' or 'He who brings into existence'. This is the greatest self-revelation about God we have. The being of God transcends time. So, I would say to you simply, if such a thing could be simple, that God wants your attention. He has a purpose for your life, and He will guide you if you trust Him and listen."

"I've done nothing worthy of His notice--nothing that could qualify me to be considered for His use," Johnny admitted, his puzzlement growing to concern. "I have faith, but not the kind Moses had." Johnny leaned forward to rest his arms along the back of the pew before him.

"If so, ask God to increase your faith. He will honor any man's sincere prayer for that, son. Romans 10:17 promises that faith will come as you hear and read His word. Expose yourself to the Bible, take a look at how Jesus lived, and do it intentionally. Don't just depend on my modest attempts at preaching on Sundays. Read the Bible for yourself. It's a living Word through which God speaks to us individually. Get to know the Savior, what He has done for us, how He lived, and what He will do today and in the future. Start with the Gospel of John," he instructed, flipping through the well-worn pages to the first chapter of that gospel and symbolically laying it on the pew next to Johnny. "Then read through all the gospels. You make choices every day. Choose to do this...if you really want to understand what God would have for you personally.

Johnny did not take the Bible up, but glanced at the chapter's familiar title, The Gospel According to John.

"I know I need to be more diligent in trying to get to it. That's a lot to think on, but I thank you, sir," Johnny said rising. "I'll do my best to make the effort."

"In your effort, Johnny, never forget the enemy of your soul. The devil's deception in this world will continue for a time, and he will mock you and try to tarnish the things you succeed in doing, for he holds the world in temporary bondage. But Christ has already won the war, and when the tempter falls, his end will be swift and complete."

(Revelation 2:10; Ephesians 2:2; 1 Peter 5:8-9)

Reverend Stoner stood and as he gave Johnny a parting handshake remembered, "Cassie Wilkerson paid me a visit while you were ill and told me a little of what was on her heart. She is young, but strong in her faith, which is another reason you may want to consider our Savior carefully."

He smiled knowingly and continued, "Young women such as Cassie usually look for men who will lead them spiritually--men who will be good husbands and fathers. It seems the hearts of men are harder to reach these days."

Melancholy touched his eyes, then he brightened measurably, again considering the man before him. "Just become what you need to become and let the Lord lead you. While He's doing that, He'll take care of that girl of yours and as you both grow, He'll handle the details. Don't obsess over Dodge Wilkerson, when it's time, he'll come around…if it's meant to be."

As Johnny walked out into the gray of the cold evening, more thoughts now heaped upon the quandaries of his life. But with the added burden, he found it strange that they did not weigh on him further, but gave him a different avenue to traverse and, though full of twists and turns which blocked any clear view now, the path proffered a measure of hope.

(Joshua 24:15)

Reverend Stoner remained quietly on the pew for a few moments, watching the orange firelight color the vertical white planks which formed the interior walls of his church, neatly fitted, strong and straight. He prayed for his small congregation, that they would be as symmetrical and as functional for the Lord as was the building. Many of the faithful were graying now, and he prayed they would persevere with the changing demographics of the town. He prayed for the deputy and for the girl he loved, and prayed for wisdom to guide them, for they would surely come to him again.

He thought of Johnny on the mountaintop and of the Ancient Voice that had puzzled the young man. He picked up his Bible, lying open on the pew, and his eyes fell on the words that gave him pause. They were awesome words, powerful in their portent, and among his favorite for they were filled with truth from God, Who had proved so faithful in his own life. Now he pondered them again, and wondered at the mysterious ways of his God, Who continued to work out His marvelous plan down through the generations.

He read through the verses slowly. John 1:6-7, "There was a man sent from God, whose name was John. The same came for a witness, to bear witness of the Light…"

20

THE TUMULT

OVER THE NEXT few days, as the weather moderated somewhat and the problems increased in town, another break-in at the Flour and Grain was reported to the marshal's office by an irate Abigail Miller whose husband was again out of town. When rounds were made early in the morning, tampering of locks on other businesses also became apparent. Nothing seemed to have been disturbed except at the Flour and Grain, where Clancy Miller's clerk, Lester, reported six bags of flour missing. Brawls at the Watering Hole Saloon became more frequent as another dealer took up residence in Sideling.

One evening as he was rounding, Johnny found Beau Brenner and Eric Flynn on the street behind the saloon, talking with two young women who had recently taken up residence in the upper rooms of the establishment. Having come through the back street, Johnny surprised the boys who were loitering with the ladies, reclining on the back steps.

"Evenin', folks," Johnny called in greeting, coming out of the shadows in the twilight.

A young woman, petite and brunette, smiled, and a blonde of more ample proportions watched the deputy approach. The brunette expressed particular interest in the new arrival.

"Good evening, sir. What can I do for you?" she replied, standing to assume a more provocative posture and smoothing her skirts.

"For starters, you can quit fascinatin' these two young men," Johnny replied, shifting his gaze toward the pair who had ceased conversing and now stood awkwardly.

"Isn't there somewhere else you boys need to be?" Johnny asked diplomatically.

Beau spoke up. "I guess it's none of your business, McLane. Ain't breakin' no laws now, are we?" Beau's eyes flashed arrogantly.

Earlier, when Johnny had found an opportunity to question him about the break-in, Beau had been vague and evasive. His attitude toward Johnny had not improved since their run-in over the alleged hawk shooting earlier in the fall. There had been a few minor skirmishes since that time, and Beau and Johnny continued to mix like scum on a pond. Recent allegations concerning a potential liaison between Cassie Wilkerson and the lawman had infuriated Beau.

Rumor also indicated that Johnny, although he wore a badge, was only a few years Beau's senior. Beau knew Eric also had designs on Cassie and figured he could handle him, but he found the particulars regarding Johnny to be troublesome. It riled Beau immensely that the deputy thought he had any claim to the girl who had been Beau's secret passion for the last two years.

"You may not be breaking any law, but I am sure your folks would prefer you spend your time more profitably. As for the ladies," he turned, directing his comments toward the women, "solicitation of minors...is a problem."

'Beautiful woman...' the thought assaulted him suddenly, and he grew uncomfortable under the brunette's gaze.

With eyes laughing, she questioned him. "A lawman, are you? Too bad, but as you can see, we were just talking--just passing the evening, getting some fresh air. It's good for the mind and soul, don't you think?"

Johnny's eyes took her in and he could not stop them from devouring her. Visions emerged, suffusing and rising from a dark vault within his core. He turned to focus on the boys. "It's late. I'm sure you're both needed at home."

Eric, who had not spoken, turned and walked away. Johnny knew that the young man stood to lose more than Beau. His father would never tolerate the heir to his large cattle ranch hooking up with painted ladies of dubious reputation, and Eric understood this well. Seeking diversion from the rigors of schooling and impending responsibilities of adulthood, Eric had formed an unlikely and inexplicable alliance with Beau which Johnny imagined was only temporary.

Johnny made no comment as he watched Eric leave, and waited for Beau to move on. Hurling a few snide comments at the deputy, followed by a few brazen remarks to the ladies who seemed to have lost interest in him, Beau departed scornfully, promising that he would return.

The blonde spoke first. "We were just having a little fun with them, Marshal, didn't mean no harm."

Johnny turned his focus to the problem at hand. "What brings you ladies to town? Are you plannin' to stay or just visiting?"

The blonde looked to the brunette, waiting for her response. Finally, after a blatant appraisal of Johnny, the latter spoke.

"Well, I'd say it depends on a few things. We have friends here for one, and the other could involve you, if you would like."

She quit being coy and now spoke frankly, scrutinizing him. Johnny was glad for the deepening twilight and found himself unsettled under her audacious gaze. He fought to control his thoughts, to control the images of what she could be, if he would only...

His flesh warred with his will. 'I love Cassie,' he chastised silently, finding it hard to concentrate on the words the brunette was speaking, and struggling to recall what questions he had asked of her. Fervor arose as images of the woman in the shadows of the hotel lobby in Laramie, and the confusions of that night in the wagon so long ago played over in his mind.

'You are no different than those boys,' his thoughts condemned, 'no different.'

She was still speaking, and he interrupted angrily. "The law in this town restricts any solicitation on the streets so you'll have to go inside," he exclaimed bluntly.

Her eyes narrowed. "Now wait a minute! I don't know what you are talking about. I was only being friendly! Don't get so edgy," she barked, with a flip of her skirt. "I didn't mention the third thing that brought us to your town." Johnny ignored the bait.

"The mountains--we love the mountain air, don't we Doris? It's good for the lungs," she sighed, taking an exaggerated breath, causing her short cloak to fall open and cling to her rounded shoulders, exposing her black-laced bodice.

"Oh, let's go in, Deena! It's too cold to waste our time out here. You're gettin' nowhere." She tipped her blonde head, tramped her way up the steps, and opened the door. "He ain't interested, Deena, so just come on!"

Johnny had one more question and he felt obliged to ask it, though he would rather be gone from her presence. "Is your 'friend' the new dealer in town?"

"Why do you care about my friends?" Her tone was hard and even.

"Just wondering if all of your friends are particular acquaintances of Mr. Leafy Misner who owns this place, or did you all just up and decide on your own that business in Sideling was too good an opportunity to pass by?"

"I am sure you are referring to my job as hostess here. To what other business or opportunity would you be referring? We all need places to live and work, so why not here? It's mountain air that brings us out here, Marshal; good mountain air, and if you would like a lesson in enjoying it, I'd be happy to oblige you."

When he did not respond, she raised a speculative eyebrow. She lifted her skirts, turned to mount the steps, and entered the doorway. Without a backward glance, she closed the door behind her.

Johnny stood alone in the street and realized two things simultaneously. First, the arrival of the new citizens to Sideling was not coincidental, it had most likely been orchestrated. Secondly, he might wear a gun and a badge, but he was still as affected and drawn to the illicit as might any other man in Sideling.

He stood perplexed as the dark fell like a curtain over the last of the sorry melodrama. A dark and pathetic spectacle, he felt himself the center of theater in the absurd and as lost as those he had just reprimanded. The difference between his life and theirs was that he knew well the pitfalls of that kind of behavior. That knowledge might deter his behavior, but it did nothing to diminish his desire for it.

He walked slowly down Main Street, toward the office and wondered what Cassie would think of him now. He tried to rid himself of the guilt but could not shake free of it.

(Proverbs 7:6-12)

Focusing on any detail of his job proved difficult. After a few minor run-ins with Sam, he found himself trying to keep out of the marshal's way and just get his work done. Catching a glimpse of Cassie became a subconscious "mind game" and wondering how she was bearing up threatened to overtake his waking thoughts. When evening came and he could be fairly certain she was not at Millie's and had gone back to the ranch, he unwittingly anticipated relief, but suppositions and expectations arrived with the night, haunting his dreams.

Again, he attempted to visit Mabel Baker at Mrs. Winkler's, but the old woman was "sleeping", having passed a restless night. Mrs. Winkler informed Johnny that Mabel asked for him frequently, and that she would be pleased that he had stopped by. "Mabel will be disappointed to have missed you."

Trying not to appear too obvious, Johnny rode past the schoolhouse, or glanced at the doorway to Miss Halstead's cabin when business carried him out of the office. He usually failed to see Cassie, except occasionally from a distance. Where was she? Injured or ill--and how would he know?

When the request came from Iron Mountain, Sam gladly sent his deputy. It would be his pleasure to spare the deputy for a day or two--or longer if necessary. In truth, Sam decided he would send Johnny on every venture he could find or conjure up, as long as it involved getting him away from Sideling. In town, Johnny had been restless, underfoot, or hard to find. He forgot almost everything he was asked to do, and unless a task could be accomplished by rote, it was often left half completed.

Sam was blindsided by all of this. Usually conscientious and dependable, it did not seem normal behavior for his deputy. Johnny had worked hard to regain his riding and shooting skills, progressing nicely over the past three weeks, but Sam could swear that the deputy had left a portion of his brain buried under the tonnage of rock atop that mountain. A day before Johnny left, Sam decided to question Doc on the matter of a damaged brain.

Doc, being a scientific man, supposed it could be possible. Little was known about the brain and its mysterious functions, however, he had another theory. He felt that the symptoms Johnny displayed came from an entirely undamaged brain, a brain which functioned quite normally and that the symptoms Sam beheld were exacerbated by an age-appropriate functioning of that cerebellum. Sam stared blankly at Doc. The practitioner rephrased his assessment in common terms, and Sam finally got the gist of it.

"Oh, for Pete's sake! I don't know if I can tolerate another year of this!"

Some days Sam caught a glimpse of Cassie, standing at the gate to Olivia Halstead's "millinery", leaning against the new signpost, staring toward the jailhouse. On one of those afternoons, he noticed Olivia come onto the porch, shake her head at the girl, and point to a hat she held in her hand. Sam supposed the millinery was suffering neglect, as was the office of deputy, but that knowledge gave him little solace. He was not much of a praying man, but he thanked God then and there that he was not Cassie Wilkerson's father. He decided he had let this go on long enough. He would have it out with Johnny when the deputy returned from taking the incoming shipment to Iron Mountain, but he did not relish the confrontation in the slightest.

21

THE EPOCH

HE DID NOT notice the sunlight as it crept across the toes of his boot until it rose, warming the cloth of his pants as he sat by the river. The sun had begun its climb over the cottonwood trees along the riverbank. The shadows cast by the trees from the east were long, the morning cool and crisp, unusually mild for early November.

'How strange the weather has been,' he thought as he rested, recalling the fierce mountain storm of another warm day in mid-October. Johnny glanced at the sky...not a cloud in sight.

So much had happened since that loss. He glanced across the small clearing, and Cody stood grazing on the sparse prairie grass. The horse had been more than adequate and Johnny, when he was honest with himself, found he had enjoyed training him.

His own body had healed to a large degree, and the training finally gave more gratification than pain, physically at least. The mental anguish remained. He did not understand why the loss of Traveller hung over him, or why he continued to feel it so keenly and tried to reason it away. This was part of life; it was not his fault. He should be able to move on, but he felt as though he had lost a part of himself.

It occurred to him that there was nothing much left of himself now, for the rest of his heart had gone to Cassie, irretrievably and totally, and without thoughts of her, there was nothing to fill his emptiness. He couldn't fill it with her presence beside him; he couldn't hold her hand or even speak with her. They had managed a few stolen sentences; a kind of code had evolved between them since their chance meeting near the office weeks ago.

It took only seconds to transmit and most of the time, seconds were all they had. "I'm doing my best," she would say. "I'm keeping my promise," he would respond, and he would wink at her. He tried to keep those brief encounters positive, but the moment she was out of sight, he crumbled inside and the emptiness returned. They had not encountered each other while riding outside the town limits. If they did, he knew he would be hard-pressed to respect her father's wishes. Time seemed his enemy, but as Marshal Brett had said, it was also his ally.

In little over a year's time, Cassie would be eighteen. But what kind of life would they have together if Dodge Wilkerson never accepted any role for Cassie other than that of a cattleman's wife? What kind of life would Johnny hand her, if she lived in opposition to her father's wishes as the wife of a lawman.

Johnny would give up nothing and gain everything that was precious to him. Cassie would be giving up everything--her comfort, a place in Sideling's society, meager though it was, and possibly her family, gaining only hardship with the union. How could he ask that of her?

Impulsively striking the heel of his boot hard against the rock, he quit his thoughts. "I've gotta stop this! My mind runs like a coonhound in a pen, round and round the truth, wearing the ground thin and always ending up where I started with no new resolution," he groused aloud.

Cody's ears twitched but the horse did not bother to lift his head or turn a sympathetic eye. With no other living thing nearby, Johnny unleashed his frustrations on the docile, grazing equine.

"Oh, yeah, fine friend you turned out to be!" Johnny snapped sourly. He had traveled for four hours, was still about two hours shy of Sideling, and bone weary from the tribulations of the last two days.

At the request of Marshal Riddick, Johnny had accompanied the marshal's speculator friend who had traveled from Salt Lake City by wagon, and had made a stop in Sideling on his way to Iron Mountain. Joining the company in Sideling, Johnny had followed the speculator on horseback in a security detail...of sorts.

After having secured the cumbersomely-loaded wagons as assigned, Johnny had been ordered to the mercantile to refortify supplies, with a list in hand. He had been mildly curious when the lawman who had accompanied the speculator up from Utah had said little, just shaking his head and heading for the saloon as they traded places on the duplicitous detail.

All had gone well until they reached Laramie City. Johnny and a small, dark Mexican, had transferred the contents of the two wagons to the Union Pacific boxcar. Johnny was never privileged to know exactly which great trunk held the silver and valuable documents that were to be conveyed by train to Cheyenne, although it was his duty to protect it, and he did his best to ascertain the facts.

The speculator was a pompous, high-hatted man, who made no bones about the fact that Johnny was there to serve. He dictated his orders while staring at some document or letter he invariably held before him, never directly acknowledging the man who stood before him. Securing food, another ream of paper, or an evening tub, were among the speculator's many demands, and led Johnny's thoughts backward along a well-trodden path. Johnny suddenly found himself wondering if the Emancipation Proclamation had been far-reaching enough.

Cody had been a different, though no less frustrating, exercise in humility. Loading him into the cattle car had been an exasperating experience for the horseman Johnny knew himself to be. He had been forced to drag the chestnut gelding up the plank as two cowboys assisted at either side with a rope behind and tugging the horse's rear. It had taken thirty minutes to accomplish the task, and Cody bucked and reared in terror until Johnny was forced to blindfold and manhandle him into the boxcar.

The horse was no fonder of the moving train than he had been of the loading experience. Johnny had spent his time on the rails precariously scrambling between the cattle car, to comfort the horse, and the boxcar, to guard the unidentified boxes of cradled valuables.

By the time Johnny unloaded the boxcar in Cheyenne, reloaded the valuables and sundries onto other wagons, helped by a boy he had bribed with a few pieces of his own scarce silver, he did not care if he ever laid eyes on Cy Riddick's speculating friend again.

The equally horrendous task of unloading the gelding had also taken a toll on the deputy. His recovering muscles burned and ached as they had not for a week, inflamed by the strenuous enterprise. However, he was able to ride Cody to Iron Mountain in relative peace, armed to the teeth, following the wagons of valuables, and away from the sight and demands of the obstreperous entrepreneur.

When they reached the small, nondescript town, Johnny's position was decidedly better as the speculator had acquaintances ready to assist, and his old friend, Marshal Riddick, to focus on. To Johnny's surprise, Riddick requested to see the deputy in his office as soon as the flurry of greetings settled.

"Good to see you up and about, Deputy McLane." Riddick rose, removing himself from behind a huge, oak desk. He offered his hand and a chair nearby, then settled himself casually on the corner of the desk, looking down at Johnny. Riddick had an easy smile and seemed genuinely glad to see the deputy. After passing a few obligatory comments, Marshal Riddick grew serious.

"I hope the trip up here was not too difficult. I heard that you had a tough time of it after the accident you had; was it last month?

Johnny thought it best not to mention his struggles on the way to Iron Mountain and referred instead to the progress he had made.

"It was an unfortunate incident, but we are both back to work now." Johnny replied levelly.

"Who was the man with you?" Riddick inquired.

"Jess Bryant, sir. He was also with us on the canyon raid. Works for Wells Fargo, has his own relay station and helps us out as needed. In fact, he's assisting Sam Brett while I'm gone. A good man, a fine scout; do you remember him?" Johnny asked.

"I believe so," Riddick replied, tightening his lips as if trying to remember. He rose to sit behind the desk, leaned forward, and placed his forearms upon the desk top.

Johnny wondered how the marshal could keep track of any one thing. Papers lay strewn at odd angles, covering the surface of his desk until not one inch of wood was visible. The marshal's hat and gloves rested atop a stack of wanted posters at one corner of the jumbled conglomeration. Marshal Riddick's eyes regarded Johnny amiably.

"How is Sideling taking the loss of the two prisoners and your recuperation process?" Johnny was surprised by so direct a question and returned his comments as evenly as he could.

"Everything seems to be quiet at least for the time being. I guess Jess and I are getting the benefit of any doubt the citizens may have."

"But you're not sure of that," Cy commented, looking squarely at Johnny.

The deputy began to feel some discomfort as he tried to process the statement, then quickly countered with a question of his own.

"Is there something specific you'd like to know? If so, I may be the wrong person to ask. I talked to Mayor Vaiden myself, and my situation seems stable, at least for now. That's all I can tell you." Johnny fixed his eyes directly on Cy Riddick's tired, deeply lined eyes which did not hold steady.

Again, Johnny was thankful for his papa's instruction. 'Look at me when I'm talking to you, son. A man can learn a lot from another man's eyes. Sometimes eyes can hold a lot more truth than mere words, for they are windows into a man's soul.'

Cy Riddick met Johnny's eyes again. "I'll get to the point. I was very impressed at your handling of the canyon raid, son, many of us were. Now, as for the transport of the prisoners, especially across a mountain range, well, that is always "iffy" business. Anything can happen; there are a myriad of unknowns…I am aware of that. I'm on the lookout for a good man for this town. I need a deputy and, frankly, you interest me. I am prepared to offer you one third more than your current salary in Sideling. Iron Mountain is a growing town, and I am not as young as I used to be. May be thinking of retiring soon. You would make a good marshal."

The surprise must have shown on Johnny's face for Cy continued in an easy manner. "Sam Brett is a good man, younger than me by a few good years, I'll admit," he chuckled, "and he's got a good reputation. He won't have trouble finding a replacement for you in town…not of your same caliber for sure, but a smart man can learn to be a lawman. You did."

Just what town did Riddick think he was talking about? Johnny had been hired as deputy only because no one else wanted the job, and he happened to have been lucky enough to shoot straight on that particular day. Had so much changed in a little over one year? Maybe many men were smart enough to learn to be lawmen, but just how many would be desperate enough to take the job?

Cy continued, "Besides, Sam knows business is business. Sideling can't afford to pay you what you're worth."

Johnny wondered at Riddick's comment. Iron Mountain was further from the railroad and major cattle operations than Sideling. The town was neither larger in population or in commerce, and had few natural resources as far as Johnny knew. Where would this kind of money come from? Was it copper, silver or gold? Maybe coal, but he decided not to address the point. Cy leaned back in his chair and smiled.

"Where is your deputy?" Johnny asked, still holding Riddick's eyes.

"Gone back east. Up and married and the Mrs. hated the constant wind out here, so they left," Cy answered casually.

Johnny could not have defined the second it happened or sworn that a change had actually occurred in Riddick's gaze, but he perceived a tiny alteration. Riddick pushed back in his chair, placed his hands behind his head, elbows pointing east and west, and gave Johnny a broad smile.

"Just think about it, son. This town's got some new business opportunities coming our way. Stay for dinner, we'll talk, and I'll show you around." Riddick rose to his feet just as a large, mustached, middle-aged man entered the office.

"Excuse me, didn't realize you were busy." In a dress coat and ruffled shirt, with a narrow tie about his throat, the man with the clipped, British accent looked out of place. His polished boots did not appear to have seen much of the mud or dust of the boardwalks of the prairie town.

Johnny stood and was introduced by the marshal. The introduction was brief and included only the man's name, Philip Joyner, but no other information.

The brisk manner by which Joyner had entered contrasted markedly with the sudden shift in his demeanor. He stared at Johnny as though he were quickly appraising him for worth, then shot Riddick a sharp glance.

"Think about what I said, Deputy McLane. I'll be in touch." Riddick said easily, dismissing Johnny with a smile.

"Good to see you, sir, a pleasure to meet you Mr...." Johnny replied, but Marshal Riddick had turned away, engaging Mr. Joyner in conversation which began with an uneven smile, and a consolatory hand on the tall man's back.

Uncomfortable with the thought that for some unknown reason he had been responsible for the change in the attitude of the encounter, Johnny had pushed away the senseless contagion from his mind, and left without comment, unnoticed by the conversing associates.

That afternoon and within the half hour, Johnny had departed, shaking the dirt from his hat with a hearty dismissal. "So much for dinner!"

Now, with the trials of the journey and quandaries of those preceding days behind him, Johnny rested by the river upon a rock. The sun climbed further into the clear sky, warming him. He thought of Cassie and as those thoughts assailed him, he felt an urgency rise within.

Maybe together, they could start a life in Iron Mountain. Cassie would be away from the pressures of her family, of Myra and the incessant friction between them, in a place where she would not be a schoolgirl: a place where there would be no rumors. She would be his wife, his to be with whenever he wanted or needed her. Impetuously, he sprang from the rock, spooking Cody. The frightened animal wheeled, bucked, and ran a few yards before calming and fixing the deputy with a doleful eye.

Heedless, Johnny ran for a deep spot in the river among the rocks, stripped off his clothing, and plunged into the frigid mountain stream, losing his breath. Oblivious to anything but the shock of cold, it took a few seconds before his instincts engaged and he began to swim. This was the merciful freedom he craved, and it lasted only minutes before the icy water began to make his bones ache and his head throb. He pulled himself from the pool and lay in the sunlight. There was nothing with which to dry himself except the chill of the breeze, and he struggled to pull his longjohns and pants over his wet body.

It had all been worth the effort. His skin tingled and he lay on his back, quiet, numb, and still...until the sun, then thoughts of Cassie, rose higher and brighter, warming him once again.

This had become the odd pattern of his life; his thoughts held him captive while he allowed circumstances to overtake him, pitching him into murky waters. He seemed to have no control, no way to free himself and gain any lasting escape.

"If you choose to do this...if you choose..." and with the remembrance of Reverend Stoner's advice, Johnny realized that to change anything, he would have to make a conscious choice, and that only he could choose to do this for himself.

He rose from the ground and walked to where Cody stood cropping the short, prairie grasses. From the saddlebag, he retrieved his small, black Bible. He returned to his place on the rock, lifted the cover of the Bible, and smoothed out the crinkled onionskin paper. How something so fragile and translucent could contain immutable ideas that were as life-changing as Reverend Stoner had indicated, he had no idea.

He thumbed through the pages, noting verses he had memorized as a child. Returning to the first page of the Book, his eyes fell upon the words, written in his mother's hand:

John Scott McLane
Born the 14th day of May
In the Year of Our Lord 1849
To Julia Rebecca Scott McLane and John Robert McLane
McLane's Mill, Virginia
In the county of Southampton

Between the flourishes and lines, she spoke unexpectedly to his heart, bringing a stab of emotion and a yearning for family and home. In a wave of debilitating loneliness, he sank to the ground, his back against the rock.

"Mama," he whispered. Beautiful mama, gone ashen and white, vacant eyes staring blindly up into the blue, prairie sky, body broken, her grace and guidance fragmented, blown away as the glitter of mica by the mournful prairie wind.

"Oh, God," he cried "Who am I now? That child is long gone...they are all gone! If I walked a thousand miles, ten thousand miles, I could never find them! I don't recognize myself anymore and You...You seem so distant, what could You want from me? Either leave me be or God, please...help me understand!" He hung his head as tears fell and rested his hands woodenly upon the open Bible in his lap, sobbing deeply.

He mourned, unaware of the sound of the rushing stream, or of the hawk which circled slowly, symmetrically, high overhead: oblivious to the shadows of the trees as they receded silently toward the riverbank, or the sun rising toward mid-morning. Images recent and from the distant past painfully assaulted him. Crashing waves, the sensation of tumbling, of lungs aching for oxygen, all merged wildly with the sharp crack of a rifle, and the scream from a dying horse, amidst thunder, lightning and hail--then the crushing weight as the mountain fell. His comrade, Saxby, with hand blown apart, lay helplessly across him as his own leg, ripped open by a Union bullet, bled on a battle-field. Thoughts of his father loomed, torn from his horse in battle, scorched in burning ash in the conflagration of the Wilderness; his father...whose wisdom and counsel died with him forever that day.

Sweet Mary Annie's haunted face rose, a spector, pale and ravaged by yellow fever, calling from the dark place. "Come find me, Johnny. It's cold and I'm frightened...it's time we go home." Her cries of desperation and his inability to help her, ushered him unwillingly into the deepest, darkest recesses of his mind; to the place he had trained himself never to go...back to the solitude of that evening, the evening of Mama's tragic death.

He lay prostrate, half-naked in the sultry heat of the confines, alone in a wagon full of her treasures but devoid of her presence, grief-stricken, chest wracked and aching with sobs, swallowed up in empty darkness.

He had passed the waning hours of the daylight similarly, unable to eat the supper brought to him by the well-meaning Mrs. Hart whose family also plodded slowly along with the stretch of wagons headed westward on the remains of the Overland Trail.

He ached with the knowledge that he had failed Mama, had failed to pro-tect her when she needed him, and that she was now gone forever. Oblivious to the circling of the wagons for the night, and the flicker of cook fires from without the wagon's canvass confines, he kept to himself.

The family had checked once again to see if they could comfort the grieving boy but realized there was nothing they could do, that his grief must be borne in his own way, alone by himself, so they had left him.

She made little sound, entering the wagon as she crawled to the spot where he lay on his belly. Coming close, she spoke softly, placing her hand on his head, stroking his hair.

"Johnny," she whispered, "it will be alright." She leaned over him, brushing her lips against his cheek, and he turned his tear-stained face away, breathing in the musty scent of the brown canvass.

"Leave me alone," he moaned, but she uncoiled, stretching out beside him.

Ellie Sinclair was an acquaintance, her family also making their way west with the small wagon train. She and Johnny had occasion to partner during the rousing reels when the other young folks, seeking release from the stress of the day, congregated as the fiddlers tuned up their instruments around evening campfires. Chronologically, Ellie was barely of age, but wise in the ways of the world, and danced provocatively at times, soliciting partners from the ranks of the young men.

Julia kept an eye on her son. In morning devotions, she increased her instruction from the book of Proverbs, warning graphically about the pitfalls which beset young men. She spoke honestly and openly on the subject with her son. Although curious, Johnny managed to sidestep the pitfalls, determined to do nothing to disappoint his mother. As far as he could figure, she had been through hell itself in the last four years. He was all she had left, and he felt both the pride and the weight of his responsibilities.

Ellie had enough sense to leave the young boys alone, except for subtle teasing and flirting when they were out of range of their mamas' watchful eyes, as they worked at minding siblings, livestock, and trod along behind the wagons in the daylight hours.

(Proverbs 7:1-5)

This night, owing to the tragedy of the day, there had been no revelry, no gaiety or dance, and at fifteen, Johnny would make the rest of this journey under no one's protective care. She eased closer, still stroking his hair and shoulder, passing her hand along the small of his back, whispering softly in his ear.

"It's alright, you're not alone now, I am here." Soft lips brushed his shoulder. "We all loved her Johnny, it's alright; it's alright now..."

He turned his face toward her empathetic whisperings, searching for commiseration, seeking a way to rid himself of the terrible pain. In the thick darkness, with overpowering need, he met her dim form. Caressing curls, infused with the pungent scent of smoke and herbs, fell softly on his cheek and bare shoulders. Her arms ensnared him, and beguiled, he exchanged truth for a lie, embracing the false security and the dissembling force of her wickedness. Yielding, the hope of comfort became the lie, driving him to rage against Providence who had taken his mother, then against the betrayal of her ideals by his own willful act.

Of the magnitude of the act and the misappropriation of the gift he possessed within him, the unsuspecting boy could not yet conceive, and the careless young woman had given no thought to the costly ramifications of her treachery. The war had eliminated his childlike wonder of the world, along with his father and siblings, and the prairie had claimed his mother. On that night of unspeakable sorrow, under an immense and starry canopy, the last remnant of his childhood was stolen away.

(Proverbs 6:16-19; 7:10-18)

He struggled upward from the dismal abyss of his soul, shutting his eyes tightly against the anguish of his past betrayal and cried out, "Oh, God, oh God!"

With a sudden gust, the wind caught the pages of his opened Bible. Lifting the corners against his fingers, swirling leaves and dirt against his damp body, it filled his nostrils until he breathed in sharply, opening his eyes to the bright light of the early November morning.

He passed a shirtsleeve across his face to wipe away the dirt and the wet of tears and sorrow. His gaze fell upon the open page in his lap. The jagged scars on his wrists contrasted sharply with the smooth white of the page and he recalled his struggle upon the mountain. Then, he remembered what he had heard that day...'I AM'. Through the eyes of his heart, he could see that the call of those words meant much more.

'I AM...your God.' Reverend Stoner had mentioned "Yaweh", and indicated this name for God also meant 'I am yours'. Intentionally, Johnny pondered these things.

(Exodus 19:4-6)

Vividly he recalled the image of the church's stained-glass window and remembered the Lord's struggle beneath the heavy beam, bearing the sins of humanity on his shoulders. He thumbed through the pages and found the gospel that Revered Stoner had shown him.

The Gospel of John, chapter one, verse one. "In the beginning was the Word, and the Word was with God, and the Word was God."

He read throughout the early afternoon, pausing occasionally to ponder a verse, rereading until its meaning became clear to him. These words, which seemed to have had little relevance previously, were now being revealed to his understanding. While he still struggled to comprehend this fully, he realized that the meanings of the precious words were being revealed to him by the power of the Holy Spirit as promised by Jesus.

Only as the late afternoon breeze picked up and the chill of the waning day settled in on him, did he lift his head to scan the horizon and to realize much of the day had passed. Marking his place with a leaf, he closed the Bible and took in the vast landscape.

It was more beautiful than he had remembered; the cottonwoods stood tall with roots sinking deep, protecting the banks at the river's edge. The golden autumn day swept majestically toward the distant purple mountains aflame with the copper and gold leaves of aspens, framed by tall, stately spruce. The sky was clear, deep, and expansive; all of this proclaimed the truth of the world in which he existed. How had he missed this truth? Even the beauty he now beheld groaned under the weight of sin, waiting for Christ to redeem and restore it at the end of the age. He recognized that if a simple, ordinary man such as he, was loved and valued more by Christ than the beauty before him, there had to be hope.

Jesus had carried that burdensome cross and died, laying down His life... for him. Johnny knew he was not worthy of this and as he pondered on it, he began to give God thanks for the great sacrifice, but most especially, for the gift of understanding it. Jesus had given volitional strength and had promised to provide him with courage, not only to seek out, but also to understand and to do His will.

(Romans 10:5-13; 5:1-8)

"I don't see how you can use a man such as me...but I am willing," he prayed earnestly. "God forgive my stubborn self, just take me and what little I have, for it's all I can bring to you now."

He sat quietly, wrapped in peace and rest. This pivotal discovery brought forth not only hope, but the character trait which had lain dormant throughout the tragedy and confusion and now would rise again to serve him well. Johnny was resilient, and with the peace Christ had given, came a rush of his God-given, natural optimism.

He reckoned that if God loved him as much...no, more than his earthly father had, then He could be trusted to treat him as a son, loving him in spite of his sorry efforts, guiding and correcting as his own father had, but with divine, transforming wisdom. God's plan was to bring him a purpose and a hope as promised in His Word, and Johnny found himself all in for it.

(Jeremiah 29:11)

He wondered that he could have thought himself worthy to court a godly, young woman such as Cassie and marveled at the fact that God had allowed her to open her heart to him. He prayed that God would help him to become worthy of her love, worthy of his work as deputy, and of the respect of a man like Sam Brett.

He knew he had been a trial for Sam of late and felt the sting of remorse. He recalled the looks Sam had given him, the times he had not realized Sam was speaking, and the duties he had to repeat. Sam had been a friend and relatively patient through all of it.

Johnny's eyes fell on his scars again. Reverend Stoner had said that it was God who drew all things into existence, and Johnny realized that just as the moon drew the ocean to high tide, surely it was God who had drawn his own frail heart to Him. He drew his finger across the length of the ragged scar and remembered.

He had been unexpectedly saved from perishing upon the mountain. Now, today, God had come to him again. He reckoned that to continue on would be a matter of faith, and possible only through trust in the God of this Bible. He realized he would have to rediscover God's expectations, and learn of His character from the words of this Book, for how could he obey or trust in One he did not know?

(John 14; 2 Corinthians 4:6)

It would not be easy, but he was determined to stay the course. He began to see that he was where he should be for now, living and working in the town of Sideling. As the town grew, he would be there for the struggle, working to provide a decent place for its citizens to live. He could not accept the offer from Cy Riddick and would not leave Sideling for a place where he detected duplicity, and where the facts did not add up. God had not called him to that.

(Hebrews 11:1)

22

THE PROTRACTION

TWILIGHT DEEPENED TO night and the lamps were lit along the streets of Sideling as Johnny rode in. The din from the saloon was raucous as Johnny passed, deciding to tie Cody outside of the office instead of stabling him immediately. As he entered the jail, Marshal Brett was wrangling two inebriated cowhands through the front cell door, slamming and locking it behind their curses.

"Rough night, I reckon?" Johnny asked as the marshal turned to face him.

"Yeah, and it was just as bad last night. Good thing you're back. Jess left to handle a problem at the relay." Sam's tone was flat and weary, and Johnny experienced a tinge of guilt, remembering his own peaceful afternoon.

"I'll take over, Mr. Brett. Go get supper, I'll handle this." Johnny said, moving to retrieve the logbook from the desk.

"I won't be long. Just find out who these men are and what outfit they are with."

Exiting the office, Sam turned to Johnny. "I want to hear how things are in Iron Mountain, and we've a few things to straighten out."

Sam returned to find that Johnny had moved the miscreants into the rear, more secluded cell. The lawmen talked quietly into the night, sorting out facts from suppositions. There were clearly increasing tensions in Sideling. The increase in complaints of missing cattle indicated that rustling might again be on the increase in their area. They had one day to come up with answers and form a strategy to present at the town council on Monday night.

As tired as Sam was, he was alert enough to perceive an unusual composure in Johnny's demeanor. His deputy carefully considered the many angles regarding the problems facing the town and remained calm as they discussed his tenuous status as deputy marshal. Sam did not think the latter would be problematic as sufficient time had passed and impassioned speculations now idled. However, Sam was surprised to hear that Johnny had spoken with the mayor, and that Vaiden had openly confessed the need for a competent deputy, having declared that nothing had proven Johnny incompetent--only guilty of human error. Nevertheless, Sam did not trust what the council would decide on any given day.

Sam began to relax and appreciated the time well spent in conversation, and as he left the office for the hotel that night, he wondered at the change in Johnny. Would it last or was it another of the recent fluctuations that Johnny would experience? Too tired to contemplate further, he removed his weapon, badge and boots, lay on the bed, and was asleep in moments.

From his cot in the backroom, Johnny was awakened by the rumblings and cursing of his drunken charges. One hour of sleep was all he had managed after Marshal Brett had left the office for the hotel. Toward dawn, both cowhands became ill and the office putrid. Feeling somewhat better toward morning, the men demanded release from the cell.

"We want outta here; you got no right to hold us any longer!" they clamored, and they rained down colorful remarks concerning Johnny's heritage.

By 5:00 a.m., the stink, his lack of sleep, and their orneriness usurped his patience, and Johnny had enough. "You'll get out of here as soon as you clean up this mess. Here's the mop and broom, use it!" he countered sharply.

"We're doin' no sech thin'; it ain't our job!" the shortest, bearded man bellowed contemptuously.

Johnny secured old rags from the closet, a half bucket of water by the wood stove, and an old bar of lye soap.

"Well, I say it is," he countered, adding his favorite old standby, "and I have the badge, the gun, and the keys! Here's the water. Start cleanin'!"

The younger of the two men, who looked to be not much older than Johnny, did the cleaning, and the bearded man assisted only under provocation. The men, anxious for freedom and fresh air, gave their names and other required information, then were turned loose.

Johnny hurried to the café for a jug of vinegar, emptied it into the rest of the water in the drinking bucket, and threw the entire concoction over the cots and onto the floor of the cell, opening the front and back doors. As the cold wind roared through the office, he swept the liquid outside. He stoked up the wood stove to blazing and walked out onto the porch to breathe.

By 7:00 a.m. Marshal Brett returned, stepping through the open front door. With a sharp expletive, he covered his mouth and nose with a hand, and turned abruptly to walk out the way he had come.

From the middle of the street, he called to Johnny. "Hey! Want some breakfast before the church service?" Johnny did not.

Sunday morning came and went. That afternoon, Johnny rode southwest toward the Wilkerson ranch. After only two hours of sleep and a hurried bath, he was assigned to assess the two largest ranches lying to the southwest of town, leaving Sam the ranches to the northeast. Johnny's motive was twofold: look for signs of rustling, and hopefully, find Dodge Wilkerson.

Johnny sighted Cassie briefly as she left the church service in the family wagon earlier that morning, but lacked the opportunity to catch her eye. He had not attended the service as he had hoped, for intending only to "rest his eyes", he had fallen asleep following the long night's escapade.

The fair weather and moderate temperatures of yesterday, which had done much to diminish the snow, had given way to cold wind and gray skies. Johnny cantered Cody along the trail, glad for the brisk, fresh air and freedom from the town. A horseman came toward him from the west, just at the southern border of the Wilkerson ranch. He reigned in as the man drew near and then hailed him.

"Afternoon, Mr. Wilkerson. I was hoping to find you."

Dodge Wilkerson maneuvered his stallion alongside Cody. Its damp, black coat glistened with sweat.

Wilkerson's eyes were hard upon Johnny's face and his expression guarded, almost angry. He finally spoke in a cool, flat tone. "What brings you out this way?"

"Business, sir. There have been more rustlings reported by ranches to the north and east. I'm here, officially, to alert you and to find out if you have seen any signs of activity."

When there was no response, Johnny continued, "Have you noticed anything unusual, signs of disturbances anywhere, campfires, or anything?"

Caught off guard, Dodge felt exposed. He resented this intrusion upon his privacy. The past two weeks had been some of the most difficult he had experienced in his life. He could handle drought, floods, even rustling with some degree of calm, knowing that these things were part of his existence as a cattleman, and his due for choosing this hard country. These things, allowed by God to refine and improve men, he accepted with some degree of understanding.

Over the past days, he had tried to lessen the pain and heartache which followed the darkness of his sorrowful thoughts, by riding the perimeters of his land. This escape helped to ease the tensions of the subtle, yet stubborn defiance of his oldest daughter. Now, Dodge was face to face with the perpetrator of and reason for the perpetuation of his misery. He fought hard for civility.

Dodge took a deep breath. "Did the marshal send you here for the purpose of warning me, or did you think it your duty to ride out to question me?" Dodge regretted the mean-spirited question almost before it rolled off his lips. "No. I've not seen anything unusual. My men haven't reported anything. I would have notified your office had there been anything to report."

Johnny nodded, but did not comment. Dodge Wilkerson sat his horse silently, sensing the young man's hesitance to depart and awaiting the question he suspected would be forthcoming. The silent moment stretched on uncomfortably until the wisdom of Dodge's years broke the stalemate and trumped Johnny's abilities to hold any command of the conversation.

"Would there be anything else?" Dodge asked, pinning the deputy with his eyes. Dodge had a naturally kind face and though his tone was stern, his round, gently contoured features never quite portrayed the turmoil inside the man.

"I'd like to see your daughter, sir," Johnny exclaimed boldly, surprising even himself.

Dodge shifted in his saddle, then glared at the deputy. "We've been over this. No, and I want you to stop communicating with her."

Johnny was quick to collect his thoughts. "That's impossible, Mr. Wilkerson. We live in the same town, ride the same roads, and have some of the same acquaintances. We both attend church. I'm asking only for permission to talk with her, sir, not just the casual 'hello' and 'goodbye' which now marks our only communication."

Dodge searched Johnny's face intently. There was no defiance in him, not in his tone or his demeanor, yet Dodge clung fast to his anger.

"What would be the point in that, Deputy? You know my desires for her." Amidst his frustration, he sought a quick end to the useless conversation. "Do as I ask; leave her alone!"

Prompted by the finality of Dodge's demand and desperate, Johnny attempted to circumvent the unreasonable request with the truth. "I have left her alone, sir. If she's as unhappy as I am, leaving her alone won't help. She is a strong, determined gir...woman," he corrected, abashed by his own use of the sensitive term, "and I don't believe she'll give in just because you, or even I, desire that of her."

"What do you mean you desire that of her?" Dodge queried, becoming incensed. "How do you know anything about her? What gives you the right to speak about my daughter as though you have any meaningful knowledge of her?"

The indignant inflection in Dodge's tone kept Johnny's courage to the forefront and he knew he had to answer with more than just his heart. This might be his only chance.

"She came to me when I was injured. She convinced Doc to let her see me, even when she knew I could not know she had come. Later, I told her I had no right to ask for her affections--after the accident and all that had happened to change my situation. She is the one who gave me back my hope in the matter, the one who made me see that there was more than just hope for a life we could share, reminding me of the changes we could bring about if we worked together for this territory."

Without hesitation, Johnny pressed on. "Last night, sir, I read from the Word that 'a cord of three strands is not easily broken.' For us, that cord of three is Cassie, myself, and God. His plan for our lives, His sustaining strength will prevail Mr. Wilkerson, and I don't believe this will change, no matter the obstacles or time that may be placed between us."

Much surprised, Dodge Wilkerson sat still in the saddle. Through the tumultuous heat of anger, he tried to understand the implications of what the deputy had said. Momentarily muted by the depth of Johnny's confessions, he watched as the deputy tipped his head respectfully, touched his fingers to the brim of his hat, wheeled his horse around, and rode away toward the southwest.

Dodge sat for a long time, numb and still, oblivious to the cold wind and the shadows lengthening across the plains. The deputy had indicated that there was a "we" and had claimed "for us", but how was this possible? When could this have come about? Had his daughter really been so forward in the pursuit of this man? As her father, how had he not known these things, or had he just refused to see the change in her? Was it sudden or had it been gradual? Did her mother not know from the beginning?

Deep within, Dodge knew he was the one who had forged Cassie into the woman she had become. She had not been a child for a long time. She had willingly accepted all of the ranching responsibilities he had doled out to her and met them with all the strength and courage of her determined character. How could he think she would respond any differently now? If she truly loved the man, he knew that no fear of danger or concern for the future would deter her from what she perceived as right and what she truly desired.

In a few sentences the deputy had been able to clarify Dodge's dilemma, forcing a turning point in his history as father and protector. Much as Lincoln had done with his brilliant, brief, Gettysburg address, Johnny had verbalized the concise, clear, unvarnished truth. The "last full measure" of Cassie's devotion would likely go to that young man. Johnny had included God in the factor, and if God had truly ordained this, Cassie and the deputy would ride out the storm, and with dreaded certainty, Dodge Wilkerson knew it.

The faces of the men around the oval table were congenial enough, but as they greeted each other cordially, Johnny couldn't stop himself from speculating what thoughts brewed behind their smiles. Of special interest to him was Cassie's father: one of two cattlemen on the board, who glanced toward him, nodded briefly, but did not smile.

Among the participants were: the banker and deacon of the church, Lance Brooks; the newspaper editor, Pierz LaFarge; Almon Baird, Sideling's only lawyer; a sprinkling of businessmen including Bradford Jones, proprietor of the mercantile, and Dean Beale, blacksmith.

With a bang of the gavel, the meeting for the month of November was convened and Mayor Vaiden greeted the council with a few brief remarks. After the reading of the last month's minutes, new business was brought forth. The mayor sidestepped the formalities and honed in on the most pressing issue.

"As you know gentlemen, we have a problem. We need answers as to who, what exactly, why, and most importantly, how we are going to deal with the crime and corruption we are experiencing."

As conversation commenced, the evening drew on and each individual concern was raised. It became obvious that there were no clear solutions, and the body politic looked to the marshal for an appraisal of the situation.

Johnny, who was out on the street a good deal in the evenings, while Marshal Brett handled traffic in and out of the office and took care of the bulk of the paperwork, had made the greater part of the observations in town. Sam Brett assured the council that investigations were in progress, and telegrams of inquiry into the background of certain individuals had been sent.

There was much speculation, but at this time, Sam preferred to keep his strategy under wraps. Some of the members objected, Sam held firm, and Johnny backed him up by declaring that "any information divulged could delay or hamper the investigation process".

Sam turned the dialogue over to his deputy, and Johnny assessed the incidences of street shootings, crooked dealers new to the area, and questionable activities abounding in the upper rooms of the saloon. Wise Sam Brett let him talk, nodding thoughtfully in agreement when he found himself being studied by the occasional, skeptical councilmember.

On the whole, Johnny's statements and opinions were accepted readily. Again, his military schooling enabled him to present the information with the same intelligent manner he had shown when the lawmen had convened before the canyon raid two months prior.

Toward the end of the evening, Sam was relieved when Mayor Vaiden thanked Johnny heartily for his assessment and then thanked God for the deputy's timely recovery. The Mayor reiterated that, "This town needs good men like Sam Brett and Johnny McLane," to the nods and muffled consent of his cronies.

As for the last order of business, the motion was brought forth and the deputy, by unanimous vote and hardy accord, would retain his position at current pay rate. He would receive only half of his compensation for October, all of which had been held in escrow at the bank, pending the results of the decision made tonight. The rest of his October reimbursement would go to Doc Cullins for services rendered. All agreed, motion carried.

It had been decided that the cattlemen would have their foremen post any extra men they could spare in the line camps surrounding their ranges. They and any sons they deemed old enough to handle a gun, would patrol their holdings frequently. Sam would handle investigation of any suspicious findings on the larger ranches to the north and east of Sideling, and Johnny would continue to be responsible for the ranches and homesteads to the south and west.

As the men slowly filtered from the council room and descended the steps onto Main Street, they talked quietly in pairs or small groups. Johnny, who had been cornered by well-meaning banker Lance Brooks, curious for details of the mountain accident, finally broke away and found himself the last to exit along with Dodge Wilkerson.

With a nod, Johnny confronted the older man. "In my time off, sir, I'll ride your boundaries and patrol for you when I can. I know you could use an extra man."

Wilkerson raised his brows and Johnny added, "I'll stay well away from the house. I won't seek Cassie out; this has nothing to do with us. You won't know I am there."

He paused and waited for a comment as Dodge considered the proposal. When none came, Johnny continued hesitantly.

"If this isn't acceptable, I understand, but I realize you have a lot at stake."

Dodge Wilkerson had not expected this. He leveled his gaze and said introspectively, "My cattle, my life's work, is at stake here. My foreman is down with a broken leg. I don't have much choice. I appreciate the offer, and just so there will be no misunderstanding, I still hold firm to what I said earlier."

"I understand, sir."

They exited and did not speak again.

Johnny chopped at the tall, dead clumps of grass which had grown up around Mabel Baker's weathered cabin. Over the short summer months, the roots had tangled and intertwined like rope netting under the soil. Although it was cold, emanating sweat caused him to remove his outer shirt, then roll up the cotton sleeves of the longjohns he wore underneath.

He was glad for the work, a chance to strike out, to pound hard dirt and fight a foe he knew he could tackle with sheer, brute strength. It was a way to gain peace. Here he could tear down, nail up, chop, and clear out things that made an immediate difference; tangible things he could see, feel, and taste-- wood, iron, and the sweat from his brow.

Only an occasional spasm clinched his muscles now, forcing him to stop and work the knot out. Mabel Baker was no longer here, but her home would be ready for her return, waiting and in good repair, should God allow that day to come. Johnny would see to that.

The town of Sideling rested quietly midweek as it had for the two days since the council meeting. Snow piled up in drifts on the prairie, leaving cattlemen to worry as to whether the taciturn creatures could find food. Johnny considered cows as he labored and thought how dumb they were. He knew they could easily starve as they would not dig away the snow to reach whatever forage that may lie beneath.

Johnny wondered at that and as he worked, figured cows weren't not much different than some men he knew. Like himself, they were too careless to uncover the good things right under their own noses and would wander around empty until they just dried up inside.

Well, he was trying, he thought, as he whacked harder with the pick and the blade of the hoe. He reflected on the verses he had studied as he worked the roots. Much like the grass roots, he wanted to be so firm in the soil, so rooted and grounded in the Word of God, that he could never be yanked up and cast out of the new understanding he had received.

(Matthew 13:18-23)

The wind had blown most of the snow away, except where it lay against the barn and fences. The front of the house stood facing westward and caught what little heat radiated down from the pale, winter sun. The air had warmed to a few degrees above freezing, but Johnny's progress was slow, and the partially frozen soil yielded little to the virility of his effort.

The truth was, he was tired of hanging around Sideling, waiting for something to happen. There had been no further incidents and no "break" in the investigation. With nothing out of the ordinary to do, the snowy days seemed interminable to him.

Yesterday, he had ridden the eastern boundary of the Wilkerson ranch but had observed nothing unusual. In the cold wind and through deep drifts of snow, riding had been difficult and in the dismal gray he had not been able to keep his thoughts from Cassie. He attempted to reflect on his spiritual state as he rode, but his mind had become like Cody's feet, impeded by drifts and stuck in his struggles.

The pounding of hooves out on the hard dirt road disturbed his contemplations and he straightened, leaning on the hoe handle as he turned toward the sound.

His belly knotted and he caught his breath. Cassie came flying up the road at breakneck speed from the direction of town. Catching sight of him she pulled up sharply, and entered through the open gate, loping toward him on Lady.

"Howdy, Johnny!" she hailed brightly.

He tried not to notice the heightened color in her cheeks or the way strands of hair, freed from a braid which had loosened in the wind, curled about her face. She was delighted at finding him there.

She came closer, and looking up, he spoke brisker words than he had intended.

"What are you doing here, Cassie? You shouldn't have come." He had spent the last days struggling to keep her from his thoughts in what had become a most futile exercise, finding that the effort only increased his dilemma and pushed his mental capacity to the limit. Now, she was before him...alive, fetching in her disarray, and still unavailable.

Desperate, he attempted to pull his wits together and tried to see her as her father might at that moment. A disobedient child who was borrowing trouble for herself. But, the only thoughts he could brook were the ones that caused heat to rise within him.

The stress of self-restraint edged his voice. "You should not be here," he repeated.

The vibrancy in her features melted away and dismay set up firmly. Surprised by his censure and clearly injured, Cassie lifted her chin, tossed her head, and yanked the loose ribbon from her braid, spilling auburn hair over her shoulders. Johnny lost the last of his reserve.

"That's why!" he barked, "That's exactly why!"

He assumed she had done this on purpose; she must have instinctively known that by doing so she could stir his passions. That she would counter attack in a way he could not, seemed suddenly most unfair.

Her brow creased, and her eyes narrowed. "What? What are you talking about? I have every right to be here," she challenged. "I come frequently; I always have, and I always will!" she exclaimed stubbornly.

Looking about her with an air of supreme confidence, she added, "I check on Aunt Mabel's chickens, you know!"

Johnny knit his brow. "For cryin' out sakes, Cassie! We both know that the chickens are almost gone, and what eggs they lay the foxes and snakes take. That's no excuse!"

"I don't need an excuse, sir," she retorted, embarrassed and sensing she was losing ground. "I'll come here any time I like and if you happen to be here, then...I am sorry!" Her attitude crumpled and to hide sudden tears of frustration, she looked away, turning Lady as she did so.

Johnny moved quickly and caught the bridle, then grabbed her arm.

"Cassie," he groaned in anguish, "it's too hard! Too hard to honor your father's request when you come around like this--when there is no one here but us, when..."

He searched her eyes, trying to organize his words, grasping for any idea that might make her understand.

She met his eyes. "Oh, Johnny!" she cried adamantly, "Right now I don't care a flick about honor! All I know is that I hate this! I want to spend time with you, to talk with you!" Prideful, she swiped at her tears.

"Cassie, I care; I care about honor. It's got to be important if we are to make any sort of life together," Johnny replied ardently, still controlling Cassie's dancing mare.

"Then you care more about honor than you do me! If you cared, you'd fix this! You'd do something!"

"I tried, Cassie. I talked to your father again Sunday afternoon, but he's not budging. He thinks he's right. I don't know what else I can do!"

With flashing eyes, she lashed back at him. "Well, do what you want to do for a change, Johnny!"

Johnny released her arm. She had ceased to make sense and would not listen to reason. Although he knew he should temper the heated exchange, her challenge had wounded him. He lost the battle and met her challenge with angry words.

"So, you want to know what I want?" he demanded, clutching the rein as Lady pivoted fearfully, trying to back away. He yanked the bridle firmly.

"Do you Cassie? See that old barn over there? I want to pull you off that horse of yours, take you in there and shut the world out--all of it! I want to be with you, to hold you through the night and never let you go! That's what I want. What is it that you want? Just what? Don't you know that's not the way it can be for us? Where would that leave us? I'd be breakin' the law--lord girl, you're sixteen! And that's only man's law, and it pales in the face of the fact that I'd be breaking the law of God! Is that the way you want it to be for us? Well, is it?"

She was crying now, and the tears she had guarded so carefully slipped down her cheeks.

"No, Johnny, no! I don't want it to be that way! I just can't bear this," she confessed in tears. "We can't even be friends anymore. It would have been better had Pa never known about us!"

He recognized her emotions and frustrations as his own and desiring to defend her against the onslaught of them, gathered her to his heart.

"Cassie, don't cry. Please don't cry." He covered her hands which held Lady's reins with his own. "It is as you said before. We are meant to be together, but we have to stand strong. I hate this waiting also, but there's no way around it. It's just as you said, remember?"

His eyes pleaded with hers, and his voice softened. "Do you remember?"

"I remember. I do."

Against winds of disaccord, they stood tentatively under the cottonwoods, his hands covering hers, attempting to buffet the turmoil between them like the last of the stubborn leaves which clung resolutely to the high branches above, unyielding in the fierce gusts of the autumn prairie winds.

In the vulnerability of her innocence, Johnny perceived a beautiful and wild creature, desiring to be freed, but caught in the restraints of a trap that he could not spring.

From the saddle she looked upon him, allowing his words to tether her soaring emotions. Set in earnest, the fine features of his face, and his near-patrician demeanor calmed her. She wished she could slip into his strength, protected by the fire and passion he held for what he believed, and find herself forever the sole recipient of the compassion reflected in his uncompromising gaze.

He felt her ease and spoke tentatively. "Now, if I turn you loose you'll stay on that horse. Am I right?" He attempted a convincing, crooked smile. He held her hands and her gaze.

"Well...I suppose I will, but just so you know, I don't agree, I..." She sniffed, wiping her nose with her sleeve. She sensed he wouldn't take lightly any fanciful whim which might induce her to trifle with him further.

"And," he continued, not altogether trustingly, "you'll go off and try not to ride like the devil himself is on your heels, am I right? Promise me."

"I promise, I suppose."

Fascinated, he watched as she raised a noble chin and from her feet to her arched brow, she became his girl again.

"But just you know this, Mr. Deputy Johnny McLane. Someday and soon, you'll be taking me into that barn, and nothing will stop us!"

She wheeled Lady around, saluting with her free hand, "Goodbye... for now!"

Cassie spurred the mare and took off. Seeming to remember her promise, she slowed just outside the weathered gate, pivoting in the saddle as she shouted over her shoulder.

"While you're remembering, just remember this!" With her arm sweeping wide, she blew an exaggerated kiss.

He leapt off the ground, stretching an arm high over his head, grabbing the air to catch it.

"Hey!" he called back, "You almost missed!" and he watched as she beamed and galloped away.

"Johnny!" Although Mabel's eyes twinkled merrily as she spoke, he was surprised at the wan hue of her face. She appeared ancient and her shoulders slumped, reminding him of a page waiting to be unfolded, its rich content hidden by the plain linen of the well-worn envelope.

"Come here, boy, let me look at you. It's been quite a while!"

Smiling broadly, Johnny crossed to the rocker, bent low and gave her a kiss on the cheek. "I'm sorry, Miz Mabel, I tried to see you earlier, but you were sleeping."

"Oh lawdy, I know, I know, and don't you let Miss Bertha keep you away any longer! It's the curse of old age. When you doze off out of sheer boredom, they think that you need the sleep and check to see if your pulse has quit! You just tell her to wake me right away. Heaven knows I need the company! Sit down please, tell me about yourself."

He took the indicated chair from the corner of the small room, pulling it up directly in front of her. Her brow furrowed in a thousand minute creases, and she took his hands.

"I wanted to hear all about everything. Oh! I want to hear it from the horse's mouth, not the rumor mill." She tipped her head slightly and beaming, studied him. "You look fine!"

Her worn face contrasted dramatically with the color and intensity of her eyes, and he was drawn into their depths. Momentarily, he caught a glimpse of the girl inside, of the beauty she must have been, mocked now by her outer shell.

"I need to tell you somethin'. Some things I think you'll be glad to hear," he began. "I'll tell you the rest later but..." Watching his eyes, Miss Mabel interrupted.

"Oh glory!" she whispered softly, her eyes misting over, and in his spirit, Johnny perceived that she already knew.

Slowly, he began to recount the details, starting from the encounter with Reverend Stoner. She sat enraptured, smiling at each success. "Oh yes!" She exclaimed intermittently as he told her of each new revelation and of the way the puzzle had fit together for him.

He finished, "I never really knew it was His voice speaking through the tragedy. I never put the pieces together. I couldn't move, I almost died on that mountain, and even then I tried to ignore what I had heard, until m' mind bogged down so heavily that it affected my job...and my relationships."

This was the first time Johnny had confided the totality of his journey, and vocalizing helped to clarify for himself the magnitude of his experience, and the depth of the chasm he had crossed. It filled him with awe and he was silenced, contemplating his own words.

"I knew God's hand was upon you! I knew you were sought by the "hounds of heaven" and praise be! You crossed that chasm, supported by the grace of God. This is only the start!"

"What if I am not able to follow through? I don't really know what I'm doin'," Johnny replied solemnly. "When I was reading the Bible, on the day

God spoke to my heart as I came home from Iron Mountain, many things I had learned as a child came to memory, and I understood the words more fully. The way to proceed seemed so clear...adherence to the precepts and commands seemed so possible, but as the days pass it seems a harder thing."

"You can do this, Johnny. The truth is you can never be good or strong enough to haul yourself through all that God will allow to touch your life, the good and the bad."

He recognized the twinkle in her eyes. It appeared whenever she had the key for unlocking a mystery, and he knew that she would keep after him until he could unlock the truth for himself.

"What are you doing each day, I mean, with the truths you've discovered so far?"

He pressed his lips together and leaned back in the chair. "Well, I read the Word, I pray some, especially quick, short prayers, when I find myself dwelling on things I shouldn't be thinking about, and doing what I shouldn't do."

He knew she had guessed his meaning, and caught in the truth, returned her understanding smile rather sheepishly.

"Ahhh," she interjected, "How can a young man keep his way pure? It is a question from Psalm 119. You study on those words; do what they tell you, but realize--those things are hard to do on your own."

"Well, that's encouraging," he chuckled wryly, giving her a wink to cover the embarrassment of his explicit honesty.

As though she was giving him an ingredient for some coveted recipe, she instructed, "What you need is righteousness!"

"Interesting, but I think that's the problem," Johnny quipped, concluding they were back to where they had begun, without any real answer.

"You must remember where righteousness comes from." She waited for his response.

"Well, I believe the Pharisees thought they had it, being religious leaders, but it seems they were good only at keeping the letter of the law and not the intent of it," he replied.

"Smart boy!" Mabel said laughing, then she grew serious. "I'm afraid they tried to regulate people's outward actions, but Jesus insisted they deal with the thoughts, emotions, and intentions of their own hearts."

Confounding him with her wit, she continued, "And you, Johnny McLane, have a most wicked heart!"

He arched his brows and gave her his best crooked grin. "Now, how did you guess? You can see right through me! It is, however, true and I'd say that's the problem," he confessed, becoming reflective.

"Well now, don't despair. Jeremiah, Chapter 17 says, 'The heart is evil above all things and desperately wicked; who can know it?' You are therefore no different from anyone else in that matter, boy, including myself," she said.

He nodded but did not comment, waiting patiently, knowing she was about to dole out a big dose of the truth. It would not take long, and like good medicine, it would be worth the wait.

"True righteousness, the kind that we need, cannot be obtained by the human heart's desire or man's efforts. It is a gift, my boy, a gift from God given through Jesus, the only righteous man who ever lived. When you accept Him, He clothes you in His perfect righteousness... sort of like those big woolen cloaks army officers wear. You are wrapped in Him, and when you are, you have the power of the Holy Spirit and the ability to overcome those sins of the heart. You won't be flawless til you are in heaven, but if you allow this, His Spirit will change you. You will grow more mature, whole in thought and in action, and you will accomplish the purpose He has for you here on Earth."

She smiled gently, then scrutinized him impishly. "As far as your thoughts, there are many verses to help you hold down that vivid imagination of yours; they will set your feet on the high road where you need trod." She looked about her, deciding on an object. "Give me that pencil and the paper also, if you please, sir...over there by the window," she directed, pointing a crooked finger.

He rose, obtained and delivered the items she had requested then sat again, watching as she inscribed the verse references from memory.

"Here! Memorize them--all of them," she instructed, "and when you are tangled up in that mind of yours, and you surely will be in many ways," she advised, glancing over the rim of her spectacles, "throw each verse verbally, right into the face of our adversary the devil, who seeks to pitch you off that high road!"

She tapped his knee twice, with a resolute hand, surprisingly strong for one so feeble. "You can do this! It is through His grace and mercy that you can succeed. Just remember, God will bring you along as steadily as you will allow Him, or leave you in trials as He must, if you are stubborn!"

Mabel Baker warned Johnny that she would be checking to see whether he stayed the course. Johnny grinned at her and laughed, declaring he would need a lot of prayer, to which she most heartily agreed.

(Romans 6:17-23;
Philippians 1:21)

Before he left, Mabel asked, "And now, how is our girl?"

Johnny's eyes softened and the merriment left them. Mabel watched as he composed his response carefully. "She is as frustrated as am I and tryin' to figure a way around the restrictions, I think. I don't know if she fully understands the gravity of her father's refusal. She behaves like a cornered cougar, and I am afraid she'll do somethin' to make her pa's restrictions more intolerable."

Johnny told Mabel of his encounter with Dodge Wilkerson along the trail. "I'm afraid he'll send her away," and as he verbalized the revelation which he had never allowed to surface, it sounded more ugly and ominous than he could tolerate.

He looked so bewildered that Mabel took her time considering words she might use to encourage him.

"Johnny, you are going to have to trust the Lord for this as you will for all things. It is hard, but it's only a matter of time."

He shook his head. "I know all of that, but there are so many considerations, even when the time comes and she is old enough to decide for herself."

He caught the reproof in her eyes as she screwed up her mouth, and looked at him as though he were a small boy who had failed to comprehend what his mama had just said.

"Despair and confusion are formidable foes, Johnny. Remember Who it is Who holds your future," she admonished, as the spark in her eyes dimmed and touched with concern.

He remembered that same caring look, when as a boy of seven, after carelessly reciting the Bible verses that had been required, he had attempted a quick escape from the dull confines of the parlor in the house used for a classroom, to the lure of open, golden fields. Aunt India Carr had grabbed him by his britches, admonishing him on the importance of taking the lovely words to heart. It had been a long while since anyone had cared for his heart in quite that way.

He had to smile. "I will, and I reckon if I want a future as a Sideling lawman, I'd better get back to work."

Mabel leaned forward slightly, her tone filled with true empathy. "I pray for you daily, Johnny. The rumblings and gunplay in the streets that awaken me occasionally at night, don't speak well of the condition of this town. What's happening?"

Johnny was slow to smile. So as not to concern her further, he kept his comments on the lighter side. "My unwelcome inquiries into those trifflin' matters are often met with terse responses and resentment from some of the folks and businessmen, but I thank you ma'am. I appreciate your prayers."

Aware of his subtle evasion, Mabel didn't press him on the issue, but nodded thoughtfully.

"Do you remember, from the Gospel of John, when the Pharisees and Levite priests came to John the Baptist in the wilderness, questioning whether or not he was the promised Messiah? John answered them with the prophet Isaiah's words from Isaiah 40:3, confessing, 'I am not.' John then declared himself the voice crying in the wilderness, proclaiming the arrival of the Messiah. Even though they were given the exciting news that the long-awaited Messiah was at hand at the time, those guardians of the law and Scriptures, who should have known this, never asked John where the promised Messiah was, nor did they ask anything else about Him! In their misplaced zeal, they seemed more anxious to discredit John and challenge his motives than to find the Lord." She paused, allowing the lesson to unfold.

Johnny's eyes never left Mabel's, and he contemplated her words and responded. "They should have known John spoke the truth, as the events had been foretold in the Scriptures, and they should have asked who and where the Messiah was. They missed the truth by asking the right person the wrong questions."

"Correct. Don't allow yourself to be placed on the defensive, Johnny, or become distracted from the truth of the matters at hand, for if you are you may never ask the right questions. And remember, it is God Who has answers to all the questions you will ever have. Don't hesitate to ask of Him. He gives grace and mercy, and the ability to move forward in all things."

(Isaiah 41:21-9)

He shook his head and sighed. "You sure left me in a pool of preponderance, but I thank you, Miz Mabel, for the lessons and encouragement. By the way, I am looking after your home- place. Everything is manageable, so don't worry."

She took his hand. "Bless you, bless you for all you do, and come back soon, Johnny… when you can, and I'll be praying! Remember, that like the strongest men, even the strongest Christians were once babes in arms!"

(1Corinthians 9:24-27)

23

THE PERSPECTIVE

THE 4:00 P.M. stage was an hour late, and it pulled in just as Johnny tied Cody to the hitching post by the front of the office. As he crossed the street headed for the stage, he pondered Miz Mabel's words, reckoning that if those ancient "wise men" looked to the Scriptures for more than just a way to reprove others, they might have saved the world a lot of confusion and strife.

Passing the din of the already crowded saloon, it struck him that he could lament over "if onlys" forever, and decided his mentation would be better spent in an appeal to Heaven, which he did quickly. He'd have a lot to deal with in just a little while, for even at this early hour, patrons of the Watering Hole chewed the rag, gambled, and queried deals loudly. He picked up his pace and headed toward the next task at hand.

After the last council meeting, he had taken to scrutinizing the arriving passengers. His goal now was to appraise the man who had just disembarked from the stagecoach, dressed in business garb and engaged in friendly conversation with the driver on the opposite side of the coach. Johnny intended to introduce himself and find out what business the man had in town. As he approached the coach, the proximal door opened, and an ankle protruded from the interior, followed by a soft green skirt.

He stepped back offering his hand, which the young woman took graciously. Deep brown eyes searched his and she smiled, revealing dimples set pleasantly in a small oval face.

She thanked him, then noticing the star on his chest asked, "Do all the new arrivals get such special attention from city officials?"

"I'd like to say so," he commented with a smile, "but I'd be lying. Welcome to town. I'm Johnny McLane, and at your service. What brings you to Sideling?"

Although his question had been casual, a flick of care crossed her eyes and he watched her demeanor change. She withdrew her hand, surprising him, for he had not realized he still held it and that they now stood alone.

"I am here only to visit a friend...could you get my things for me?" She turned her back on him, looking up at the driver who now loomed above them. Johnny called up to Rufus, who hauled a large trunk forward, placed the wobbling object on the luggage railing, and almost lost it over the edge before Johnny could reach up to help support its weight.

"Good golly," he exclaimed, "you must be visiting for quite a while." He struggled under its bulky weight, placing the trunk on the ground beside the young woman.

She looked around as though she expected someone would arrive to help her, but she said nothing and stood quietly.

"Is someone meeting you this evenin'?" Johnny asked, and from her expression he knew there would be no one. When she stood silent, he tried again.

"Is there some place in town you intend to stay?"

She looked indecisive then threw together a quick response. "Could you just place this over there for me? I reckon no one is meeting me." She motioned toward the saloon as she spoke, and Johnny's suspicions were validated.

With the trunk borne on a shoulder, he hauled it onto the porch of the saloon, placing it against the wall some feet away from the doorway. Two gloved and chapped cowpokes came through the doorway, raising their hats and leering at her. Johnny turned and searched her face. The tiny lines of her frown and the brush of shadows beneath her eyes were hardly concealed under the light powder she wore. She appeared young and vulnerable, but looked after the men. Johnny sensed a fire in her, banked, just awaiting the gust that could spring it to life. Spontaneously, he caught one of her hands in his. He wished to keep her from entering the saloon, but simultaneously knew it was not his place and released her.

"I hope you'll find what you're searching for," he said quietly, and owing to the furrowing of her brow, added, "And that you'll be safe."

She lowered her eyes and without comment, hurried around the corner to the business entrance of the saloon. He stood for a moment, watching her leave and wondering what events in her life had colluded to bring her to this place.

He would check the passenger roster for names and points of departure. Investigate. It was something he could do, yet he felt unsettled and inadequate against the force of things he could not control.

Still standing on the boardwalk before the saloon, he turned to glance after the departing stage. The businessman was gone, but Cassie stood diagonally across from Johnny, on the hotel porch, watching him. His heart leapt at the sight of her and he raised his arm in greeting.

She did not move, but held him in her gaze, then turned away decidedly, walking quickly along High Street and disappearing behind the mercantile.

Why had she not acknowledged him? Her reaction prompted a sharp recollection of her solemn plea and at once he understood: "Promise me you'll tell me if you stop loving..."

But how had she misinterpreted this? Johnny left the boardwalk, crossing Main Street at a run, headed straight for Cody, and lifted into the saddle just as Marshal Brett stepped out of the office.

"I'll be right back!" Johnny spurred Cody hard to the west and overtook Cassie as she neared the gate by the millinery sign.

"Cassie!" He called, but she ignored the oncoming horse and refused to look up as she hurried for the gate.

He came off the saddle rapidly, stumbled, and found his footing as the horse veered to miss the fence. Johnny overtook Cassie at the gate. He held the gate closed and she struggled to get by him, fumbling to open it.

He grasped her shoulders, and breathless, turned her to face him. "Cassie, you know better than this!" She struggled to free herself but he held her firmly, and when she finally raised her widened eyes to meet his, she was trembling.

"Know better? I saw you with her, walking with her, talking with her! She didn't look like a stranger--the way you stared after her! I never believed Eric and Beau when they told me you knew the girls in the saloon very well...so do you?" she paused, "Know them?'

"They told you what?" Astonished, Johnny held her off and continued rapidly. "Cassie, it's my job to know what goes on in there. I watch all of the passengers who come and go. She just arrived on the stage and knowing who comes and goes is a part of solvin' the problems here in town!"

She stiffened and fired back. "It looks like it's a problem--a big one. Those women, they are..."

"I know what they are. You don't need to say it!" he retorted, watching the anger battle the hurt in her eyes.

"Cassie, don't do this. Don't look for things that aren't there, it won't help us." He pulled her wooden form to him. "I can't say it any other way. I love you."

She lifted her head and closed her eyes, squeezing them tight against the conflict. Involuntary tears slid down her cheeks.

"It...it looks so awful. I know the boys live to torment, but what they indicated, how they said it, was so horrible, and as I watched, it just got the best of me. I don't know why I said what I said. I'm sorry," she cried, placing a defeated brow against his shoulder.

She softened in his embrace, and with great difficulty, he released her, slipping his hands from around her to capture her wrists. He stepped back. A coppery strand of her hair held fast to the star on his chest.

"Look at me; look into my eyes, Cassie." Intently, he searched her hesitant face. "This job is full of ugly things, and some of those things you'll just have to trust me on. I'm committed to you, but it'll take a lot of faith and prayer on the part of both of us to make this work. We haven't yet begun a life together! You need to consider all of this. Can you do it? Can you watch me involved with the affairs of this town, see all the hard things and trust me for them? Trust God for us? Can you?"

In the deepening dusk, she tried to step toward him, gathering her imaginations and feelings, desperate to sort through them in the shelter of his arms. His hands went to her shoulders, and he held her off relentlessly, desperate for her affirmation, yet knowing it was unfair to ask those things of her. She shrugged his hands away and came to him.

"Don't tempt me girl; I can hardly bear it," he said wearily, still trying not to pull her close. "I have to go. Things are happenin'. Go home. It will be dark before you know it. Go now. It's not safe out here at night."

"I had to help Miss Olivia earlier this evening, and I'm spending the night at Millie's tonight. I..." He cut her short.

"Come on then, I'll take you toward Millie's." His tone softened, "please... come now," and he helped to untangle her tresses from his badge.

He fetched his horse and mounted, removing his left boot from the stirrup and offering his hand. Cassie placed her foot in the empty stirrup and Johnny swung her up behind him. She put her arms about him, pressed her cheek against his back, and held on tightly.

Through the last of the twilight, they trotted along High Street and Johnny slowed Cody to a walk. They circled the secluded area behind the hotel, headed for the cover of the stand of pine trees in front of the hotel's front porch, just across from Millie's house. Snuggled against him, Cassie inhaled deeply the combined scents of leather, wood smoke, and the raw earthy pungency of the wilderness and the man. The scent was the sum of the things she loved, and it fully engaged and comforted her.

The press of her against him and the rocking motion of the horse were overwhelming, rendering him nearly beside himself. Having seared his emotions, she now wreaked havoc with his passion.

Tense, he instructed her gruffly. "I'll be stopping under the pines. I'll watch as you cross to Millie's."

Under the concealing branches adjacent to the hotel, he halted. She said nothing and did not stir. He nudged her with an elbow, "Cassie, did you hear me?"

Dislodged from her fantasy, she realized that he was speaking but still did not move. Her words rose, muffled by his coat.

"I heard," she answered softly.

"Well, go now. It isn't safe on the streets. I know you aren't afraid, but things are changing."

He helped her swing down from the saddle, supporting her arm, while his hand slid along the length of her coat sleeve until she stood steadily on her feet. He clutched her gloved hand firmly, and they held fast for a moment.

With a sardonic edge, he warned, "It won't do for anyone to see us out here. Go on now. If your pa catches me with you he'll likely blow me out of the saddle."

It had been too long since she had been cradled or held, and overcome with a sudden emptiness, Cassie ached for more. She missed her father's touch, the casual way he would stop to drape an approving arm about her shoulders as they worked side-by-side in the barn. Now, they had grown distant, separated by a chasm. He had attempted to breach it, but she had refused.

She stood looking up at Johnny through the dim light and held his hand and his eyes intentionally, conscious of the warmth they invoked and of the way he seemed to complete her.

Undone by the need in her expression, he murmured, "Oh, hang this town, anyway," and remained mounted while holding her hand as she walked by Cody's side. Crossing Main Street, they headed straight for Millie's front gate, scrim-like forms beneath the pale, rising moon.

Two sets of eyes, each unaware of the other, watched the tender scene; one through a slow-rising cloud of pipe smoke, the other through the inky shadows from the recesses of the mercantile.

Just before daybreak, the smell of pork belly frying drew him like an ant to a summer picnic cloth. Reaching the Sideling Café, he poked his head through the kitchen's swinging doors.

"Mornin' Miss Frances, my breakfast ready yet?" Johnny queried, winking at the cook who turned from the stove, placed a hand on her rounded hip, lifted a large frying pan, and shook it menacingly above her curly head.

"Go on boy, git before I beam you with this! It's too early; you know what time I open! Been openin' same time ever' day since you worked here--before Sam Brett lost his mind and gave you that tin star!" she barked, in mock agitation.

"Aw, come on now, I'm perishin' here. Have some sympathy for a dyin' man!" he countered, making as pitiful a face as he could muster.

"Johnny McLane! When you gonna grow up? Sam never comes beggin' at my door. Go take a lesson from him!"

"But he's still in his blankets, and I gotta hit the trail early. It's cold out there, Miz Frances; help me out some!"

He screwed up his mouth. "Aw, please?" He knew it would not be long in coming.

"Oh, all right! Anything to stop your whinin'! Get you a plate!" and he was at the cupboard faster than she could finish her instruction.

He didn't need it. He knew the kitchen well. For the past year, after having discovered that cheap, good food came readily from this buxom, able cook, who secretly delighted in feeding the lawman, he had been making tracks to her kitchen like a coon to a garbage heap.

And she loved him, for he would appear in the fat times when he had a little extra time and a little extra cash, as well as the lean times when all he could give her was a hand with the dishes and a song. She never had children of her own, and her dormant mother's heart was pleased by his foolish, teasing ways and boyish charm.

He presented a welcome change from the boredom of the kitchen and the run of the mill patron. He would show up at odd hours to torment her, entertaining her with his stories and music while snatching warm biscuits from the pan so quickly, all that was left was the aroma. Then just as quickly, he'd disappear, but never before thanking her. He ate anything she cooked with surprising relish...and he pleased her.

He sat on the stool by the counter, enjoying a plate of pork and some hoecakes while she flipped cakes and sipped coffee. The pale light eased through the windows giving form to the day and dimming the glow of the lantern.

"Notice anythin' out of the ordinary aroun' town, Miz Frances?" he asked, narrowing his eyes.

"Well, things are more raucous at night," she replied. She frowned slightly, paused from her task, and continued. "These evenin's seem to go on into the early mornin' hours! I was thinkin' yesterday, that the only benefit seems to be more customers orderin' bigger cuts of steak. But, I'm gettin' too old to stay up half the night, disturbed by the goings on. Oh, and remember Pete Worrell's little brother? I saw him in town late one night. Thought it odd he'd be out so late; he can't be more 'an fourteen, but who knows what's happenin' to those kids with their brother locked up? Don't think Miz Chenette has much luck controlling him. You and Sam gonna do anything to fix these matters?" She pumped water into the sink, looking at him over her shoulder.

"We have a few ideas, but other than the certainty that the makeup of the town's population seems to be shiftin' from desirable to the opposite, nothin' else is clear."

He had seen Matt Worrell ride through town and had tried to hail him, but the kid had taken off. Thus far unable to break through the crust of Matt's hatred, Johnny didn't want to discuss that situation now. Feeling he was responsible for sending Pete to a dank prison cell, he shoved the burden to the back of his mind and the rest of a hoecake in his mouth, then stood and washed all of it down with a gulp of coffee.

"Well, you'll be gettin' rid of me now, and I thank you kindly." He placed his plate in the sink, giving her a peck on the cheek. "You're the best cook east of the ole Jim River!" he exclaimed.

"Where 'ere that's at," she murmured, then watched as he turned to go. "Now don't go stealin' that cup! Seems I miss another one ever' time you show your triflin' self in this kitchen! What do you do? Eat 'em, too?" she asked puckishly.

"I'll round them up. There're a few at the office...I forget to bring 'em back," he laughed lightly.

"You should be in that jail, not behind that badge, boy!" she chided, her eyes twinkling with merriment.

On the other side of the swinging door now, Johnny chirped over his shoulder, "Save me the scraps--I'll be back!" and he was gone.

He rode to the southwest of town, through the early morning chill, toward the cut-off which marked the northern border of the Wilkerson ranch, keeping an eye out for any signs of intrusion on the range. Well-fed, and content to be out of town, all was well until he remembered it was Friday, and that most likely the town would become hellish as dark approached.

He succeeded in pushing the thought aside, for he found himself in the midst of that particular meteorological phenomenon he found most interesting. The ground lay locked in cold, and a gray fog rose, penetrating the pant-legs above his boots, chilling his bones, and leaving his toes numb. Meanwhile, the sun shone brightly through the clear air above, warming his thighs and shoulders, soothing his soul.

Maneuvering toward a goal always improved his humors, and now as he moved forward, the rhythm of hooves on frozen ground provided the means to bring him closer to what could be a clue to the rustling mystery as well as in closer proximity to Cassie.

If he could not be with her, he reasoned, at least he could attempt to protect her from the relentless hand of lawlessness which bore down upon the territory. Tyranny's grip--it could stifle one until there was no air left to breathe. The weight of two separate remembrances shackled his senses. Hollow-eyed men and emaciated soldiers long gone, still haunted him, but out here in the vast freedom of the high plains, he was determined never to see that way of life again.

His mind churned with the second oppressive event of the day, conjuring up Cassie's face and reliving the heights of the moments they had spent together the previous evening-- reviving the feelings she had evoked in him. He reprimanded himself--remembering Doc had cast him into a subjacent valley earlier this morning, after leaving the café.

Doc had caught him on High Street just shy of the livery doorway, as he led a big, brown Yorkshire, headed for his waiting rig.

"I wanted to see you, Johnny, just didn't expect it to be this soon. I'm on my way out of town for a day or so. Fortunately, you found me."

"What can I do for you, Doc?" Johnny asked, happy to oblige the kindly practitioner. As Doc's eyes searched his, a prick of apprehension began to gnaw at the comfort of Johnny's day. Doc's face was just inches from Johnny's.

"It's more of a matter of what you can do for yourself, I'd say, boy," he continued, ignoring the quizzical stare Johnny returned. "I happened to be on the porch last night, taking in the late evening air when I noticed you and Cassie entwined on that horse of yours." Doc paused for effect.

Johnny shook his head. "It's not what it looked like, Doc." Thinking to put the matter to rest, he rushed on. "I was only..."

"Hold up! In case you have lost the ability to reason, let me tell you what it did look like, and pretend for a moment that I am Dodge Wilkerson." In an ominous, low tone, Doc blocked Johnny's defense and proceeded.

"She was wrapped around you like a blanket, boy, so what would you expect one to think? I don't know where you both came from or how she got on that horse without your absolute knowledge of it, but you, Deputy, are the responsible party here and need I remind you, that if you are still struggling with issues of impropriety, you are not making this easier on yourself! Do you want that girl for your wife? If ever you have a chance of convincing Dodge Wilkerson to change his mind, boy, you better wake up and swallow the bitter pill of restraint--the sooner the better!"

Johnny opened his mouth to respond but found it dry and lacking any verbiage that would make a pittance of difference.

"At the risk of repeating myself, it was a good thing it was I who saw the two of you. I can't squelch the rumor mill forever, and you're trying my patience. Stay clear of her for now, boy, and that's about it." Doc had turned and left him standing there.

Just then, oddly enough, one, and only one thought was able to eke its way into his perplexed mind. How was it that over the course of at least 1,800 miles and a span of just over four years, he had been demoted to "boy" from "Sir", "Deputy Marshal", "Mister", "Cadet Corporal McLane", or even from the title he had gained by age twelve: "Master McLane"--almost every time someone addressed him?

He shook off the turbidity of his thoughts and concentrated on the land-scape, scouting for signs of disturbance. Mountains rose to the northwest, snow-capped and golden in the morning light, serene and enduring. Nothing out of place, everything ordered, following the pattern of the seasons, and day after day, pouring forth the glory of God. It was humanity that brought dis-order, he concluded for the "umpteenth" time.

Breathing in the pungent fragrance of the pine, he tried to picture the town without moral decay but only caught the vision of Cassie walking through mud and mire. He knew that he could not protect her from the images and realities, as the town degenerated further.

As sure as night followed day, they would cross paths again, and he knew he had done what was necessary the previous evening. Cassie would not stay at home any more than he could hole up in the office. She loved to ride, enjoyed her work at the shop in the house positioned diagonally behind his office, and he knew she would never allow herself to be held hostage by what she perceived to be injustice.

He would have to trust God to take care of their relationship, for he could not stop life as it moved them along uncertainly day by day. As far as the rumors they would encounter, the conclusions folks would draw as the days progressed as he and Cassie struggled through the maze of impediments and restrictions, he couldn't stop those either. What Sideling folks perceived was not more important than the reality of the situations they both faced. He would protect her when he needed to, because he loved her more than he loved his own life.

Beyond that truth, in the crystal clarity of the radiant morning, came the realization that their battle wasn't physical so much as it was spiritual.

"I can't do this alone," he uttered, and his spirit cried out to Jesus and His righteousness to give him strength to guard his own integrity and to honor Cassie's father. For as much as Johnny loved Cassie, he knew from the Word, that God loved her more.

(2 Corinthians 10:3-5)

Sam Brett met Mayor Vaiden for dinner, then took the late rounds. Johnny checked for ammunition, then replaced the last of the rifles in the gun rack behind Sam's desk and went to the backroom to fetch his Henry. He preferred his rifle over the Winchesters, thinking of it as his right hand and appreciated that it spoke authority loud and clear without so much as a breath. He stepped onto the porch and took in the lively scene before him.

Across the street, the broad backsides of at least a half dozen horses, shifting weight from one leg to the other, stood saddled and hitched to a rail. With heads drooping and tails swatting an occasional fly as they waited docilely, they rested themselves through the long Friday evening before being obliged to carry confused, inebriated men out onto the plains in search of their outfits in the early morning hours.

Silhouettes in the windows moved haltingly or danced animatedly, backlit by the glow emitted from within the saloon. The accompanying music and raucous laughter were quelled by frequent oaths and challenges flung about the establishment. The soft glow through heavily-curtained windows above, punctuated the scenes within.

Truculent men milled about the streets and several fights broke out, forcing Johnny to lock up transient and citizen alike. Ebenezer Smith challenged the blackjack dealer when faced with the loss of his homestead as settlement for debt incurred at the table. Gunplay had barely been averted.

Johnny leaned against the outside balustrade of the saloon porch, hoping his presence would deter the hostilities and impetus of the night's fray. Tired of being jostled by patrons as they made their way in and out of the saloon, Johnny moved from the post by the door and rested in the shadows, against the outside wall of the establishment. Closing time had been posted at midnight, but by eleven o'clock he found himself weary.

One of the swinging doors at the front of the saloon opened slightly, and a small figure slipped from the interior, turning in haste, bumping into Johnny and pressing him against the wall. With a startled cry, dark brown eyes looked into his, registering instant recognition. Her face was pale and contorted in fright.

"Oh, God, please help me, help me!" She sobbed coming into his arms. "I can't do this anymore!" Quickly she turned away from him, flattening her back against the wall beside him, trying desperately to get behind him. He turned to shield her.

"What's wrong? Is someone after you?" he asked, taking her by the shoulders.

Sobbing, she clung to him desperately. "He said it wouldn't be like this; he said it would be different here, but it's not...not at all. Please don't let them see me! Get me out of here!" she whispered frantically.

"Who are you talkin' about?" Johnny questioned, "Who is he?"

"I can't say now; please get me away!"

"How can I help you if you don't tell me who's after you? I could arrest him, you'd be safe then."

"You don't understand," she breathed. "He's not here now, but he'll come; he'll come for me! Just help me now!"

She was on the verge of hysteria and shaking so violently that he stopped his inquiry. Placing his arm around her shoulders, Johnny kept her near the wall in the shadows, walking her to a darkened spot on the porch, well away from the door. She clung to him, desperate to stay hidden.

"I can't stay here, he'll find me and kill me, I know he will! The day I arrived, you asked me if I was alright. No, I'm not! I'm not, please help me," she pleaded trembling.

She had no coat and was dressed scantily. Johnny removed his coat and wrapped her in it. "I'll take you to the office. We can talk there," he said, trying to reassure her, but she resisted and stepped back.

"No, no! You have prisoners there and they'll tell him. They'll recognize me from the saloon and tell him--he always knows everything, always gets answers!"

Johnny tried, but could not reassure her. "I don't know where to take you." Then, he remembered Doc's office, just to the north of the hotel.

"Come on, don't be afraid," he said, shielding her as they hurried along the boardwalk. Stepping into the side street, they quickly crossed High Street and entered the deep shadows of the pines in front of the hotel. She stumbled in the dark, and he pulled her upright, then suddenly halted.

"Doc's gone," he thought aloud, and then with a flicker of hope, kept the course and passed the hotel, following the curve where High rejoined Main Street not fifty yards from Doc's porch. Distraught and trembling, Rosalyn stayed in the wing of his arm. Unnoticed, they reached the office porch. There was no flicker of flame from the sentinel globe that usually burned nightly in the window. Undeterred, Johnny knocked loudly on the door.

They were both gone. He groaned and held her close, turning to face the direction from which they had come.

"Got an idea," he whispered, urging her forward.

"No! Don't take me back there," she pleaded, trying to turn him around.

"Stop! Just listen to me!" He held her shoulders speaking emphatically. "If I'm gonna help you, you'll have to trust me!"

Those words came back to haunt him; he had spoken the same words the previous evening when another young woman had struggled in his grasp. The thought struck like a bullet in the dark, passing through his gut, leaving him wary. He wondered, 'How can you trust a man with no real answers?' Now, he needed a quick solution to another problem...another cloaked in mystery, without a face.

"The marshal and I have a room at the hotel. I'll take you there til I find a better place for you."

He tucked her under his arm, away from view. They retraced their steps quickly to the shadow of the pine grove, then around the back of the hotel, entering the rear door and ascending the steps to the first room adjoining the landing.

He ushered her through the doorway, and she stepped aside, fitting her back against the inside wall, uneasy and awaiting instruction. He moved to scoop his pants from the floor, grabbing two shirts which lay upon the bed and hanging all three items on the bedpost. Removing a newspaper and two books from the rocker by the window, he turned toward her and offered her the seat. She slipped his coat from her shoulders and held it out to him.

She was diminutive, very pretty, and so scantily dressed that he dropped his gaze. In two quick strides, he was at the dresser, yanking open the middle drawer and fumbling through it. Finding no clean shirt, he handed her one from the bedpost.

"Put this on, it will...keep you warm. I'll be right back." Stumbling over those words, he masterfully took his next thoughts in hand.

"Lock this door, and don't open it until you hear my voice, or until the marshal comes. You must know who he is; his name is Sam Brett. I'll try to get word to him about you, but I am not sure how long this will take. There's water in the pitcher over there. Sorry, that's all we have." She watched as he exited rapidly, closing the door.

Once down the back steps, he left the hotel and ran across the way, gaining the porch at the mercantile and hurrying toward the marshal's office where Cody stood tied to the rail. Perusing the office from the porch outside the window, he spotted four perpetrators locked up behind the closed cell door, but there was no sign of Sam Brett.

Departing from High Street at the rear of the office, Johnny and Cody took Center Street, which sliced through the town vertically and separated the Livery from the Flour and Grain. At the end of the street, at the top of the hill, Reverend Stoner answered his poundings on the church door.

The Reverend was sorry not to be able to give refuge to the girl for he had no wife, and his living quarters at the rear of the church accommodated only a small sitting room and a lesser bedchamber. Nevertheless, he did offer a suggestion.

Johnny groaned. "In a devil's jig!" he exclaimed in dismay, then tempered his speech. "I don't mean to be disrespectful, sir, but Myra Davis would be the least likely of souls to help me out."

"Sorry, son, I can't think of anyone else. She is the only single woman of propriety who would possibly consider aiding a female fugitive of questionable repute."

With a sense of impending doom, Johnny left the church knowing he had no choice. It would do no good to attempt to try to clear up misconceptions concerning the young girl's character, and as far as Johnny knew, the clergyman was correct in his assumption.

Surveilling the town quickly, he rode along Main Street through the relative calm of the moment. Sam was still nowhere to be found. He spurred Cody westward, passing the schoolhouse, then turning north toward Myra's cabin which rested in the wilderness little more than a mile distant, along a narrow, rough road.

The windows of the small log cabin radiated with the warm glow of lamplight. With his second attempt to rouse her, Myra answered from behind the closed door.

"Who's there?"

"It's Johnny, Johnny McLane."

"Just a moment," she replied, and shortly Myra stood in the doorway, backlit by the glow of lamplight. Dressed in nightclothes, her dark blonde hair hung loosely over her shoulders, and she held a leather-bound volume in her right hand. She was obviously surprised by his appearance, so he answered the question in her eyes.

"I am here on business, Myra," he began, "what I need...is a favor."

She considered his request for a moment and said with a slight smile, "Then I suppose you'll have to come in," and she stepped back, opening the door wide but not moving from the doorway.

It occurred to Johnny that tonight held some firsts for him. The first time to ever be alone with a prostitute in a hotel room, and the first time to stand alone in a room with Myra--familiar Myra, dressed only in her nightdress and light wrap.

He found his mind drifting from the tyranny of the urgent. She held his eyes, and he struggled to keep them level with hers. Why had he come; why had he risked this? In her desperation, the young woman from the saloon had driven him to face his unsettled past. He had difficulty concentrating.

Myra stepped closer, and Johnny stood hesitantly.

Searching his eyes, she knew she had him, if only for the moment. Instinctively, she recognized that this might be the last time her provocative powers could hold him. She parted her lips, tilting her head slightly.

"What do you need, Johnny?" She placed her hands on his forearms and as he stood still, pressed herself to him, kissing his lips tenderly.

He inhaled the familiar scent of a lemon orchard, a forewarning borne on the rushing breeze that precedes a summer storm, and took a slight step backward. She moved with him, until feverishly, he gripped her shoulders. Drawing her to him, he yielded, returning her kiss.

'I promise...' eclipsed the fire in his brain, 'I promise I will tell you...'

He released her suddenly, slipping his hands from her shoulders to grip her arms roughly.

"No! What are we doin'?" He demanded angrily.

"You want this as much as I do, Johnny, and you know it!" she retorted, eyes imploring, yet aflame with accusation.

"Myra! What man wouldn't? Want it, I mean, but I don't love you. I won't do that to you-- or to myself. It would be meaningless to me, and you'd hate me in the long run. I love Cassie, Myra! I want to be with her, and that is all there is."

His eyes were hard upon her now and she shuddered, then fired back angrily. "Then what on earth are you here for? What business do you have out here in the middle of the night?"

He recognized the hurt in her eyes, closed his own momentarily, then held her gaze again. "There's a girl in town, I don't even know her name..."

Myra sat with a blanket wrapped about her as Johnny gave the few facts he knew. It took the better part of an hour he did not have to calm her. True to form, she questioned him intensely, implying indiscretion on his part and implicating him in the troubled girl's affair, suspicious of the vague facts he presented. He tolerated this, holding his rising anger at bay, knowing she wanted the upper hand and would keep at him until she felt she had it. Realizing she was his last best hope, he answered her evenly, remaining remarkably imperturbable, maintaining a calm he did not feel, until she settled as she always had, conceded, and allowed him to present his hastily-contrived plan.

She threw one final barb as he exited. "You don't mind putting me in danger just to save this girl, do you, Johnny?"

"Myra, there is no other way," he replied wearily. "Thank you for this."

"Oh, certainly! You are welcome," she said acrimoniously. "The whole world is welcome." She closed the door on him.

She walked to the chair, sat down, placed her head in her hands and cried for what she had carelessly thrown away. Unless she left town, she would probably live with these disappointments for the rest of their lives.

Vexed by the emotional battle and consequences of the last few hours, Johnny tried to concentrate on getting the woman, who had identified herself as Rosalyn Blackbridge, to Myra's house in the middle of the night. A buckboard, an old woolen army blanket, and a couple of bales of hay had been the camouflage. Her clothing and every belonging she owned had to be left at the saloon.

Rosalyn entered Myra's cabin at 3:00 a.m., dressed in Johnny's spare shirt which she had used to cover her scanty costume. Recognizing the shirt, Myra cut her eyes from the girl to Johnny, shook her head, and tightened her lips.

While Johnny caught the inference, the exhausted girl did not and Myra, recognizing the young woman's fragile state, softened toward her, offering coffee and buttered bread. It was agreed that Myra would go to the school as she did each morning, and Rosalyn would remain sequestered in the cabin with the curtains drawn. Johnny promised to keep an eye on the school and the cabin when he could, then left the two women with an extra rifle. Later, he would have to find a way of convincing Rosalyn to entrust him with the name of the oppressor. For now, he needed to get back to Sideling.

24

THE COMPLEMENT

"THE MARSHAL'S BEEN shot!"

Sherm McNeil dashed onto Main Street as Johnny entered town, running full tilt, and grabbing at Cody's reins in a bizarre attempt to stop the horse and deputy. Cody shied from the running man, almost unseating Johnny.

"How bad is he hurt?"

"We've been huntin' all over for ya, Johnny! Doc's gone, so they carried Sam to your office."

Not waiting for the breathless man to answer him, Johnny spurred Cody toward the office, leaping from the horse onto the porch, and bounding into the jail. He followed the voices which came from the backroom.

Sam sat in a chair, pale faced but alert, being attended to by Hyrum Brown who had seen the marshal go down. Frances Kelly had run to her bedroom window above the café after hearing the shot, just as Sam struggled to his feet and staggered toward the office. Charging carelessly down the steps, without thought for life or limb, she ran into the street, following Sam as she hollered for him to stop.

Now, as her graying curls poked out at odd angles from under her night cap and her bright, red-checked flannel nightgown flowed from under a hastily applied shabby-brown, wool wrap, which barely concealed her ample frame, any inkling of past quizzical musings by the male gender present, were forever quenched. Nobly, she held a white cloth, pressing it firmly against the marshal's left shoulder, taking command of the situation.

Johnny crouched before Sam, placing a hand on Sam's forearm which was elevated on a pillow.

"You hurt badly? Are you alright?"

Sam shook his head. "No, they just grazed me. I'll be fine." He winced as Frances removed the cloth to assess for bleeding, then replaced it, firmly pronouncing the seepage as having "almost quit". Johnny's heart hammered in his chest, and he sought Frances' eyes for confirmation, silently thanking God for the life of his friend.

"I am sorry I wasn't here. Do you know who did this? Did he get away?"

Etched with anger, Johnny's face warned Sam to keep his tone light. There was no suspect, his injury was minor, and Sam meant to defuse the situation.

"I think it was a stray bullet. If someone had wanted to kill me, they could have. They only winged me," he said with finality and a wry smile.

Frances bandaged Sam's shoulder with a clean, torn strip of sheet. After she finally consented, Hyrum and Johnny helped Sam from the backroom toward the hotel room. Frances begged Johnny's attention, instructing him to take care.

"I only have two hands, and Doc won't be home until tomorrow, at the earliest!"

Without replying, Johnny nodded and watched as Frances exited the back door, intending to return to her room. Through the eyes of his worn mind, he envisioned a grizzly sow in red and white circus frills, lumbering back to her cage. He found himself amazed at the variety in women's nighttime attire and shook his head.

"Oh, me," he exhaled, and wondered briefly if after all he'd seen and done this night, he'd ever truly be comfortable outside the realm of masculine society.

"Whoa son; what have you been up to in here?" Sam asked, squinting his eyes and wrinkling his nose as they entered the small hotel room. "This place reeks like a ladies parlor."

Hyrum Brown raised a speculative brow at the deputy, and Sam loosed himself from his assistants, sitting heavily on the bed.

Johnny grimaced. "It's a long story and I'll tell you in the mornin'. Right now I need to get back on the street--unless you need my help here, Hyrum."

The wiry man declined and Sam sent them both along, declaring his need for sleep only. Johnny was back on the street, just as first light split the wee morning hours.

"I Corinthians 10:13," Johnny proclaimed, concentrating his aim on the row of tin cans spaced out along the supine tree trunk which had fallen beside the dilapidated barn.

"'No temptation has overtaken you that is not common to man.'" He squeezed the trigger. Crack! The first tin can propelled into the air, landing with a clunk on a rock some 60 paces out.

"'But God is faithful, who will not allow you to be tempted beyond what you are able to endure.'" Crack!

"Dang it!" Lowering the barrel of the rifle, Johnny shook out the cramp from his right hand, then leveled the barrel again, took a breath, and aimed. Releasing his breath slowly, he squeezed the trigger. Crack! Another tin can flew into the air.

"'But with the temptation will provide a way of escape...that you may be able to bear up under it.'" Crack!

"Yeah!" He finished with another shot, pleased that he had borne the challenge of rifle to target, but only daring to hope that the Bible verses would sink in to strengthen his moral capacities.

He had not borne up under temptation. In fact, he had failed miserably, and in the early morning hours, he had risen from his cot in the backroom, dismayed over his carelessness and indiscretion. Unable to sleep, he read and reread the Bible verses which Miss Mabel had written out so carefully, mindful of the instruction that he commit them to memory.

(Proverbs 9:9-10)

He needed a sword and a shield. Was that not how Miss Mabel had described God's Word? "'Sharper than a two edged sword,'" he recited aloud, "'rightly dividing the word of truth,'" and the winds took his prayer for Cassie and the confessions of his miserable failings heavenward.

"'Our warfare is not of the flesh, but divinely powerful for the destruction of fortresses. We are pulling down every thought and lofty imagination that is lifted up against the knowledge of God!' James...somethin' or other." Crack! The next bullet slammed the target, and another can flew airborne.

"O God," he cried out to the gun and the target. "How many times will you have to drag me to my feet? Help me to stand strong. I'm tired of tossin' like a wave on the ocean!"

The mist of frustration veiling his eyes made it difficult to sight the target. He blinked, then lowered the barrel, striding toward the fallen tree and placing the rifle against the stump. Returning to his original spot, he sighted the remaining can.

"Proverbs 4:23, 'Keep your heart with all diligence...'" From the hip, he drew his colt and fired. Blam! The can remained on the log, winking wickedly as the sun's rays sent mocking glints of gold his way.

"'...For from it flow the springs of life.'" He drew and fired again, blasting the offending can from the log.

With practice, he hoped to strengthen his hand and improve his aim, but it wasn't enough. The battle was not only physical, it was one for his soul, and he needed strength to fight against those fiery darts Satan hurled his way. He holstered the weapon then sat upon the stump, opening his small Bible, and pouring over its promises.

Concealed by the barn, Dodge Wilkerson stood watching in silence. He had come upon the unusual display as he passed Mabel Baker's cabin on his return from Sideling and had stopped to discover the source of the gunfire. Struck by the intimacy of the situation, his first inclination was to leave as silently as he had come. But his heart had been pricked by the young man's struggle. He knew the deputy had been fighting to regain strength, to hold his job and serve a town that would have disregarded his courage and good character, casting him aside for his one mistake, if ill winds had not blown the need for protection back into their society.

(Proverbs 20:27)

It was not a question of Dodge's regard for Johnny. It was, he confessed, his own unwillingness to release his dream for a precious daughter to so harsh a reality. He had done all he could to justify his decision, and had sought advice from those he trusted most--Reverend Stoner, Doc Cullins, even Sam Brett. All had understood his position and agreed he was most probably correct in his assessment of the difficult path which lay ahead should Cassie continue to desire this liaison.

The crux of the matter was that he could stop them now, but the clock would keep ticking and calendar pages turning, and soon she would come of age. For Dodge, the question became, 'Am I willing to lose the warm attachment which has blanketed Cassie and me through the years?'

He had made of her both cherished daughter and replacement son, and right or wrong, this was how it was. He knew her as he knew himself. She would not change her mind, and he could not bear her cool disregard.

(Colossians 3:12-15;
Philippians 2:3-4)

A leader in the town, Dodge was also a deacon in the church. As deacon, he had accepted the privilege of helping to guide and encourage the flock and now, he questioned himself about his own commitment.

"How can I turn away, as I watch a young man struggle physically and emotionally in his search for God? I am my brother's keeper," he whispered softly.

He had judged the deputy even more harshly than had the town's cruelest critic, and his motives for judging had arisen from his own selfish desires and conceit. 'I want this...not that. I have achieved this...he has not.' As his prejudices were revealed, his discomfort grew. Stiil, he struggled to reconcile this truth with his nature and desires.

Dodge realized that the purpose for the church was reconciling man to God, but he knew there was more. He contemplated the man before him.

'If anyone is sick...' The young man had certainly been buffeted by ill winds--physically, morally, and as he now saw, spiritually. However, until Dodge had come face to face with the suffering before him, he had not considered the harsh dynamics of it and his own duty towards it. '...Let him call for the elders of the church, and let them pray over him.'

Dodge knew these scriptures well, but the boy evidently had not known to do this. As a believer in Christ, Johnny had access to the enabling framework of the Christian community, to men blessed with Christian maturity--responsible men, of which Dodge was a part. But how would the young man know this if no one cared to pursue him or model these truths for him? And how would he learn to do this for others? Wasn't that what Jesus had commanded of His disciples? Of Dodge himself?

(James 5:14-15, Proverbs 21:1-3;
Colossians 3:12-15; Philippians 2:3-4)

Now, God had brought him to this place at this time. He stepped from the shadows.

"Hello the barn!" he called in the time honored pronouncement for safe passage, but Johnny had already dropped and sheltered behind the stump, finding Dodge Wilkerson's head square in his rifle's sights. Sweating, Johnny collected his wits and stood. Raising a deliberate, tremulous hand in greeting, he could only thank God he had not fired on the man. He did not speak as he watched Dodge come toward him.

"I'm sorry, Deputy. I didn't mean to startle you." Dodge offered his hand in rectitude, even as a flicker of question crossed his mild, blue eyes. "This abandoned farm is the last place I expected to hear shots, and I suppose gun play is on everyone's nerves about now," he offered, a hint of apology in his tone.

Having accepted his hand, Johnny agreed. "And, I suppose I'm a little jumpy. I figured this to be an out of the way place to strengthen my hand--practice my aim, but I guess I wasn't far enough from the road. Since the accident, I've had some...difficulty," and he added quickly, "although, I have improved measurably. I was actually on my way to check the southern ranges before I return to Sideling. I thought I'd get some practice in first."

It was the truth, but it sounded apologetic, even to his own ears. He wondered just what the man before him might be thinking, then simultaneously wondered why he felt the need to defend his actions.

Dodge kept an unpretentious gaze on Johnny, as if waiting for a further account. None came, and in a moment, he smiled easily.

"I do appreciate that, son. Shorthanded as I am, I've had little time to patrol those borders, so I'll ride with you if you don't object. I'm down to one man at each line camp and I believe two sets of eyes patrolling for anything out of the ordinary will be better than one."

Astonished by the proposition, Johnny hesitated, then nodded his consent. He returned Wilkerson's smile, gathered his rifle, and fetched his horse.

(Proverbs 20:29)

They talked generally of the town's problems as they rode through the afternoon, and the sun drifted downward, seeking its resting place upon the rim of the mountains. At last, Dodge confided his deep concern.

"You gave some good insight into the problems we face at the council meeting, Johnny. When you went to Iron Mountain, how did you find things to be there? I wonder if other towns are experiencing as much difficulty, besides the rustling issue."

Johnny answered the inquiry as vaguely as he could, for although he had hunches, he preferred to keep them to himself. He had spoken only briefly to the marshal concerning Iron Mountain and never of the job offer he had received.

After finding nothing unusual on the range, they parted company. They had not spoken of Cassie, but neither had Johnny felt the distrust or seen the hard attitude displayed by Dodge on their last encounter. The change in Cassie's father seemed a marked one. Johnny smiled at the irony of riding with Dodge congenially along the prairie, talking as compatriots, just as though the older man didn't hold the key to his sanity.

Then he remembered. He had asked God for help. Had he not expected an answer? He had hoped for one, and this time, it had come immediately.

"Man's ways are surely not God's ways," Johnny quipped, and he laughed out loud, inviting Cody's ears to twitch attentively. He had begun to believe he could trust this God of surprises, this God who was faithful to answer, and Who also seemed to rule with a pretty darn good sense of humor.

(Jeremiah 33:2-3;
Romans 11:33-36)

The morning was cold. Cody picked up a rock, and Johnny stopped to remove it with his knife. As Johnny dropped the hoof, Cody pawed at the ground frost impatiently.

"Easy son," Johnny crooned. "You don't want this day over any worse than I do."

The horse swung his large head, and with a rough nudge, shoved Johnny so hard that he had to brace himself with his hand to keep from toppling where he crouched in the road. With a commiserating, wet snort from his flaring nostrils, Cody stared at Johnny with a doleful eye. Johnny stroked the crooked, white snip on the chestnut's face. Skep had been correct. The young horse was proving a good fit.

As he mounted, he thought of Traveller, sure that there could never be another like him. As he rode along, he allowed things he had loved and lost to play through his mind like a tired old song. When the sense of her came, bringing the image of Cassie to mind, it doused him like ice water.

What would she think if she knew? She would have been hurt deeply had she seen. He shook the thoughts away, refusing the condemnation and unable to consider the possibility of further loss. He didn't understand why he had lost control with Myra that night, for it had been months since he had even considered her, and he did not want to explore the motive behind his indiscretion. He wanted to have the whole incident over and done with, never to think on it again.

He had waited until mid-morning, knowing Myra would be teaching and giving Miss Blackbridge time to awaken, dress, and consider the importance of the information she harbored, not only for her own safety, but also as a possible means of lending insight into the mystery which blanketed Sideling.

How should he approach her? The subject would need to be broached carefully. He could not afford to frighten her or seem threatening in any way. He had with him sourdough bread, apples, and coffee beans, the only things he had been able to pilfer from Frances' kitchen before daybreak. If he were to receive answers, he would have to be sure the girl was not famished and unable to think. He had no idea if Myra stocked her pantry for guests, for until last night, he had never made a social call to her home unexpectedly--not ever.

A yellow, striped cat ran between his feet and yowled, nearly tripping him as he stepped onto the low porch. He knocked on the door, and a curtain ruffled at the window. He identified himself, and the door creaked as Rosalyn opened it cautiously.

"I'm alone; no one followed me," he offered reassuringly. "I brought food in case you're hungry. I need to talk with you."

She stood behind the door, opening it further, and he stepped inside. It took a moment for his eyes to adjust to the dim light of the cabin, and he set the wrapped provisions upon the table in the center of the room then turned to face her.

Large brown eyes stared out from a pale face. Her hair was pulled back and twisted in a knot at the nape of her neck. She wore a simple, cotton-print dress which swallowed her petite form, and Johnny was amazed at how young she appeared. It occurred to him suddenly, that she was someone's daughter, maybe someone's sister, or friend; and those who loved her would be as afraid for her now as she was for herself. He understood the loss and loneliness portrayed in her face, for he had experienced it many times in the years past.

"Please, Miss Blackbridge, sit down. I need to talk with you," he requested gently. Hesitantly, she sat on the settee and he drew up a straight-backed chair opposite her.

"Were you able to sleep?"

She nodded and whispered, "Please...please get me out of here." Large tears welled in her eyes and slipped like oval jewels down her cheeks and onto her bodice. Johnny watched, helpless to stop them and unsure of how to proceed.

Registering little emotion, he continued gently. "Miss Blackbridge, if I am going to help you, I'll need to know something about you--where are you from, who sent you here?"

Neither spoke for a moment. She regarded him solemnly as though she understood that to commit to his line of questioning would send her on an irreversible course. He grew warm, stood, unbuttoned his coat and removing it, placed it on the opposite end of the settee. As he turned toward her, she flinched and drew herself into the corner of the couch.

"No, I...I'm not going to hurt you, I only want to help." Realizing he had frightened her, he added, "My job is to uphold the law, to help you. How old are you, Miss Blackbridge?" he asked, patiently.

She studied him intently. "Why does it matter? And as for you being a lawman, it never seems to matter what men are or what they do. They all want the same thing, and they don't care about age or much else!" She glared, anger edging her frustration.

His first thought ran to the defense of his gender and for himself particularly, but he remembered Myra and as much as he wanted to deny Rosalyn's sweeping censure, he could not bring himself to do it. He tried another avenue.

"You want to get out of here; I understand that," he replied, appealing to her sense of reason, "but that will take some planning. I have to know where to send you and figure out how to get you safely there. If I don't know who is after you, it will be much more difficult to make the right choices." His eyes remained fixed on hers.

He watched as she eased herself from the corner of the settee ever so slightly. He said nothing more, waiting patiently and allowing her to safely settle with his words and presence.

"You don't know this man. He can't be fooled. He has eyes everywhere. He will kill me before he lets me out of..." and reconsidering, she restated, "Before he lets me go."

"Out of what?" Johnny asked intentionally.

"Please," she cried pitifully. Tears fell and she dropped her gaze. "Please, just get me out of here."

She drew herself into the corner of the settee again, crying softly, and trembling like a lost, frightened child. He fought the instinct to comfort her and didn't move. Remembrance of the boy he had been, of the wagon train and how grief and need had mingled until they had become indistinguishable, warned and halted the impulse.

He confronted her gently. "Then...I may not be able to help you. You can't hide out here much longer. This is a small town, Myra teaches, and children come and go from her cabin for various reasons. It's only a matter of time before you're discovered. Let me help you figure a way out." He turned the chair around, straddling it and giving her time to consider what he meant.

She stood shakily, then walked behind the settee, turning to face him. "I should have stayed home. Being there was no worse than being here," she whispered, and he strained to hear her.

She looked past him into a distant place. "At least I knew what I faced. Marriage to him would have been better than this. My pa...he insisted that I marry him. He's ugly, old, and rough! I don't care that he owns cattle and mining shares. It won't be Pa who must withstand his nasty ways!" she confided desperately. Johnny dropped his gaze as her meaning became clear.

Rosalyn noticed his discomfort, and found herself wondering if this man might truly be different from the others she had known. His eyes held something intangible. Not the flash of desire or of raw greed she encountered unexpectedly on the streets or found with strangers behind locked doors in the harsh light of a stale room, but a kind of warmth and inner light, which seemed to pacify and bid her to trust him. She had never experienced this, in anyone.

He considered her, steady in his valuation, her story striking an empathetic chord within him. "I experienced something similar, though very different, when I was fifteen. The details aren't the important thing, but from the experience I learned what love is not. No one wants what you've described. I reckon no one should be bound unwillingly...to anything or anyone. I left that situation, or rather, was taken out of it, just as you can leave the mess you find yourself in now. But you have to help yourself."

She was taken aback by his honesty and after a moment, sat down across from him. "His name was Smith or Jones--a simple name, I remember," she replied softly, as though the walls around them could absorb and convey the facts abroad by some mystical messenger on the wind.

"I met him in Iron Mountain, but I don't know anything about him. He was not the original man who interviewed me for the job, but came in as we were finishing. I remember him as he dressed differently and spoke with an accent."

She trembled, took a wrap from the back of the settee, and placing it about her shoulders, sheltered within it.

Johnny did not register surprise at the description, but asked, "How did you come to meet these men?"

"I answered an ad in a newspaper I picked up in Cheyenne. It was for young women seeking employment as maids or receptionists in hotels. Afterward, I went to Iron Mountain, applied and was hired, and they sent me here. I found out that housekeeping was not all we had to work at. I was broke and the money was good. I believed that I wouldn't have occasion to be with...many men...that I wouldn't have to..." Her eyes, dulled with self-awareness, fell on the hands in her lap.

"I don't need details," Johnny concluded, inviting no further response. "I understand the circumstances, but tell me--did you catch the name of the man with the accent?" Rosalyn shook her head.

"Do you have any idea what sort of accent he had?"

"I don't know for certain, maybe English. The man who interviewed me called his name. I think it began with a 'J'. I remember because he looked austere and out of place. He leered at me, never spoke, and then left."

"Can you describe the man who interviewed you? Is he the man you're afraid off?"

"Yes, but I'm not sure which man is most dangerous. All the girls say both men are ruthless. No one seems to know, but all are afraid. The man who interviewed me was of average height and heavily bearded--nondescript really, no accent."

"I see. Where are you from, Miss Blackbridge?"

"Grand Encampment. Do you know of it? It's on the western side of the Leviathan." A spark of hope touched her expression.

"I know of it," Johnny replied, flatly. It occurred to him that getting her home would not be easy on any level, for he had been to that copper mining settlement on the mountain to hunt, using wildlife and rutted wagon trails. The ride over the mountain was rough, and there was no stage line that serviced that route. No matter, though, as he had no money for her passage, even if one did traverse the steep mountain. They would have to take the southern route through the foothills.

"Did you manage to save any money?" he asked, and she disengaged her eyes from his.

"No," she said, "and what I do have is in that saloon's upper room and I won't ever go back there."

She looked at him hopefully. "I have an aunt in Virginia Dale."

"Where?"

"It's in Colorado, though not far from here. Somewhere south of the Wyoming border. They used to have a stage running through the town, but it quit a few years back."

Her eyes were large and round like saucers, dwarfing her fine features. "Could you take me there?"

Perplexed, he studied her. Although she had finally admitted to being one year his junior, he was cloaked in a haze of doubt. She looked like a kitten in a rain storm. He would be needing advice from Sam.

Cassie and Mary sat on stools in the dark of the cold barn. The only light came from a lantern on the floor between them, bathing the straw beneath in warm orange-gold before its ring of color wandered off to be swallowed up in deep shadow. The occasional flap of bat wings high above their heads, and the singing of the rhythmic 'ting', as milk shot from the udders into the tin pails, were the only sounds to break the silence. Cassie tried to remain civilized and had quieted briefly, giving thought to Mary's accusation.

Now she spoke crossly, addressing the audacity of the provocations. "I don't know why you'd say that Mary! I never gave him the time of day, and especially not in that way!"

"But you know of his affection for you! Pa is just waiting to give his consent, should Eric ask."

"He won't ask Mary, he knows I'm not interested, so quit talking about it! You are so full of fantasy, dear sister, you can't keep your mind on anything important. Wait til Pa sees your marks in history--they're deplorable! You did bring the paper home, didn't you?"

"Me? Me?" Mary cried, ignoring the question, flinging her hands in the air, and tipping the stool. In an attempt to catch her balance, her foot struck the bucket before her, tipping it precariously as Cassie reached out quickly to steady it. The bulky cows sidestepped, lowing discontentedly at having been interrupted.

"I am not the one who dreams and moons endlessly, sulking over a man! It's you, dearest sister--you!" Mary exclaimed resentfully. She bunched up her face, swiveling around to face Cassie, pushing away the wisp of hair that threatened to enter her mouth.

"I think you just want all the boys to like you! And if I were you, there would only be one for me!"

Cassie was on her feet. "I don't want to hear any more, Mary! I don't want to court Eric or any boy in school, so please! Just leave me alone! I don't want to talk about this now or ever!"

She lifted her pail and stalked through the barn, away from the flicker of the lamp, making her way into the shadows and out into the night.

"Yeah," Mary muttered to herself alone in the gloom. "You don't have to talk about it because all the boys like you! Well, I hope you do cave in and marry ole Eric one day. I hope you do--cause that will leave Johnny McLane for me!"

From under the hayloft in the recesses of the barn, a dull thud sounded.

"Darned ole cats!" Mary exclaimed sourly, standing and moving her bucket to the side. Leading the cows back into their narrow stalls, she slid the crossboards that confined them in place. Disturbed by a soft thump and rustle of hay just beyond the lantern light, she paused a moment, listening.

Hearing nothing further but the usual moan of wind through the rafters, she raised the lantern, took her bucket and left the barn, closing and latching the heavy door behind her. Half way across the yard, the low creak of the huge barn door stopped her in her tracks and she turned.

"Oh, bother! Drat that stinkin' door!" she exclaimed angrily and began to retrace her steps.

She caught sight of a dim apparition sailing around the corner of the barn, dissolving in the inky recesses of the narrow passageway next to the chicken coop. Terrorized, the chickens squawked and flapped from their roost. With heart hammering, Mary ran for the house, sloshing milk over her dress, onto her shoes and in a trail behind her. Still holding the swinging pail, she kicked wildly at the kitchen door.

"Open up! Open the door!" she screamed.

Cassie appeared in the window pane, then in the doorway. "Quick!" Mary shrieked, "Get Pa! Someone just ran from the barn!"

Dodge Wilkerson rousted the only hand not out on the line camp. Old Bill came groggily, limping from the bunk room cabin with shotgun in hand, but the search of the barn and remaining out-buildings turned up nothing.

Dodge questioned his winsome daughter, thinking perhaps she might have imagined the incident but grew uneasy after Mary confided she had heard something as she finished the milking and witnessed the "flight" after Cassie had left the barn, confessing it to be, "Much bigger than a rat, I'd say!"

Cassie listened to the exchange without comment until asked if she had noticed anything unusual.

"No, nothing at all," she replied, but as the words left her lips, her stomach knotted and she became queasy. She hadn't thought much about Beau, or regarded his threats as meaningful on that early morning weeks ago. She had given no further thought to it in the days that followed, chalking it up to Beau's bravado and stupidity, that is, until she suspected that Johnny somehow knew about it. But Beau had not been to school for many days since, and she had forgotten the incident until she encountered him again with Alden at The Flour and Grain. Johnny had never mentioned Beau when they spoke, and she felt that if it was important enough, he would have found the time. It was silly to think that Beau may be in some way connected to this incident, but still she wondered. She said nothing. It just couldn't be. Beau was a braggart, but certainly not dangerous.

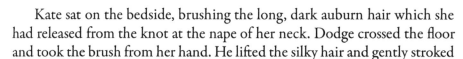

Kate sat on the bedside, brushing the long, dark auburn hair which she had released from the knot at the nape of her neck. Dodge crossed the floor and took the brush from her hand. He lifted the silky hair and gently stroked it with the soft bristles, from the crown of her head to the tips.

"I love it when you do this." Smiling, Kate studied his reflection in the mirror. "You haven't done this for many a day."

"It's true," Dodge replied quietly. "I'm so short of help and ranching has been so demanding that I haven't had much time for you." His eyes held the smile that his lips did not.

"Events in the town have concerned me much. I don't think there is much to Mary's story, but I will check the barn and grounds in the daylight. If need be, I'll report my findings to Sam Brett." He lay the brush on the bed and sat beside Kate, encircling her waist with his arm.

"Kate," he said softly, "I feel I am losing myself. I may have already lost Cassie, and I feel I'm at odds with the younger girls as well. I've been hasty and judgmental...and selfish," he added.

When Kate looked as though she would protest and took his hand, he interrupted.

"I've seen the disapproval in your eyes, and do me the honor of not denying it." He hugged her tenderly and they sat in silence for a long moment.

She studied his face, aware of how worn he appeared. "I'll not deny it, Dodge. This has been an unexpectedly hard time for the both of you. But Cassie knows you love her and that you want the best for her. One day she will see it clearly."

He began again. "I have considered every option I can. I've even considered sending her to Wolf Hall in Denver. Perhaps the Episcopalians could drive some sense into her. She wouldn't stay. No, Kate. I am going to give my permission to Johnny McLane...to court Cassie."

Kate's lovely features registered surprise then softened in the lamplight, but she did not interrupt him. "However, only when she turns seventeen, if she still insists on such a difficult thing. There will be stipulations, of course, and he will have to agree, but I think he will. I rode out on the range with him today. He is a fine young man. I wish I could change some things about him, however," Dodge lamented solemnly, but the corners of his mouth upturned.

Kate searched his eyes and smiled slightly. "Such as?" she asked.

"The awful job he has chosen and the fact that he doesn't have two nickels to rub together and most likely never will. Other than that, he's about as honest a young man as I've ever known. He cares about the town, he's respectful and most importantly, I believe he seeks to honor God with his life."

Dodge did not tell Kate all he had observed earlier at Mabel Baker's farm, but confided enough to satisfy her curiosity as to why he had suddenly changed his mind.

"I am glad, Dodge. We have to trust Cassie. She is strong, independent, and although she is young, knows her mind. I have spoken with her and I trust she is sincere in her beliefs. Have you told her of your decision?"

"No, I want to speak with the deputy first. I must be sure he understands and realizes that she'll not marry until she is eighteen. I am firm on that. I will have all my daughters educated and of an age to know their own mind, regardless of what the norm may be. Cassie has a little less than a year and a half to see the truth of his life. Perhaps she'll change her mind." Dodge sighed and shook his head slowly. Tenderly, Kate kissed his cheek.

They talked into the night and as he held her, they celebrated their love, thankful for one another. Despite the unknowns that lay ahead, they expressed their gratitude for the life they had been allowed to build together throughout the years of toil and faith.

(Proverbs 5:15-19)

25

THE DELIBERATION

EXHAUSTED AND GLAD for the solitude, Cassie flopped down carelessly, sinking into the down mattress. She rolled onto her back and lifting one knee then the other, untied and loosened the laces of her boots, kicking them off to land with a 'thunk' upon the wide floorboards of the bedroom she shared with Mary. Sinking her stockinged heels into the counterpoint covering, she maneuvered around until her head was positioned directly below the small window.

Heavenward, a swath of pale stars ribboned the sky, the largest shimmering like diamonds in the velvety blackness beyond the square glass panes, while the cool, white moon hung in relief against eternal night. She contemplated the loveliness of the heavenly order.

"Diamonds," she whispered morosely, "not at all like me. I've become so ugly inside...so flat and stale. Just like that awful cake," and the mortification came upon her once again as she remembered that day. In her effort to surprise Ma, she had in haste, omitted the baking powder and added too much salt. When Ma returned from Aunt Mabel's and Cassie had opened the oven door, the sad, flat thing was rendered useless as a birthday treat. Even the goats had rejected it, and as Ma held her, wiping away the tears, Cassie had refused to believe the day could ever be redeemed.

She had been a child. 'Anyone can overlook a childish mistake, but now I'm a woman,' she chided, and found it difficult to forgive herself for the tastelessness of her current attitude.

Now, nothing pleased her on the ranch or at school, and very little about the millenery projects appealed to her of late. It had been difficult to tolerate the little girls, and she was at odds with Mary.

Ma's steady and pleasant attention to the details of daily life unexplainably frustrated Cassie to no end. She wondered whether her mother ever desired anything out of the plain ordinary.

However, it was Pa that burdened her more than any single thing. She could not understand him, but she had not tried to chip away at the granite wall they had thrown up between themselves. She hated herself for her emotions. Tears filled her eyes as she grabbed her worn baby doll, pressing it to her bosom.

"I want to feel differently--I just can't," she lamented to the distant stars. She set the floppy doll aside and stretched an arm high above her head. Spreading her fingers to grasp the starry heavens, she longed to join them in their luminescence and float weightlessly in the sky.

"Please, God," she pleaded softly.

Her eye fixed on a brilliant star shining between her outstretched fingers. She moved her hand ever so slightly until that star glimmered between her ring and middle finger.

"Oh, please, God! Let Johnny place that diamond on my finger!" Squinting her eyes, the star and her finger merged into the happy illusion.

"Mrs. Johnny McLane," she whispered dreamily, and then more reverently, "Mrs. John McLane."

He had to have a middle name, for she had heard that southerners always had them, and sometimes more than one.

"But I don't know what his could be..." and she realized there was much she didn't know about him.

In the solitude of her room, she rolled onto her stomach and slipped quietly to the floor upon her knees. "Please, God," she whispered, "please help me to be the woman you want me to become. I can't do this by myself. I feel...so divided, so addled and foolish, yet hard and cold. I don't want to live for myself. I'm tired of thinking only of myself and my desires. Please, Jesus, help me to fit into this family again. Change this, Lord; change me! And bless Johnny. I pray you'll keep us together," and even as she uttered the request, the words she knew she must confess came hard. "Unless it is not in your plan...not your will for us. Then change my heart to want what you want for me."

The tears came softly as she climbed into bed. Drifting toward sleep and floating high into the night sky, she grasped the diamonds, sifting them like glittering mica through her fingers, gathering the most beautiful, and offering them lovingly back to God.

"I'm not sure how to get Miss Blackbridge back to Grand Encampment," Johnny answered wearily. "No stage travels in that direction. I suppose that she could travel in a mining or timber wagon, but I wouldn't trust sending her alone. The men would want payment, and since she has no funds, they'd demand she pay up in another way."

Sam realized the truth of Johnny's statement, and listened to his deputy ponder on the matter. Johnny recounted as much of the saga of the previous night as he could, leaving out the abstruse details relating to Myra.

"The man who hired Rosalyn and terrifies her so may be Philip Joyner. Ever heard of him?" Johnny added. "He's in cahoots with Riddick in some fashion, and you can bet on it."

Sam sat in his swivel chair nursing a shot of whiskey. He shook his head, finding it difficult to concentrate. Now and then he turned to fetch a paper from the broad desk top or bent to open a desk drawer and winced in pain with the effort.

"The force of that bullet must have bruised you pretty good," Johnny noted, observing the sweat beads gathering along Sam's brow and letting the previous discourse die. The marshal's shirt was draped over the bulky bandage on his right shoulder, and the arm was secured to his chest by bandages, leaving his only free arm in the opposite sleeve.

"Take this blasted thing off, Johnny. The bandage is in the way and I'll heal better without all these trappings. I can't do a damn thing; I can't move!" Sam tossed his pencil on the desk in disgust.

"Oh no, not me!" Johnny exclaimed, throwing up his hands in benedictory fashion. "I'm not high up on Doc's list about now, and I don't want to lose my kitchen privileges by peevin' Miz Frances. Nope, you're on your own if you want to tangle with those two, sir."

"Humph," Sam grunted. "I won't be much good later on, and if things hold true to usual, the town should start hoppin' in an hour or so. At least you can get those old wanted posters out of the middle drawer, can't ya? I can't tug it open," Sam charged gruffly, getting back to the problem at hand.

"What did you say that fellow's name is? Joyner?"

"Yeah, Philip Joyner. Marshal Riddick introduced me to him very briefly at Iron Mountain. He's a real dandy, dressed to the hilt when I met him, and seems on friendly terms with the marshal. He's got a British accent, I believe," Johnny offered, attempting to hand the retrieved posters to Sam who waved them away with a stern, "You do it."

They sat in silence. Sam remained behind the desk, resting his head against the wall and closing his eyes. With legs outstretched and feet crossed before him, he emitted an occasional grunt or groan as he tried to find a comfortable position in the hard chair.

Johnny remained stretched out in a chair by the wood stove with his stockinged feet elevated on the railing. Heedlessly, he thumbed through the old posters with his mind on Rosalyn Blackbridge's plight.

"Miss Blackbridge says she has a relative in Virginia Dale and..."

The office door swung wide, admitting the grinning face and lanky body of Jess Bryant.

"Good evenin', gents! I come bearin' gifts!" Before him, he held out a round object draped with a large, white napkin.

With a flourish, he removed the cloth, exposing a delicacy that brought Johnny immediately to his feet. From a round, deep pan, the creation arched skyward and from its vented expanse, small rivulets of an amber honey-toned goo flowed lava-like, emitting the rich aroma of apples, bathed in cinnamon and butter. Piled high, the contents could barely fit under the lumpy blanket of flakey, golden crust, stretched thin, with lovely fluted edges. Jess placed the toothsome temptation on the desk before Sam and quickly removed a small bottle of Kentucky Bourbon from his coat pocket. Johnny reached the desk, took a great whiff, then cracked a grin.

"Well, well, Pard, didn't know you could bake! A talent you've concealed lo these many months. Let's have at it!"

Jess tossed the napkin in Johnny's face and replied, "Keep those secesh' mitts off, Virginia, it ain't for you! Sodie baked it for the marshal." Addressing Sam, he finished, "It's a 'get well pie', or somethin' such, and she says she hopes you're better soon, but *this*," he added, grinning conspiratorially, "is from me! I know it's been rough around here, so I figured you could use this as well!" He placed the bottle on the desk.

Sam tried to extend a hand, then grimaced from pain. "Thank you, Jess, and thank Sodie kindly for me." He sat back, displaying a rare grin.

Jess drew up a chair. "I'm free tonight so if you need some extra help keepin' order, I'm available".

"So," Johnny responded mildly, "it's Saturday night and you're free as a bird, huh? That must mean either Sodie is busy, or most likely, that she came to her senses and dumped ya."

"Neither assumption is correct, son. There just happens to be a meeting at the schoolhouse. I believe the older girls are making costumes for somethin', and Sodie volunteered to help out. They were supposed to meet at Myra's place, but she has unexpected company--a cousin or someone, so they switched their meeting place to the school."

Johnny shot a quick, hard glance at Sam, catching his eye, and Sam responded with a casual, noncommittal grunt.

Jess turned on Johnny. He pulled a nonchalant face and said smoothly, "So, it should be kinda interestin', don't you think, John Scott? I mean, both of your 'la…dies', together under one roof at a social gatherin'? We might yet have a skirmish in the town tonight!"

Johnny bunched his brow and shot back. "Quit trying to make somethin' out of nothin', you ignorant Texican. You know I haven't been seein' Myra for months, and besides, Myra is with Cassie during part of most every school day, anyhow."

"I can just hear the conversation now, risin' above the ting of needle against thimble," and Jess equivocated girlishly, "'So, what's new with you deary, bless your little heart? Got you a new beau, you say? Oh, my! Tell me all about him!'" When he was unable to ruffle Johnny, he switched tactics.

"Oh, and by the way, son, I take offense at your reference regardin' the great state of Texas. It's an insult, boy, and I could call you out on it if I'd a mind to. Texicans, we are no longer, and I'll thank you to remember that since William Barrett Travis stood against Santa Anna at the Alamo, along with Bowie, Crockett, and others, we are Texans, sir, Texans! Would you like me to spell it out for you? T-E-X…"

"As far as callin' me out goes," Johnny interrupted, "I think there is no honor to be found in your dying in the street like a dog. Aside from that, I am surprised at your prowess in spellin'. Never figured you for a scholar, but then again, your lack of historical knowledge proves me right--as usual. Few of those boys were from Texas--not Crockett, or Bowie, or even Travis himself. They might have won their cause, but they did lose the battle, or did you forget that little detail?"

"Well, bless me, John, if you ain't the one to talk about losing battles! It's about time you raised that soggy, rebel brain of yours out of that tidal-swamp water. I know they weren't all from Texas, but they made the stand and won their independence, unlike some others I know."

"Enough!" Sam Brett exclaimed, fatigued by his discomfort and the monotonous discourse. "You boys have got to quit fightin' wars that have long since been decided and casting aspersions on the dead! This town has enough conflict without the two of you snarlin' and scrappin' like cur whelps!"

Sam stood, picked up the pie, then headed for the door. "I am going to where I can eat my pie in peace!"

When faced with the loss of the only pleasure likely to present itself over the course of the long evening ahead, Johnny and Jess grew less philosophical, protesting loudly.

"We weren't serious, Mr. Brett, we were merely killin' time!" Johnny defended, with astonishing conviction.

Jess issued his own urgent plea. "He's right--don't go, he'll quit!"

Sam Brett turned back impatiently, staring down the contrite faces before him. He filled the doorway with his six-foot frame, and with unusual theatrical flair, using his good arm, he held the enormous pie before him, breathing out a challenge.

"While you're rememberin', and seem to be in need of conflict of some sort, just remember the flag that flew high above that great cannon so sought after in the first battle in Gonzales, Texas. And picture, if you will, John Henry Moore holding that famous flag upon which was inscribed the words I now leave with you boys--'Come and Take It'!"

He glared at their stun forms for a moment, turned and left, and before his hirelings' eyes, the pie vanished, carried away in the breeze like the last skein of smoke from that lost cannon.

"Now you've done it, Jess! See what just happened?" Johnny howled, exasperated over the flight of his sustenance.

"Go on after him, Johnny," Jess urged.

"You ain't talkin' to me, son. You go after him!"

Sam felt no better as he took that short walk in the shadows of the boardwalk. In fact, his shoulder throbbed with the effort it had taken to wrangle the pie out of the office. What stuck in his brain and bothered him most was the mysterious circumstances surrounding Miss Blackbridge, and especially, what might lay in store for Sideling as the night drew on. Women working away unsuspectingly in the brightly-lit schoolhouse on the edge of town was not going to help the situation, and he had seen the truth of it reflected in Johnny's glance. He turned back for the office. They would need a plan.

True to their word, Johnny and Jess quit their foolishness, and as they sat around the desk with the great pie diminished by half, they ate and discussed the potential complications likely to arise as the night hours dragged on.

Johnny expressed concern for the women, for the windows of the schoolhouse would be awash in light, and the lovely silhouettes would likely draw roving eyes as the cowhands made passage to and fro by the southern entrance to town. He rose, walked to the stove, and chucked another fat stick of wood into the conflagration. Shivering, he buttoned his vest, then found his boots and pulled them on.

"How is it you spend most of your time barefooted, son?" Jess began. "It don't seem to matter what the temperature is, you can be found shuckin' your boots."

"Can't stand the constant confines of the things. Guess I just came up that way. Never wore shoes much as a child, except of a Sunday when I had to," Johnny replied evenly.

"I swear if I can understand how the Union is able to embrace as uncivilized a population as resides in the state of Virginia," Jess baited coolly.

Johnny shook his head, started to comment, caught the look on Sam's face and declined rebuttal. There was still pie left in the tin.

Johnny, Jess, and the marshal patrolled the town streets in three concentric circles, reminiscent of the long, lonely times Johnny had night-herded as a youth in Montana. At that time, he had contented the bovine with his song; now he could hardly hear himself think over the din of contention.

Sam took the center of town while Jess patrolled the east side and hotel. Johnny, trusting no one but himself for the task, took the western section which included the schoolhouse.

They passed each other only briefly as they circled on foot, breaking up any unruly gatherings and tamping down the spark of argument before it could erupt into trouble. Though the saloon was Sam's, they all watched it carefully. On the third pass, Johnny and Sam paused to confer. It was decided that, due to the increased boisterous activity flowing from the saloon into the street, Johnny would inform the ladies who where housed at the school of the potential dangers they faced.

The sounds and sights hibernating within the schoolhouse, starkly contrasted with the ominous finger of licentiousness uncurling toward it. Easy chatter and laughter filled the air as Johnny stepped from the pale glow of the cloakroom into the lambency of the classroom.

The desks had been placed in a circle in the center of the room and facing the entrance, Sodie was the first to notice him.

"Why, Johnny, what brings you here?" she asked, rising and coming to him with a welcoming smile as others raised curious faces.

Johnny caught Cassie's questioning eye, and with a lift of his brow and a quick nod, telegraphed his desire to gain her understanding and was rewarded by her astute appraisal. She did not move. He returned his gaze to Sodie's anxious face.

"Jess?" she asked breathlessly.

"He's fine." Johnny answered. A quick smile played along his lip line as he realized her first thoughts would be concern for his friend. Immediately Myra walked up to stand beside Sodie.

"I need to talk with Myra," Johnny advised quietly, and Sodie returned to the circle of seamstresses.

Myra's questioning eyes found his, and involuntarily he glanced toward Cassie whose gaze held both of them. Johnny took Myra's elbow and moved her toward the cloakroom, turning his back to the women.

"There's likely to be trouble in town tonight, Myra. When I leave, lock the door and don't open it for anyone you don't know really well. It would better if you all would leave now."

With a harsh whisper, she interrupted him. "You know why we are here! I had no choice. You need to get her out of my house and out of this town. Just when is that supposed to happen?"

In a low, controlled tone, he replied, "Soon. I have a plan, but for now, if you stay here you must listen, and please, do as I say. What time can you be finished here?"

"I don't know," she answered impatiently, "we've got a lot of planning to do as we sew..."

Johnny interrupted, "We'll give you until 9:00, then we're coming back. You'll have to leave--all of you. It's rough out there, and stability decreases by the moment." He thrust the rifle he held toward her. "Take it. Use it if you have to, on anyone coming through that door uninvited."

"I..." she began.

"I don't have time to convince you, Myra. Just do it!" Johnny replied tersely. He stepped forward as if to leave, then turned and caught Myra's arm, fishing something from his coat pocket.

"I forgot. Take this and buy some sort of wrap for Miss Blackbridge." Her confusion was obvious. He pressed four coins into her palm.

He lowered his voice. "I'm gonna try to get her out of town early Monday morning. I'll bring an extra horse to your place beforehand, under the cover of night, and hope no one becomes suspicious."

"Don't come for her too early," she whispered, standing closely. "The mercantile won't open until 9:00 a.m. and I teach, you know."

"Just do the best you can. I'd do it myself, but that would raise suspicion. Tell her to look for me. I'll come to your cabin as early as I can get away. No one can know about this, Myra," he advised seriously, pinning her with his eyes.

"You seem to forget who is harboring her, Johnny, and I want her gone as much as you do!" she whispered shortly.

"I'll return. Be ready at 9:00, and lock that door," he warned. He did not trust himself to look toward Cassie.

Myra followed him through the cloakroom, and as he exited, he listened for the turn of the key in the sturdy lock.

As the evening wore on, disputes erupted in the streets. One man suffered a gunshot wound, and two were arrested on drunk and disorderly charges. Aggravated, Johnny threatened one with "inciting a riot" and the man reluctantly staggered back into the saloon.

A small fire of unknown origin broke out in the alley beside the Flour and Grain, bringing citizens out from their homes and causing further commotion. Sam Brett was the first to spot the flames that were extinguished before flame or ash could leap across the road and torch the hay mounds by the livery.

It was 9:15 p.m. before Johnny raced to the schoolhouse where the ladies huddled behind the locked door, ready to depart. Jess came up behind him, and with guns drawn, they dismissed the women, using themselves as shields between the town and the waiting horses and wagons.

"Hurry ladies," Jess directed. "Anyone going southwest, go quickly. Those going northeast and through town will need our escort."

Coming down the steps, Cassie ran for Johnny, who caught her outstretched hand with his free hand.

"Where's your wagon?" he asked, drawing her to his side.

"I'm staying with Millie tonight, I..." He nodded, acknowledging Millie who had suddenly come alongside them. Cassie grasped Johnny's wrist, and looked apprehensively toward the schoolhouse door.

"Where's Mary? She's supposed to stay with us tonight, but I don't know where she has got to!"

Millie moved quickly, calling back over her shoulder as she gathered her skirts and bounded back up the stairs. "Miss Myra is still inside! I'll check for Mary!"

"We'll move out along the back street," Johnny said, thinking outloud. Cassie finished his unspoken thought.

"Just as we did the other night," she commented softly. "Remember?"

"Yeah, I do," Johnny replied, watching the fray around him while sheltering Cassie between himself and the white, clapboard structure behind them.

"Here we are!" announced Millie, as she came rapidly down the stairway with Mary on her heels. Johnny extended his gun hand and swept the lot of them behind him.

"Get back toward the wall," he commanded. Myra Davis appeared behind Johnny and drew up closely, forcing Cassie to release his wrist.

"You're going southwest, Myra. You'll be alright, but go now."

Not to be rushed by his hasty instruction, Myra paused and said pointedly, "I'll see you *early* Monday morning, Johnny."

With a forced smile, Myra turned her attention on the three girls. "Take care and be safe. We'll finish up later."

Uncharacteristically, Mary stood mute and watched in fascination as the melodrama played out. When no one responded to Myra, Millie added hastily, "Be safe also, Miss Davis."

Myra tried to catch Johnny's eye, but his mind was elsewhere, and in the dim of the lamplight, he never noticed. Without another word, she turned in stiff regality, brushing past Cassie and nodding a farewell to all as she left for her rig.

The wind howled through the streets as snow undulated and swirled wildly, lifting then falling. Minute particles of ice joined the fray, stinging at what little skin remained exposed to the elements. Johnny stood just outside the doorway in the mid-morning light. The air was frigid, but welcomed after the stagnancy of the jail, and he breathed deeply.

Jess had departed, headed for the relay and his bed. Sam had gone to Doc's to check on the injured man and have his own wound redressed. Before their release and under Johnny's scrutiny, the jail had been scrubbed by the inebriated cowhands, but it would be some time before the scent of wood smoke, gunpowder, or freshly-brewed coffee would veil the stench of them.

He glanced toward Millie's house, invisible now through the scrim of snow. The town seemed to disappear a few yards from where he stood, lost in a pale gray. A lone rider appeared suddenly in the street, bent against the wind. Johnny wondered if Cassie and Mary would try to make it back to the ranch through the storm. He hoped they would not. He closed the door and returned to the chair behind the desk.

He rested his elbows on the desk, his head cradled in his hands. Three hours of sleep had not been enough. "She's so close--just yards away," he mused, wondering what Cassie might be doing at the moment. What did girls talk about when they were together? What might they be doing now? Cooking or sewing--what was she thinking about? It was most unlikely that she would be dwelling on the same things he was. It was so cold, and she would be so warm.

He had to set those thoughts aside for now. One day there would be an appropriate time for those things, but that time was not now. He rose sluggishly and added wood to the potbelly stove.

The town was sick, riddled with unrest, and it needed healing. But how? They could struggle with the evil, but how could they prevent or even hold it at bay? When had it begun, and why had they not noticed the subtle changes? They had muddled their way through the previous night and had changed nothing, only reacting to the tide of violence which had flooded the streets. His mind was numb, mired in remembrance of quick decisions made in the heat of last night's confusion.

Toward evening, the wind began to die down. Johnny cleaned his gun, spinning the cylinder and meticulously wiping away any signs of residue.

Sam worked on the office ledger, leaned back in his chair, and tossed the pencil onto the desk. "We're gonna need a new ledger before the year is out if we can't settle this town down," he complained wearily.

The door to the office flew open, arcing wide. It slammed into a chair which fell back against the railing, causing the oak door to rapidly rebound, its heavy weight impeding the intruder.

"Oh! Ooh," and with a deft boot, the invader gave another swift kick to the offending door, which duplicated its trajectory.

With a leap, Johnny was at the door, catching it as he pulled the laughing girl into the office.

"Wow, gal, you alright?" he exclaimed, as he looked with surprise into the laughing, flushed face of Mary Wilkerson.

"That door's dangerous; you should have it fixed!" she exclaimed, holding forth a basket covered with a white dishtowel.

"Unless it's assaulted by a banshee, it usually works quite well," Johnny grinned, releasing her arm.

She gave him a brilliant smile, then marched toward Sam, and sat the basket on the desk before him.

"These are for you, Marshal Brett, sir, from me, Millie, and Cassie. We baked them special. They're sugar cookies! We hope you're on the mend and that these cookies will help."

Mary backed up and perched upon the railing in front of Sam, waiting for his appraisal of her offering. Sam lifted the towel, took a whiff, and popped a fat cookie into his mouth.

"Fine! They're very good," he complimented, and Mary smiled broadly, then regarded Johnny.

"A little milk would go well with them. They're for you also, Johnny McLane," she instructed, smiling sweetly. "Oh, and so is this. I almost forgot!"

Mary fished an envelope from her pocket and handed it to Johnny. "It's from Cassie."

Her eyes widened, and her checks budded rosily as Johnny thanked her and remembered to apologize for the lack of milk. He inquired whimsically as to whether or not coffee would be an acceptable substitute. Mary pulled a self-conscious smile, but Johnny's attention remained fixed on the letter in his hand.

Mary ignored Johnny's question, noting he didn't seem to care if she answered, and watched as he tucked the small envelope into the breast pocket of his vest. When he raised his eyes expectantly, her animation had faded. Under the scrutiny of the two lawmen, she seemed suddenly at a loss for words.

Alighting quickly from her perch, Mary recovered enough to curtsy a quick farewell.

"I'm supposed to stay--only for a moment, I'm told," she confessed earnestly.

"I hope you recover soon, sir," she repeated, moving quickly for the door.

From over her shoulder, she cast a quick, unsubtle glance toward Johnny, then pulled the heavy door closed as she exited. Sam stared inquisitively at his deputy, but Johnny's focus was on the envelope he had retrieved from his pocket.

"I'll make rounds. Maybe the town will stay quiet tonight for a change," Johnny uttered distractedly, replacing the letter in his vest pocket and fetching his coat.

Sam nodded, too tired for inquiry or supposition, and pacified himself with another sugar cookie.

An argument kept Johnny at the saloon far longer than he wished, and returning to the jail, he found the marshal headed for the hotel. He bade Sam "good night" and locked the door. Extinguishing all but one lamp, he retired to the backroom.

Cassie's unread correspondence warmed his vest pocket like a live coal. Enveloped in the flickering lamplight, he lay on the cot, bunched the pillow under his head, and unsealed the envelope.

Unfolding the cream-toned, faintly lilac-scented paper, Johnny found the words of a poem inscribed with perfect, delicate penmanship:

> 'What if heaven be that, fair and strong
> At life's best, with our eyes upturned
> Whither life's flower is first decern'd
> We, fix'd so ever should abide?
> What if we still ride on, we two
> With life forever old yet new,
> Changed not in kind, but in degree'
> The instant made eternity—
> And heaven just prove that I and she
> Ride, ride together, forever ride?
> (Robert Browning, 1855)

In the same delicate hand, Cassie closed with, 'Remember our rides together. I hold them in my heart. Forever Yours.'

He closed his eyes and watched as the two of them rode through the evening on the dim path toward the Wilkerson ranch, into the shadow of the large barn, then through the bright-white snow as they raced down the road to Sideling. This was how they had been found together and for her to touch upon it in verse, stirred him deeply.

Cassie was the epitome of his freedom, and as he watched them ride across the plane of his thoughts, he prayed that heaven would prove they would ride together...forever ride.

About midnight, a loud pounding upon the office door jarred Johnny to consciousness. Struggling into his pants as he went, he thumped his way through the semi darkness.

"I'm comin," he yelled, grabbing his rifle and pulling the door wide.

An urgent voice called to him from the street. "There has been a break-in at the mercantile! I smell smoke, but I see no flame. I'll ring the alarm an' rouse the boys!" Sherm McNeil ran toward the backstreet.

Johnny sprinted down the boardwalk, fumbled with his key chain, and gained entry into the storefront. The atmosphere was smoke-filled, but as he opened the door to the storage room, a billow of thick black smoke plumed outward. Preceding heat and searing flame, it sucked away his breath, choked his lungs, and burned his eyes.

Coughing violently and managing to close the door, he stumbled back to the entrance, stepped out onto the porch, and slammed the door behind him. The side window shattered as he circled the structure. Watching the rear entrance give way to the axes, he joined the men as they vigorously pumped the wooden handles of the town's one water wagon in an attempt to douse the leaping flames.

Within the next hour, the fire was extinguished. The proprietor and Sam surveyed the soggy scene by the dim light from two lanterns. With most of his reserve merchandise destroyed, and much of the rack goods damaged from smoke, Bradford Jones was beside himself.

Johnny found it difficult to inhale, coughing fitfully while he and Sherm questioned the locals at hand. No one had seen anything unusual or even admitted to being on the streets before the spectacle had drawn them from their homes.

As Sherm entered the telegraph office, Johnny followed, questioning him. Sherm turned on him gruffly. "I was just leavin' the office. I had to set up for the mornin'. You ain't the only one who's had a rough night of it, and don't forget--I'm the one who reported this. Surely you aren't questioning my involvement, are ya Johnny?"

Irritable and perplexed, both young men realized the absurdity of the questions. Johnny apologized to his friend, then returned to help secure the broken, charred rear door and smashed windows of the mercantile. By 4:00 a.m. the town had settled.

Exhausted and plagued with coughing fits, Johnny returned to the office and sat on the cot, propped up against the back wall. He sipped watered-down corn whiskey to numb the pain in his chest and tried to doze off.

Rosalyn Blackbridge had been ready since daybreak, but it was after 10 a.m. before she and Johnny left Myra's cabin. Hugging the wooded areas of the mountain base, Johnny took as many obscure trails as possible.

The coat Myra had purchased fit adequately over the plain, gray dress she had given the girl, but the hood blew off constantly as the wind hurled gusts at the two southbound riders. Taking pity on the reddening ears of Miss Blackbridge, Johnny gave her his woolen scarf, drawing his coat collar up and tipping his hat against the wind.

To his dismay, he found that Miss Blackbridge was no horsewoman and required frequent stops to adjust her clothing and relieve her sore body. She had difficulty keeping pace with Johnny, so eventually he took her rein and led her horse at his side. When he glanced sidelong at her, chin tucked to her chest and eyes squinted tight against the elements, he knew she was unaccustomed to frequent exposure on the harsh winter prairie. He wondered at the harshness of life, which had brought her to this place, and again felt the need to protect her.

He spoke with the wind. "What will you do after reaching your aunt in Virginia Dale? Do you have a plan?" A coughing spasm choked off the last of his words.

She looked at him through watering eyes. "I can't think past this need to get away...to get to safety," she replied stiffly. "If it wasn't for you, I'd have died. I still can't believe he won't find me."

The fear in her voice reminded him of his own past times of desperation. "Everyone needs to be rescued at one time or other, Miss Rosalyn," he rasped.

She stared evenly at him. "Oh, is that so? And how would you know that? I could bet you never have."

"You're wrong about that. I've had some fairly dark days of my own--times when I felt I wasn't gonna make it."

"Look, Johnny, I got myself into this horror story and now I am so...so used...that I can't expect anyone would want to rescue me. So, what makes you consider helping me? I can't stand who I've become, and I don't see any way out!" She wiped her eyes angrily with her sleeve.

"There isn't a human alive who hasn't made mistakes or who has the right to judge you for the mess you've found yourself in," he answered sympathetically.

"Oh really? Is forgiving and forgetting that easy? What about you?" she challenged, rushing on. "You want to rescue me? Now, would you stay with me, be with me and accept me, or ever feel that you could make a life with me?"

When he did not respond immediately, she lashed out angrily. "I didn't think so! All those things you say! They are just words!" Hurt and anger captured her features, and she turned her face away.

"No, Rosalyn, they are not just words. I am in love with someone else, but..."

"I know," she interrupted, "Myra. I thought as much."

"No, not Myra, and it doesn't matter who it is. The point is, no person can really rescue another person. Not in the way that has a long-term effect or that matters in the end."

She looked at him dully, and he struggled to continue, losing momentum from the pain in his throat. Coughing, he forced his next words. "I got you out of Sideling. I could do that, but I can't keep you safe forever. I'm limited by time and space like every other man. You need someone who can rescue you from more than this world or the men in it. And," he added pensively, "we all need to be rescued from ourselves."

"You remind me of the preacher in my church back home. Are you talking about God? God, the rescuer? He, least of all would want me now!" She laughed bitterly.

"You are wrong about that. He hates what you've allowed in your life, its sin and He can't look on it, but He loves you. Most of all, He wants to restore you, to bring you to Himself and give you a hope and a future. I believe the Bible says this in the book of Jeremiah. You can read it for yourself."

(Acts 17:30-31; Jeremiah 29:11)

Between the coughing fits and in a rasping voice, Johnny told her briefly of his own experiences, and she began to listen intentionally. She asked hard questions; for some, he had no answers. He did his best to reply honestly, telling her about Jesus Christ and how his own heart had been changed.

"I have a lot more to learn about this myself, but if there is a church in Virginia Dale, you could get a Bible and start from there," he concluded.

Rosalyn spoke no more, retreating into her thoughts as the wind picked up steadily, and conversation for Johnny became nearly impossible. The throbbing in his head compounded with his coughing, and even the watered-down whiskey could not touch the ache behind his eyes.

The hovel of a cabin sat in a rocky clearing on the outskirts of the small village.

Non-descript and drab, it was inhabited by Rosalyn's ancient wisp of a great aunt who was not pleased to see her and displayed no eagerness to take the girl in. She did not invite him into her quarters, and they stood in the gloaming as she bombarded Johnny with pointed, irrational questions.

Who was he, and why was "the girl" in trouble with the law? Was she in a "desperate way" and if so, why had he brought her there? If he cared enough to haul her all the way to Colorado, why did he not just keep her?

It had been a bizarre experience, and when the hag wanted to search the palm of Johnny's hand to divine his "spirit" and bring back "rebel" family members from the dust of the "terrible war", he had refused, and she blasted him with accusations. The 'conversation' had been almost a monologue, delivered by the withered, old crone. Rosalyn had contributed little.

Before he mounted Cody, Johnny caught Rosalyn's hand and asked if she was sure he should leave her. She glared at him, and her eyes filled with tears.

"Just go..." she replied numbly.

"Remember, Rosalyn. Remember what I said. It's a matter of God's grace. It's clean, simple freedom." He released her hand, and she turned away speechless.

The late afternoon brought deepening cold, with the promise of a crystal-clear night and plummeting temperatures. Johnny rode into Virginia Dale, leading the horse he had commandeered from the Sideling livery for Rosalyn's escape. The town appeared deserted. Tumbleweed caught in a picket fence surrounding a hand-hewn, unpainted church. A lone gravestone, inscribed with the rough, chiseled letters, "A.W.", sat within the perimeter of the crooked fence, presenting a bleak sight in the twilight. Small cacti grew among the scattered rocks and prairie grass stubble. Beyond the churchyard, a few log cabins and small wooden structures stretched out in a lopsided square. At one corner, an adobe-like structure bore a shingle that hung from the porch and creaked in the wind. Upon it was the only apparent written communication to be found in the hamlet, the single word: SHERIFF.

"'Evenin'. What can I do for ya?" The sheriff glanced at the clock on the wall as Johnny entered the office. "Time sure gets away from me when I do these accounts," he groused, rubbing his face and yawning. He lay his pencil down and pushed back in his chair, looking at Johnny with eyelids at half-mast. "So, how can I help you, son?"

As Johnny came closer, the badge on his chest caught the sheriff's tired eye. "I'm Johnny McLane, deputy marshal from Sideling, Wyoming."

"Well, pleased to meet ya." The man stood to shake Johnny's extended hand. "Adam Lundquist, Sheriff. Come on, have a seat. What brings you down this way?"

The warmth of the small office was a relief, and Johnny removed his hat and gloves, taking the chair closest to the stove.

"I'm just passin' through on business. I had hoped to make it back to Sideling tonight but I..." The deep, racking cough hit him, and he stopped. Finally able to catch his breath, he continued. "I'm sorry, this cough has the best of me, and I don't think I could sit a saddle for much longer."

"You sound kinda rough. You best lay over for the night. We have a widow woman who lets rooms on occasion, and I'm sure she'd be able to put you up," Lundquist advised amiably, his blue eyes taking in the haggard deputy before him.

Johnny took a breath, putting the sheriff in mind of an old accordion sucking at air after having dried out in its confines for years. "I am short of funds, sir, and was gonna ask if I could use an empty cell to catch a couple hours of sleep. Then, I'll head north."

Adam Lundquist regarded the deputy for a moment, seemed to be considering the matter, then closed his eyes nodding slowly. Johnny wondered if the man was about to doze off. But his eyelids fluttered, and he came to life just as Johnny was deciding to lay himself on the cot in the small cell without permission, for fear he might be the one to pass out.

"I'll do ya one better, son. I got a little house at the rear of the office, just down the path. You can use the room to the left in the back. My daughter's recently married and moved away. It was her room, and no one will bother you as my wife has gone to visit her in Denver."

"I'd appreciate that, sir," Johnny rasped. The dull ache that had plagued his head throughout the day now pounded like a bass drum, leaving him dizzy and queasy.

"I've got some sandwiches and hot coffee. You look like you could use some nourishment as well," the sheriff said with a wry grin. He stood and fished in his vest pocket for a key which he handed to the deputy.

"Don't think I could tolerate food, but I'll kindly take you up on that bed," Johnny replied.

"Everything you need and probably a lot more should be there--help yourself. I'll point the way." He led Johnny past a single cell and out the back door.

"I'll be over later. Need to get through these books--not my favorite part of the job!" Johnny thanked him again.

The key slipped easily into the lock, and the door swung open. The small living area was dim and sparsely furnished. Johnny found the room to the left and entered. The last gleam of evening sun shone through the frilly curtains and fell upon the colorful patchwork quilt. He navigated around the boxes stacked by the bed and moved the small pile of books from the coverlet. Untying his bedroll, he tossed it on the coverlet and removed his coat, gunbelt, and boots. Not bothering to undress, he met the woolen blanket in relief. His stomach churned, and he prayed he would not be sick, knowing he would never be able to get up in time. Closing his eyes, the dizziness slowly subsided, and he sank into darkness.

"Hey!" Lundquist called from the doorway, "You dead or alive?" In two strides, the wiry sheriff was by the bed, shaking Johnny's shoulder. "McLane, you alright?" he repeated.

Swimming to semi-consciousness, Johnny raised himself to his forearms, and the bright sunlight shot through his eyes like the flash of a sword. He turned from his stomach to his side, squinting up at the sheriff's animated face.

"Where...?" Johnny mumbled, then dropped his head and turned on his stomach, becoming inert once more.

"You're in Colorado, son, and half the day is spent. It's fine with me, but I figured you'd want to be getting' back to Wyoming. Get yourself together and come over to the office. Got some coffee on." Johnny made no response and did not move.

"Hullo! You hearin' me?" the sheriff asked jovially.

"Yes, sir," Johnny mumbled. "I'm comin.'" Through the fog, Johnny heard the water splashing into a bowl and the distant voice of the sheriff, and in seconds he drifted away, sinking down into muffled confusion.

The sun's last golden rays reached his face, and he raised his head from the bed just in time to observe the crest of its brilliant orb sink behind the mountain range far to the west. A plate of beans and pork belly sat covered with another tin, warming on the wood stove as Johnny stumbled into the sheriff's office.

"Well, I guess I don't need the undertaker after all," Lundquist chuckled. "Your supper is on the stove. I've just about finished mine," he said, wiping his mouth with a bandana and laying aside his fork. "Cup's over there near the coffee--what's left of it. Help yourself."

"I'm sorry, sir." Johnny felt the need to apologize, for the day was gone and he found himself in an awkward predicament once again. "I thought I was getting up, but I was asleep again before I knew it, and so here I am now."

By the look on the sheriff's face, Johnny knew he was still vaguely incoherent, so he gave up and got the last of the coffee from the pot. The coffee was strong and did the trick.

"Well, I'm glad for the company and that's the truth. Now that you're revived, tell me, what's new from up your way?" Lundquist's tone was pleasant, and he continued as if he thought it was necessary to help the deputy organize his thoughts. "I hear rustlin's been a problem up north."

"Yeah, that and other things. Sideling used to be a quiet town but that's changed, not really sure why."

"You got a marshal? Maybe I know of him."

"Sam Brett," Johnny replied.

Lundquist nodded his head. "Heard of Sam. I believe he was in Arizona before. So he went to Wyoming, did he? Good man."

Johnny contemplated the man before him for a moment, quickly deciding this sheriff and his town most likely were not connected with the tumult taking place in Albany County.

"Sideling is not on the Union Pacific line? You say it's southwest of Laramie City? In the shadow of the Leviathan..." Lundquist contemplated, as he admiringly watched Johnny put away his dinner.

"Sorry you can't eat up that pan too. Breakfast and dinner are the big meals around here. You just got the benefit of a few scraps there," he joked.

"It's fine, sir, and thanks for it. I appreciate all you've done."

Lundquist waved the comment away like a bothersome fly. "Glad to do it. You know, a fellow passed this way, oh, I'd say it's been about a month ago now. Said he was on his way to Grand Encampment. Was going up in them mountains. Said something about silver or copper. Don't hold me to it, but I believe that's where he said he was headed."

"Have you seen others coming through, heading that way or up the valley toward Laramie?" Johnny asked, his interest piqued.

"I seen a few pass through, but I don't much care where they are headed as long as they pass by peacefully." He grinned.

Johnny thought on the matter. "Did they have families with them or mining equipment? Did you notice anything unusual?"

"They all had picks and shovels, most do, but nope, just men passin' through," he said. "Sorry, but nothin' out of the ordinary." He fell silent, studying on his thoughts. Johnny sipped his coffee, grateful for the effects of the caffeine.

"A town, even a small place like yours, so close to the mountains, could provide a lot of what a man would desire," Lundquist contemplated.

"We have timber and water," Johnny replied thoughtfully, "and there aren't many towns can claim those commodities on the high plains."

"Yeah, and throw in a little iron ore to boot and bam!" The sheriff looked up from under his bushy brows.

"Ever'one out here's lookin' for the mother lode. But you got somethin' there maybe worth goin' after. A town like that would be a boom for greedy men, but with two honest lawmen standin' in the way, well, that ups the ante a bit."

As they talked, Johnny was surprised to find that he was tired, so it did not take much convincing on the sheriff's part to get him to agree to layover for another night. His cough still lingered, but feeling better than he had in days, he planned for an early morning start back to Sideling.

Although experiencing a prick of guilt for leaving Sam alone in Sideling, the bed was warm and soft, and he stretched out on it determined to enjoy the sensation. Virginia Dale was quiet...eerily quiet. Johnny had no responsibilities, leaving him with a sense of dissociation and freedom. Drowsy, relieved of the burning in his lungs and fairly free of the cough that had plagued him since the fire, he wondered idly if he could exist in such a condition for very long. As he relaxed, he began to sense that he was lacking something. In the midst of all the comfort, he was totally alone and totally lonely.

Quietly, her overwhelming presence filled his senses as she came through the dimness, gliding gracefully toward him, and she was laughing. The expressive bow of her lips decreased demurely into a delicate smile, while her eyes flashed and danced above her freckled nose. Soft hair blew like angel wings about her, captivating him with the vision. Fire within lit him like a flame.

He groaned and forced himself up, swinging his feet onto the cold floor. Moving quickly to the dresser and dipping both hands into the cold water, he bent to splash his face repeatedly. From his saddlebag on the back of the chair, he removed his small Bible, taking from it the worn page of verses tucked randomly within. He sat on the chair, reciting the verses and praying for strength, attempting to commit to memory those he had not quite mastered.

He raised his fist and with outstretched arm and thumb pointed upward, extended his index finger toward the lacey curtain that framed the night beyond. "Proverbs 5:21," he recited, "A man's ways are before the eyes of the Lord." With his thumb, he cocked the imaginary hammer. "And, he pondereth all his going."

Needing more ammunition, he recited, "James 1:12. 'Blessed is the man that endureth temptation, for when he is tried, he shall receive the crown of life which the Lord promises to them that love Him.' Blammm..." he said softly, pulling the imaginary trigger, and he watched as Satan's torturing minions scattered, dispersing through the walls and into the four winds.

315

The morning was frigid and as the dark fled, gray clouds scudded in from the west, promising snow. After partaking in biscuits, molasses, and coffee, Johnny bade Lundquist farewell and rode northeast from the hamlet of Virginia Dale.

He smiled and waved to the children playing in the churchyard and watched as a woman came from the sanctuary to the doorway, calling the children together. School had been conducted in Sideling in much this way, before the new schoolhouse had been erected on the edge of town. As he rode, he pondered on it.

When the school had been removed from the church building, it had given more space and had clarified the purpose of both structures, but was the split significant for another reason? Myra taught from the classics, with a heavy emphasis on the modern philosophies of pragmatism and even transcendentalism. He knew this because, when they had first begun to see each other, he had foolishly consented to monitor her class for an afternoon while she handled some supposed "emergency". Finding him suitable for her purposes, she had soon insisted on a repeat performance. He had firmly denied her request, begged her forgiveness, lied outright and quickly contrived to leave town to keep from the task. She was infuriated.

He knew she instructed from the Bible sparingly, nor not at all. This was not the case when he was coming along. He had learned to read from the Scripture's elegant phrases, studying the moral lessons derived from the Psalms and Proverbs. He had been schooled in grammar and sentence structure by writing the verses repeatedly, and had studied the magnificent forms of poetry contained within the pages.

In the solitude of the Colorado morning, he wrestled with the new philosophies. If the function of human thought had become man's guide to action as some believed, and if truth was tested by the consequences of actions resulting from belief, where was God with His unchangeable character, commands, and laws in the pragmatic approach?

If man was to depend on his own intuition and personal reflection by simply immersing himself in nature as a means to bring about truth, as in the transcendentalist's approach, he wondered how this could possibly square with the Word of God. If the fallen nature of man in general, and of himself in particular, was any indication of the potential of man living solely on his own merits, then woe be it to mankind!

The Bible had long been the instruction manual and the standard for the society he had grown up in, and he wondered when it had become a separate thing…a Sunday thing? When had this changed for him? Through the terrible war, he studied the Bible at the military institute. Using its principles, he and the young men who were his comrades had been trained to become soldiers and gentlemen in a world gone mad. Had the truth of the Word of God become less important to him after he had been forced to flee from the military academy? Was it after his mama's death and the termination of her instruction?

Early on, he had studied the Reverend Jonathan Edwards' stirring of the American colonists to a "Great Awakening". Later, he read of Reverend Samuel Johnson's moral philosophies, which declared that the essence of true religion was morality. Somewhere along the way, the road map to a walk with God had slowly faded for him. Likened to the approach of a late afternoon storm upon the clarity of a beautiful day, the changes seemed to have brought a cloud of obscurity to the Word of God, for he had not clung to the Word through the storm.

It occurred to Johnny that regardless of when things had changed, it seemed to have been a sweeping, transforming change. He did not see how the transformation had been for the better, for it seemed to him that what he had observed of men in general, and from some of the population of Sideling in particular, was an indifference to biblical principles. He found himself wondering if anyone else in Sideling saw things in this light. Sideling might be desirable for water, timber, or precious metals, but were those things more precious than character and integrity? And how many lives would be ruined in the struggle for material things when in the confusion, men became mired in deceit and considered their own needs and wants as more important than that of the next man?

What would become of Rosalyn Blackbridge, and others like her who were used like chattel for the gain of others? When they had parted, she seemed no closer to making better choices for her life. He had dumped her on a bitter, old woman, and it bothered him to have done so. Yet, he knew he could not be responsible for her actions, and he could not judge her. That was for God to do.

"We enforce the law, we don't make judgments. There are courts for that." This was the edict he had learned from Sam in his early days of apprenticeship.

He rode on through the tranquility of the early morning even as his solemn thoughts rained down hard. 'I did what I came to do,' he assuaged, even as he saw the irony of the situation. Rosalyn was in no less danger of being harmed all these many miles from Sideling. Why had she not listened to him or understood that he had told her truth in an attempt to help her? There were two forms of death, but she seemed not to understand. No, he would not judge her. 'We'll all stand before the Great Judge one day,' he thought, 'and evidently, many of us will be tried and found wanting.'

(Acts 17:30-31)

Cassie watched as her black boots sank into the snow. The ice crunched beneath her weight as she stepped from the porch in front of Olivia Halstead's cabin. She untied and mounted Lady for the short ride to Mrs. Winkler's gate. As she passed the marshal's office, she slowed. A lone horse was tied to the hitching post, and it was Sam Brett's gelding that cast a calm eye toward Lady as they passed.

Her heart sank. Johnny had been gone for three days now. Perhaps his horse was in the livery...perhaps she should have taken the back street past the weathered barn, but what reason could she give for entering the structure?

Frustrated, she trembled in the cold. "Please God, let him be safe. Let what they said not be so." She pulled Lady up to the gate.

"I'm delighted to see you, Cassie!" Mabel held out a frail hand, and her eyes twinkled brightly.

"I'm sorry my hands are so cold, it's fearful outside." Cassie took the aged hand, and sat on the bedside next to Mabel's rocker.

"You should have gone home, not come to visit an old lady on such a miserable day!" Mabel's eyes had clouded briefly but brightened again as Cassie smiled. "However, I'm mighty glad to see you," Mabel added.

"I've missed you...our talks and your encouragement," Cassie replied, leaning forward and placing a kiss on Mabel's gaunt cheek, then settling on the bedside.

"How are things at home with you and your pa? I've kept both of you in prayer. Are things improving?" Her brow drew into a mass of soft crevasses.

"I haven't seen much of him for the last two days, but we talk and he is civil. I try, but something is broken between us. I hate it, but I can't change it without denouncing my love for Johnny--which I certainly will never do!"

Cassie's burst of passion dissolved and her resolve slackened, saddening the old woman's heart. She squeezed Cassie's hand. "Oh, my girl," she lamented, "you mustn't be angry with your father. I know this is difficult."

"There is another concern, Aunt Mabel. Johnny has been gone for all of three days now."

"Well, Cassie, you know he often leaves town on business. This is not surprising, nor is it unknown to you," she reminded gently. "What has happened to concern you so?"

With a stricken look, Cassie studied her own hands. In a moment she answered softly. "I overheard Miss Davis and Sodie Duane in conversation. Millie and I were finishing up instruction for some of the younger students, and Sodie stopped by the school to bring more fabric for the costumes. I doubt Sodie knew we could hear them, or even if she knew we were there, as they conversed briefly in the cloakroom and didn't come into the classroom."

Cassie gathered her thoughts, and Mabel waited patiently. "They talked briefly about the town ruckus Saturday night, then Sodie mentioned that the marshal was concerned because Johnny had not returned. I heard Miss Davis comment that it was just like Johnny to go off, but what was worse, I heard her say that he had gone off with some woman, and she indicated that he would likely take his time returning."

Cassie paused, and Mabel waited.

"Well, Sodie seemed surprised at Miss Davis' poor assessment of Johnny. She said that Jess was forever teasing Johnny about being "an overly virtuous man". Then, Miss Davis said there were two sides to every coin, and they just may be surprised."

"What do you think of that?" Mabel asked evenly, and watched as Cassie's defenses rose.

"It can't be true! I know Johnny is not that sort of man. At first, I was stunned because I know Miss Myra knows him rather well, but oh, why would she say such a thing? She must be wrong, but then I wonder if perhaps I don't know him as well as I thought, and perhaps..." her voice trailed off softly.

"There are a thousand 'perhaps'. Life seems to call them up when we are concerned. You must keep your relationship with the Lord strong, then bathe the relationship you hope to have with Johnny in prayer. You must decide to trust God with all of this."

"I try! I try my best, but sometimes I can't feel settled in my soul, and I struggle with doubt again. I know that I have no right to know where he is, no real claim to him. Suppose he is injured? Suppose he..."and she gave up suppositions for facts.

"Waiting is so horribly hard!" she exclaimed, then the corners of her mouth drew up in a purposeful bow, and determination fixed her features. "You must pray for my courage, Aunt Mabel, for talking with you helps. I will learn to keep a smile...can you see? I will trust, I'll be confident, even if I faint trying!"

Persisting throughout her breathless statement, the contrived smile lingered, even as tears stung her eyes.

Mabel embraced Cassie's resolve. "You have the answers, sweet-one, you just need to continue with the same determined trust. Remember that if you feel anything toward your teacher, it must be compassion. I think she may still have feelings for the deputy, so this will be hard for her also. Remember, God is in control. Myra is in a hard place and may say some hard things because she desires what she cannot have.

"Be respectful to your father and your teacher, and wait for God's perfect timing. If you will, walk one mile further. Honor them with your words and actions. By these things you honor our Lord, and when you need to talk, remember, I am here to listen."

Cassie's eyes shone through unshed tears. "You are my Naomi, Aunt Mabel," she said softly. "Caring for me and guiding, just as Naomi did for Ruth in ancient times."

"Well then, child, I will say to you just what Naomi said to her daughter-in-law, Ruth. Let me see..." Mabel picked up the worn black book from the bedside table, thumbing the pages carefully. "Ah, here it is. The book of Ruth, chapter three. Listen now, and recall that Naomi was referring to Boaz, whom she trusted God would give to Ruth as a kinsman redeemer, an appropriate husband for Ruth, after the death of Naomi's own son. Listen to verse 18: 'Then said she, Sit still my daughter, until thou know how the matter will fall: for the man will not be in rest, until he have finished the thing this day.'"

Cassie thought for a moment. "Be still and you will see...how beautiful, thank you," Cassie leaned forward to kiss the soft cheek.

Mabel took Cassie's hands and held them firmly, looking deeply into her eyes. "You go now, daughter, if I may call you daughter. Remember to trust and to sit still, and I believe your young man will not rest until, like Boaz with Ruth, he claims you for his own.

26

THE ENTERPRISE

"OWW! DANG IT all!"

While he tried to flick the splats of boiling water off one hand, water from the pail he held in the other hand sloshed onto the floor. He set the bucket down and grabbing another stick of wood from the box, tossed it into the inferno, slamming shut the iron door with his knee. With a long wooden dowel, he gave a hearty swish to the shirts bathing in the soapy water of the large, black pot atop the stove. With a string mop, he swabbed the puddle which had formed on the floor. Noticing the brown tinge of the water wicking into the twisted, cotton fibers of the mop, he took a small pail and dipped it into the steaming pot, drawing out a substantial amount of the soapy water. Pouring it on the dirty floor, he pulled the mop back and forth across the floorboards. He halted, still holding the mop with one hand and swished the soggy shirts using the dowel stick with his free hand as the boiling water erupted in blobs from the pot, hissing as it met the hot surface of the stovetop. Continuing to mop, it occurred to him that he should have swept the floor first. Too late, he decided, vigorously repeating the mopping process. The office door swung open and Sam Brett stepped through the doorway, dispersing the humidity with a blast of fresh air.

"Well, you've returned. I was ready to send a posse out after you, Johnny. What in Sam hill are you doin'?" he asked, as he watched Johnny orchestrate in hodgepodge confusion.

"Hey! Sorry for the delay, but I'll explain after I finish up here. Was everything stable while I was gone?" Johnny asked, starting with the mop on another section of the floor.

"Things were fair, I guess. What are you cookin'?" Sam asked, coming toward the stove.

"Stop!" Johnny admonished, "Don't walk on ma' clean floor, it'll be dry soon. And, I'm not cookin', I'm washin' my shirts."

Sam took in the scene before him. "That floor may eventually dry, but from the looks of that mop, I doubt it'll be clean."

321

"Did you see my extra pair of pants anywhere?" Johnny asked distractedly, placing the mop against the corner wall.

"You've got stuff everywhere, boy--slung over chairs, balled up in corners in the backroom, and at the hotel. I wouldn't begin to know how to find them."

"Yeah, sorry. I left in a hurry the other mornin'."

Back at the stove, Johnny lifted his dripping shirts with the dowel, and dropped them one by one into the pot of clean water on the floor by the stove.

"You do realize that Sideling has a laundry for this process," Sam asked dryly, "Why are you doin' this?"

Johnny slipped out of his shirt, adding it to the simmering pot, and turned to face Sam. "I need to save some money, and I figured now's as good a time as any," he explained, turning to retrieve the mop again. "I'm taking care of Cody at the livery which should save a couple 'a bits a month."

"Huh," Sam muttered noncommittally, "and where do you intend to dry those shirts?"

"I'll string em' up across a rope in the backroom. That should do it."

Sam shook his head, "Well, that's good news. If you have to jump up to run after somethin' in the middle of the night, you'll hang yourself."

Johnny stared at him, decided the marshal's comment wasn't worth debate, and replied, "I've got to get to the livery. I'll do rounds on my way back, then I'll finish this." Looking about him, he contemplated how best to get out of the corner he had mopped himself into.

Sam watched with detached curiosity as Johnny removed his boots and socks, drowning the socks in the steaming pot with the shirts, and then walked barefooted across the wet floor to the backroom. Johnny returned, took up his boots, and buttoning his coat up to the bandana at his throat, walked through the doorway, commenting as he departed.

"I shouldn't have washed that shirt. It was the only one left."

"How would you even know?" Sam muttered, picking up the newspaper and settling back in his chair.

An hour later, Johnny returned to the aroma of fried chicken and sour-dough biscuits. Sam sat writing and eating at the desk. Johnny's stomach rumbled uncomfortably reminding him that he hadn't eaten since breakfast.

"It's frigid out there," Johnny observed, shaking the snow off his hat. He walked to the stove and found that the coffee pot had replaced the black pot that held his shirts. The pot now sat with its contents, cold and still upon the floor. Pouring a steaming cup, he noticed a tin pan on the stove, covered with another of the exact size.

"What's this?" he asked.

"Your dinner--from the café. Frances sent it over," Sam replied simply. Johnny stared at the plate and closed his eyes, giving immediate but silent and profound thanks, not only for the food, but for Sam Brett's perception of the facts.

"Thanks for bringing it, sir," Johnny said with relish, as he picked up the pan and lifted the inverted lid. Mouth-watering and fragrant, the spectacle tantalized his senses. Just as quickly, he replaced the makeshift lid, and set the pan down with a plunk.

"Ah," he groaned, "I forgot to feed Horse Handler's crazy mare! I'll be right back. Don't let this pan out of your sight!"

Disgusted with himself for the oversight, he vacillated a moment as the aroma of the chicken lingered about, and held his retreat even as he willed himself gone. Caught in a flash of indecision, he breathed in deeply as though to preserve its wonder, but just as quickly the instruction ingrained by his father since boyhood returned, staying the impulse to indulge himself first.

"Feed the animals in your care first, son, and then yourself." He relinquished the pan to the stovetop, and returned to the cold barn.

Interspersing words with yawns and stretches, Sam and Johnny conversed until midnight. They were interrupted only briefly by a domestic dispute of no lasting consequence, except possibly for Hyrum Brown who had been unable to recoup his losses after a rare pilgrimage to the gaming table, which was discovered by his wife, Euphony.

Johnny told Sam of his conversation with the sheriff in Virginia Dale, and about the questions Lundquist had raised relating to the possibility that Sidling's many resources could be a reason for criminal interest in the town. They questioned whether the fires in Sideling had been set as distractions from the bigger problems that plagued the town, or as retribution against business owners who had been "hold-outs". But to whom or what exactly?

They reviewed the cases of domestic unrest, historically not much of an issue for the town, and poured over the disputes and complaints against and from the business owners to see if they could make any correlation between them. There seemed a few.

The only names to reoccur were those of the Englishman, Philip Joyner; of Leafy Misner at the saloon; and Clancy Miller at the Flour and Grain. Johnny could connect Misner and Miller, and their access through their business involvements to information relating to local cattle dealings, but if they were paid for this information, he did not know.

When Sam sent wires to a few trusted lawmen throughout the territory, the information he received on Joyner was already surmised. Joyner was an Englishman, spending English money on American soil, buying up sections of railroad-owned land, easily obtainable because in the previous year, the American banks had been reluctant to make loans backed by gold to citizens. This enabled Joyner to begin a major cattle endeavor, and import breeding stock from England. Was Joyner intending to breed his English stock with easily stolen, hearty American longhorns? If so, from whom was he receiving the information as to the whereabouts of valuable stock, and the movement of the herds around south-central Wyoming? It very well might be from Miller or Misner. Until the lawmen had this piece of the puzzle, and it could be proven, they would lack the ability to further clarify the big picture.

Clancy Miller had been the victim of two break-ins at the Flour and Grain, and had been the supposed target of the small fire. Why? Leafy Misner hired and fired from the saloon on a regular basis and had conflicts with just about everyone he had ever dealt with. Johnny thought there had to be money coming from an outside source to pay for his sudden influx of new employees. Why were they needed, except for the corruption of the town's citizens? When Sam and Johnny tried to factor in exactly "who", they had a problem they could not quite figure.

The known factors had begun to have devastating consequences on the town.

Uncharacteristically, a few men began to spend hard-earned wages on gambling and drinking to the neglect of their families. One young husband had struggled with his angry and embarrassed wife over a dalliance with a prostitute in the saloon late one evening. His gun had accidentally discharged, killing him and leaving her uncharged in the incident, yet a widow with young mouths to feed.

More than once, Sam was asked by banker and council member, Lance Brooks, to evict a family from their homestead for delinquent mortgage or rent payments. The banker frequently butted heads with Sideling's inflexible, hard-nosed lawyer, Almon Baird,

If things did not turn around, nonpayment of taxes would be next to afflict the folks. While local rustlings seemed to have decreased somewhat, possibly as the result of frequent patrolling, the degeneration of the cattlemen's cowhands had not, and weekend fistfights and gunplay in the streets had increased.

A brief discussion was raised by the town council regarding gun confiscation at the saloon and in the town's business establishments. It was dismissed as the business owners, led by Leafy Misner, rallied and argued in defense of Second Amendment rights. Olivia Halstead was the only business owner in favor of confiscation. Leafy swore such "asinine ignorance" would reduce their profits as customers would refuse to frequent the establishments, and was "unconstitutional to boot".

Sideling's two lawmen had been forced to spread their time and talents thin. The town council was dissatisfied, and Sam Brett was frustrated and worn out.

"I'm going to bed, Johnny, the town is all yours tonight," Sam commented, one night in mid-week. "Oh, by the way, I received a telegram from Cy Riddick yesterday. He's coming to town, day after tomorrow."

When Johnny questioned why the marshal from Iron Mountain planned an unexpected visit, Sam had no idea.

"The telegram said little else, but I doubt it is a social call." He pulled his coat and hat off the peg and walked out, leaving Johnny to his thoughts.

Staring into the orange flames in the wood stove, Johnny stretched out his hands toward the warmth.

"I never mentioned the job offer; I wonder what else Riddick wants," Johnny pondered aloud, feeling he should enlighten Sam before Riddick did.

He stretched his legs and flexed his muscles, seeking comfort in the chair, disheartened by the weight of responsibility and the burden of indecision he found himself shouldering.

Until his reimbursement from the city kicked in again with the beginning of the next month, just how would he feed himself and afford the few provisions he would need? He couldn't depend on the handouts from the marshal and Frances Kelly forever. Caring for horses, mucking stalls, training the "crazy mare" belonging to Horse Handler as payment for Cody's feed and board, and doing his own laundry could keep him afloat for now, but how could he keep up the pace?

"No money is a hard thing," he advised the hissing, leaping flames miserably, and could almost swear he was staring into hell incarnate.

He shook off the thought and tossed another stick of wood into the fire, then yawned and sat back with a firm proclamation. "Tomorrow will be here soon enough. Each day has enough trouble of its own, and I don't need to add any more to this one."

As he watched, the flames lick the dry wood until it roared to a blaze, crackling and popping in the iron confines, sending an occasional bright, hot spark to threaten a pant-leg or boot. A mouse scurried from the darkened corner, into the orange glow of the flames reflected upon the floor, disappearing into the darkness beyond.

"Yeah, run and hide, you varmint; sometimes I wish I could--away from the condition of this town, this contained inferno." As the blaze shot hotter, glowing sparks his way, his weary musings began to alter. "Untamed, consuming," he murmured, "and necessarily confined. Somewhat...like Cassie."

———————◆———————

Marshal Riddick's first visit of the day was not to the Sideling Marshal's Office. It was early afternoon before Johnny returned to find Sam behind the large, oak desk and Marshal Riddick opposite him. Although the conversation seemed pleasant enough, Johnny sensed the tension between the two men.

Earlier, at sunrise, as Johnny engaged in his indenture to Horse Handler in the livery, he had noticed another horse, unfamiliar to him. The animal had not been there at suppertime the evening before and had obviously been ridden hard. Dirt and sweat had dried and matted its coat, especially at the saddle mark and on the animal's legs and underbelly.

A quick check of the hotel registry revealed Cy Riddick's name, dated the evening before. He had come a day earlier than the telegram had indicated. The reason was not obvious and should not have been weather related as the snow had tapered off by noon yesterday. With no threat of further foul weather, and the wind insuring drifting and piling of the snow against the foothills, the road from Laramie City where Cy had most likely overnighted on his journey from Iron Mountain would surely almost have been somewhat cleared. Staying out of sight, Johnny had observed Riddick's visits to the Flour and Grain, the bank, and the Watering Hole Saloon.

"I don't know about that," Sam was concluding, as Johnny entered the office.

Sam stood up, directing his next comment to Johnny. "I believe you can take over from this point." The corners of his mouth turned up slightly then firmed again. There was steel in his eye.

"How are things, Deputy?" Riddick greeted amiably, rising to shake Johnny's hand.

"Tolerable, sir." Johnny accepted the friendly greeting with a smile.

Interjecting a farewell as he moved for the door, Sam nodded and left the office with a parting comment. "Stop in again."

Cy took his seat, with his attention on Johnny, as the deputy lowered himself into Sam's vacated chair.

"I don't think he meant it," Cy chuckled and continued, "I think matters in this town have Sam a little jumpy. Been quite busy around here, I understand." There was cold merriment in his eyes as he fixed his gaze steadily.

"You seem to know quite a bit about our town, Marshal," Johnny said evenly. "How is that?"

"Well, son, people come and go, seeking places to live and homestead-- word gets around out here. I know a lot of folks around your town."

Johnny caught his mocking undertone and strove to keep the challenge from his words. "Yeah, some of our folks have just recently come from Iron Mountain, so movin' must be in the blood. They must have a thirst for adventure, as you say," but he could not arrest his anger or stay the barb, for he hated deception. "It's sort of like a man thirsts for a good, cold drink of water on a hot day, especially when there's none available."

The marshal held his easy smile, but his eyes narrowed slightly. He took a breath as if clearing away an unpleasantness and changed the subject.

"Deputy, did you give further thought to my offer, or does Sideling's wild side appeal to your sense of adventure?"

Johnny fought down his ire, holding Riddick's gaze. The depreciation of an entire town did not seem humorous to him, and he questioned how a man who called himself a peacemaker could be so indifferent to lawlessness and destruction, no matter where it took place. He disliked this man who mocked with his eyes and his twisted words.

"I never took your offer seriously as the whole proposal seemed illogical to me. I don't see how you could justify a salary, such as you suggested, in a town as limited in resources as Iron Mountain," Johnny answered directly.

Riddick's jaw twitched. "Let me worry about that, and I assure you I would not have made the offer if I was not able to back it up. I have discussed this with Sam, and as I thought, he says the decision is entirely yours."

The harshness in Riddick's eyes eased a bit. "I don't deal from the bottom of the deck, son," he added, as he waited for Johnny's response.

Johnny answered reticently. "No, I'm not interested."

Cy Riddick leaned forward slightly, speaking slowly and intentionally. "You are makin' a mistake, Deputy. Look around you. Sometimes you need to look for the signs; sometimes what you think is worth fightin' for, well, just isn't."

He sat back and cut his eyes toward the door before returning a hard gaze on Johnny. He added sardonically, "You should realize this better than most, after what you encountered in the Confederacy."

Johnny had much practice tolerating this particular indignation, still it stung him coming from a man who should have elicited his respect. He did not react.

"You better think long and hard, boy, I won't be askin' again." Riddick let his intimidation hang heavy in the air.

Johnny rose dismissively. "I don't need to think on it. I won't consider it, and I won't change my mind." His eyes remained on Cy Riddick. The marshal's gaze fell to his hands, each spread out covering a knee. He flexed his fingers claw-like, and raised his eyes to Johnny, his features frozen in an iron mask. He stood slowly, drawing himself to his full height and towered imposingly over the deputy. Picking up his hat, he turned and without further comment, scraped the soles of his boots and his spurs along the floorboards, pausing in the doorway.

"You're too smart to make a stupid decision," he spat out tersely.

"That's why I'm stayin'," Johnny answered, thumping the desk with the knuckles of his fisted hand.

Steam rose from the hot potatoes, but did not diminish the aroma of the large steak Frances Kelly placed before Johnny as he sat for supper with the marshal and Miss Lauren Blaine at the rear table of the café.

"There you go, Johnny, and I'll see you later tonight," Frances said, moving along toward the next table to further unburden the metal serving tray.

Sam eyed Johnny suspiciously but said nothing, turning his attention to the lovely Miss Blaine who was fixated on the twin dinners on the large plates before two men.

"I've rarely seen such appetites," she appraised, in clipped British syllables. "And so much beef!"

"Don't you have anything but scones and tea in England?" Sam asked, with a rare twinkle in his eye.

"Why, of course. We have a bit more variety, I believe. Goose, venison, and fine spring lamb," she replied pleasantly, for which she received an immediate verbal assault.

"Sheep?" Johnny and Sam asked in unison. Lauren Blaine smiled, pleased that she elicited such a hardy response.

"Well, don't say it too loudly, Miss Lauren." Johnny laughed easily. "Wyoming cattlemen aren't too fond of 'woolies.'"

"I'll never understand it. It's a good industry and could be quite profitable if prejudges weren't so rampant," she teased.

"It's a matter of opinion," Sam offered mildly. "Cattlemen won't graze their herds near sheep, or even walk them on ground where sheep have trodden. There have been fearsome words over the matter."

Hunger got the best of both men, and the threesome fell silent as Miss Lauren sipped her tea.

A tall, striking woman, who Johnny surmised might be as old as thirty, Miss Blaine had come to Sideling to visit her brother. She caught the eye and revived the imagination of Sam Brett during a chance encounter one mid-day, as Sam made the obligatory rounds.

Afterward, Sam found himself obliged to keep a watchful eye on the school-marm from Laramie City, whenever she made her now frequent weekend visits. They seemed to enjoy each other's company, and Johnny noticed Sam whistling about the office of an afternoon, something that seemed as out of character for the marshal as a well-cut waistcoat or a 4:00 p.m. tea and crumpet respite.

Lauren, obviously curious about Sam's young deputy, and desiring pleasant conversation, unwittingly halted the repast by asking, "Are you seeing anyone special in town, Johnny? A young, handsome deputy is bound to attract attention," Lauren commented affably.

A chunk of steak, impaled on the tines of his fork, paused in midair. "Ah, no, not currently; not at the present," he answered uncomfortably, stirring up Sam's resuscitated, clever sense of humor.

"What did Miss Frances mean when she said she'd see you tonight? I don't recall giving you the evening off to be with her," Sam said docilely.

Johnny would rather face Cy Riddick on the opposite side of a firing squad than to go down this road with Sam's new lady present. He was greatly relieved, but only momentarily, when Leafy Misner burst upon the scene, red-nosed and furious.

Borne on the hand at the end of his thin, bony arm, Leafy stretched out a long index finger, wagging it vigorously before Johnny's face. "You gotta get him out of my saloon, and get him out now!" he yelled, his florid face contorted.

Sam, who sat toward the rear of the small, round table, was shielded by the gentle presence of Miss Blaine, and Johnny immediately realized that this escapade would fall to him.

The enraged proprietor continued. "He's stinkin' drunk and tearin' up my place!"

"Who you talkin' about?" Johnny asked, remembering Miss Lauren, and trying to adopt a reasonable tone.

"Ebenezer Smith!" the excited man exclaimed. "Ain't ya gonna do somethin'?"

"Just how drunk can he be?" Johnny asked, pushing down his vexation. Sam watched the encounter behind a deadpan expression.

"Drunk is drunk, now git over there, and git him gone!" Misner cried.

Johnny glared at the bartender and pointed to the clock on the wall, contesting hotly. "For cryin' out loud, Misner, it is only five forty! And tell me, how does a man get 'stinkin' drunk' this early, unless some fool plies him with alcohol all afternoon, or gives him more when he staggers in already shot in the neck and beggin' for more?" The loss of his half-eaten steak was not the least of his concern.

"Are you accusin' me of mismanagin' my saloon? You yahoo! Haul your perfidious hide over there now! I pay your salary, you know!"

He whirled on Sam. "Damn it, Sam, just get somebody over there now! I ain't arguin' about this!" He turned and stormed out in a whirlwind of black wrath.

Sam breathed easily. "I hope you'll excuse the unpleasant encounter, Lauren. I'm sure Johnny will attend to this matter quickly. Am I correct?"

He retrieved his steely gaze, casting it levelly at his deputy who sat for a moment staring down at the steak and potatoes which would soon elude him as quickly as had his civility.

"Enjoy your dinner, Miss Lauren," Johnny replied politely, rising, then turning to pontificate.

"If you think you can manage it *sir*, hold my dinner. This won't take long."

The water was steaming in the pan placed in the large sink, so Johnny pumped a gush of cold water into it. He lost his hands in the soapy bubbles as he washed dish after dish, placing them on the drying rack. Frances stood in the empty dining area and poked her head through the swinging door.

"That's the last of them, Johnny. Sorry, you didn't get your supper earlier. It's a sin and a shame to do all this and never get to eat!" she chortled.

Balancing four plates on the edge of the sink then losing the dishrag to the floor, Johnny sneezed into his bent arm and wiped the suds from his nose.

"Now, don't you go breakin' my plates! You're on probation, and damaging the wares could get you fired!" Frances puckered her mouth in warning, even though a hint of merriment touched her brows.

"You know you couldn't live without me, Miss Frances," Johnny returned, sneezing again. "And I vow, it'd be hard to fire a man, then have to watch him starve to death."

"Well, you're wrong on both counts so don't go bettin' on my good nature and generosity. Now, when you finish up, be sure to put out the lamps and lock up good," she instructed, heading for the staircase and her bed.

"Ya seem to forget who patrols this town nightly," he called over his shoulder, toward her retreating form.

A moment later, her curly head returned, poking officiously through the kitchen door. "Guess I did forget and you'll have to excuse me--I just couldn't see your shiny star 'neath all those suds, dish boy!" He could hear her cackling as she made her way back through the dim establishment and climbed the steps to her silent chambers. It was 1:00 a.m.

Johnny shook the old man who sputtered and squinted his eyes against the early morning light. He turned away from the stench of stale alcohol and filth to catch his breath, as the weathered, rumpled man muttered and groaned.

"Get up, Mr. Smith," he urged. "You'll be needin' to get home to your boy."

Young Tad Smith held a warm spot in Johnny's affections, and he hated to think that the small boy's father cared so little for him that he could drink himself into oblivion.

"Get up now; I'm releasin' you. Go home and take care of your family. Can you stand now?" Johnny asked, hoisting the man to his feet in the cell.

Unstable and needing assistance, Ebenezer Smith made his way to sit heavily on the chair by the desk, and Johnny gathered the man's personal effects. He poured a cup of coffee, handing it to Smith who stammered his weak thanks and sloshed the hot liquid on his soiled pants. He did not seem to notice. He sat without another word, until Johnny enquired about Tad.

"Boy's growing like a weed, but he'll not amount to nothin'," Ebenezer mumbled. "He's a dreamer, and all he wants to do is play with that pup of his."

"I know he's fond of the pup. Most boys have a playful side," Johnny replied, hoping to encourage the man, "but maybe he could learn--workin' alongside you at your farm. My father did that for me, and I believe he taught me a fair measure about responsibility. He was a good example."

331

"His ma babies 'im," Ebenezer slurred. A silvery thin, viscous thread anchored to his lower lip and clung to his suspended coffee cup, which trembled precariously in his hand and threatened to slosh over again.

"They are two peas in a poc...ket," Smith drawled, his reddened eyes staring off.

It was 7:00 a.m., and Johnny was as weary from Smith's hopeless recitation as though he had spent the whole night talking with him. He took Ebenezer's coffee cup and handed him his gunbelt and hat.

"Go home, Mr. Smith, there's nothing else you can do here today." He helped him clear the doorway. "Just go home," he repeated glumly.

After rounds, Johnny conferred with Sam, and finding no real reason not to, he spurred Cody toward the Baker place. Fresh air and hard work should do the trick. It was the only remedy he had found to ease his restlessness. He had not been able to help Smith, could not make a better life for Tad, or hold Cassie in his arms. However, he had discovered he could sweat and numb his restive soul with hammer and nails, the blast of a good shotgun, and Bible verses.

For a good two hours he labored under the pale, winter sun in his shirt sleeves, warmed by the vigorous mending of the barn door and the shoring up of the sagging loft, which bore the burden of old hay, moldy and dank underneath, rotting from the effects of leakage from several worn places in the old tin roof.

Using an old pitchfork, he tossed the sour hay to the ground. He paused a moment and looked down from his perch. Minute, floating particles, suspended in filtered sunrays which shot through the jagged holes in the roof, caused his chest to tighten as he inhaled. He swung down from the ladder, leaving the gloom of the interior behind him and stepped out into the sunlight.

Taking in the fresh air, he coughed, spit, then found the hammer and an old box of penny nails and began to repair the fence. It was a two-man job and he thought again of Tad. Had the boy been with him, a hundred questions would have sprung from the kid, like popcorn from a kettle. Johnny enjoyed finding answers for the imaginative child. As for the times he could not, he would answer with a catchy tune, or blow his harmonica, then laugh at Tad's attempts at mimicking him. They had not spent much time together, and Johnny wished now that those times had been more frequent. No use regretting what was past, he would see if he could catch up with Tad in the schoolyard, one day...soon.

"Good morning, Johnny."

He startled at the voice from behind, and turned quickly to find Dodge Wilkerson only a few yards away.

"Good morning, sir," Johnny returned, astounded at how easily he had been caught off guard by a rider on a horse.

Dodge nodded, and from his horse, offered Johnny his hand. "I know that Mabel appreciates your help here." He looked around him appreciatively. "You'd make a fine rancher."

"I can't imagine that runnin' cattle is any less difficult than keepin' law and order," Johnny replied pleasantly. "It may seem less risky, but it has its hazards as well."

"I believe the compensation for ranching may be better, but we are agreed. There are plenty of pitfalls with both occupations." Dodge, tidy and well groomed, sat his handsome, buckskin gelding. Johnny became conscious of his own poor appearance which contrasted markedly. He felt the pressure of the conversation, but gave Cassie's father the benefit of the doubt, deciding that the older man had not intended to debate him. Still, he felt the need to defend his position.

"This is a wild country as you have said, sir. It has the potential to give a body everything, then to take it all away again. It's not just the lawlessness. There's also disease, injury, and natural disasters. The clouds can bring the last of summer to dead winter in half an hour's time. Nothin' is predictable, nothin' is safe."

Dodge nodded, shifting in his saddle. "All of that is true, son, but why take risks with life that you don't need to take? Why put yourself deliberately in harm's way?" He spoke decidedly but not unkindly, and Johnny tensed imperceptibly, feeling the need to hold his ground.

"I guess it's kind of...a calling. I never questioned becomin' a peace officer, just always moved toward it. It's a necessity for this territory, for this country, for the people who want to live and work here. It costs like the day is long to get people to look for the truth, to maintain the rules of God and man. I don't know if it can be done, but I know I have to try. Maybe it's just what I'm called to do."

The corners of Dodge Wilkerson's mouth tightened ever so slightly, and Johnny watched as Dodge dismounted and stood before him. His next statement and subsequent question took Johnny by surprise.

"You say you love Cassie. What are your intentions when she turns eighteen?"

Johnny tried to gather his whirling thoughts and stared at the man for a long moment. Having brooded over this quandary for two months, he found himself indecisive, and desperate for resolution.

"I'm unsure how to best answer that question, sir. I lost my family at about the age Cassie is now," he said hesitantly, "and I don't want to see her lose hers through alienation. She thinks she can bear it; I don't believe she can."

The admission of that truth weighed on his heart like an anvil and he was silent.

Dodge pushed on steadily, his gaze intentional. "So, what do you intend to do about that?" Dodge saw the clench of Johnny's jaw convey pain to his eyes, and watched him struggle, patiently awaiting his response.

Johnny wanted to throw off the weight, to flee from the stifling conversation for which he had no other answer, but he remained. Standing silently, he knew this man held all the high cards, and whatever card Johnny now chose to play would make no difference. Suddenly, his frustration with the seeming futility of the situation poured forth.

"What is it you wait for, Mr. Wilkerson? What would you have me to say? I've said it all before. She's your daughter. Send her away if that's what you need to do. Send her off to school somewhere, and maybe she'll forget about us. She'll make a new life, new friends in a new place. I can't change how I feel about her...I can't change her mind, and God knows, I no longer want to! I love her. You're her father! You make the decision and do what you think is best for her."

Wiping his shirt sleeve quickly across his face to clear away the wet of angry frustration, and embarrassed because of it, Johnny turned away, picking up the hammer and nails. Dodge stepped forward, placing a hand on his shoulder. He felt Johnny's muscle tighten.

"I'm sorry, son. I had to push you hard. I had to know."

Dodge dropped his hands to his sides. "I wanted to hear you say exactly what you just said. This...this is hard for me also, and maybe one day you will understand. I had to know if you cared more for her well-being than you do for your own."

Dodge went silent, and Johnny turned to face him. Dodge's features had softened and with eyes round and compelling, he searched Johnny's face.

"I could no more send Cassie away than I could stop you from being a lawman. She would wither in the city, away from the prairie and the home she loves. Cassie is a good many things," he confessed, looking out over the field, "but most of all she is passionate to a fault. When she loves, she loves with her whole heart, with all that she is, be it horse, cow, or man. She is fierce in her allegiance. I can't change her mind any more than you can, for she sees you as..." he hesitated, then spoke precisely.

"I know she believes she loves you. I will give my permission for you...to court her *when* she becomes seventeen at the end of this month, *and* if she still desires it," Dodge stated calmly.

Johnny's lips parted but he did not speak. Dodge continued as though he was setting the terms for goods he intended to purchase, but not for a cent more than was his predetermined price. "There are stipulations, and if you agree to them, and all of them, which I trust you will, then we can strike a deal that will stand."

Johnny found his voice, asking Dodge Wilkerson for clarification of what he feared he had heard incorrectly. Then Dodge repeated his proposal, proceeding cogently into the stipulations.

"First, remember, she is not yours; you only have permission to be with her, to get to know her and she will, of course, begin to know you. You are not to touch her inappropriately, and I believe we both know what that means. I am going to ask that you not kiss her as well. Before you object, let me say this--kissing is a bonding of sorts. I don't want Cassie to be blinded to who you are--your character, and your reasoning. I want her to be able to think clearly, not through a veil of emotion. This is true for you as well. And, being men, we know where a kiss can take us."

Johnny listened intentionally, attempting to absorb the dictum as Dodge continued steadily.

"Cassie is still very young and inexperienced in these matters, and I desire she remain that way for now. She may yet change her mind, and I don't want her to have any...not one, reason for regret, and nothing she may feel sorry for later or any reason to feel...obligated. Use good judgment concerning where you take her; try not to be alone with her often. I know of the temptations, as I am sure you do. I don't know much about your past, Johnny, but I must believe that she will be courting a gentleman... and if I have cause to think otherwise, I will end it. Do you understand? Can we agree on this?"

Behind Dodge Wilkerson's penetrating gaze was an emotion Johnny had not encountered since the battlefield. He couldn't name it, but it propelled him to decided action and revived his stunned, reasoning abilities. He jutted out his hand and answered adamantly.

"You have a deal, sir, a most definite deal! You are sure about this?" Johnny added hastily.

"No," replied Dodge Wilkerson, shaking the hand before him. "I am sure about nothing. I can't put into words what Cassie means to me...she is the first of my daughters. But, I won't break the deal and be sure that you do not. I'm holding you to your word as a gentleman."

"You have my word, sir. Have you told her of your decision?" Johnny asked, as the man slowly mounted, taking up the reins. "If not, I'd appreciate the opportunity."

The buckskin side-stepped nervously. Dodge fingered the leathers and pondered the request. His eyes held a vague reservation.

"Alright, just remember all I've asked of you." He turned his horse uncertainly, then circled Johnny where he stood, and spurred the mount forward.

Johnny stood for a long moment, watching until the horse and rider disappeared down the road and around the bend. He shook his head in amazement. The sun played on the ripples in the weathered watering trough, casting glints of gold his way.

"Remember," Dodge had cautioned.

The weighty yoke Johnny had borne for the last months, heavier than the beam in the dilapidated old barn, lifted as Dodge Wilkerson's words of consent sank in.

"Remember" had been Cassie's very own words to him.

He lifted his eyes to the cloudless sky, raising his arms high and wide, palms upward, fingers spread to the heavens and remembered God's mercies. "Thank you, God! Thank you!" he shouted with victorious gratitude.

(Psalms 105:1-8)

"Just hold on a minute, can't ya? Take a breath!" Sam commanded, as Johnny burst through the doorway with a fleeting explanation, the end of which was lost as he disappeared into the backroom. "You like to give me heart failure, exploding through the door like that!"

Johnny reappeared, toting a bucket of water.

"I hate to throw cold water on your enthusiasm, son, but just how do you intend to finance this 'courtship' of yours?"

Johnny stoked up the fire and poured the water into the black, iron pot. "Don't have a clue, but I have some time to figure it out. She won't be seventeen for three weeks."

He stepped up to the small mirror by the barrel of drinking water and examined his face. Rubbing his hand across the stubble on his jaw, he disappeared into the backroom, and returned with a straight-edged razor.

"I suppose you're not gonna use the bathhouse either, are you?" Sam asked, hazarding a guess as to what would happen next.

"Nope, just this bucket in the backroom--a bath is costly, and I can do it here," Johnny replied, retrieving the lukewarm water from the stove and pulling his shirt off over his head.

"Besides, I need to get to the Wilkersons to talk with Cassie before evenin' rounds."

"In all your conservation efforts, just remember this is a public building and you're a government official," Sam cautioned dryly, shaking his head at his half-naked deputy.

Johnny disappeared with the razor and the bucket, returning in less than five minutes. His smile had dimmed, and he held a small piece of rag to his clean-shaven chin. Fully clothed, he stood mutely, staring thoughtfully in Sam's general direction, and the marshal took his suspension as a quest for approval.

"You look...clean, real clean," Sam encouraged, nodding his head affirmatively.

"Suppose she says no? What if after all of this, she changes her mind?" Johnny asked flatly.

"Go on, get out of here. You won't know til you ask her."

Sam watched as Johnny closed the door behind him.

27

THE DEAL

CASSIE THREW THE pitchfork pole to the ground, the head and tines of which had disconnected and remained imbedded in the hay bale, mocking her effort.

"I can't do anything right!" she wailed angrily. A gust of cold wind blew her apron into her face, and she dissolved into tears. Stomping her foot, she gave a swift kick to the head of the pitchfork, dislodging it from the hay and sending it into the pathway of the chickens pecking and scratching benignly in the barnyard dirt.

A plump, red hen flapped and squawked frantically, clearing a path for the sailing tines. The sight of its panic made her tears flow all the more.

"I'm sorry, Matilda," she cried in remorse, taking steps toward the offended hen who scurried away, squawking indignantly.

Cassie quit the pursuit, jamming her cold, bare fists into her apron pockets, then quickly removed a hand to swipe at a bothersome drip from her damp nose with the sleeve of her dress. Picking up the head of the pitchfork, she attempted to reset it to the pole with a hard thump to the ground. It held until she thrust it deep into the hay mound and tried to lift the bulk toward the waiting wheelbarrow. The head and hay dropped to the ground and she wept anew, tears stinging her eyes and coursing down her cheeks.

Her abdomen cramped and her head ached. "Oh...if I were a man I wouldn't be plagued with this curse!" The milling chickens ignored her lament, and she threw the pole to the ground, pushing the offending thing away with a boot.

Aware of the warning signs last evening and true to the calendar on the wall, she had been forced to rise at 4:00 a.m. to change her gown and bedclothes. All morning she had struggled with impatience, feeling too unwell for her millinery chores or school, and had wept over the most mundane occurrences.

Frustrated, she bent impulsively over the hay mound and scooped up a large armful of hay, dumping it into the wheelbarrow. Straightening, she brushed the hay from her sleeves and fought the wind, pushing back the wisps of hair from her eyes. Minute, itchy particles stuck to her lips, nose, and damp cheeks, and she wiped at them with her apron. Sneezing violently, she sniffed raggedly.

The distant, rhythmic thud of hooves signaled the approach of a horseman, and Cassie turned, horrified to see Johnny and Cody approaching rapidly. Her hands flew to her face and wiping her nose, she quickly tried to smooth her hair and brush away the tear streaks from her grimy cheeks, but Cody and Johnny were upon her before she could collect her wits. The chestnut came to a halt not three feet from where she stood and dropped his head to snatch at the loose hay.

Johnny swung a leg over the pummel of the saddle, dropping easily from Cody's shoulder and landing squarely and gallantly before her. His crooked smile and sparkling eyes greeted her.

"Hey, Cassie..." but his smile faded at the sight of her tear-stained face, and he caught her by the shoulders. "What's wrong? Are you hurt?"

He attempted to draw her to him, but she resisted, looking about apprehensively. "What are you doing coming here like this? Pa should be home anytime now! Suppose he sees you here--catches us like this? Her tone was unintentionally harsh, then she burst into fresh tears.

"What's wrong, Cassie? What's happened? Tell me," he implored. Still holding her shoulders, he studied her quickly from side to side and then tried to turn her, but she resisted, pushing his hands away.

"No! Stop!" she commanded, "I'm alright."

The blue-green of his eyes changed in intensity, and her heart caught in her chest as she watched him frowning in concern.

"It's just...just this stupid pitchfork...it broke, and I tried..." Cassie stammered, her breath coming in ragged hiccups, "to fix it... but it just..."

"What? Is that it? The pitchfork has you weepin'?" he asked incredulously, and he began to laugh, this time pulling her to him. She didn't resist and buried her face in his coat. He smoothed her hair and tried to sooth her countenance.

"Hush now, it's nothin' can't be fixed. It's just a pitchfork," he offered tenderly, "nothing worth all those tears. It'll be alright now." Lifting her chin with a gloved finger, he gazed into her eyes.

"No! It's not alright! Oh, don't look at me, Johnny, I'm a mess! Pa will be home any minute, and he'll shoot you if you don't leave now! I just can't bear this any longer," she moaned raggedly.

Amidst her grievous confession, and as he held her captive, she caught a flash of merriment in the depths of his blue-green pools, and that he dared to think this in any way humorous revived her indignation.

He pulled her close, and she shoved him hard. "Stop teasing me; why are you doing this?" she asked angrily.

"Well, stop fightin' me and give me a chance to tell you," he replied. "I've got good news!"

Searching her eyes, he instinctively suppressed a desire to ask her to guess what the glad tidings might be, deciding to deliver the message quickly.

"Your pa...he has given permission for us to court!" But the words seemed not to penetrate, for she was not smiling.

"All is well! Things are fine now," he added earnestly. "We have to wait until your seventeenth birthday, but he gave his permission this afternoon! Good news...isn't it?"

His enthusiasm waned as her face set in disbelief.

"This isn't humorous, why are you teasing me? Pa has told me no such thing; he's not even hinted at such a thing!" Bewildered, she blinked and fresh tears made tiny rivulets through the dirt on her cheeks.

"I swear it! Look here, look at me." He raised his brow and pinned her with all the sincerity he could muster.

The incredulous look on her face, mixed with a spark in her eye, begged of hope-- contrasting fancifully with stubborn bits of hay and tears. He tried to suppress a grin.

His effort and the hint of a grin, which she could never quite fathom, raised umbrage. "Do you mean this? If you are lying, Johnny McLane, I'll stab you with this pitchfork before you can ride outta' here!"

"Let your yes be yes," he stated biblically, and then he laughed.

"Where's your faith, girl? You were the one who first insisted that God meant this for us, and now you don't believe it?" He became serious. "I'd never lie about this," he said tenderly, removing a stub of hay from her curl.

She studied him for a moment, attempting to collect her wits. Her brow bunched as he released a tendril which had caught on his badge, and she pushed his hand from her hair. She strove to regain her dignity by attempting to straighten her soiled apron, then began to cry in earnest.

His heart turned to stone as he watched her. "Why are you cryin'? Don't you want this? Has somethin' changed?"

"Oh, no! What must you think of me! No, no! Nothing has changed... except I'm such a mess, I..." She brushed a hand over her dusty sleeves, and pushed the hair from her eyes. "How can you bear to look at me?"

He moved toward her, encircling her waist, then lifted her, twirling around and around.

"You are the most beautiful, wonderful, glorious girl I've ever known! I love every speck of dirt, hay, and all your mess!" Slowing, he lowered her, drawing her close.

Beginning to believe him, warmed by news she thought was impossible and the fact that he held her so closely, Cassie tipped her head back, exploring his eyes. Enchanted with the minute, brown flecks she discovered in their blue-green depths, and surprised by the urgent force of internal, unexplored glimmerings of secret things she could not pretend to ignore, her lips, just inches from his, parted. Finding it hard to breathe, she closed her eyes and whispered expectantly, "Oh...Johnny."

In an instant he had her by the shoulders, stepping back and holding her off firmly. "I can't...I want too, but I can't!"

Startled, she asked, "What? Can't what?"

"I promised your pa that I wouldn't...Cassie--no kissing! I had to promise." Johnny tried to explain. It was almost beyond him that she stared at him blankly and did not seem to immediately grasp the reason for her father's edict, so he continued awkwardly. "Kissing leads to other things...and you, well, you...just stand there, and don't come at me, at least for now."

Johnny's words and truth of them swirled through Cassie's mind. Although he had delivered them with about as much effort as it took to tan a tough piece of rawhide into soft leather, it seemed important to him that she should grasp his meaning. Suddenly, this touched her deeply. She thanked God again for the steadfast man before her. Her face softened, and her eyes lit and glowed with the passion he had longed to see.

Everything he desired he held, and Johnny knew this joyous moment would long be imprinted on his soul. An awesome prick of responsibility caught him up as he held her, for behind the lovely form of his wild, prairie maiden he perceived a precious lamb. He realized that he could easily lose his way in the deep shadows of desire, unless he trod the path carefully, shepherding and following the voice of the Shepherd of their souls along the road that would bring glory to the Lord. This must be, if ever Cassie was to be bound honorably and safely to him. Silently, he breathed his petition to God.

"Cassie, I love you." It was all he could think to say.

(Proverbs 3:21-27;
Psalm 25:4-7, 12-15; Psalm 23)

The story continues in the next book of the No Shadow of Turning series

FREEDOM'S SONG

JOHNNY WAVERED, AND Dodge stepped forward helping to get him into Doc's office. Cassie stood alone on the porch lost in a void in the night, feeling diminutive, useless, and cold. There had been little warmth even as she had supported Johnny with her arm about his waist. The chill of his damp clothing against her hands and cheek, the hard iron of the weapon at his right hip, and the cold rim of bullets along his gunbelt where her fingers had rested were material things that that signified who he was. As cold as they seemed, they were life and felt warmer than being excised so quickly from his side to stand alone on the porch like a castaway. Muffled masculine voices sounded from within the office.

Hard things, cold things, dead things... rolled in stiff, dry canvass. Cassie had seen them there, but what she saw had not registered in her thoughts until now. She began to tremble; her legs went weak. She leaned against the side of the building. She had believed there was nothing else to learn. Working beside her pa, accompanying him to the various businesses where he traded, becoming familiar with the harsh language of men, and observing the heated bargaining over the price of cattle in a predominately man's domain was within her scope. But this--this death and destruction was a part of the world of men she had never experienced, and it appeared they accepted it without tears or complaint. How? She willed herself to breathe and think. "I will not cry. I can be brave...if I love him, I must deal with this." Maybe it would be more difficult than she had imagined.

In a rush, Myra Davis dropped her book retrieving it quickly and brushing the snow from its cover. Climbing into her rig and settling herself on the seat, she paused a moment to look around. She shivered and drew the hood of her coat over her head.

Several times throughout the last week, the same eerie chill had blanketed her as she left the schoolhouse in the late afternoon twilight. Alone now, a premonition as though someone watched settled over her, and she shuddered again. It would be dark before she could make the mile-long journey to her cabin to the southwest of the schoolhouse. She chided herself for her lack of prudence, for she had lingered too long after having dismissed the children. Assuaging her fears, she picked up the reins and urged the horse forward into the lengthening shadows.

Brim tipped low and collar upturned, the watcher moved cautiously in pursuit. He stopped suddenly to reconsider and then slipped unseen back into the stand of pinons. The trespasser turned and chose a similar path, dissimilar in direction, though most decidedly equivalent in ominous intent.

The first item in the small, neatly packaged box was a letter. Unfolding it, Johnny held it a moment to examine the fine script, searching desperately for his sister's face through the veil of time. Finding only her essence, he began to read....

At last, Johhny unwrapped the tarnished, yellow pocket watch revealing the triangular point of white, embroidered stitching rising diagonally from the base of the fragment of blue bunting beneath it. Lifting the lid of the watch, the gleaming metal of the underside held an inscription. Sudden tears blurred the words, and Johnny took a ragged breath. In an instant, he was on his feet knocking the box to the floor. Sam grabbed Tad's arm before he could reach the deputy.

BIBLIOGRAPHY

Balfour, Daniel T. *Southampton County and Franklin, A Pictorial History*. Brookfield, MO: Donning Company Publishers, 1989.

Conrad, James Lee. *The Young Lions: Confederate Cadets at War*. Columbia, SC: University of South Carolina Press, 2004.

Dabney, Virginius. *Virginia The New Dominion*. Charlottesville, VA: University Press of Virginia, 1971.

Davis, William C. *The Battle of New Market*. Baton Rouge, LA: Louisiana State University Press, 1983.

Dobson, G.B. "Wyoming Tales and Trails." *Wyoming Tails and Trails*. Last modified 2015.

Duke University Library Digital Collections. "Salt Peter." *Salient Points*. Last modified August 11, 2010. https://salient-points.blogspot.com/2010/08/salt-peter.html

Duncan, Mel. *The Medicine Bow Mining Camps*. Jelm, WY: Jelm Mountain Publications, 1990.

Evans, Tim, and Barbara Allen Bogart. *Saddles, Bits & Spurs: Cowboy Crafters at Work*. Cheyenne, WY: Wyoming State Museum, 1993.

Gorzalka, Ann. *Wyoming's Territorial Sheriffs*. Glendo, WY: High Plains Press, 1998.

Henry, Matthew. *Matthew Henry's Commentary on the Whole Bible*. Grand Rapids, MI: Zondervan Publishing House, 1960. http://www.wyomingtalesandtrails.com

"History." Wells Fargo. Accessed November 7, 2017. https://www.wellsfargohistory.com/history/

Ketchum, Richard M. *American Heritage Picture History of the Civil War*. New York City: American Heritage Publishing Co, 1960.

Kinnaman, Daniel L. *Rawlins Wyoming, The Territorial Years 1868-1890*. Rawlings, WY: Kinnaman Supply Company, 2013.

Larson, T. A. *History of Wyoming*. Lincoln, NE: University of Nebraska Press, 1990.

Lavender, David Sievert. *American Heritage History of the Great West*. New York City: Simon & Schuster, 2005.

McDowell, Bart. *The American Cowboy in Life and Legend*. Washington, DC: National Geographic Society, 1972.

McMillen, Sally G. *Motherhood in the Old South: Pregnancy, Childbirth, and Infant Rearing*. Baton Rouge, LA: Louisiana State University Press, 1997.

Mountain, Mary. *Laramie Plains Museum, Early Laramie*. Laramie, WY: Modern Printing Company, 2013.

Thomas, Emory M. *The Confederacy as a Revolutionary Experience*. Columbia, SC: University of South Carolina Press, 1991.

U.S. Department of the Interior. *Wyoming Historic Trails*. Wyoming State Office.